POPULATION REDISTRIBUTION AND PUBLIC POLICY

Brian J. L. Berry
and
Lester P. Silverman
Editors

Assembly of Behavioral and Social Sciences
National Research Council

NATIONAL ACADEMY OF SCIENCES
Washington, D.C.   1980

NOTICE: The project that is the subject of this report was approved by the Governing Board of the National Research Council, whose members are drawn from the Councils of the National Academy of Sciences, the National Academy of Engineering, and the Institute of Medicine. The members of the Committee responsible for the report were chosen for their special competences and with regard for appropriate balance.

This report has been reviewed by a group other than the authors according to procedures approved by a Report Review Committee consisting of members of the National Academy of Sciences, the National Academy of Engineering, and the Institute of Medicine.

Library of Congress Cataloging in Publication Data

National Research Council. Assembly of Behavioral and Social Sciences.
  Population redistribution and public policy.

  Bibliography: p.
  1. Migration--Internal--United States--Addresses, essays, lectures. 2. United States--Population density--Addresses, essays, lectures. I. Silverman, Lester P. II. Berry, Brian Joe Lobley, 1934- III. Title.
HB1965.N4 1979 304.8'2'0973 79-25533

ISBN 0-309-02926-0

Available from

Office of Publications
National Academy of Sciences
2101 Constitution Avenue, N.W.
Washington, D.C. 20418

Printed in the United States of America

CONTENTS

iii

PREFACE

The Assembly of Behavioral and Social Sciences commissioned the papers in this volume to help fulfill a need on the part of policy makers and social scientists to understand better how the significant population redistribution trends of the 1970s will affect and be affected by areas of public policy. To provide a common base of information for the authors, the significant population redistribution trends of the 1970s were detailed by Brian J. L. Berry and Donald C. Dahmann. Their paper in this volume is an important starting point for the reader.

A workshop was held in June 1977, before the papers were written, to provide the authors with a broad overview of the policy and methodological issues that might be explored. The participants in each workshop session represented academia, research and other nonprofit institutions, and various levels of government. Discussion at the workshop focused on the Berry-Dahmann paper and on outlines of the other papers. The participants specifically discussed: the implications of population redistribution for various public policies; the effect that various alternative policies would have on contributing to or reversing the observed trends in population redistribution; and the particular implications of public policies for major age, racial, and income groups.

Following the workshop, the authors completed the papers in this volume. While there were efforts in the early stage to provide a common data base and guidance with regard to the general outline of the papers, the authors inevitably drew on sources unique to each topic. Furthermore, the different intellectual perspectives of the academic disciplines represented by the authors are evident. We have not attempted to reconcile conflicting viewpoints and conclusions or to remove the duplication from these papers.

Population redistribution has continued and, in fact, the trends may have shifted somewhat since the initial preparation of the Berry-Dahmann paper and the workshop. For example, there has been considerable recent discussion about the repopulation of some central cities by middle-income whites and the associated displacement of inner-city minority groups. Therefore, some of the data and observations in these papers may be somewhat out of date; however, there is no question that the major trends identified in this volume are dominant.

Financial support for the 1977 workshop and for the papers came from the program planning and development funds made available to the Assembly of Behavioral and Social Sciences by the Ford Foundation, and from the U.S. Department of Housing and Urban Development. We thank Wendy H. Siniard of the Assembly for administrative and secretarial support throughout this project, and Barbara S. Davies and Eugenia Grohman for editorial assistance.

Lester P. Silverman
Brian J. L. Berry

INTRODUCTION

Brian J. L. Berry and *Lester P. Silverman*

Significant changes have taken place since 1970 in the composition and spatial distribution of the U.S. population.
These changes reflect, in part, decades of public policy
at all levels of government in all areas of our lives. Inevitably, these changes are placing new stresses on social
institutions and the services they provide, hence providing
the stimuli for further policy changes to try to solve new
problems.

Each of the papers in this volume examines both the effects of population redistribution on public services, institutions, and policy, and the effect of potential policy
changes on population redistribution. After summarizing
the major demographic changes in the 1970s that are the
starting point for and the focus of this volume, this introduction presents some observations about the role of public
policy.

POPULATION REDISTRIBUTION IN THE 1970s

This volume focuses on changes occurring in the 1970s in
the spatial distribution of the nation's population--among
regions of the country and between metropolitan and nonmetropolitan areas. This redistribution must be viewed,
however, in the context of several other important changes
in the composition of the U.S. population.

Brian J. L. Berry is Williams Professor of City and Regional
Planning, Harvard University. Lester P. Silverman is Director, Office of Policy Analysis, Department of the Interior.
He was formerly Associate Executive Director of the Assembly
of Behavioral and Social Sciences, National Research Council.

1

Dominating all other national demographic trends in the 1970s is the continuation of a long-term decline in the rate of population increase. During the 1950s, the national population grew 19 percent; during the 1960s, it increased by 13 percent; and during the 1970s, it will likely have increased only by 8 percent. The long-term decline in population growth is expected to continue, although previous fluctuations in birthrates, e.g., the postwar baby boom, will continue to affect the nation's demographic profile. The aging of these cohorts, together with their greater life expectancies, will play a major role in increasing the median age of the nation's population.

These shifts in the age structure of the nation's population are occurring at the same time that fundamental changes in the structure of marital and household living arrangements are taking place. Since 1970, the largest increase in family groups has been among those headed by women who do not have husbands living with them; half of this increase was accounted for by women who were divorced. Other national trends, which are contributing to an overall decline in the number of persons per household, are increased numbers of people delaying marriage and both greater numbers and larger proportions of the elderly maintaining their own households.

Within the context of these fundamental compositional trends, this volume focuses on two major trends in the spatial distribution of U.S. population in the 1970s: the movement to the Sun Belt region and the movement out of metropolitan areas. The South is experiencing net migration gains from all other regions in numbers that are more than double the net gain to the West--the only other region now experiencing a net migration gain. The growth rate of the West continues to be the highest in the country, but the most rapid growth within that region has shifted from the coastal states to the Rocky Mountain states. The net flow of migrants from the Northeast and North Central regions during the first half of the 1970s was almost double that of the last half of the 1960s; this reflects both an increase in migration from the North to the South and a substantial decrease in migration from the South to the North. Significantly, the long-term trend of out-migration by blacks from the South to the North was reversed during the first half of the 1970s.

Since 1970, the metropolitan areas of the United States have grown more slowly than the nation as a whole and substantially less rapidly than nonmetropolitan America, a development that stands in sharp contrast to all preceding decades back to the early 19th century. The overall

decline in the rate of growth of metropolitan areas is
largely accounted for by the largest metropolitan areas,
particularly those located in the Northeast and North Central regions. While the populations of central cities of
all the nation's metropolitan areas grew at an average
annual rate of 0.6 percent between 1960 and 1970, they
declined at an average annual rate of 0.4 percent since
1970 (annexations excluded).

There has been rapid growth in some smaller metropolitan
areas (particularly in the South, Florida especially, and
the West) and in exurban counties located immediately outside metropolitan areas that have substantial daily commuting to metropolitan areas. High growth rates also prevail
in certain nonmetropolitan areas, especially those with
manufacturing, centers of higher education, resources for
recreational development, and retirement centers. The long-
term shift away from agricultural employment has also tapered
off, adding to rural population retention.

Although most developed countries of the world are experiencing declining birthrates and decentralization of their
populations, the factors underlying these trends are varied
and complex. We understand very little about how people
make decisions about locational preference or household and
family arrangements and about the role of public policies
in affecting the costs and benefits--or the perceptions of
those factors--that are weighed in making such decisions.
The knowledge base that would allow better understanding
of individuals' goals and expectations for social and economic improvement and the relationship of these to choice
of life-style and geographic area is widely scattered among
the behavioral and social science disciplines.

POPULATION REDISTRIBUTION AND PUBLIC POLICY

The national demographic trends--both compositional (lowered
birthrates, increasing numbers of elderly persons, changes
in family structure) and spatial (movements to the South
and West, shifts from metropolitan to nonmetropolitan
areas)--have already had, and will continue to have, important consequences for the nation into the 1980s and beyond.
The papers in this volume document four major effects of
these trends.

The first effect is on the demand for goods and services
(primarily those that are provided predominantly by the public
sector), since the groups being served have changed. Katzman
notes that declining school enrollments are likely to continue

for metropolitan areas (central cities and suburbs), with
stable or declining populations for some time to come.
Fauth and Gomez-Ibanez argue that spatial population shifts
contribute, along with other factors, to a sustained and
continuing shift from public transportation to private automobile use, a trend that will be resistant to even large
increases in the price of gasoline. Mills notes the effects
of the shifts in continuing a trend toward greater per-capita
land use.

The second effect concerns the cost of providing those
public goods and services as the clientele groups have
shifted. Perlman notes the tendency toward equalization
of welfare and related benefits across regions of the country. Loftin documents the increased per-capita law enforcement expenditures in shrinking areas. The third effect
results from the pressures placed on local governments as
their resources, including financial, labor, and capital
infrastructure (e.g., schools, transportation networks) become ill-suited to evolving demands for services. Peterson
and Muller document the adjustment problems faced by local
governments because of the lag with which fixed costs can
be rendered variable. Greenwood discusses the employment-
related pressures caused by the quite different characteristics of those who move and those who do not.

Finally, there is the effect of the redistribution of
the nation's resources--including income, nonpecuniary
amenities, and other aspects of social life (e.g., status,
mobility)--that accompany the dramatic changes. Keyes
documents that although regional shifts are not likely to
have much effect on national air and water quality, they
present the potential for significant savings in fossil
fuel. Sampson explores some of the possible implications
of population redistribution for racial-minority and low-
income groups in society.

As the effects of the demographic changes of the 1970s
have become evident, the definition of the "problem" to which
public policy has been addressed has shifted dramatically.
Title VII of the Housing and Urban Development Act of 1970
(Public Law 91-609, 84 Stat. 1791; 42 U.S.C. 4501) states
in Section 702:

> . . . the rapid growth of urban population and un-
> even expansion of urban development in the United
> States, together with a decline in farm population,
> slower growth in rural areas, and migration to the
> cities, has created an imbalance between the
> Nation's needs and resources and seriously threatens

our physical environment . . . the economic
and social development of the Nation, the proper
conservation of our natural resources, and the
achievement of satisfactory living standards depend upon the sound, orderly, and more balanced
development of all areas of the Nation . . .
The Congress . . . declares that the national
urban growth policy should--(1) favor patterns
of urbanization and economic development and
stabilization which offer a range of alternative
locations . . . (3) help reverse trends of migration and physical growth . . . (4) treat compre-
hensively the problems of poverty and employment
. . . associated with disorderly urbanization
and rural decline . . .

Only 8 years later, in March 1978, President Carter's Urban
Policy Group issued a report, *A New Partnership to Conserve
America's Communities: A National Urban Policy*, that de-
clared:

Three major patterns of population change can be
traced in the Nation today: migration from the
northeastern and north central regions of the country to the south and west; the slower growth of
metropolitan areas and the movement from them to
small towns and rural areas; and movement from
central cities to suburbs . . . Today's widespread
population loss in the Nation's central cities is
unprecedented . . . the thinning out process has
left many people and places with severe economic
and social problems, and without the resources to
deal with them . . . Our policies must reflect a
balanced concern for people and places . . . to
achieve several broad goals: (to) preserve the
heritage and values of our older cities; maintain
the investment in our older cities and their neighborhoods; assist newer cities in confronting the
challenges of growth and pockets of poverty . . .;
and provide improved housing, job opportunities
and community services to the urban poor, minorities
and women . . . If the Administration is to help
cities revitalize neighborhoods, eliminate sprawl,
support the return of the middle class to central
cities, and improve the housing conditions of the
urban poor it must increase the production of new
housing and rehabilitation of existing housing for

the poor in cities and suburbs, and increase the
production of new housing and rehabilitation of
existing housing for middle class groups in cities
. . . We should favor proposals supporting: (1)
compact community development over scattered, frag-
mented development; and (2) revitalization over new
development.

Reversals of demographic trends produced, in only half a
decade, an apparent about-face in urban policy.

If urban growth and rural decline were the problems of
1970, and their obverse, urban decline and rural growth,
are the problems today, what is left? Are all types of
change problematic, calling for corrective policies? Or
have urban policy makers somehow missed the boat? If so,
what of policy makers elsewhere in the federal government?
To begin to ask such questions is, ultimately, to begin to
ask about the role of the government in a democratic country
that is undergoing rapid changes.

In a market economy such as the United States, the key
premise underlying policy development is that solutions to
the nation's needs must be found, for the most part, in the
private sector. Market processes are relied upon to allocate resources efficiently and to provide new jobs, rising
incomes, and improving quality of life. An essential pre-
requisite is the necessary mobility of capital and labor to
realize differential market opportunities. One role of government is thus to preserve, support, and enhance those opportunities: to provide information if it is lacking on
the part of buyers or sellers; to prevent emergence of undue
concentration of economic power, which results in higher
prices and fewer services than if competition prevails; to
reduce market fluctuations and uncertainty; and to facilitate mobility. In this sense, the government has a stake
in change. Its other roles arise if public welfare is
endangered by change and if adequate remedies are not available in the marketplace. The need for government intervention may arise (1) if market prices do not reflect the full
social costs or benefits of development because of congestion or external costs such as pollution, noise, hazards,
etc., so that too much or too little of a good or service
will be provided unless corrected; (2) if there is an inability to determine or collect a proper price, as in the
case of a public good whose consumption by one individual
does not reduce the consumption of it by others; (3) if
there are demonstrable advantages to society from maintaining
minimum levels of service to population groups or communities

that otherwise would be unable to obtain it (frequently such minimum levels of service are characterized as basic rights); (4) if market fluctuations give rise to periodic problems or unemployed resources; or (5) if rapid changes in the market produce short-term hardships.

The roles of the government, therefore, are as regulator and facilitator in the interests of the mainstream; as social engineer pursuing related objectives of stability and growth; as arbiter of competing interests (as between polluter and pollutee); and as supplier of public goods and services. The question of the relationship between demographic change and public policy may be viewed, in light of these roles, on a different plane, for the government clearly has a stake both in change and in its consequences. Are demographic shifts an expression of market choices and resource mobility? If they are, should there be any intervention designed to enhance or retard them? Are there problems of short-term adjustment, of underutilized resources, or of social costs that require correction? If so, what are they, where are they, how best might they be addressed, and by which level of government?

The papers in this volume dramatically document the gaps in substantive research about the links between demography and public policy. To assert in a volume of this type that more work needs to be done may seem trite, but the reality of such a statement cannot be dismissed. Yet to conclude on such a note would be to downplay the contributions that the authors of these papers have made, notwithstanding their disagreements. Together, they provide a more comprehensive assessment of the implications of the post-1970 demographic changes than has been available so far--an assessment based on the relevant bodies of theory and focused on the role of and implications for public policy.

The papers in this volume will help provide a basis for the long, tedious, and painful process by which our nation will arrive at answers to these questions.

POPULATION REDISTRIBUTION IN THE UNITED STATES IN THE 1970s

Brian J. L. Berry and *Donald C. Dahmann*

INTRODUCTION

In 1975, the population of the United States was 215 million persons, 5 times greater than it had been a century before and 85 times greater than it had been in 1776. In 200 years, the nation's population density had increased from an average of 2 to more than 60 persons per square mile.

As the United States annexed territory from the Atlantic to the Pacific, new regions were settled and the geographical center of the nation's population shifted westward. At the time that the 13 colonies declared their independence, the center of population was located east of Baltimore; at the close of America's first century, the center was near Cincinnati; today, according to current calculations, which include Alaska and Hawaii, the center lies just southeast of St. Louis--750 miles west of its location in 1776--reflecting the fact that the central and western regions of the country have continually increased their proportion of the nation's total population relative to the Atlantic seaboard concentration.

Concurrently, as the economy shifted from one based on agricultural production to one dominated by industry and an increasingly important service sector, the levels of urban concentration increased. In 1800 the United States was 6 percent urbanized; today, more than 75 percent of the nation's population resides in urbanized areas.[1] Metropolitan

---

Brian J. L. Berry is Williams Professor of City and Regional Planning, Harvard University. Donald C. Dahmann is with the Center for Demographic Studies, U.S. Bureau of the Census.

[1]The nation's urban population includes individuals residing either in places with 2,500 inhabitants or more or in the densely settled fringes of such places.

areas (defined below) have come to dominate the urbanization pattern: by the close of the 1960s, nearly 70 percent of all Americans resided in the nation's metropolitan areas. Today, 44 percent of the total population reside in the nation's 30 largest metropolitan areas (each of which contains 1 million or more residents), and 27 percent are concentrated in the eight largest metropolitan areas (each of which contains more than 3 million residents).

Since 1970, major changes in the nation's settlement pattern have been occurring. Although the West received the largest net flow of migrants in the country as recently as the latter half of the 1960s, since 1970 the volume of net migration to the South has increased to more than double that to the West. Thus, the South has now emerged as the region experiencing the largest population gains and the center of population has begun to move southward. During the first half of the 1970s, interregional migration alone produced a population increase in the South of more than 1.8 million.

Significant change has also occurred since 1970 in the overall growth rate of the nation's metropolitan areas. For the first time, the growth rate of metropolitan areas has dropped to below that of nonmetropolitan areas. More significantly, the long-term net inflow of persons from nonmetropolitan to metropolitan areas has been reversed; as recently as the 1960s, there was a net flow of migrants from nonmetropolitan areas. Since then, however, these areas have added residents largely as the result of increased outmigration from the nation's metropolitan places.

Organization

This paper examines changes in the nation's settlement patterns through 1975. First, current national population trends (including the declining growth rate for the nation as a whole, alteration of the population's age structure, and change in composition of households) are reviewed as an introduction to the documentation of changes now occurring in the patterns of settlement. Evidence relating to the current restructuring of settlement patterns is presented in the next three sections: the first presents patterns of decline and growth in central cities, nonmetropolitan areas, and the four major regions of the country; the second presents recent patterns of residential mobility and their effect on the structure of settlement; and the third reviews the changing character of central-city,

suburban, and nonmetropolitan residents. A summary of
regional and metropolitan and nonmetropolitan changes
concludes the textual presentation. The appendix presents
1977 data for the major tables (Tables 1-7) in the body of
the report. The appendix also provides population figures
and components of population change (natural increase and
net migration) for individual metropolitan areas with
populations over 1 million and for various categories of
metropolitan and nonmetropolitan areas.

Definition of Terms

Throughout the paper, the definitions used are those of
the U.S. Bureau of the Census. In the Bureau's classification, the United States is divided into four major geographical regions and nine divisions. A list of the
regions, the divisions, and the states that comprise them
follows. (For complete definitions and explanations of
terms, see U.S. Bureau of the Census [1970].)

West Region
Pacific Division: Washington, Oregon, California,
                                    Alaska, Hawaii
Mountain Division: Idaho, Nevada, Utah, Arizona,
                                    Montana, Wyoming, Colorado,
                                    New Mexico

North Central Region
West North Central   North Dakota, South Dakota,
  Division: Nebraska, Kansas, Minnesota,
                                    Iowa, Missouri
East North Central   Wisconsin, Illinois, Michigan,
  Division: Indiana, Ohio

South Region
West South Central   Texas, Oklahoma, Arkansas,
  Division: Louisiana
East South Central   Kentucky, Tennessee, Alabama,
  Division: Mississippi
South Atlantic Division: West Virginia, Maryland,
                                    Delaware, District of Columbia,
                                    Virginia, North Carolina,
                                    South Carolina, Georgia,
                                    Florida

Northeast Region
New England Division: Vermont, New Hampshire, Maine,
                          Massachusetts, Connecticut,
                          Rhode Island
Middle Atlantic Division: Pennsylvania, New York, New
                          Jersey

The Bureau also divides the United States in terms of
two population concentrations: metropolitan and nonmetropolitan areas. A metropolitan area, briefly defined, is a
Standard Metropolitan Statistical Area (SMSA), which consists of a county or group of contiguous counties that contains at least one city of 50,000 or more residents or two
contiguous cities with a combined population of at least
50,000. Contiguous counties are included in an SMSA if they
are economically and socially integrated with the base county.
The nonmetropolitan area is all territory outside metropolitan areas.
    Metropolitan areas are subdivided into two parts: the
central city and the suburban area. The largest city in
the metropolitan area is designated as the central city,
although additional cities within the metropolitan area may
be included as part of the central city if they are of sufficient size. The suburban area is all remaining territory
within the metropolitan area.

NATIONAL DEMOGRAPHIC TRENDS

Dominating all other national demographic trends is the
continuation of a long-term decline in the rate of population increase. The population of the United States continues
to grow, but at a steadily decreasing rate. During the
1950s, the national population grew 19 percent; during the
1960s, 13 percent; and if current growth rates continue
through the close of this decade, the nation's population
during the 1970s will have increased 8 percent.
    Each of the components of population change--birthrates,
death rates, and immigration rates--contributes to the current low rate of population increase. The annual death rate,
after falling continuously since 1900, stabilized during the
1950s at about 9.4 deaths per 1,000 and then dropped again
to a level of 8.9 deaths per 1,000. The nation's birthrate
has returned to its previous trend of long-term decline following the anomaly of the post-World War II baby boom. The
birthrate stood at 19.4 births per 1,000 in 1940 and rose

to 24.9 births per 1,000 in 1955, but has declined continuously since then, dropping to 14.7 births per 1,000 by 1975, the lowest level in American history. The eventual number of births that women now moving into their child-bearing years expect to have averages 2.1, a figure barely at the replacement level for a stable population. Immigration rates are based on quotas that are fixed by law, and legal immigration currently averages 400,000 persons per year. Of the nation's total population increase of 1.7 million during 1975, 1.2 million resulted from natural increase (an excess of births over deaths), while immigration accounted for the remaining 0.5 million (including 130,000 Vietnamese refugees).

These declining rates of population growth have caused the Census Bureau to issue a new series of three population projections that adjust expected national population growth downward. Each of these current projections, Series I, II, and III, assumes that annual net immigration will continue at 400,000 per year and that a slight reduction will occur in future mortality rates. The three projections differ only in their assumptions about future fertility rates, ranging in their assumptions from a high of 2.7 lifetime births per woman in Series I to a low of 1.7 lifetime births per woman in Series III. These projections suggest that the nation's population by 2000 may total between 245 and 287 million (although totals outside these bounds cannot be ruled out).

Due to a lowering of expected lifetime fertility rates, these current population projections are significantly lower than ones made as recently as the latter half of the 1960s. At that time, projections of the nation's total population by 2000 ranged from a low of 283 million (Series D) to a high of 361 million (Series A), which exceed current projections by as much as 25 percent.[2]

The long-term decline in population growth is expected to continue, although previous fluctuations in birthrates (for example, the sharp rise in the number of births following World War II after which the birthrate dropped to an all-time low) will continue to affect current changes in the nation's demographic profile. The subpopulations of individuals aged 18 to 24 and 25 to 34, age-groups now consisting of members of the postwar-boom cohorts, have

[2]See U.S. Bureau of the Census (1975c) for comparisons between current and earlier projections and the assumptions underlying each series in the two sets of projections.

grown 13 and 23 percent, respectively, since 1970. The
aging of these large cohorts, together with their greater
life expectancies, will play a major role in increasing
the median age of the nation's population.

Changes in the size of other age-groups during the first
half of the 1970s include a decline in the number of youths
and an increase in the number of elderly persons. The lower
birthrates of the latter half of the 1960s have produced a
decline of 8 percent in the number of children aged 13 and
under, while the declining mortality rate and the increased
size of the cohort of elderly persons have served to increase the size of the age-group of those 65 and over by
12 percent. Continued declines in the birthrate, along
with either a constant or slightly dropping death rate,
will produce a population that contains proportionately
more elderly persons year by year. The median age of the
total population, which dropped from 30.2 years in 1950 to
a low of 27.9 years in 1970, has already begun to rise and,
as of 1975, stood at 28.8 years.

These shifts in the demographic structure of the nation's
population are occurring at the same time that fundamental
changes in the overall structure of marital arrangements
are emerging. As the large birth cohorts of the late 1940s
and early 1950s are advancing through young adulthood, the
nation's marriage rate is declining (having peaked in 1972);
the median age at first marriage is increasing; the divorce
rate is increasing (from 2.2 per 1,000 population in 1960
to 4.8 per 1,000 in 1975); more young unmarried adults are
maintaining their own homes; and more children are living
with a single parent. Since 1970, the largest increase
in family groups has been among those headed by women
who do not have husbands living with them; half of this increase was accounted for by women who were divorced. The
combination of falling birthrates and changing household
composition (especially the increase in one-person households) is reflected in the declining numbers of persons per
household (Ross and Sawhill 1975).

These national demographic trends--lowered birthrates,
increasing numbers of elderly persons, changes in family
structure--carry with them consequences for the nation in
the 1970s as well as long-term consequences. Although current low birthrates imply lowered future levels of household
formation, the 7.7 million new households formed since 1970
represent an increase of 12.2 percent over the number that
existed at the beginning of the decade. Most households,
in 1975 as well as earlier, were maintained by two or more
related family members (primary family households); however,

a growing proportion was maintained by persons who lived
alone or with nonrelatives only (primary individual households). Between 1970 and 1975, the number of primary family
households increased 8 percent, and the number of primary
individual households rose 30 percent. These different
growth rates have reduced the proportion of households composed of related family members by 3 percent in just 5
years (U.S. Bureau of the Census 1976).

Although households headed by primary individuals still
account for less than one-fourth of the total number of
households, they have accounted for half of the increase
in new household formations since 1970. Considering national trends of increased numbers of individuals delaying
marriage, higher divorce rates, and both greater numbers
and larger proportions of the elderly maintaining their
own households, one may expect that the size of households
will continue to decline and the demand for dwelling units
will continue to rise at rates that are higher than the
rate of total population growth.

PATTERNS OF DECLINE AND GROWTH

Signs of the shift away from the long-term trend of metropolitan growth exceeding that of nonmetropolitan areas first
appeared during the 1960s. During this time, several nonmetropolitan regions experienced a reversal from population
decline to modest increase, and it appeared that, in at
least some of these areas, out-migration had peaked during
the previous decade. The metropolitan population growth
of 22 million during the 1960s resulted in part (one-third)
from growth through the addition of new land area, but two-
thirds was derived from population increases within the
1960 boundaries. Of the growth within the 1960 boundaries,
three-fourths was due to natural increase; of the remaining
one-fourth, a larger proportion resulted from immigration
than from the in-migration of former nonmetropolitan-area
residents. Thus, only a small proportion of the increase
in America's metropolitan population during the 1960s can
be attributed to out-migration from nonmetropolitan areas.

While the nation's total population increased 13.3 percent during the 1960s, the number of individuals residing
in metropolitan areas increased 16.6 percent, a rate of
increase that was 8.5 times the rate for nonmetropolitan
areas. Since 1970, however, a reversal has occurred; as
a result, the growth rates for nonmetropolitan areas have

exceeded those of metropolitan areas. Nationwide statistics
for the first half of the 1970s indicate that population
has increased 7.1 percent in nonmetropolitan areas and only
3.9 percent in metropolitan areas (see Table 1).

The Decline of Central Cities

When the nation's metropolitan areas are divided into their
central-city and suburban areas, it is readily apparent
that the current lower rate of growth of metropolitan areas
has resulted from a combination of the depopulation of the
central cities and the slackening growth boom in the suburbs.
Between 1970 and 1975, central cities experienced an absolute
population loss of nearly 2 million, or approximately 3 percent of the total number of their residents at the beginning
of the decade. Net migration from central cities to suburbs
and nonmetropolitan areas during this same period was more
than 7 million persons (gains and losses for each residential
category are presented in Table 1).

Although the current national trend of an absolute decline
in central-city population is new, the proportion of metropolitan area residents living in central cities rather than
the suburbs has declined continually since reaching a peak
during the 1920s. In 1920, central-city residents accounted
for 66 percent of America's metropolitan-area residents; by
1960, metropolitan-area residents were about equally divided
between central cities and suburbs; and by 1975, central-
city residents accounted for only 43 percent of the nation's
metropolitan population.

Although absolute population declines in selected central
cities occurred prior to 1970, gains in other central cities
more than offset those losses, resulting in overall central-
city growth. During the 1950s, absolute population declined
in 56 central cities while the nation's total number of
central-city residents increased 11.6 percent. During the
1960s, the number of central cities whose populations declined increased to 95 (39 percent of all central cities),
while the national central-city population increased 6.5
percent. Altogether, there were 47 central cities whose
populations declined continuously during the 20-year period
from 1950 to 1970. Since the total central-city population
declined by 2.7 percent between 1970 and 1975, it is likely

TABLE 1 Population of the United States, 1950-1975 (in thousands)[a]

Residential Category	1975[b]	1970	1960[c]	1950	Percentage Change 1970-1975	Percentage Change 1960-1970	Percentage Change 1950-1960
Total U.S.	209,682	199,819	179,971	151,235	4.9	13.3	19.0
Metropolitan	142,461	137,058	119,595	94,579	3.9	16.6	26.4
Central-city	61,154	62,876	59,947	53,696	-2.7	6.5	11.6
Suburban	81,307	74,182	59,647	40,883	9.6	26.7	45.9
Nonmetropolitan	67,221	62,761	60,384	56,656	7.1	6.8	6.4

[a]Population data for 1977 are presented in Table A-1 of the Appendix.

[b]Data for 1975 are April-centered averages from the Current Population Survey; 1970 data are also from the Current Population Survey and have been adjusted by excluding inmates of institutions and members of the Armed Forces residing in barracks for comparability with 1975 data.

[c]Data for 1960 and 1950 are total population counts from the two respective decennial censuses. The total population counts for 1970 were used to calculate the 1960-1970 percentage changes rather than the Current Population Survey figures shown.

SOURCES: U.S. Bureau of the Census (1972, 1975d).

that the number of central cities experiencing population
losses has been increasing.[3]

While central-city population losses during the 1950s
and 1960s occurred in a relatively large number of metropolitan areas, they were largely confined to the industrial
heartland cities of the North Central and Northeast regions
of the country. During the 1950s, 81 percent of the central
cities that lost population were located in this northern
area extending from the Midwest states through New England.
During the 1960s, this concentration of declining central
cities in the North lessened somewhat to 74 percent. Of
the nation's central cities that lost population during
both decades, 90 percent were located in this northern area.
Large central cities in this area that lost population during both the 1950s and 1960s include Baltimore, Boston,
Buffalo, Chicago, Cincinnati, Cleveland, Detroit, Minneapolis,
Philadelphia, Pittsburgh, and St. Louis.

In the 1970s, the greatest concentration of central cities
that are losing population continues to lie within this
northern industrial area. In the South, the central cities
in metropolitan areas with more than 1 million residents
have lost population, while the central cities of metropolitan areas with less than 1 million residents have gained
population--resulting in only a slight decrease in the total
number of southern central-city residents. In the West, the
number of residents in metropolitan areas of all sizes has
increased, with the largest gain occurring in the central
cities of metropolitan areas with less than 1 million residents. Population changes during the 1970s for central
cities, suburbs, and nonmetropolitan areas by size of metropolitan area for each region of the country are presented in
Table 2.

The Growth of Nonmetropolitan Areas

Throughout the 1940s and 1950s, the nation's nonmetropolitan
areas experienced high levels of out-migration. Some nonmetropolitan areas reached a turning point during the 1960s
in that they were no longer losing residents, but since 1970
nonmetropolitan areas as a whole have not only retained

[3]Neither the Current Population Survey nor the Federal-
State Cooperative Program for Local Population Estimates
permits intercensal estimation of central-city population
changes for individual cities that are strictly comparable.

TABLE 2 Population as of 1975 and Percentage Change in Population Between 1970 and 1975 for Selected Categories of Metropolitan and Nonmetropolitan Counties by Region of the United States

Region	All Metropolitan Areas			1,000,000 or More		Less Than 1,000,000		Nonmetropolitan Areas[a]			
	Total	Central Cities	Suburbs	Central Cities	Suburbs	Central Cities	Suburbs	Total	Less Than 2,500	2,500-24,999	25,000 or More
1975 Population:											
Total U.S.	209,682	61,154	81,307	32,589	48,408	28,565	32,899	67,221	7,957	40,530	18,733
Northeast	48,184	15,858	22,128	10,975	13,931	4,883	8,197	10,198	101	4,098	5,999
North Central	56,714	15,718	21,746	8,591	13,518	7,127	8,229	19,250	2,471	12,523	3,855
South	67,047	17,810	20,019	5,626	8,975	12,184	11,044	29,217	4,641	18,263	6,313
West	37,737	11,768	17,413	7,397	11,984	4,371	5,429	8,556	744	5,246	2,566
Percentage change 1970-1975:											
Total U.S.	4.9	-2.7	9.6	-5.0	7.2	0.0	13.4	7.1	10.7	2.0	18.2
Northeast	-0.3	-7.0	2.3	-8.4	1.0	-3.5	4.6	5.6	-50.0	20.4	39.3
North Central	0.8	-16.7	7.1	-7.4	6.0	-6.0	8.9	3.4	11.4	5.0	-5.9
South	8.8	1.1	19.1	0.7	17.1	1.3	20.8	7.5	15.2	3.0	16.4
West	10.7	3.6	12.8	-1.0	9.4	12.3	21.2	17.2	0.4	15.6	27.1

[a]Nonmetropolitan areas in this table are groups of counties with either no place of 2,500 or more residents (less than 2,500), counties with a place of between 2,500 and 25,000 residents (2,500-25,000), or counties with a place of more than 25,000 but less than 50,000 residents (25,000 or more).

SOURCE: U.S. Bureau of the Census (1975d).

residents but also have experienced a gain in population through migration from metropolitan areas.

The number of persons residing in the nation's nonmetropolitan areas during the 1960s grew by 6.8 percent, a rate of increase that was half the national average. During the first half of the 1970s, nonmetropolitan population increased 7.1 percent, compared to the national average of 4.9 percent and an increase of 3.9 percent for metropolitan areas.[4]

More significant for nonmetropolitan areas than their current relatively higher growth rate is the reversal that has occurred in migration between the nonmetropolitan and metropolitan areas of the nation. Increased mechanization of farming since World War II has led to a decrease in the size of the farm population and contributed to rural out-migration. During the 1950s, nonmetropolitan areas experienced a net loss of more than 5 million persons through out-migration. High levels of out-migration continued into the 1960s, when the nation's farm population declined at an annual rate of 4.8 percent; since 1970, however, the farm population has declined at an annual rate of only 1.8 percent. (Farm population is now at an all-time low of 8.9 million, 4.1 percent of the nation's total population.) With fewer out-migrants and increased numbers of in-migrants, nonmetropolitan areas have experienced net migration gains of approximately 2 million persons since 1970, thus reversing the trend of population loss that had existed since the 1940s.

Although not all nonmetropolitan areas are now sharing in this new pattern of growth, it is true that migration reversals have occurred in almost all nonmetropolitan areas of the country. Nonmetropolitan population increases in the four major regions vary from a low of 3.4 percent in the North Central region, to 5.6 and 7.4 percent, respectively, in the Northeast and South regions, and a high of 17.2 percent in the West. Increases are now being registered in all classes of nonmetropolitan counties--from the most sparsely settled counties (those with settlements of

[4]These changes are within metropolitan and nonmetropolitan areas as defined for the Census of 1970. Between 1970 and 1975, counties whose status changed from nonmetropolitan to metropolitan shifted 114,719 square miles of land area and 9.4 million persons to the metropolitan category. Population growth between 1970 and 1976 for nonmetropolitan and metropolitan areas is virtually equal when these territorial changes are included (U.S. Office of Management and Budget 1975).

2,500 persons or less) to those with a settlement of over
25,000 residents (see Table 2).

Generally, those areas located immediately adjacent to
but outside metropolitan areas (which account for 52 percent of all nonmetropolitan residents) have experienced
the highest nonmetropolitan growth rates: a 4.7 percent
increase from 1970 through 1973 compared with a 3.7 percent
increase for counties not adjacent to metropolitan areas
(Beale 1975). In particular, nonmetropolitan areas whose
residents are relatively more integrated into metropolitan
labor markets have experienced higher rates of recent growth.
Through 1975, population increased 10.1 percent in those
nonmetropolitan counties in which 20 percent or more of the
residents commute to a metropolitan area for work and dropped
to 5.9 percent in those counties in which less than 3 percent
of the residents commute to metropolitan areas (see Table 3).
However, even this lowest nonmetropolitan growth figure of
5.9 percent is greater than the 3.9 percent growth experienced by metropolitan areas during the same time period
(Forstall 1975).

The areas of nonmetropolitan America that have undergone
reversals from population decline to growth in the 1960s
and 1970s are both diverse and widespread (Beale and Fuguitt
1975). In the South, an area extending from the Ozarks
through eastern Texas that contains a predominantly white
population shifted from reliance on agricultural employment
to development of manufacturing and new recreational areas.
The Upper Great Lakes area, bordering the southern coast of
Lake Superior, has also experienced growth primarily as the
result of manufacturing decentralization and the development
of recreational facilities and retirement communities. The
nonmetropolitan areas of the Blue Ridge-Piedmont, Florida,
the Southwest, and the northern Pacific Coast have all

TABLE 3   Growth of Nonmetropolitan Counties by Level of
Commuting to Metropolitan Areas, 1960-1975

Level of Commuting[a]	Population			Percentage Change	
	1975	1970	1960	1970-1975	1960-1970
>19 percent commuters	4,407	4,009	3,655	10.1	9.7
10-19 percent commuters	10,011	9,349	8,705	7.1	7.4
3-9 percent commuters	14,338	13,497	12,805	5.9	5.4
<3 percent commuters	28,197	26,628	26,207	5.9	1.6

[a]Percentage of counties' work force commuting to a metropolitan area for
employment. Based on 1970 Census commuting data.

SOURCE: Forstall (1975).

experienced growth resulting from the decentralization of
manufacturing, recreational and retirement developments,
the opening up of new resources, or the expansion of improved transportation facilities (for example, the interstate highway system) that enable persons to live in rural
areas and commute to metropolitan labor markets. (Since
1970, nonmetropolitan growth has not only exceeded its
1960s level but has also spread to a larger number of areas;
for example, a new growth axis now cuts through central
Maine along the route of the interstate highway.) While
only the six nonmetropolitan areas mentioned above experienced net migration gains during the 1960s, only one of the
nation's rural areas now continues to lose population through
out-migration: the old Tobacco and Cotton Belt extending
from the North Carolina Cape to the Delta area of the Mississippi River. This area, which contains a large rural black
population, has not benefited significantly from the decentralization of manufactuirng and continues to lose residents
through out-migration to cities of both the North and the
South.

Regional Growth

Figure 1 presents the population of the United States by
residence in the four major regions for each year since
1940. The long-term faster growth trend of the West, the
recently increasing growth rate of the South, and the declining growth rates of the Northeast and North Central
regions are evident.

Figure 2 presents the percentage of each decade's population increase accounted for by the individual regions
and divisions. This shows that the North Central region
(the East and West North Central divisions combined) increased its share of the nation's population growth during
the 1950s but has since seen its share decline relative to
those of the West and the South. Population growth in each
of the three divisions of the South during the 1960s and
1970s occurred at higher rates than in any of the other
divisions of the country; since 1960, these three divisions
have doubled their share of the nation's total population
growth. Growth in the West, while continuing to account
for a large share of the total population expansion, has
shifted markedly from Pacific to Mountain divisions since
the 1960s.

Only three divisions of the country have exhibited significantly declining shares of the nation's new population

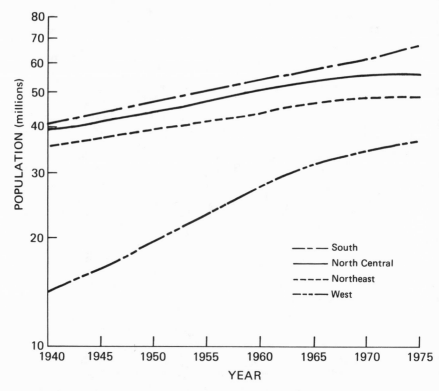

FIGURE 1   Total population of the United States by region, 1940-1975 (U.S. Bureau of the Census 1975a, 1976).

growth since the 1950s.   The first is the East North Central division, which includes Ohio, Indiana, Illinois, Wisconsin, and Michigan.   It first experienced a declining share of the nation's population growth during the 1960s and more recently its share has decreased even more.   The second division to experience relatively slower growth has been the Middle Atlantic division (New York, New Jersey, and Pennsylvania), whose share of national growth has declined, especially recently.   The New England division's share of national growth has also decreased during the 1970s.   The area formed by these three divisions, extending from New England to the Mississippi River and north of the Ohio River, encompasses the nation's industrial core, whose urban centers, as was previously shown, have experienced

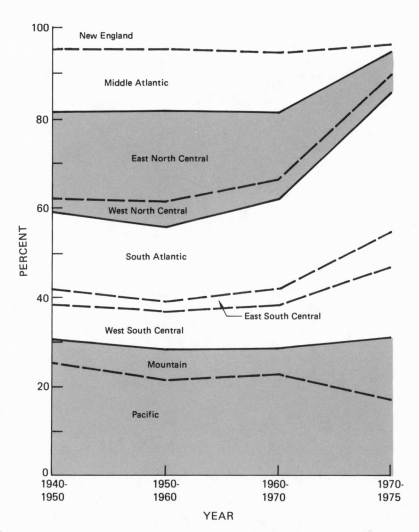

SOURCES: U.S. Bureau of the Census (1975) *Historical Statistics of the United States: Colonial Times to 1970.* Washington, D.C.: U.S. Department of Commerce. U.S. Bureau of the Census (1976) Population profile of the United States: 1975. Series P-20, No. 292 in *Current Population Reports.* Washington, D.C.: U.S. Department of Commerce.

FIGURE 2   Percentage of Total United States Population Growth, 1940-1950, 1950-1960, 1960-1970, 1970-1975.

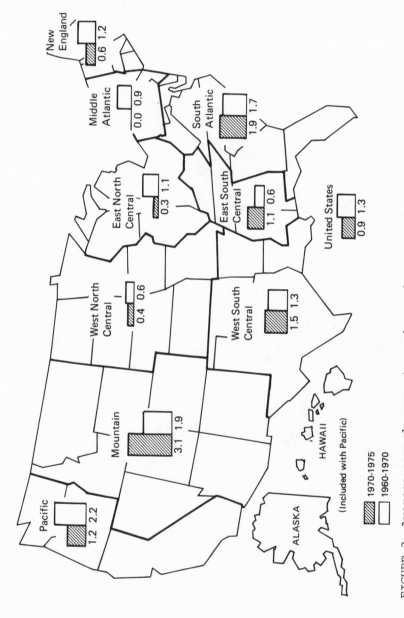

FIGURE 3 Average annual percentage change in population: 1960–1970 and 1970–1975
(U.S. Domestic Council 1976).

the slowest growth of any of the nation's metropolitan
areas (see Table 2).

The average annual growth rates for the nine divisions
of the country during the 1960s and the first half of the
1970s are shown in Figure 3. During the 1960s, the divisions covering the northern section of the country, extending from New England to the Rocky Mountains, experienced
annual growth rates that were lower than the national average of 1.3 percent. Outside the North, only the East South
Central division, composed of the four states of Kentucky,
Tennessee, Mississippi, and Alabama, experienced growth at
a rate lower than the national average. Since 1970, the
average annual growth rates of the northern section of the
country have accounted for an even smaller percentage of
the national population increase. The Middle Atlantic
division has in fact experienced zero population growth
since 1970.

Meanwhile, 1970s' growth rates across the South and in
the Rocky Mountain states have all increased above their
1960s' levels. The Rocky Mountain states are now experiencing the nation's fastest growth, an average annual rate
of 3.1 percent--more than three times greater than the
national average. Growth rates during the 1970s for each
of the divisions in the South and West have exceeded the
national average, and only in the Pacific division of this
entire section has the annual growth rate diminished since
the 1960s.

Interregional Migration

Population change is the result of three major processes:
natural change (births and deaths), interregional migration,
and international migration. Because regional variability
in natural increase has diminished over the past 3 decades
and international migration (although it does not add equally
to the population of each region) totals only about 400,000
immigrants and is relatively stable, neither seriously
affects differential regional growth. The truly dynamic
component of regional population change thus lies in interregional migration. Interregional migration rates (measured
as a percentage of all residential moves) have remained
approximately the same in the 1970s as they were in the
1960s, but the volume of interregional flows, especially
those to the South, has changed dramatically in the 1970s.
Interregional migration flows between the four regions for
both 1965-1970 and 1970-1975 are shown in Table 4.

TABLE 4   Interregional Migration: 1965-1970 and 1970-1975
(in thousands)[a]

Residence in 1965	Residence in 1970			
	Northeast	North Central	South	West
Northeast	--	450	1,064	474
North Central	397	--	1,282	982
South	626	1,007	--	853
West	250	567	796	--
Residence in 1970	Residence in 1975			
	Northeast	North Central	South	West
Northeast	--	380	1,508	511
North Central	313	--	1,638	975
South	544	848	--	861
West	200	503	936	--

[a]Interregional migration data for 1975-1977 are presented
in Table A-2 of the Appendix.

SOURCES: U.S. Bureau of the Census (1972, 1975b).

While the volume of interregional migration demonstrates
the scale of long-distance mobility in the United States
(the volume in and out of the South during the period, for
example, exceeded 4 million in-migrants and 2 million out-
migrants), the regional effects can be seen in the net
differences in the volume of interregional migration, shown
in Figure 4.   During both 5-year periods, 1965-1970 and
1970-1975, the Northeast region experienced net migration
losses to each of the three other regions; the North Central region experienced net migration losses to the South
and the West; and the South and the West showed net migration gains.   Since 1970, the small net residual flow between
the South and West has reversed itself.   In the 1970s, the
South has become the only region of the country with net
migration gains from all other regions.   Furthermore, the
flow of persons into the South from both the North Central
and Northeast regions (which represents the largest in-
migration streams) has increased over 1960s' levels.

RESIDENTIAL MOBILITY

Residential Decentralization

In 1975, 44 percent of the nation's civilian noninstitutional population over 4 years of age resided at a different

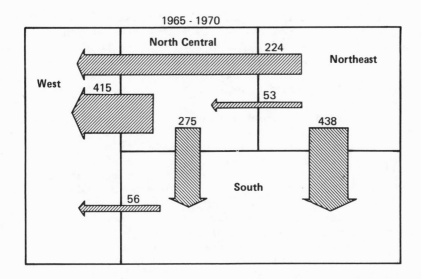

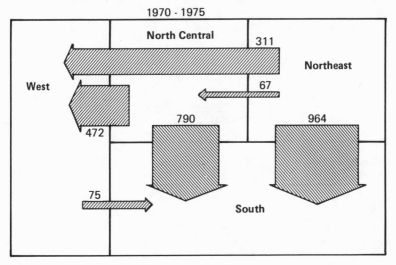

NOTE: Width of arrows is proportional to volume of net interregional migration flows. Figures accompanying arrows indicate numbers of net interregional migrants (in thousands). Total numbers of interregional migrants for both periods appear in Table 4.

FIGURE 4 Net interregional migration: 1965–1970 and 1970–1975 (U.S. Bureau of the Census 1970, 1975b).

dwelling than in 1970.[5] In Table 5, these movers are divided into the three residential categories of central city,
suburb, and nonmetropolitan area according to the locations
of their 1970 and 1975 residences. Of all moves, 85 percent were within the same residential category, for example,
moves from one suburban area to another suburban area or
moves within the same suburban area. Of the 15 percent who
relocated to a different residential category, the pronounced
trend consists of a centrifugal shift from the central city
to the suburbs, and, on a larger scale, from metropolitan
areas to nonmetropolitan areas (see Figure 5). Between 1970
and 1975, a total of 13 million persons moved out of central
cities, three-fourths of them to the suburbs and one-fourth
to nonmetropolitan areas. At the same time, only 6 million
persons moved into the central cities--a net loss of 7 million residents through migration.

During this same 5-year period, the suburbs experienced
a net migration gain of 5.4 million persons. This net gain
resulted from the in-migration of 12.7 million and the out-
migration of 7.3 million persons. Of those who moved to the
suburbs, 77 percent were former central-city resedents; and
of those who left the suburbs, about equal numbers moved to

TABLE 5 Residential Mobility, 1970-1975 (in millions)[a]

| Residential Category in 1970 | Residential Category in 1975 | | |
	Central City	Suburb	Nonmetropolitan Area
Central City	[17.1][b]	9.8	3.2
Suburb	3.8	[18.2][b]	3.5
Nonmetropolitan area	2.1	3.0	[19.0][b]

[a]Data on residential mobility for 1975-1977 are presented
in Table A-3 of the Appendix.

[b]Figures in brackets are movers who remained in same residential category during relocation.

SOURCE: U.S. Bureau of the Census (1975b).

[5]Estimates of residential mobility reported in this section
are derived from the Census Bureau's annual Current Population Survey (U.S. Bureau of the Census 1975b).

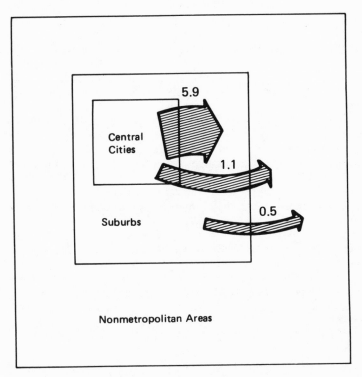

NOTE: Width of arrows is proportional to
volume of net flows among the three areas.

FIGURE 5   Net residential flows, 1970-1975
(in millions) (U.S. Bureau of the Census
1975b).

central cities and nonmetropolitan areas. The net migration gain of 1.6 million persons to nonmetropolitan areas
(the result of out-migration by 5.1 million and in-migration
by 6.7 million) consisted of approximately the same number
of individuals from both central cities and suburban areas.
Of all individuals who changed their residential category
between 1970 and 1975, 26 percent moved from metropolitan
to nonmetropolitan areas, 20 percent moved from nonmetropolitan to metropolitan areas, 38 percent moved from central cities to suburbs, and 16 percent moved from suburbs
to central cities. Relocations outward from the urban center outnumbered relocations inward by a margin of 2 to 1.

Labor Force Migration

Residential decentralization in the United States has been
accompanied by similar shifts in the work place of the labor
force (see Figure 6). Comparing the national work-force
migration patterns of 1960-1963 with those of 1970-1973 reveals a dramatic reversal: in the earlier period, the central counties[6] of metropolitan areas gained 104,000 workers
and nonmetropolitan counties (areas) lost 106,000 workers;
in the more recent period, central counties lost 84,000
workers and nonmetropolitan counties gained 19,000 (see
Table 6).

This reversal in labor-force migration between the central counties of metropolitan areas and nonmetropolitan
areas has been most dramatic in the nation's largest cities.
During the 1960-1963 period, the work force in central
counties of metropolitan areas with populations of 2 million or more was increased by 25,000 workers who moved
there from nonmetropolitan areas. In the 1970-1973 period,
however, these same central counties lost 54,000 workers
who shifted their work place to nonmetropolitan areas, plus
an additional 76,000 who relocated to jobs in the suburbs
(see Table 7). These work-force migration patterns reflect
the accelerated decentralization of manufacturing and related activities out of central cities--especially out of

TABLE 6   Net Migration of Work Force for Metropolitan and
Nonmetropolitan Counties: 1960-1963 and 1970-1973 (in
thousands)[a]

| | Metropolitan Counties | | | | | Nonmetro- |
| | Central Counties of SMSAs with Populations of: | | | | Suburban | politan |
Years	2 Million or More	1 Million- 1,999,999	0.5 Million- 999,999	Less Than 0.5 Million	Counties	Counties
1960-1963	-27.1	71.9	28.0	31.3	55.4	-159.5
1970-1973	-270.8	46.8	85.8	54.5	64.4	19.3

[a]Positive numbers indicate net in-migration and negative numbers indicate net out-
migration.

SOURCE: Regional Economic Analysis Division (1976).

[6]Central counties are those counties within metropolitan
areas that most closely approximate the central city (Regional Economic Analysis Division 1976). These data on
worker migration are derived from the Social Security
Administration's Continuous Work History Sample.

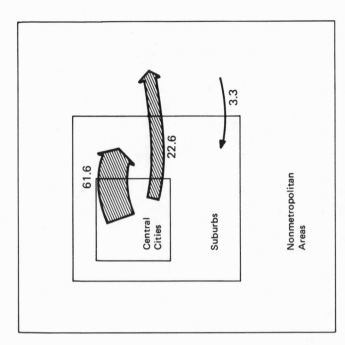

1970-1973

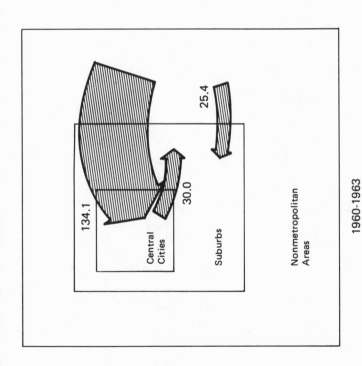

1960-1963

NOTE: Width of arrows is proportional to volume of net flows between the areas.

FIGURE 6 Net work-force flows, 1960-1963 and 1970-1973 (in thousands) (Regional Economic Analysis Division 1976).

TABLE 7 Place-to-Place Net Migration of Work Force for Metropolitan and Nonmetropolitan Counties: 1960-1963 and 1970-1973 (in thousands)[a]

	Metropolitan Counties								Suburban Counties		Nonmetropolitan Counties	
	Central Counties of SMSAs with Populations of:											
	2 Million or More		1 Million-1,999,999		0.5 Million-999,999		Less Than 0.5 Million					
	'60-'63	'70-'73	'60-'63	'70-'73	'60-'63	'70-'73	'60-'63	'70-'73	'60-'63	'70-'73	'60-'63	'70-'73
Central counties of SMSAs with populations of												
2 Million or more	--	--	0.1	73.7	-10.4	47.1	-3.1	20.7	65.1	75.8	-24.6	53.5
1 Million-1,999,999	-0.1	-73.7	--	--	1.5	-3.2	-19.3	16.5	-23.7	12.6	-30.3	1.0
0.5 Million-999,999	10.4	-47.1	-1.5	3.2	--	--	0.6	-13.7	-1.2	-11.6	-36.3	-16.6
Less than 0.5 million	3.1	-20.7	19.3	-16.5	-0.6	13.7	--	--	-10.2	-15.7	-42.9	-15.3
Suburban counties	-65.1	-75.8	23.7	-12.6	1.2	11.6	10.2	15.7	--	--	-25.4	-3.3
Nonmetropolitan counties	24.6	-53.5	30.3	-1.0	36.3	16.6	42.9	15.3	25.4	3.3	--	--

[a]Positive numbers indicate net in-migration, and negative numbers indicate net out-migration.

SOURCE: Regional Economic Analysis Division (1976).

the nation's largest ones—that has been occurring during
the 1970s.

Characteristics of Movers

Previous research has demonstrated that, typically, persons
who move differ from those who do not move and, as a result,
have an impact on areas of origin and destination greater
than their numbers alone would imply.[7]

Age The highest levels of mobility are usually found
among persons in their 20s, reflecting the establishment
of new households by young adults who have recently completed their schooling, married, or entered the labor force.
During the first half of the 1970s, 72 percent of all persons aged 25 to 29 resided at a location in 1975 different
from that in 1970, compared with just over 40 percent of
the total population (over 4 years of age). Persons in
their early 20s and early 30s were also highly mobile during this period: about 60 percent of both groups changed
residence. The high mobility rates of younger adults are
also reflected in the mobility rates of their children,
which are higher than those for adolescents whose parents
are older.

Race Residential mobility levels differ by race as well
as by age. Between 1970 and 1975, more blacks changed
their residence than whites (46 compared with 41 percent),
but they tended to move shorter distances; 36 percent of
all blacks aged 4 and older moved to a new residence within
the same county, compared with 23 percent of all whites.
However, the long-distance moves, represented by intercounty
and interstate migration, were more frequent among whites
than blacks (18 compared with 10 percent and 5 compared with
3 percent of each respective subpopulation).

Education Educational attainment is another factor influencing the likelihood of migration. College graduates are
more likely to move between counties and states than high
school graduates, who, in turn, migrate more often than

[7]A summary of earlier research on the levels of geographical mobility of specific subpopulations is presented in
Taeuber and Taeuber (1957); statistics for the 1970s are
from U.S. Bureau of the Census (1975b).

persons whose formal schooling ended at the primary level.
Among all persons aged 18 and older, 30 percent of those
with 4 or more years of college moved to a different county
between March 1970 and March 1975, compared with 16 percent
of those who had completed 4 years of high school and 9
percent of those with 8 years of education or less.

Family Structure   The presence and age level of children
are additional factors influencing the spatial mobility of
families. Among married men aged 25-34 living with their
wives, those with no children under 18 are more mobile than
those with children under 18. Husband-wife families (head
aged 25-34) whose children are all under 6 are also more
residentially mobile than those with children over 6.
Thus, the presence of school-age children appears to reduce
the spatial mobility of families.

Characteristics of Subpopulations of Movers   Not only do
more mobile individuals differ from those who are spatially
stable, but also subpopulations of the spatially mobile
differ among themselves in the direction of their moves.
For instance, persons moving to central cities tend to be
slightly younger than persons moving from central cities.
In the 1970-1975 period, the median age of central-city
in-migrants was 25.1 years, compared with 27.6 years for
out-migrants. Blacks are relatively more numerous in the
migration flow to, rather than from, central cities. Between 1970 and 1975, blacks constituted 12.3 percent of.
the in-migrants to central cities and 7.5 percent of the
out-migrants. Continuation of these particular migration
patterns by blacks and younger individuals, accompanied
by the higher rates of natural increase associated with
both groups, will contribute to raising the proportion of
youths and blacks residing in central cities.

Directions of Residential Changes

Suburbanization Trend   Those who make short-distance
moves, especially those who remain within a single metropolitan area while changing residence, contribute more to
the suburbanization trend than those who move long distances (e.g., interregional migrants). Among those who
moved within the same metropolitan area during the 1970-
1975 period, those moving from the central city to the
suburbs outnumbered those moving from the suburbs to the
central city by 3 to 1. Among interregional migrants, on

the other hand, persons shifting to the suburbs outnumbered those shifting to central cities by only 2 to 1. This difference between short- and long-distance movers produced a net shift to the suburbs that was 42 percent higher among those who remained within a single metropolitan area than among interregional migrants.

Metropolitan/Nonmetropolitan Shifts   A similar trend was evident during this period among individuals who changed their residential location between metropolitan and nonmetropolitan areas. The proportion of movers shifting from metropolitan to nonmetropolitan areas while remaining within the same region was 14 percent higher than the proportion of those who stayed in the same residential category while migrating between regions. Among persons shifting both from central cities to suburbs and from metropolitan to nonmetropolitan areas, short-distance movers exhibited the greater tendency to shift away from the central city. These differences between local and long-distance movers are at least partially explained by the fact that interregional migrants continue to include individuals seeking the opportunities traditionally associated with central cities, such as schooling and better employment. For the black poor leaving rural areas (especially those of the South), accessible housing and personal contacts are often found in the inner city. These overriding decentralization trends should not obscure the fact that some 61 percent of all interregional migrants who had resided in nonmetropolitan areas in 1970 were by 1975 living in metropolitan areas.

Black Migration   The movement to metropolitan areas was most apparent among black migrants from the South, who continue to maintain migration streams from rural areas to the cities of the North.[8] However, even this pattern is changing. During the 5-year period from 1965 to 1970, the black population of the South decreased by 216,000 due to outmigration, but since then the South has gained 14,000 blacks from other regions of the country. Comparing the first half of the 1970s to the last half of the 1960s, in-migration by blacks to the South increased 86.4 percent and out-migration decreased 23.8 percent.

---

[8]See U.S. Bureau of the Census (1975b) for data documenting the continued long-distance moves to central cities from rural areas.

Economic Aspects of Population Shifts

These population shifts have broad economic consequences
for central cities. During 1970-1975, the mean family income of black migrants leaving nonmetropolitan areas for
central cities was $5,037 or about half that of blacks al-
ready residing in central cities. This continuing flow of
low-income persons will continue to add to the financial
burdens of central cities. The economic problems of cities
are also affected by the fact that more families and unre-
lated individuals are leaving the central city than are
moving to it, and the income levels of in-migrants are in
general lower than those of out-migrants.[9] The previous-
year mean income level of families and individuals who
moved to central cities between 1970 and 1974 was about
$10,300, compared with $12,500 for those who moved from
central cities. During this 4-year period alone, central
cities experienced a net loss of $29.6 billion in the ag-
gregate personal incomes of their residents, due to the
differential income levels between in-migrants and out-
migrants and the greater number of out-migrants than in-
migrants.

Conclusion

Overall, the decentralization trend has been greatest among
movers who change residence within the same region of the
country, while at least some interregional migration continues to include people moving from rural areas to central
cities. More blacks, more poor, and greater numbers of
younger persons are moving to, rather than from, central
cities. The suburbs receive proportionately more whites,
the more affluent, and families rather than single persons.
    It has been suggested that these current patterns of
decentralization represent continuations of previous trends
--that what is now being referred to as nonmetropolitan
growth is simply growth at the exurban fringes of metropolitan areas. However, longitudinal analysis of data from
1900 through the 1970s, which document levels of population
concentration, forces us to conclude that what we are now
witnessing is something more than the continued expansion

[9]See U.S. Bureau of the Census (1975d) for more detail on
the income differences between central-city, suburban, and
nonmetropolitan residents.

of metropolitan areas. The data consist of indexes of
population concentration at each of several levels (scales)
of spatial disaggregation, with the coarsest level consisting of the nine geographical divisions used by the Census
Bureau and the finest consisting of county units. Analysis
of changes in those indexes shows that population concentration has declined throughout this century at the division and state levels, reflecting the general deconcentration
that has accompanied the expansion of settlement to the West
and the South. During the 1940s, population dispersal also
occurred at the county level, reflecting the suburbanization
movement. On the other hand, analysis of population concentrations at a level termed economic subregions (which
divide the country into approximately 100 areas centered on
metropolitan economies) shows continually more concentration
between 1920 and 1970, indicating that period's widespread
trend of rural-to-urban migration (Duncan et al. 1961,
Vining and Strauss 1976).

Since 1970, however, deconcentration has occurred at
all of the spatial levels--from the county through the
divisional. This represents a clean break with the previous trends indicating continued urbanization in the form
of rural-to-urban migration. For the first time in this
century, population deconcentration is now occurring at
all levels of regional disaggregation. Although population
concentration continues in some of the most rural states,
e.g., New Mexico and North Dakota, the trend toward decentralization in the more urbanized states far outweighs these
counterflows and indicates that the current changes represent a genuine turning point from the nation's preceding
trends toward urbanization and metropolitan concentration.

CHARACTERISTICS OF METROPOLITAN-AREA RESIDENTS

Halfway through the current decade, the central cities of
metropolitan areas lost 2.7 percent of their 1970 residential population. During the same period, suburban areas
gained 9.6 percent. As a result, the suburbs contain 33
percent more residents than do central cities; 39 percent
of the nation's population reside in suburban areas, compared with 29 percent in central cities and 32 percent in
nonmetropolitan areas. The differences between central-
city and suburban residents are significant.

Income

The median income of families residing in the suburbs is
now $14,007, 23.5 percent higher than the average of $11,343
for central-city families.[10] The difference between the
average suburban and central-city family's income was 17.8
percent in 1970. In the 1970-1975 period, suburban incomes
increased 4.6 percent and central-city incomes diminished
an average of 0.3 percent.

Contrary to popular beliefs, current differences between
central-city and suburban incomes are of a similar magnitude
for both black and white families. The median income of
suburban black families is now 20 percent higher than that
of black families residing in central cities, and the median
income of suburban white families is 15 percent higher than
that of white families living in central cities. The generally lower income levels for both central-city blacks and
whites should not, however, lead one to conclude that higher-
income families have altogether deserted central cities.
As of March 1974, when the median family income nationwide
was $12,000, one-third of all central-city families (almost
5.3 million) had annual incomes in excess of $15,000, and
17 percent had annual incomes over $20,000.

Although the number of persons with incomes below the
poverty level has actually decreased during the 1970s (from
27 million or 13.7 percent of the total population in 1969
to 23 million or 11.1 percent by 1973), the portion of that
population that resides in metropolitan areas has increased
from 56.2 percent to 59.9 percent, and the largest share of
the increase has occurred within the central city. Central
cities, with 29 percent of the nation's population, now
contain 37.4 percent of its poor, an increase of 3.2 percent of the total since the beginning of the decade. Just
over 10 percent of all central-city families now receive
some form of public assistance income, while the proportion
of suburban families receiving such assistance is 3.9 percent

Race

Not only do central cities contain a disproportionate number of the nation's poor, but they are also the home of a

[10]All figures in this discussion of income levels are in
constant 1973 dollars (U.S. Bureau of the Census 1975d).

majority of the nation's blacks. Of the total black population, 58 percent now reside in central cities compared
with 25 percent of all whites, while 17 percent of all
blacks and 42 percent of all whites reside in the suburbs.
The number of black persons residing outside metropolitan
areas continues to decline, and the white nonmetropolitan
population is now increasing at a higher rate than that of
the 1960s.

Although the number of blacks residing in suburbs relative to the number of whites remains small, the suburban
growth rate of blacks has exceeded that of whites during
both the 1960s and 1970s. During the 1960s, black suburban
population grew at an annual rate of 3.2 percent compared
with 2.3 percent for whites; since 1970, black suburban
population growth has increased to an average of 5.2 percent per year, while growth in the number of whites residing
in the suburbs has decreased to an annual rate of 1.6 percent. Thus, black suburbanization rates have increased
during the 1970s at a time when white suburbanization rates
have dropped.

This increased rate of suburbanization by blacks, coupled
with a central-city growth rate that has dropped from 3.1
percent per year during the 1960s to 1.9 percent per year
in the 1970s, is now producing a decline in the concentration of blacks residing in the central city for the first
time in this century. The central-city concentration of
blacks reached its peak in 1970, when 80 percent of all
blacks living in metropolitan areas resided in central
cities. Since then, the level of central-city concentration of blacks has dropped to 74 percent, placing it below
the levels of the 1940s.

Blacks are not the only minority group concentrated in
metropolitan areas. Persons of Hispanic origin are more
concentrated in metropolitan areas than either blacks or
whites; however, they are not as concentrated in central
cities as blacks. Of the nation's total Hispanic origin
population, 81 percent now reside in metropolitan areas,
but only 49 percent reside in central cities, compared with
58 percent of blacks and 25 percent of other whites.

Age

Similarly, the decline in the total population of central
cities during the 1970s has not been distributed equally
among all age-groups. The number of young adults aged 25-
34 has increased, while the number of youths through age 17

and adults aged 35-64 has decreased, due to generally lower
birth rates and the general suburban shift of families.
The median age of the central city's declining population
remains slightly older than that of suburban residents, but
this gap has narrowed since the 1960s as the proportion of
young children in the suburbs has declined. The proportion
of elderly persons (65 and over) among the residents of
central cities remains large, with 22 percent of all central-
city residents receiving part of their income from social
security, compared with 18 percent for suburban dwellers.

Family Structure

The final set of differences between central-city and suburban residents relates to family structure. The nationwide increase of 1.2 million families headed by women in
1970-1975 is equal to the increase in such families that
occurred during the entire decade of the 1960s. The largest
proportion of this rise (83 percent) has occurred in metropolitan areas, where 74 percent of all female-headed families
resided in 1974. Female-headed families accounted for 19
percent of all families in the central cities and 10 percent
of all families in the suburbs.

The difference in the number of female-headed households
in the suburbs and the central cities can be attributed to
differences in black and white family structure; 39 percent
of black families living in central cities are headed by
females, whereas 14 percent of white families in central
cities are headed by females.

SUMMARY

Significant changes have taken place in the nation's settlement patterns since 1970. The two major categories of
change involve the population distribution among regions
and between metropolitan and nonmetropolitan areas.

Regional Changes

   ● The South is experiencing net migration gains from
all other regions in numbers that are more than double the
net gain to the West--the only other region now experiencing
a net migration gain. Significantly, the long-term trend

of out-migration by blacks from the South to the North was
reversed during the first half of the 1970s.

• The growth rate of the West continues to be the highest in the country, but the most rapid growth within that
region has shifted from the coastal states (Pacific division) to those of the Mountain division.

• The net flow of migrants from the Northeast and North
Central regions during the first half of the 1970s was almost double that of the last half of the 1960s. This increase has resulted primarily from a rise of 34.1 percent
in the migration from the North to the South coupled with
a decrease of 17.3 percent in migration from the South to
the North.

Metropolitan and Nonmetropolitan Changes

• Since 1970, the metropolitan areas of the United
States have grown more slowly than the nation as a whole
and substantially less rapidly than nonmetropolitan America, a development that stands in sharp contrast to all
preceding decades back to the early 19th century.

• On a net basis, metropolitan areas are now losing
migrants to nonmetropolitan areas, although they still
show slight population increases due to natural increase
and immigration.

• The overall decline in the growth of metropolitan
areas is largely accounted for by the largest metropolitan
areas, particularly those located in the Northeast and
North Central regions. Through 1975, the 8 metropolitan
areas exceeding 3 million in population added only 270,000
residents to a 1970 population base of 52 million, while
their central cities had absolute declines in population.
All central cities of the nation's metropolitan areas grew
at an average annual rate of 0.6 percent between 1960 and
1970 but have declined at an average annual rate of 0.4
percent since 1970 (annexations excluded). Much of the
decrease is attributable to the post-1970 decline in the
number of white central-city residents, which has occurred
at a rate of 1 percent per year.

• Rapid growth has taken place in some smaller metropolitan areas, particularly in the South (especially
Florida), the West, and in exurban counties located immediately outside metropolitan areas that have substantial
daily commuting to metropolitan areas.

• Particularly noteworthy are the reversals in migration trends in the largest metropolitan areas and the

furthermost peripheral counties. The metropolitan areas
with populations exceeding 3 million gained migrants in
the 1960s but have lost residents since 1970; the nation's
peripheral nonmetropolitan counties lost migrants between
1960 and 1970 but have gained migrants since 1970. The
balance of migration flows has been reversed.

● High growth rates prevail in certain nonmetropolitan
areas, especially those with manufacturing, centers of
higher education, resources for recreational development,
and retirement centers. The long-term shift away from
agricultural employment has also tapered off, adding to
rural population retention.

We must learn more about the causes of the redistributions and their implications, for if the nation's settlement patterns are changing, urban policy should be shaped
to deal with these changes.

APPENDIX

TABLE A-1 Population of the United States, 1970-1977
(in thousands)^a

Residential Category	1977	1970	Percent Change 1970-1977
Total U.S.	211,792	199,819	6.0
Metropolitan	143,182	137,058	4.5
Central-city	60,334	62,876	-4.0
Suburban	82,848	74,182	11.7
Nonmetropolitan	68,610	62,761	9.3

^{a}For population of the United States, 1950-1975, see Table 1

SOURCES: U.S. Bureau of the Census (1972, 1975e). Figures
updated through 1977.

TABLE A-2   Interregional Migration: 1975-1977
(in thousands)[a]

Residence in 1975	Residence in 1978			
	Northeast	North Central	South	West
Northeast	--	278	902	395
North Central	247	--	1,136	788
South	466	707	--	718
West	183	498	843	--

[a]For 1965-1970 and 1970-1975 interregional migration data, see Table 4.

SOURCE: U.S. Bureau of the Census (1978).

TABLE A-3   Residential Mobility: 1975-1978 (in millions)[a]

Residential Category in 1975	Residential Category in 1977		
	Central City	Suburb	Nonmetropolitan Area
Central city	[15.2][b]	7.5	2.4
Suburb	3.7	[16.7][b]	2.9
Nonmetropolitan area	1.6	2.6	[17.5][b]

[a]For 1970-1975 residential mobility data, see Table 5.
[b]Figures in brackets are movers who remained in the same residential category during relocation.

SOURCE: U.S. Bureau of the Census (1978).

TABLE A-4 Population, Population Change, and Components of Change for Selected Categories of Metropolitan and Nonmetropolitan Counties: 1960-1970 and 1970-1975 (in thousands)

Location	Population 1975 (Provisional)	1970 (Census)[a]	1960 (Census)	Population Change 1970-1975 Number	Annual Percent[b]	Population Change 1960-1970 Number	Annual Percent	Natural Increase 1970-1975 Number	Annual Percent	Natural Increase 1960-1970 Number	Annual Percent	Net Migration 1970-1975 Number	Annual Percent	Net Migration 1960-1970 Number	Annual Percent
UNITED STATES	213,051	203,304	179,311	9,748	0.89	23,993	1.25	7,281	0.67	20,466	1.07	2,467	0.23	3,528	0.18
Metropolitan areas[c]	156,098	149,826	127,943	6,272	0.78	21,883	1.58	5,575	0.69	15,548	1.12	696	0.09	6,335	0.46
Over 3 million[d]	53,135	52,865	45,766	271	0.01	7,099	1.44	1,635	0.59	5,042	1.02	-1,364	-0.49	2,057	0.42
1-3 million	41,402	39,341	32,403	2,061	0.97	6,939	1.98	1,451	0.68	4,066	1.13	610	0.29	2,873	0.80
0.5-1 million	23,782	22,548	19,386	1,234	0.10	3,162	1.51	922	0.76	2,425	1.16	312	0.26	736	0.35
0.25-0.5 million	19,554	18,223	15,803	1,331	1.34	2,420	1.42	798	0.80	2,062	1.21	533	0.54	358	0.21
Less than 0.25 million	18,225	16,849	14,585	1,376	1.49	2,264	1.44	770	0.84	1,953	1.24	605	0.66	311	0.20
Nonmetropolitan areas	56,954	53,475	51,368	3,476	1.20	2,110	0.40	1,706	0.59	4,918	0.94	1,770	0.61	-2,808	-0.54
Counties by level of commuting to metropolitan areas:															
20 percent or more	4,407	4,003	3,651	404	1.83	353	0.92	115	0.52	312	0.82	289	1.31	41	0.11
10-19 percent	10,011	9,349	8,705	662	1.30	644	0.71	267	0.52	760	0.84	395	0.78	-116	-0.13
3-9 percent	14,338	13,497	12,805	841	1.15	692	0.53	431	0.59	1,238	0.94	410	0.56	-546	-0.42
Less than 3 percent	28,197	26,628	26,207	1,569	1.09	422	0.16	893	0.62	2,607	0.99	676	0.46	-2,186	-0.83

NORTHEAST[e]	54,849	54,289	48,989	559	0.20	5,301	1.03	1,267	0.44	4,561	0.88	-708	-0.25	739	0.14
Metropolitan areas[f]	47,021	46,980	42,264	41	0.02	4,716	1.06	1,087	0.44	3,998	0.90	-1,046	-0.42	718	0.16
Over 1 million	34,772	35,024	31,464	-251	-0.14	3,560	1.07	811	0.44	2,493	0.92	-1,063	-0.58	517	0.16
New York SCSA[g]	16,365	16,701	15,126	-337	-0.39	1,576	0.99	369	0.46	1,347	0.85	-706	-0.81	229	0.14
Philadelphia SCSA	5,635	5,628	5,024	7	0.02	604	1.13	140	0.47	506	0.95	-133	-0.45	98	0.18
Boston NECMA	3,915	3,849	3,457	66	0.32	392	1.07	82	0.40	331	0.91	-16	-0.08	61	0.17
Pittsburgh	2,316	2,401	2,405	-85	-0.69	-4	-0.02	24	0.19	162	0.68	-109	-0.88	-166	-0.69
Washington (pt)	2,018	1,989	1,495	29	0.27	494	2.84	86	0.82	255	1.46	-57	-0.54	239	1.37
Baltimore	2,137	2,071	1,804	66	0.60	267	1.38	55	0.50	213	1.10	11	0.10	54	0.28
Buffalo	1,527	1,349	1,307	-22	-0.31	42	0.32	26	0.36	124	0.94	-48	-0.70	-82	-0.62
Hartford NECMA	1,060	1,035	847	25	0.45	188	2.00	29	0.53	105	1.11	-5	-0.08	83	0.89
0.5-1 million	7,328	7,206	6,453	122	0.32	753	1.10	159	0.39	559	1.02	-28	-0.07	194	0.28
0.25-0.5 million	3,059	2,971	2,760	88	0.56	211	0.74	77	0.49	241	0.84	11	0.07	-30	-0.10
Less than 0.25 million	1,863	1,780	1,587	83	0.87	193	1.15	49	0.51	156	0.93	34	0.36	37	0.22
Nonmetropolitan areas	7,828	7,310	6,725	518	1.30	585	0.83	180	0.45	563	0.80	338	0.85	22	0.03
20 percent or more	1,288	1,127	929	161	2.53	198	1.93	27	0.42	78	0.76	134	2.11	120	1.17
10-19 percent	2,006	1,889	1,734	117	1.14	155	0.65	41	0.40	127	0.70	76	0.75	28	0.15
3-9 percent	2,174	2,060	1,929	115	1.03	131	0.66	50	0.45	157	0.79	65	0.58	-26	-0.13
Less than 3 percent	2,360	2,234	2,133	126	1.04	101	0.46	62	0.52	201	0.92	63	0.52	-100	-0.46
NORTH CENTRAL	57,665	56,593	51,619	1,072	0.36	4,974	0.92	1,953	0.65	5,657	1.05	-882	-0.29	-683	-0.13
Metropolitan areas	39,902	39,408	34,859	494	0.24	4,548	1.23	1,550	0.74	4,362	1.18	-1,055	-0.51	187	-0.51
Over 1 million	26,123	25,996	22,948	127	0.09	3,049	1.25	1,004	0.73	1,867	1.17	-877	-0.64	180	0.07
Chicago SCSA	7,623	7,611	6,794	12	0.03	817	1.13	295	0.79	823	1.14	-283	-0.71	-6	-0.01
Detroit SCSA	4,701	4,669	4,122	32	0.13	547	1.24	195	0.60	532	1.21	-163	-0.66	15	0.03
Cleveland SCSA	2,912	3,000	2,732	-88	-0.56	267	0.93	94	0.62	304	1.06	-181	-1.17	-36	-0.13
St. Louis	2,369	2,410	2,144	-41	-0.33	267	1.17	78	0.81	242	1.06	-119	-0.95	30	0.11
Minneapolis	2,027	1,965	1,598	62	0.59	367	1.61	86	0.71	250	1.10	-23	-0.22	118	0.52
Cincinnati SCSA (pt)	1,376	1,362	1,238	14	0.19	124	0.96	51	0.64	152	1.16	-37	-0.52	-26	-0.20
Milwaukee SCSA	1,602	1,575	1,421	28	0.33	154	1.03	53	0.77	183	1.22	-26	-0.31	-29	-0.19
Kansas City	1,287	1,274	1,109	13	0.20	165	1.39	52	0.86	135	1.13	-39	-0.57	31	0.26
Indianapolis	1,147	1,111	944	36	0.61	167	1.62	51	0.90	128	1.25	-15	-0.25	38	0.37
Columbus	1,077	1,018	845	59	1.08	173	1.85	49	0.83	121	1.30	10	0.18	52	0.55
0.5-1 million	3,966	3,874	3,393	72	0.45	481	1.32	172	0.74	450	1.24	-80	-0.39	32	0.09
0.25-0.50 million	4,645	4,536	4,055	109	0.45	481	1.12	179	0.73	502	1.17	-70	-0.29	-21	-0.05
Less than 0.25 million	5,168	5,001	4,463	166	0.62	538	1.14	195	0.73	543	1.15	-29	-0.11	-5	-0.01

TABLE A-4 (Continued)

Location	Population 1975 (Provisional)[a]	Population 1970 (Census)	Population 1960 (Census)	Pop. Change 1970-1975 Number	Pop. Change 1970-1975 Annual Percent[b]	Pop. Change 1960-1970 Number	Pop. Change 1960-1970 Annual Percent	Natural Increase 1970-1975 Number	Natural Increase 1970-1975 Annual Percent	Natural Increase 1960-1970 Number	Natural Increase 1960-1970 Annual Percent	Net Migration 1970-1975 Number	Net Migration 1970-1975 Annual Percent	Net Migration 1960-1970 Number	Net Migration 1960-1970 Annual Percent
Nonmetropolitan areas	17,763	17,185	16,760	577	0.63	426	0.25	404	0.44	1,296	0.76	173	0.19	-870	-0.51
20 percent or more	1,322	1,241	1,163	81	1.20	78	0.65	33	0.49	85	0.71	48	0.71	-7	-0.06
10-19 percent	3,378	3,249	3,031	129	0.74	217	0.69	93	0.53	255	0.81	36	0.20	-37	-0.12
3-9 percent	4,550	4,412	4,239	138	0.59	173	0.40	110	0.47	334	0.77	28	0.12	-162	-0.37
Less than 3 percent	8,513	8,284	8,327	229	0.52	-43	-0.05	168	0.38	621	0.75	61	0.14	-664	-0.80
SOUTHEAST[h]	28,210	25,450	21,648	2,859	2.03	3,802	1.61	992	0.70	2,675	1.14	1,867	1.32	1,127	0.49
Metropolitan areas	17,544	15,550	12,154	1,994	2.30	3,396	2.45	609	0.70	1,616	1.17	1,385	1.59	1,780	1.29
Over 1 million	6,471	5,493	3,849	978	3.11	1,644	3.52	171	0.55	457	0.98	807	2.57	1,187	2.54
Washington (pt)	999	921	602	77	1.53	319	4.19	54	1.06	131	1.71	24	0.47	189	2.48
Miami SCSA	2,301	1,888	1,269	413	3.76	619	3.92	27	0.25	107	0.68	386	3.51	512	3.24
Atlanta	1,806	1,596	1,169	211	2.36	426	3.09	95	1.06	193	1.40	116	1.30	233	1.69
Tampa-St. Petersburg	1,365	1,089	809	277	4.30	279	2.94	-4	-0.06	26	0.28	281	4.36	253	2.67
0.5-1 million	3,414	3,184	2,687	230	1.33	497	1.69	145	0.84	386	1.31	85	0.49	111	0.38
0.25-0.5 million	3,999	3,533	2,907	465	2.35	627	1.95	159	0.81	397	1.23	306	1.55	230	0.71
Less than 0.25 million	3,660	3,340	2,712	320	1.74	625	2.08	134	0.73	376	1.24	187	1.02	252	0.83
Nonmetropolitan areas	10,766	9,900	9,494	866	1.60	406	0.42	383	0.71	1,059	1.09	483	0.89	-653	-0.67
20 percent or more	661	607	592	54	1.62	15	0.25	21	0.64	61	1.01	33	0.98	-46	-0.77
10-19 percent	1,993	1,784	1,662	209	2.11	123	0.71	59	0.59	166	0.96	150	1.52	-44	-0.25
3-9 percent	2,713	2,482	2,362	231	1.69	120	0.49	90	0.66	259	1.07	141	1.03	-140	-0.58
Less than 3 percent	5,399	5,027	4,878	372	1.36	149	0.30	213	0.78	573	1.16	159	0.58	-424	-0.86
SOUTH CENTRAL[i]	34,398	32,133	29,001	2,265	1.30	3,131	1.02	1,495	0.86	3,728	1.22	770	0.44	-596	-0.20
Metropolitan areas	21,392	19,770	16,775	1,623	1.50	2,995	1.64	1,085	1.00	2,502	1.37	538	0.50	493	0.27
Over 1 million	6,379	5,845	4,445	534	1.67	1,400	2.72	334	1.04	699	1.36	200	0.62	701	1.36
Dallas-Ft. Worth	2,553	2,378	1,738	174	1.35	640	3.11	133	1.03	273	1.33	41	0.32	368	1.79
Houston SCSA	2,479	2,169	1,571	310	2.54	598	3.20	142	1.17	271	1.45	168	1.37	328	1.75
New Orleans	1,094	1,046	907	48	0.85	139	1.43	50	0.88	129	1.32	-2	-0.03	11	0.11
Cincinnati (pt)	253	251	229	2	0.12	22	0.90	9	0.65	26	1.09	-7	-0.53	-5	-0.20
0.5-1 million	5,488	5,173	4,488	315	1.13	685	1.42	247	0.88	596	1.23	68	0.24	89	0.18
0.25-0.5 million	5,017	4,639	4,057	379	1.49	581	1.34	258	1.02	620	1.43	121	0.48	-38	-0.09
Less than 0.25 million	4,508	4,113	3,784	395	1.75	329	0.83	246	1.09	588	1.49	149	0.66	-259	-0.66

Nonmetropolitan areas	13,005	12,363	12,226	642	0.96	137	0.11	410	0.62	1,226	1.00	232	0.35	-1,089	-0.89
20 percent or more	1,082	979	928	103	1.90	51	0.53	32	0.59	86	0.90	71	1.30	-35	-0.37
10-19 percent	2,206	2,074	1,985	132	1.18	89	0.44	61	0.54	181	0.89	71	0.63	-92	-0.45
3-9 percent	3,189	3,059	3,024	130	0.79	30	0.10	109	0.66	326	1.07	21	0.13	-296	-0.97
Less than 3 percent	6,528	6,251	6,284	277	0.83	-34	-0.05	208	0.62	633	1.01	69	0.21	-667	-1.06
WEST	37,831	34,818	28,053	2,992	1.57	6,785	2.16	1,573	0.82	3,844	1.22	149	0.74	2,941	0.94
Metropolitan areas	30,238	28,119	21,891	2,119	1.38	6,227	2.49	1,244	0.81	3,070	1.23	875	0.57	3,158	1.26
Over 1 million	20,791	19,847	15,462	944	0.88	4,387	2.49	766	0.72	2,042	1.16	178	0.17	2,345	1.33
Los Angeles SCSA	10,317	9,983	7,752	334	0.63	2,231	2.52	412	0.77	1,060	1.19	-79	-0.15	1,172	1.32
San Francisco SCSA	4,580	4,424	3,492	156	0.66	932	2.36	142	0.60	444	1.12	14	0.06	488	1.23
Seattle SCSA	1,822	1,837	1,429	-15	-0.16	408	2.50	53	0.61	174	1.06	-74	-0.77	235	1.44
San Diego	1,587	1,358	1,033	230	2.97	325	2.72	62	0.80	156	1.31	168	2.17	169	1.41
Denver	1,404	1,239	935	165	2.38	305	2.80	62	0.89	140	1.29	103	1.48	165	1.51
Portland	1,082	1,007	822	75	1.36	185	2.03	29	0.53	69	0.75	46	0.83	117	1.27
0.5-1 million	3,586	3,111	2,366	475	2.70	745	2.72	207	1.18	435	1.59	267	1.52	310	1.13
0.25-0.5 million	2,835	2,545	2,024	290	2.05	520	2.28	125	0.88	303	1.33	165	1.17	218	0.95
Less than 0.25 million	3,026	2,615	2,039	411	2.78	575	2.47	145	0.99	290	1.24	264	1.79	286	1.23
Nonmetropolitan areas	7,593	6,720	6,162	873	2.32	558	0.87	329	0.88	775	1.20	544	1.45	-217	-0.34
20 percent or more	55	49	38	6	2.18	11	2.50	2	0.66	2	0.55	4	1.53	9	1.95
10-19 percent	427	353	293	75	3.65	60	1.86	14	0.67	32	0.99	61	2.98	28	0.87
3-9 percent	1,712	1,485	1,247	227	2.71	238	1.74	72	0.86	161	1.18	155	1.85	77	0.57
Less than 3 percent	5,999	4,833	4,585	565	2.10	249	0.53	241	0.90	579	1.23	324	1.21	-331	-0.70

[a] Includes corrections in local and national totals determined after 1970 Census complete-count tabulations were made.

[b] Average annual percent change.

[c] Metropolitan areas defined as of December 31, 1976. Data refer to standard consolidated statistical areas (SCSAs) where they have been defined. Data for New England's metropolitan areas refer to New England-county metropolitan areas (NECMAs). Some metropolitan area titles have been abbreviated.

[d] Population size classification of metropolitan areas is as of the Census of 1970.

[e] Expands Northeast region to include Delaware, Maryland, and the District of Columbia.

[f] New England county metropolitan areas (NECMAs) in New England.

[g] Excludes portion located in New England division.

[h] Includes all states in South Atlantic division except Delaware, Maryland, and the District of Columbia.

[i] Combines East South Central and West South Central divisions.

SOURCE: Unpublished data provided by Richard L. Forstall updating Forstall (1975).

REFERENCES

Beale, C. L. (1975) *The Revival of Population Growth in Nonmetropolitan America.* Economic Research Service, ERS-605. Washington, D.C.: U.S. Department of Agriculture.

Beale, C. L., and Fuguitt, G. V. (1975) The New Pattern of Nonmetropolitan Change. CDE Working Paper 75-22. Madison: Center for Demography and Ecology, University of Wisconsin.

Duncan, O. D., Cuzzort, R. P., and Duncan, B. (1961) *Statistical Geography.* Glencoe, Ill.: The Free Press.

Forstall, R. L. (1975) Trends in Metropolitan and Nonmetropolitan Population Growth Since 1970. Revision of paper delivered at the Conference on Population Distribution, sponsored by the Center for Population Research, National Institutes of Health, 29-31 January 1975 (revision dated 20 May 1975).

Regional Economic Analysis Division (1976) Work-force migration patterns, 1960-1973. *Survey of Current Business* October: 23-26.

Ross, H. L., and Sawhill, I. V. (1975) *Time of Transition: The Growth of Families Headed By Women.* Washington, D.C.: Urban Institute.

Taeuber, C., and Taeuber, I. B. (1957) *The Changing Population of the United States.* Washington, D.C.: U.S. Government Printing Office.

U.S. Bureau of the Census (1970) *1970 Census User's Guide.* Washington, D.C.: U.S. Department of Commerce.

U.S. Bureau of the Census (1972) *Census of Population: 1970.* Washington, D.C.: U.S. Department of Commerce.

U.S. Bureau of the Census (1975a) *Historical Statistics of the United States: Colonial Times to 1970.* Washington, D.C.: U.S. Department of Commerce.

U.S. Bureau of the Census (1975b) Mobility of the population of the United States: March 1970 to March 1975. Series P-20, No. 285 in *Current Population Reports.* Washington, D.C.: U.S. Department of Commerce.

U.S. Bureau of the Census (1975c) Projections of the population of the United States: 1975 to 2050. Series P-25, No. 601 in *Current Population Reports.* Washington, D.C.: U.S. Department of Commerce.

U.S. Bureau of the Census (1975d) Social and economic characteristics of the metropolitan and nonmetropolitan population: 1974 and 1970. Series P-23, No. 55 in *Current Population Reports.* Washington, D.C.: U.S. Department of Commerce.

U.S. Bureau of the Census (1975e) Social and economic characteristics of the metropolitan and nonmetropolitan population: 1974 and 1970, updated to 1975. Series P-23, No. 53 in *Current Population Reports*. Washington, D.C.: U.S. Department of Commerce.

U.S. Bureau of the Census (1976) Population profile of the United States: 1975. Series P-20, No. 292 in *Current Population Reports*. Washington, D.C.: U.S. Department of Commerce.

U.S. Bureau of the Census (1978) Mobility of the population of the United States: March 1975 to March 1978. Series P-20, No. 331 in *Current Population Reports*. Washington, D.C.: U.S. Department of Commerce.

U.S. Domestic Council (1976) *Report on U.S. National Growth and Development*. Updated through 1975 with data from the U.S. Bureau of the Census, Series P-20, No. 292 in *Current Population Reports*. Washington, D.C.: U.S. Government Printing Office.

U.S. Office of Management and Budget (1975) *Standard Metropolitan Statistical Areas*. Revised ed. Washington, D.C.: U.S. Government Printing Office.

Vining, D. R., Jr., and Strauss, A. (1976) A Demonstration That Current De-Concentration Trends Are a Clean Break With Past Trends. RSRI Discussion Paper No. 90. Philadelphia: Regional Science Research Institute.

POPULATION REDISTRIBUTION AND THE USE OF LAND AND ENERGY RESOURCES

Edwin S. Mills

INTRODUCTION

The so-called Sun Belt trend and demetropolitanization
trend, as identified by Berry and Dahmann in this volume,
are examined in this paper in terms of their implications
for government policies relating to the use of land and
energy. The two trends have different causes, different
results, and, to a considerable extent, different policy
implications. Hence these trends are discussed separately
within the section on land use policy and within the section on energy policy.

The Sun Belt trend is conceptually straightforward and
is well established by census data; for many decades the
predominant pattern of migration was from the South to the
North, but in the 1970s, large numbers of Americans have
been moving from the colder to the warmer parts of the
country. The causes of this dramatic reversal of migration trends are not well understood and deserve careful
study. However, the implications of the Sun Belt trend
for uses of land and energy resources are relatively easy
to analyze. These implications will be the subject of
subsequent sections of this paper.

The demetropolitanization trend is conceptually more
complex than the Sun Belt trend. Berry and Dahmann show
that the nonmetropolitan population grew much faster than
the metropolitan population during the first half of the
1970s. Were that trend to persist through 1980, this decade would be the first since the census began in 1790 in

---

Edwin S. Mills is Professor of Economics, Princeton
University.

which rural population grew more rapidly than urban population.[1]

However, the demetropolitanization trend may be largely a statistical illusion. The dispersion of population and jobs from the center to the periphery of metropolitan areas is well established and has proceeded for at least a century. In each census, more land is included in most metropolitan areas than in the previous census. Berry and Dahmann have shown that the most rapid nonmetropolitan growth is occurring in counties adjacent to metropolitan areas. By 1980, the Census Bureau will probably conclude that the main trend is not demetropolitanization but an expansion of metropolitan areas into formerly rural areas. Whether population growth just outside a metropolitan area should be identified as enlargement of the metropolitan area or as rural growth is a subtle issue. The Census Bureau programmatically bases its decision on the extent of the interdependencies between the new settlements and the metropolitan area.

Perhaps the time has come for revision of the criteria used to determine which settlements are parts of metropolitan areas. The density of metropolitan areas in the United States is extremely low when compared with that of metropolitan areas in most other nations. The densest parts of many U.S. metropolitan areas currently are less dense than rural areas in many of the world's more populated countries. In the context of the United States in the last quarter of the 20th century, a determination of what constitutes a metropolitan area must be based on careful analysis, for the trend toward urbanization is strong and pervasive throughout the developing and developed world. In the absence of a man-made or natural catastrophe, a fundamental reversal of that trend would be among the most dramatic events of the 20th century. Until much better evidence is available, the demetropolitanization trend should be assumed to be a continuation of the longstanding trend toward dispersal of population to the peripheries of metropolitan areas. That assumption will be maintained throughout this paper.

[1] The terms "rural population" and "nonmetropolitan population," as defined by the U.S. Bureau of the Census, are not synonymous. My use of these terms conforms with the definitions used by the Bureau of the Census.

TRENDS IN URBAN LAND USE

Urbanization

The United States has urbanized rapidly and steadily during its 200-year history. In 1790, 5.1 percent of the
population resided in urban areas; by 1975, urban areas
housed 75 percent of the population. The pattern of growth
in the United States consisted of a rapid increase in the
percentage of urban growth during the years when rapid
industrialization was taking place (approximately 1820-1920)
and a slower but substantial increase in the percentage of
urban growth since that time. This pattern is typical of
high-income industrialized nations. Japan and most of the
countries of northern Europe have displayed similar patterns, although compared with the United States, the pattern developed earlier in Europe and later in Japan. During
the middle half of the 20th century, the pattern also has
been observed in rapidly developing countries such as Brazil
and South Korea. Growth in the percentage of urban growth
decelerates after reaching about 50 percent and increases
very slowly after reaching about 70 percent.[2] By the end
of the century, about 80 percent of the population of the
United States will probably live in urban areas.
      Urban land is expensive compared with rural land in all
countries in which land markets are permitted to record
land values and allocate land. The cost of land along with
other factors results in greater land economy for urban activities. Residences in urban areas, in contrast with rural
areas, are surrounded by less land that has not been used
for buildings. Given land areas are used to provide more
square feet of floor space in urban areas than in rural
areas. Similarly, manufacturing and service activities
employ less land relative to output and other inputs in
urban areas than in rural ones. Thus, urbanization is, in
part, a shift from land-using to land-economizing activities.
Contrary to the popular notion that urbanization swallows
up open space, urbanization decreases the amount of space
needed to provide housing and employment for the population.
Thus, the predominant implication of urbanization for land
use is that it frees land for recreational purposes, for-
ests, or nonuse.
      The size distribution of urban areas is among the most
stable social phenomena. An examination of any country

[2]See Mills (1972a) for detailed data and comparisons.

during any period of history reveals that size distribution
is always highly skewed to the right, with the largest
urban area having many times as many people as the mean or
modal urban area. The Pareto distribution with an exponent
between 1 and 1.5 provides a close approximation to the
distribution. The pattern has persisted throughout the
200-year period for which usable data are available, under
greatly varying levels of economic development and across
an astonishing variety of cultural and political organizations. Many scholars have fitted a variety of statistical
frequency distributions to urban size data, and all have
concluded that the best fit is provided by the Pareto distribution or ones that are closely related (Rosen and
Resnick 1979).

In the United States, the size distribution of urban
areas follows the pattern found elsewhere. The distribution and, to a lesser extent, the positions of particular
urban areas in the distribution are highly stable. Large
and high-income countries tend to be less primate than
other countries, meaning that the urban population is less
concentrated in the largest urban area or areas. As U.S.
population and real income per capita have increased,
smaller urban areas have grown faster on the average than
larger urban areas. New York has been the country's largest metropolitan area since the founding of the nation,
but for many decades it has become steadily smaller relative to other metropolitan areas and to the total urban
population (Mills 1972b). The right tail of the size distribution of urban areas has become gradually less promi-
nent. Census data show that from 1940 to 1970, the period
for which data are best, the population of the New York
metropolitan area fell as a percentage of total U.S. metropolitan population from 18.6 percent to 11.8 percent.[3]
During the same period, the population of the 10 largest
metropolitan areas fell as a percentage of total U.S. metropolitan population from 51.8 to 39.3. These data indicate
a very rapid decrease in primacy. But this long-term trend
is to be distinguished from the events of the 1970s. All
of the five largest metropolitan areas in 1970 lost population by 1974. This loss is, in all probability, mainly
the result of the severe 1974-1975 recession and will almost certainly not continue. Between the mid-1970s and
1990 or 2000, the trend probably will be for slow growth

[3]The population of New York is that of its standard consolidated area.

of the largest metropolitan areas and faster growth of
smaller metropolitan areas.

The move to the Sun Belt is a continuation of the trend
toward decreased primacy in the size distribution of urban
areas. Small metropolitan areas are concentrated in Sun
Belt states, as are most of the fastest growing metropolitan areas. Los Angeles, Phoenix, Houston, and Miami have
risen in rank among metropolitan areas in recent decades,
whereas Baltimore, Boston, and other northeastern metropolitan areas have fallen. The Sun Belt trend is, to some
extent, a reallocation of population growth from large
metropolitan areas to small and medium ones. Such a reallocation of urban population growth is precisely the mechanism by which primacy decreases. As a result of increased
migration to the Sun Belt, the ranks of metropolitan areas
in the Sun Belt will almost certainly continue to rise and
the ranks of metropolitan areas in the Northeast and North
Central regions of the country will, in all probability,
continue to fall.

There are two probable explanations for the increased
migration to the Sun Belt. One is the phenomenon described
by Perloff et al. (1960) as the growing importance of footloose industries. As the economy grows, services become
an increasing fraction of employment and output. The location of services is influenced by the location of consumers
because services are consumed in the act of production and
therefore production must take place close to consumption.
However, the location of services is not dependent on proximity to natural resources and bulk transportation facilities. Furthermore, such proximity is becoming increasingly
less important for many manufacturers. As the economy
develops, materials are subjected to an increasing number
of steps between extraction and consumption. As a result,
a growing proportion of manufacturing output and employment
is not dependent on proximity to natural resources and bulk
transportation facilities. Both the growth of service
industries and the decreased dependence of manufacturing
on proximity to natural resources permit employers to locate where people want to live. Most people, other things
being equal, probably prefer relatively warm and perhaps
dry parts of the country. Hence the trend toward footloose
industries is an important factor in the increased migration to the Sun Belt.

A second and perhaps more important factor is the tendency to decreased primacy. As was stated previously,
countries become less primate as they urbanize and as real
income per capita grows. Nobody knows to what extent the

move to the Sun Belt is a consequence of decreased primacy.
Phenomena such as the Sun Belt trend are frequently attributed to highly localized causes. It is important to
recognize that generalized phenomena such as decreasing
primacy may influence the Sun Belt trend and that local
causes may be less significant than they first appear.

Primacy decreases with development for many reasons.
The largest urban areas reach sizes at which the costs of
living and the costs of production become increasingly
expensive because of growing congestion, deteriorating
environment, and perhaps other disamenities. The greatest
population and employment growth then takes place in smaller
metropolitan areas. In the United States, the South has
been less urbanized and less industrialized than the North
and typically has smaller metropolitan areas. The relatively small urban areas of the Sun Belt are, therefore,
likely places for growth to occur.

Considering that the size distribution of urban areas
is a rather abstract notion, primacy is a remarkably controversial subject. Among the most persistent beliefs of
our time is that unless governments act to control metropolitan growth, an excessive number of people and jobs
will be concentrated in the largest metropolitan areas.
The belief is held by public officials, scholars, journalists, and others in the United States, Europe, and most
developing countries. Most countries have more or less
thoroughly formulated and enforced government programs to
control the growth and sizes of their largest metropolitan
areas. Perhaps the most articulate advocate of this position in the United States is Sundquist (1975).

The desire to control populations of large metropolitan
areas is based on the concept that residents of large
metropolitan areas are victims of disamenities--particular-
ly congestion and pollution--that are outside the control
of market forces. Pollution, congestion, and other disamenities are somewhat worse in large metropolitan areas
than elsewhere, but the conclusion that government should
control population in large metropolitan areas does not
follow. Tolley (1974) has shown that government programs
to control disamenities might increase or decrease the
population of large metropolitan areas. Pollution abatement
programs, for example, make production more expensive in
large urban areas than elsewhere, but they also improve
the environment more in large metropolitan areas than elsewhere. The former tends to decrease the population of
large metropolitan areas and the latter to increase it.
The net result depends on the magnitude of the two forces.

The basic point is that if pollution is excessive, governmen
programs should be directed at pollution abatement, not at
metropolitan populations. Pollution results mainly from
the manner in which resources are allocated, not from the
size of an urban area. Reducing the size of the largest
metropolitan areas would be very disruptive and would
have little effect on pollution levels, whereas a direct
attack on pollution could have large beneficial effects.

Although many have advocated government programs to
control populations of large urban areas, market forces
have for decades been accomplishing just that. The relative sizes of our largest metropolitan areas have fallen
in recent decades even without a government policy on the
matter. By now, the United States is among the world's
least primate countries. No rational basis exists for
developing a government program to control the relative
sizes of urban areas.

Suburbanization

The second important trend in urban land use has been the
dispersion or suburbanization of people and employment from
the centers toward the peripheries of metropolitan areas.
When Americans think of suburbanization, they think of
movement from the jurisdictions of central-city governments
to those of local governments in the surrounding area.
But boundaries of local government jurisdictions are moved
frequently and, in the United States, the part of the metropolitan area that falls within the boundaries of the
central city varies greatly from one metropolitan area to
another. In addition, in most countries a single local
government jurisdiction includes the entire metropolitan
area. For these reasons, movement among jurisdictions is
an unreliable measure of suburbanization.

For a quarter of a century, economists have instead
measured suburbanization by changes in parameters of a population density function. The most common such function
is the negative-exponential,

$$D(x) = D_O e^{-bx},$$ (1)

where $D(x)$ is population density at distance x from the
center of the metropolitan area, e is the base of the
natural logarithm, and D_O and b are parameters estimated

from the data. In this equation, *b* is the percent decrease
in density per unit of distance from the center and is
always positive. Equation (1) is usually found to fit
the data about as well as any comparably simple function.
This equation has been estimated for 19th- and 20th-century
cities in Europe, North America, Asia, and elsewhere.

In equation (1), *b* is a simple measure of suburbanization. Of two metropolitan areas with the same total population and radius, the one with the larger *b* has more
people within any given distance of the center. Thus, a
highly centralized metropolitan area has a large value of
b and a decentralized metropolitan area has a smaller
value of *b*. In the limiting case in which *b* is zero,
density is constant throughout the metropolitan area. We
term *b* the density gradient.

Estimated values of *b* have fallen dramatically in
American metropolitan areas. In *Studies in the Structure
of the Urban Economy* (1972c), I was able to estimate equation (1) for four metropolitan areas from 1880 to 1963.
The average value of *b* for the four metropolitan areas
fell from 1.22 in 1880 to 0.31 in 1963. Much better data
are available for the 20th century, particularly for the
period since World War II. Many scholars have estimated
density functions and all have concluded that American metropolitan areas have decentralized rapidly during the 20th
century and that rapid decentralization probably has been
taking place since about the middle of the 19th century.
Although European metropolitan areas are more centralized
than American metropolitan areas, the same process of decentralization has occurred there. Recent studies of Japan
(Mills and Ohta 1976) and Korea (Mills and Song 1979) show
that metropolitan areas in both these countries are much
more centralized than metropolitan areas in the United States,
but that they are undergoing very rapid decentralization.

Three factors are mainly responsible for decentralization.[4] First, as metropolitan areas grow, subcenters for
employment and shopping can be supported in locations outside the center of the metropolitan area. Once these subcenters are established, the advantage of proximity to the
center for workers and shoppers is reduced. Second, as
real incomes rise, the demand for housing grows, and much
of the demand is directed toward housing on the periphery
where land values are low. Third, as transportation improves, the cost of trips from the periphery to the centers

[4]See Mills (1972d) for a precise statement.

of the metropolitan areas falls, thus reducing the disadvantage of residential locations on the periphery.

The pervasive causes of suburbanization, like those of the Sun Belt trend, have little to do with localized phenomena. Racial tensions and high local taxes in central cities may contribute to suburbanization in the United States, but they should not be considered primary factors. Similarly, the automobile is not a primary factor. Transportation improvements, whether they consist of road or subway construction, also contribute to suburbanization. Japanese urban areas, where public transit accounts for the majority of trips, have suburbanized rapidly as public transportation has improved. Metropolitan areas in the United States are more decentralized than those in Europe and Asia, largely because in this country land values are much lower in relation to incomes. Among industrialized countries,[5] the United States is almost uniquely rich in land and therefore all activities, urban and rural, take place at remarkably low densities. In Japan, which contrasts sharply with the United States in terms of density, land values relative to incomes are 20 times as high as they are in the United States (Mills and Ohta 1976).

Metropolitan decentralization is a controversial phenomenon. The major concern is whether metropolitan decentralization results in land being used for urban purposes that could be better used for agricultural purposes. There can be no doubt that suburbanization and the related declines in urban population density increase the amount of land used for urban purposes and that agricultural uses are frequently the alternative to urban uses. Some of the most valuable agricultural land is that land close to cities because prices reflect proximity to markets. Furthermore, land that is particularly valuable for urban uses is frequently also valuable for agricultural uses; for both urban and agricultural uses, the best land is relatively flat, well drained, and near good natural transportation routes such as navigable waterways. Thus, urban decentralization often conflicts with agricultural land uses. Central to the controversy is the extent to which land prices reflect the most valuable use of the land. If prices are an accurate reflection, then urban uses outbid agricultural uses only when urban uses are more valuable, and it is in

[5]Canada and Australia also have low densities, but much of their land is almost uninhabitable.

these instances appropriate to convert agricultural land
to urban uses.

POPULATION TRENDS AND GOVERNMENT LAND USE POLICIES

Demetropolitanization and Government Policy

Because government taxation and land use policies distort
land prices, prices may not reflect the value of land for
alternative uses. The issue is complex because all economic activities are taxed and all take place on land.
Virtually all taxes distort demand and supply of taxed
activities and therefore distort prices and uses of land
on which the activities take place.

Of all taxes and land use controls, those directed at
housing are most likely to distort the prices and uses of
urban land. Housing is by far the largest single use of
urban land; about half the land developed for urban purposes is used for housing. Housing is among our most heavily taxed commodities. Urban real estate taxes average
about 3 percent of the market value of the property, which
means that the annual tax is equal to nearly 25 percent of
the annual cost of the property. Such high taxation substantially reduces the demand for housing and consequently
the amount of urban land used for housing. Offsetting high
real estate taxes is the favorable treatment of owner-
occupied housing in the federal income tax laws. Aaron
(1972) estimates that the federal tax "subsidy" equals about
15 percent of housing costs of owner-occupiers. Thus, the
net tax burden on urban housing would be 15 percent of
annual housing costs if all urban residents were owner-
occupiers. However, only about two-thirds of urban residents are owner-occupiers and the net tax burden therefore
exceeds 10 percent.

Agricultural and other rural real estate is also subject
to real estate taxes and to preferential treatment under
the federal income tax. In most states, both law and custom
dictate that agriculture be taxed at a lower percentage of
market value than urban real estate. Furthermore, owner-
occupancy is more common in agricultural than in urban areas,
and the preferential federal tax treatment of owner-occupants
is therefore probably more important in agricultural areas.
Thus, the net tax burden on agricultural housing is probably
less than on urban housing, and these taxes, therefore,

probably discourage conversion of some agricultural land
for urban uses.

In addition to taxes, government policies on land use
also affect the amount of land used for urban residential
purposes. Most of the land in metropolitan suburbs in the
United States is zoned for low population densities in
order to exclude racial minorities and people with low
incomes. Two- to six-acre zoning and the exclusion of all
but single-family detached dwellings are not unusual.
Zoning, combined with a plethora of other land use controls, has been successful as a technique for restricting
residential areas to high-income citizens. (Mills 1972d,
1979). However, urban land use controls have had the un-
intended results of producing excessively low suburban
population densities and excessive use of land for suburban
residences. Land use controls are relatively unimportant
in rural areas and therefore no rural programs have been
developed to encourage excessive use of land for housing.

Nobody knows the net effect of land use regulations
on land use for urban housing. My judgment is that the
effect is a modest but significant overuse of land in U.S.
suburbs. However, even in the absence of land use controls, suburban population densities would be lower than
those in central cities because suburban land costs less.
Furthermore, the density in Houston, which has no zoning,
is not notably higher than the density in comparable cities
that have zoning. Thus, at the present time, the excess
use of urban land that results from zoning and other land
use controls probably is modest, but the subject needs
further study. The modest effect of land use controls on
excess land use should not be permitted to obscure the
considerable social effect that such controls have on excluded minorities and other low-income urban residents
(Downs 1973).

The Sun Belt Trend and Land Use Policies

It has been pointed out earlier that the move to the Sun
Belt is in part a move from relatively large metropolitan
areas to relatively small ones, and that the Sun Belt trend
reinforces the trend toward decreased primacy. The move to
the Sun Belt will increase urban land use for two reasons.
First, population densities are lower in small metropolitan
areas than in large ones and the move to the Sun Belt is,
therefore, a move from high-density metropolitan to low-

density metropolitan areas. As a consequence, the amount of land used for urban purposes will increase. Second, metropolitan areas of given population in the Sun Belt are much less densely settled than metropolitan areas of similar population in other parts of the country. For example, the Baltimore and Houston metropolitan areas each had about 2.1 million people in 1973, but the population density of the Baltimore metropolitan area was three times that of Houston. As a second example, the Akron and Jacksonville metropolitan areas each had populations of just over 640,000 in 1973, but the density of Akron was more than three times the density of Jacksonville. These examples, which are typical, suggest that the Sun Belt trend represents a shift in population from high-density metropolitan areas to low-density metropolitan areas even when the trend reflects movement between metropolitan areas with populations of equal size.

Since the rate of residential density in northern metropolitan regions is three times the rate of residential density in the Sun Belt, a typical individual who moves to the Sun Belt would use three times the amount of land for residential purposes that he would have used if he had moved to a northern metropolitan area.

Why are the population densities of metropolitan areas in the Sun Belt so low? The explanation generally given is that because much of the growth of metropolitan areas in the Sun Belt has taken place in recent decades, these areas are products of the automobile age. It is claimed that these areas developed a low-density land use pattern that was appropriate for transportation systems based on the automobile. In contrast, much of the growth of older metropolitan areas in the North occurred before the automobile had become the predominant mode of urban transportation. These northern areas therefore developed high-density patterns appropriate for transportation systems based on public transit.

This explanation has some validity. Patterns of land use change slowly in older urban areas and land use patterns in metropolitan areas of the Sun Belt are better suited to automobile travel than the patterns of northern metropolitan areas. However, the explanation overlooks the most important determinant of population density--namely, land prices. Land costs much less in metropolitan areas of the Sun Belt than in metropolitan areas in many other regions of the country because the Sun Belt has lower population densities, less industrialization, less productive agricultural land, a large supply of flat land suitable for

urban development, and so forth. However, where land is
cheap, households and businesses use a great deal of it.

Dramatic verification of the importance of land prices
in determining population densities is obtained by comparing Los Angeles and Chicago. Los Angeles is popularly
viewed as a metropolitan area that is completely dependent
on the automobile. It is the largest metropolitan area in
the country without a subway system, and its bus system is
primitive. In contrast, Chicago has both a subway system
and an elaborate bus system. The populations of the two
metropolitan areas are approximately the same size and the
population densities are identical. The density of Los
Angeles is high despite the area's reliance on the automobile because Los Angeles is an exception to the rule of
low land values in Sun Belt metropolitan areas. The Los
Angeles basin is an especially attractive place to live
and produce, and the area is highly industrialized and
heavily populated. Thus, the cost of land is high and
residents and businesses economize on land, thereby creating population densities that are high. Because Phoenix,
Albuquerque, and Dallas are in regions where population is
low and the productivity of agricultural land is low, the
cost of land is also low.

The Sun Belt trend represents not only a shift from
high-density metropolitan areas to low-density metropolitan
areas, but also a shift from regions where land costs are
high to regions where they are low. Where land values are
low, patterns of residential and commercial land use are
entirely appropriate. The low densities of the Sun Belt
are not caused by a "frontier outlook" that leads residents
to squander land; rather, the densities are the result of
an appropriate response to inexpensive land. As Sun Belt
metropolitan areas grow, land values will rise and land
uses will gradually become more intensive.

The low densities of metropolitan areas in the Sun Belt
do not provide governments with a reason for rationing
land or for otherwise encouraging high-density land use.
But if Sun Belt metropolitan area governments decided they
wished to encourage high density, the land use controls
necessary for achieving this goal would be very different
from those used elsewhere for exclusionary purposes. As
indicated earlier, suburban jurisdictions exclude low-
income families by zoning regulations that establish minimum lot sizes and that permit only single-family detached
houses. To encourage high-density development, governments would have to require maximum lot sizes and multi-
family housing.

Suburban land use controls have been less important in
the Sun Belt than elsewhere for several reasons. Urban
areas in the Sun Belt have until recently been small, and
land use controls are relatively unimportant in small urban
areas in all regions of the country. Second, local governments in the Sun Belt receive a large part of their revenues
from state and federal funds, and the fiscal incentive to
exclude people with low incomes is probably less strong
than in areas where local governments raise most of their
revenues from local real estate taxes. Furthermore, the
extremely low densities permitted by inexpensive land
probably result in people's being less sensitive to differences between themselves and their neighbors.

I believe the federal government should attempt to ease
exclusionary land use controls in the North and prevent
them from becoming more important in the Sun Belt. I see
no justification for land use controls to force high-density
development in Sun Belt metropolitan areas. There is no
reason to believe that market choices lead to excessively
low densities. Furthermore, history shows that land use
controls, although introduced for legitimate purposes,
quickly come to be used to exclude people who are not wanted
because of their race or income level (Mills 1979). Recently, the courts, in such cases as *Southern Burlington County
NAACP* v. *Mt. Laurel, N.J.*, have begun to chip away the most
extreme land use controls. Undoubtedly, the number of such
cases will increase and more zoning restrictions will be
invalidated by the courts. But I do not believe that the
courts can significantly alleviate the essential harm done
by exclusionary controls.[6] The other branches of the federal government could do much to prevent land use controls
from becoming important in the Sun Belt.

POPULATION TRENDS AND GOVERNMENT ENERGY POLICIES

Both the move to the Sun Belt and suburbanization have
implications for energy use. Each will be discussed in turn.

The Sun Belt Trend

In order to determine the effect of the Sun Belt trend on
energy use, the amount of energy used in the Sun Belt for

[6]See Mills (1979) for a detailed historical and economic
argument.

heating and cooling and the amount used for transportation
must be compared with the amount of energy used for the
same purposes in other parts of the country. Heating costs
are obviously lower in the Sun Belt than in other regions
of the country. An Arthur D. Little study (1974) shows that
about twice as much energy is needed to heat a house of a
given type (e.g., single-family detached) in the Northeast as in the South. Comparisons between the cold North
Central region and the South result in greater differences
while comparisons between the relatively warm West and
the South result in smaller differences. The relationship
does not vary much by fuel or by house type, provided the
combination of fuel and house type is the same for all
regions being compared. The differences for employment
facilities are similar.

Although energy use for space heating is less in the
South than in the North, energy use for space cooling is
obviously greater in the South. When the combined energy
use of the Sun Belt for heating and cooling is compared
with that of other regions, the Sun Belt still uses less
energy. The ratios resulting from regional comparisons
of total energy required for heating and cooling do not
vary much according to house type but do vary according
to fuel type. For most combinations of fuel and house
type, 60-90 percent as much energy is required for heating and cooling in the South as in the Northeast. Again,
comparisons between the North Central region and the South
yield lower ratios and comparisons between the West and
the South yield higher ratios. Thus, the Sun Belt trend
offers a distinct potential for saving energy, particularly
because most migrants come from the cold Northeast and
North Central regions, not from the moderate West region.
Use of energy for other household purposes does not vary
by region.

Two other factors relating to space heating and cooling
will influence the effect of the Sun Belt trend and energy
use. First, the amount of energy used for heating and
cooling greatly depends on the construction of the house
and on the difference between inside and outside tempera-
tures. Because heating and cooling costs are lower in
the Sun Belt than elsewhere, the return to the owner from
investment in insulation and other energy-saving improvements is less in the Sun Belt. Therefore, tax credits for
insulation expenses and other government measures designed
to induce homeowners to economize on household energy use
may be less effective in the Sun Belt than elsewhere.
Second, solar-energy technology for heating and cooling is

likely to improve greatly in coming years. Solar energy undoubtedly has its greatest fuel-saving potential in the Sun Belt, especially for use in cooling. A consideration of the various factors influencing energy use leads to the conclusion that the Sun Belt trend will probably substantially contribute to the conservation of energy used for heating and cooling purposes.

The Sun Belt trend affects not only the amount of energy used for heating and cooling but also the amount of energy used for transportation. In the Sun Belt, public transit is used less relative to the automobile than in other regions. Since the energy efficiency of buses and subways is greater than that of cars, the energy consumption for transportation purposes will probably increase as a result of the Sun Belt trend. Use of public transit in Sun Belt metropolitan areas is low mainly because the densities of these areas are low. Efficient use of public-transit systems requires high densities at origins and destinations along transit routes. Public transit is efficient in terms of economics and energy only if ridership is large. Operating buses and subways that are mostly empty does not save energy. But in low-density areas, ridership cannot be large enough to make public transit more energy-efficient than cars. Because the density of Sun Belt metropolitan areas is only one-third the density of other metropolitan areas, public transit in the Sun Belt is doomed to fail. If the low densities of Sun Belt metropolitan areas resulted mainly from their small size, the problem would solve itself as Sun Belt metropolitan areas grew. However, the low densities result mainly from the low cost of land. Many decades will pass before land prices rise enough to produce density levels adequate to support public transit. Meanwhile, federal subsidies for transit systems in metropolitan areas of the Sun Belt will be wasted money. The future of public transit in Sun Belt metropolitan areas is bleak unless a dramatic change, such as a tripling of the price of gasoline, occurs.

The amount of energy used for transportation purposes is also affected by the average trip lengths that result from the density levels of the Sun Belt. In principle, the length of urban trips depends not on density but on the distances from origins to destinations. For example, work trips can be short in a low-density metropolitan area if workplaces are close to residences. However, in U.S. metropolitan areas, workplaces tend to be segregated from residences and commuting is common practice. Under circumstances that require commuting, the length of the trip

increases as density decreases. Although I have seen no
data, I am confident that average trips tend to be longer
in Sun Belt metropolitan areas than in other metropolitan
areas of similar population.

One additional aspect of the Sun Belt trend will affect
the amount of energy used for transportation: in the Sun
Belt more cars are air conditioned, and air conditioning
reduces miles per gallon by approximately 15 percent.

I am unable to provide good evidence on the greater
energy use for transportation in Sun Belt metropolitan
areas than elsewhere. The Arthur D. Little data (1974)
showed that the move of a family from the Northeast to
the Sun Belt decreases energy use for space heating and
cooling. On the other hand, I have suggested that the
Sun Belt trend would result in increased driving and greater
use of air-conditioned cars. The increase in the amount
of energy used for transportation would probably equal the
decrease in the amount of energy used for space heating
and cooling. Since total energy used for space heating
and cooling is about the same as that used for automobile
travel, the move to the Sun Belt would probably have little
effect on energy consumption.

Thus, federal energy officials should not expect the Sun
Belt trend to have significant effect on energy use. However, I believe it would be a mistake to encourage energy
conservation by subsidizing public transit in most Sun
Belt metropolitan areas. Unless gasoline becomes much
more expensive or scarce, public transit has little potential for success in most Sun Belt metropolitan areas; and
if gasoline should become much more expensive or scarce,
subsidies for public transit would be unnecessary.

Suburbanization

Because suburbanization results in low densities, it has
important implications for energy use. As was pointed out
earlier, low densities make public transit impractical,
encourage automobile use, and necessitate daily trips of
greater-than-average distance.

Local government regulations controlling land use have
greatly exacerbated this situation. Low-density zoning
has reduced suburban densities below the level that would
result from free-market choices. Without these regulations,
average trips would be shorter and public-transit ridership would be greater. More importantly, land use controls
have resulted in excessive segregation of workplaces and

commercial centers from residences, thereby necessitating
lengthy trips for commuting and shopping purposes. In
many U.S. suburbs, zoning is so stringent that an individual store may not be located within walking distance of
residences.

Although excessive land use controls have probably
caused more important distortions in energy consumption
than in land use, they waste both land and energy. Federal
programs should encourage substantial relaxation of land
use controls by local government in order to improve the
use of land and energy and provide better social organization in the suburbs.

As pointed out earlier, suburban zoning excludes all
but single-family detached housing. Furthermore, such
housing is excessively encouraged by several federal programs. Americans, like people in many other countries,
have a traditional attachment to single-family owner-
occupied housing. This attachment results in part from
economic motivation; owner-occupied housing is among the
most profitable investments available to people with little
capital. Thus, high levels of owner-occupancy would occur
without government encouragement, but government programs
have contributed to the current levels. In addition, preferential treatment of owner-occupied housing amounts to
about a 15-percent reduction in the costs of such housing
to the average homeowner. Owner-occupied housing is by
no means identical to single-family detached housing, but
ownership is technically easier to define, and consequently
easier to finance, with single-family detached housing.
In addition, FHA and VA mortgage insurance from the Federal
Housing Administration and the Veterans Administration have
encouraged owner-occupied housing.

Although the amount of single-family owner-occupied
housing that results directly from federal and local preferential treatment is unknown, it must be considerable.
Since World War II, the importance of federal income taxes
and suburban land use controls has increased greatly. From
1900 to 1940, the percentage of housing that was owner-
occupied showed no trend, hovering around 45 percent. After
World War II, the percentage climbed steadily to about 65
percent. These figures suggest that the percent of housing units that are owner-occupied as a result of government
programs may be as great as 20. The percentage of owner-
occupied housing and single-family housing is about equal.
In the 1960s, the trend in housing construction was strongly toward multi-family dwellings. Many people felt the
era of owner-occupied housing was ending. But since about

1974, the trend has been reversed, and the 1977 boom in
housing construction was based almost entirely on construction of single-family units.

In terms of energy used for space heating and cooling,
the distinction between single-family and multi-family
structures is important, whereas ownership is irrelevant.
The Arthur D. Little study (1974) ranks housing types by
energy efficiency: high-rise multi-family dwellings are
the most energy-efficient, low-rise multi-family dwellings are second, single-family attached dwellings are
third, and single-family detached dwellings are last. The
data show dramatic differences in energy use for heating
and cooling by housing types: a single-family attached
dwelling typically might require 75 percent as much energy
for heating and cooling as a single-family detached dwelling, a multi-family low-rise dwelling might require half
as much, and a multi-family high-rise dwelling might
require one-third as much. The key parameter in such data
is the amount of outer wall area. The ratios are only
slightly dependent on region or fuel.

Because space heating is the single largest energy use,
a shift in the proportion of single-family detached dwellings and multi-family dwellings could result in tremendous
energy savings. Beyond a doubt, removal of preferential
programs for single-family detached housing is the single
most important measure available to governments for energy
conservation. For example, if newly constructed single-
family detached dwellings reverted to their prewar percentage of the total housing stock, only about half of
new dwellings would be single-family detached, as contrasted with the present level of about 78 percent. If
the proportion remained constant, by 1988, single-family
detached dwellings would be 58 percent of the total housing stock as contrasted with the current level of about 68
percent. The result would be about a 10-percent drop in
total energy used for residential space heating and cooling.

Thus, I conclude that an important ingredient of government policies on the use of land and energy must be abandonment of programs that have exacerbated the problems.

REFERENCES

Aaron, H. (1972) *Shelter and Subsidies*. Washington, D.C.:
    The Brookings Institution.

Arthur D. Little, Inc. (1974) *Residential and Commercial Energy Use Patterns, 1970-1990.* A. D. Little Report C-77101. Cambridge, Mass.: Arthur D. Little, Inc.

Downs, A. (1973) *Opening Up the Suburbs.* New Haven, Conn.: Yale University Press.

Mills, E. (1972a) City sizes in developing countries. In *Conference Papers: Rehovot Conference on Urbanization and Development in Developing Countries.* Rehovot, Israel: The Continuation Committee of the International Conference on Science in the Advancement of New States in cooperation with the Settlement Study Center.

Mills, E. (1972b) Economic aspects of city sizes. Pp. 383-394 in Commission on Population Growth and the American Future, *Population, Distribution and Policy.* Vol. 5. Washington, D.C.: U.S. Government Printing Office.

Mills, E. (1972c) *Studies in the Structure of the Urban Economy.* Baltimore, Md.: Johns Hopkins University Press for Resources for the Future.

Mills, E. (1972d) *Urban Economics.* Glenview, Ill.: Scott, Foresman and Co.

Mills, E. (1979) *Economic Analysis of Urban Land Use Controls.* Pp. 511-541 in P. Mieszkowski and M. Straszheim, eds., *Current Issues in Urban Economics.* Baltimore, Md.: Johns Hopkins University Press.

Mills, E., and Ohta, K. (1976) Urbanization and urban problems. In H. Patrick and H. Rosovsky, eds., *Asia's New Giant.* Washington, D.C.: The Brookings Institution.

Mills, E., and Song, B. N. (1979) *Korea's Urbanization and Urban Problems.* Cambridge, Mass.: Harvard University Press.

Perloff, H., Dunn, E., Jr., Lampard, E., and Muth, R. (1960) *Regions, Resources and Economic Growth.* Baltimore, Md.: John Hopkins University Press for Resources for the Future.

Rosen, R., and Resnick, M. (1979) The size distribution of cities, the Pareto law and primate cities. *Journal of Urban Economics* 6.

Sundquist, J. (1975) *Dispersing Population.* Washington, D.C.: The Brookings Institution.

Tolley, G. (1974) The welfare economics of city bigness. *Journal of Urban Economics* 1(3):324-345.

THE ECONOMIC AND FISCAL ACCOMPANIMENTS OF POPULATION CHANGE

George E. Peterson and *Thomas Muller*

INTRODUCTION

The force of demography in shaping economic and fiscal adjustments often is underestimated. The baby boom of the post-World War II years will leave its imprint on the country in wave after wave of policy repercussions. This population bulge, which has progressed through successive age cohorts, has disrupted one national institution after another. In the 1950s and 1960s, it created problems of expansion for the public schools and universities--institutions that more recently have had to cope with the ordeal of shrinking as their user populations have subsided. When the population crest reached the 18-24 age bracket, it multiplied crime rates and redirected national job creation efforts to the alleviation of youth unemployment. Perhaps the greatest adjustments for public policy lie ahead--when the babies of 1950 become the aged of the year 2015. One projection estimates that if the federal budget holds steady at approximately one-fifth of gross national product and if federal programs for the aged already on the books are maintained in their present form, the share of the federal budget spent on the aged will have to rise from 26 percent at

George E. Peterson is Director, Public Finance Program, The Urban Institute. Thomas Muller is Principal Research Associate, The Urban Institute.

present and 32 percent in 2005 to 63 percent in 2025.[1]
Political pressure almost certainly will prevent such a
reallocation of federal resources from occurring, but the
figures indicate the magnitude of the adjustment in
social security and other domestic programs for the elderly
that will be necessitated by the baby boom.

Geographical shifts in the nation's population have
brought with them the need for almost equally large economic and fiscal adjustments. Differences in rates of
regional growth, and the burdens heaped upon some of the
nation's older population centers as they wrestle with decline, promise to provide a focus for domestic policy for
at least the next generation. In some respects, the full
implications of these geographic movements are more difficult to unravel than those of the nation's shifting age
profile. Except for the uncertainties of illegal immigration, the age distribution of the nation's population is
known in advance and is largely unresponsive to current
events. All of those who will be elderly in 2025 are now
alive and available for enumeration. In contrast, the
future geographic distribution of the population is a variable yet to be determined and one that will respond sensi-
tively to the locus of job opportunities and to other
factors, many of which the government will try to influence
through its domestic policies. In order to use demographic
trends to help frame a national economic development policy
or to plan for fiscal assistance to state and local governments, it is necessary to understand the market forces that
have produced these trends and determine whether (with or
without government intervention) they are likely to persist.

This paper treats four issues that are fundamental to
the interrelationship between population change and national
economic development policy. The first section examines
the extent of economic adjustment that already has accompanied geographical shifts in the nation's population. It
attempts to distinguish whether the current trends have produced convergence toward income equality or have triggered
a new and unstable imbalance in regional and local incomes.

---

[1]Background memorandum prepared by the U.S. Administration
on Aging. This projection assumes that medical prices rise
at a rate that is 3 percent per year higher than the rate
for other prices. If medical prices are assumed to rise at
the overall inflation rate, the federal budget share claimed
for the aged is less but still substantial--46 percent of
total federal outlays in 2025.

The second section investigates the role migration has played in local growth rates and local unemployment rates. In principle, labor migration (as well as capital movements) should be a strong equilibrating force. But most development policy discussions in this country assume that private market job opportunities are shifting too swiftly to be absorbed by the private market through worker migration and that, as a consequence, high unemployment has become a permanent way of life in the Northeast, older central cities, and other selected areas. Indeed, migration often is accused of exacerbating regional and local imbalances. If this is so, there is a *prima facie* case for government subsidies to create jobs in areas of excess labor supply. However, if private market adjustments already are successfully matching jobs with people through migration, government efforts to balance regional or local economic growth may represent no more than a costly and unproductive attempt to preserve traditional regional economic roles.

The third section of this paper examines the factor cost adjustments that have accompanied different rates of economic and population growth. The best hope for the future of the Northeast and the older central cities may well lie in restoration of their cost competitiveness in producing for national markets. It therefore is of interest to determine whether the economic pressure of recent years has lowered production costs in these regions relative to the costs in regions of the country that are growing. Such an adjustment is part of the competitive market model, but its lessons extend to government actions as well, for government is now an important part of the cost calculations of the private sector.

Finally, different growth rates have major repercussions for the fiscal costs and revenues of local governments. The federal government first became involved in the formulation of a national urban policy in an attempt to shield state and local governments from the fiscal impacts of economic decline. Population loss, unemployment rates, and laggard job growth have been proposed or written into federal-aid formulas as elements entitling local governments to greater federal assistance. Compensation paid to local governments for such conditions, in fact, remains the cornerstone of the nation's urban policy. It is appropriate, therefore, to take stock of these indexes of fiscal weakness and to assess the long-term consequences of disbursing federal aid in proportion to them.

The recent trends in population distribution have been an amalgam of three separate movements: a movement of

population from the North to the South and West; a movement from large metropolitan areas to smaller metropolitan
areas and to nonurban locations; and within metropolitan
regions a movement from central cities to suburbs. Although
these population movements are occurring simultaneously and
result from many of the same causes, their effects on economic and fiscal conditions are often quite different.
Generalizations about the economic or fiscal effects of
population change must be approached with skepticism.

ECONOMIC CONVERGENCE OR A NEW DISEQUILIBRIUM?

Differences in regional and local rates of population growth
would cause little concern if not for the fact that these
differences in population trends are usually accompanied
by parallel differences in economic growth. As Tables 1
and 2 show, population growth and per-capita income growth
tend to be closely related. Between 1969 and 1977, 23 of
the 31 states with above-average population gains also had
above-average income gains. The states losing population
were more evenly divided between gainers and losers in per

TABLE 1   Population Change and Per-Capita Income Growth
by State and Region, 1969-1977

	Population Gain	Per-Capita Income Gain	
Region and State	%	%	Index Relative to Total U.S.
United States	7.5	91.4	100
New England	4.3	79.8	87
Connecticut	3.6	73.7	81
Maine	9.4	91.5	100
Massachusetts	2.3	81.5	89
New Hampshire	17.3	84.9	93
Rhode Island	0.3	86.0	94
Vermont	10.5	78.9	89
Mideast	0.8	82.5	90
Delaware	7.8	80.3	88
Maryland	7.0	89.9	98
New Jersey	3.3	83.4	91
New York	-1.6	74.1	81
Pennsylvania	0.4	92.8	102

TABLE 1 (Continued)

Great Lakes	2.9	88.9	97
Illinois	1.9	84.1	92
Indiana	3.6	91.7	100
Michigan	4.0	92.3	101
Ohio	1.3	87.5	96
Wisconsin	6.2	96.4	105
Plains	4.2	99.4	109
Iowa	2.6	99.9	109
Kansas	4.0	105.6	116
Minnesota	5.8	100.5	110
Missouri	3.5	94.7	104
Nebraska	5.9	93.8	103
North Dakota	5.2	110.0	120
South Dakota	3.1	105.8	116
Southeast	12.3	103.1	113
Alabama	7.3	108.6	119
Arkansas	12.1	115.6	126
Florida	27.3	94.5	103
Georgia	10.9	94.3	103
Kentucky	8.1	107.4	118
Louisiana	8.3	108.3	118
Mississippi	7.6	16.2	127
North Carolina	9.8	98.2	107
South Carolina	11.9	104.8	115
Tennessee	16.3	101.1	111
Virginia	11.3	101.9	111
West Virginia	6.5	118.8	130
Southwest	17.1	106.3	116
Arizona	32.2	96.6	106
New Mexico	17.7	107.7	118
Oklahoma	10.9	106.6	117
Texas	16.2	107.7	118
Rocky Mountain	19.6	102.9	113
Colorado	20.9	102.8	112
Idaho	21.2	99.9	109
Montana	9.7	95.5	104
Utah	21.1	102.3	112
Wyoming	23.4	122.0	133
Far West	11.6	89.7	98
California	11.1	88.3	97

TABLE 1 (Continued)

Nevada	31.9	87.9	96
Oregon	15.2	101.5	111
Washington	9.4	92.7	101
Other			
Alaska	37.5	151.7	166
Hawaii	18.7	84.1	92

SOURCE: Compiled from data presented by the U.S. Bureau of Economic Analysis (1978).

capita income, but most of the states in the Northeast performed below the national average on both counts.

The relationship between population growth and per-capita income for growing and declining cities is even more regular. Between 1969 and 1974, cities growing in population had above-average rates of income gain. Cities losing population had lower-than-average income growth—especially those cities that lost population at a rapid rate. In Table 2, the category "rapidly declining" is used to describe cities in which population loss between 1970 and 1975 was 10 percent or greater. Money income per capita in these cities grew approximately one-fifth more slowly than it

TABLE 2 Population Change and Per-Capita Income Growth for Cities over 100,000

Population Trend, 1970-1975	Number of Cities in Category	Money Income Per Capita, 1974 (dollars)	Percent Growth in Per-Capita Money Income, 1969-1974
Growing	57	4,692	49.1
Declining	84	4,767	44.0
Rapidly declining[a]	11	4,092	38.7
All cities	152	4,690	45.5

[a]More than 10 percent loss in population

SOURCE: U.S. Bureau of the Census (1977c).

did in cities that increased their population. Even this
comparison is greatly distorted by the large amounts of
transfer income received in the declining cities. For
example, during the early 1970s income from government
transfers rose 4.4 times as fast as income from private
earnings in Philadelphia, 3.3 times as fast as private
earnings in St. Louis, and 2.8 times as fast as private
earnings in Suffolk County (Boston) and Baltimore (Peterson et al. 1980). Private earnings did a much better job
of keeping pace with transfer income in cities with growing populations.

Many factors contribute to the observed association between changes in population and changes in income. Because
movers tend to have above-average incomes and education,
the mere influx of movers into one area and their loss to
another tends to raise average incomes in the first location and lower them in the second.[2] In addition, economic
opportunities play a large role in inducing migration.
The prospects of above-average economic growth attract
population to growing parts of the country. In some cases,
the broadening of markets that accompanies in-migration
may itself stimulate further economic gains, even when
measured on a per capita basis.

Although the connection between population and income
gains appears logical, Table 1 shows that there is no in-
eluctable bond between the two. During the last decade
the Plains states have benefited from strong demand for
U.S. agricultural products. Per capita income in each of
these states rose at above-average rates between 1969 and
1977 despite continued lags in population growth. At the
other extreme, California has continued to have above-average
population growth despite slowing income advances. In the
states of California, Arizona, Hawaii, and Florida, life-
style, as much as job opportunities, has encouraged in-
migration.

Exceptions to the association between population and
income change are also found at the city level. Indeed, it
is unclear whether the historic correlation will apply at
all in the future. In some cities, almost the entire population loss can be attributed to the fact that smaller and
often more affluent households are replacing previous residents of the city's housing. An extreme example is afforded

---

[2]As Alonso (1978) has emphasized, such a change in average
incomes may leave the incomes of all individuals unchanged
and be a misleading index for policy decisions.

by Minneapolis, which lost 13 percent of its population between 1970 and 1975 but actually experienced increases in the
number of households in the city and in the number of employed
residents. Under these conditions population decline need
not have adverse impacts. Population change in the past has
been a convenient rough index of the direction of local economic movement, but national development policy must be based
on fuller and more direct measures of economic condition.

Convergence or Disequilibrium

Implicit in much of the debate over national development
policy is disagreement over the proper interpretation of
the economic trends summarized in Tables 1 and 2. One
interpretation suggests that the different rates of economic growth have succeeded in narrowing long-standing
inequalities, thereby causing convergence toward a rough
balance in the economic prosperity of different regions
of the country. An alternative interpretation finds that
recent trends have already overshot convergence, creating
a new regional imbalance that threatens to widen at an
alarming rate unless the government intervenes.

　　Tables 3 and 4 provide a long-term perspective on regional per-capita incomes. They show that the predominant
trend of the last half century has been one of convergence.
Fifty years ago the relative gap in per-capita incomes between the Southeast and Middle Atlantic states was more
than four times as large as it is now. Incomes in other

TABLE 3　Regional Per-Capita Income as Percent of U.S.
Average

	1930	1950	1960	1970	1975	1977
New England	130	107	110	100	103	102
Mideast	141	117	116	113	109	107
Great Lakes	110	111	108	104	104	105
Plains	62	95	93	95	98	97
Southeast	50	68	73	82	86	86
Southwest	64	87	87	89	93	95
Rocky Mountain	86	97	94	91	94	94
Far West	131	120	116	111	111	111

SOURCES:　U.S. Bureau of Economic Analysis (1978); early
years from Bureau of Economic Analysis (unpublished tables).

TABLE 4   Median Household Income by Region[a] (constant 1975 dollars)

Region	1955	1965	1970	1976	Percent Change, 1970-1976	Mean Income 1977 Current Dollars
Northeast	9,481	12,943	14,825	14,573	-1.7	16,680
North Central	9,543	12,456	14,314	15,081	+5.3	16,474
South	7,206	9,568	11,859	12,694	+7.0	15,069
West	9,678	13,140	14,239	14,648	+3.1	16,627
Percent South of Northeast	76.0	74.0	80.0	87.1		90.3

[a]Census regions in this table do not correspond fully to regions in Table 3. Approximate correspondences are as follows: Northeast = New England, Mideast; North Central = Great Lakes, Plains; South = Southeast, Southwest; West = Rocky Mountains, Far West.

SOURCES: U.S. Bureau of the Census (1977b, 1978).

regions, too, have moved markedly toward the national mean. This comparison is as true when incomes are measured for household units (Table 4) as when they are measured in per-capita terms (Table 3). By either measure, the convergence process has continued into the 1970s. A comparison of nominal incomes, moreover, reveals no evidence of unstable overshooting. The regions of the country that historically have enjoyed above-average incomes continue to do so, although the margin of their advantage has greatly diminished in recent years.

The pattern of convergence in national economic growth is actually stronger than the pattern of regional economic change and stronger than the association between population and income change. Of the 48 contiguous states, 42 saw their per-capita income levels move toward the national mean between 1969 and 1977. Three exceptions were the New England states of New Hampshire, Vermont, and Rhode Island, which began the period with below-average income levels and fell further behind. Other exceptions were Wyoming, Washington, and Michigan, which began the period with above-average incomes and enjoyed above-average gains (though narrowly so in the case of Washington and Michigan).

One objection frequently raised to comparisons of the type reported in Tables 3 and 4 is that they overlook regional differences in the cost of living. Although regional

cost differentials exist, their measurement is presently
uncertain. The most common measuring stick is that provided by the family budgets developed by the Bureau of
Labor Statistics (BLS). These budgets are prepared for
households of two different age compositions and three
standards of living in selected urban areas. However, the
BLS household budgets cannot be used directly to convert
nominal incomes to their real equivalents for states or
regions. For one thing, cost levels differ greatly within
regions--by size of urban area and presumably between urban and rural areas as well. Any regional averaging of
consumer budget costs therefore involves considerable
speculation concerning how the data obtained from a few
urban areas should be generalized. Another difficulty is
posed by the bundle of consumption items priced in the BLS
studies. These do not (and very likely cannot) take into
account all of the variations in local or regional spending
patterns. The differences in consumption become particularly important in pricing such items as housing in urban
budgets. The BLS method assumes that households of the
same budget class consume the same type of housing, regardless of where they live. [3]

These caveats should be kept in mind by the reader when
examining Table 5, which presents regional per-capita incomes indexed for differences in the cost of living. Such
corrections show that the present range of regional income
differentials is smaller than that suggested by comparisons
of nominal income. The adjusted figures raise the possibility that the convergence process has indeed overshot
equilibrium, bringing with it a new regional imbalance.
With the cost-of-living adjustments shown in Table 5, New
England has the lowest per-capita income level as well as
the slowest rate of income growth. A comparison with the
growth rates presented in Table 1 shows that New England
and the Mideast, on this measure, are now falling further
behind the Southwest and other parts of the country in per-
capita real income.

When the focus of attention shifts to the cities, the
evidence of unstable overshooting is clearer. There was

---

[3]The BLS budget costs also include taxes paid to state and
local governments. If these are viewed as voluntary burdens selected by the local citizenry to finance public services, their inclusion as "costs" in adjusting local incomes
may be inappropriate for purposes of federal-aid legislation
or other federal policy.

TABLE 5   Regional Per-Capita Incomes, 1977 (Indexed),
Nominal and Adjusted for Cost of Living

Region	Nominal	Adjusted
New England	102	88
Mideast	107	98
Great Lakes	105	103
Plains	97	98
Southeast	86	93
Southwest	95	101
Rocky Mountain	94	98
Far West	111	106

SOURCES: Cost-of-living adjustment based on Grasberger
(1978); comparison adapted from Advisory Commission on
Intergovernmental Relations (1978).

a time when the northern cities that are currently suffering population losses enjoyed a decided edge in income
levels over cities elsewhere in the country. As Table 2
demonstrates, this is no longer the case. Cities suffering
from rapid population loss already trail other cities by
a significant margin in per-capita income. Corrected for
cost-of-living differences, the entire set of declining
cities would clearly lag behind other cities, both in income levels and in income growth. Greater divergence in
income levels would have occurred if not for the infusion
of government transfer funds into declining cities.

Whether recent income trends have tended to narrow or
widen income differentials depends on one's perspective.
From a broad regional point of view and from the perspective of several decades, the pattern that prevails is one
of convergence. From a perspective that emphasizes growth
in the 1970s or focuses on individual cities, the pace of
convergence may seem unduly accelerated and likely to over-
shoot equilibrium, creating new imbalances that work to
the disadvangtage of the older parts of the country. For
the cities with the most rapid population decline, the
unstable overshooting beyond income equality already has
occurred.

THE ADJUSTMENT PROCESS: MIGRATION AND UNEMPLOYMENT RATES

In a smoothly functioning national market, factor migration
is crucial to restoring regional and other geographical

balance. Capital and labor will flow between geographical
locations in response to differences in earnings opportunities. As long as all factors are fully mobile, the outcome
of this migration process will be twofold: full employment
of resources, including labor; and factor price equalization between regions (Borts 1960). Factor movements under
these conditions produce equal earnings opportunities for
labor and capital in different parts of the country. This
equality of earnings opportunities, of course, can be associated with vastly different local growth rates, when measured in terms of aggregate income.

Although few studies have examined the responsiveness
of capital flows to regional differences in rates of return,
it is generally assumed that capital investment is indeed
highly sensitive to relative profit rates and that, consequently, regional variations in the return to capital
are quickly eliminated.[4] Much more doubt exists about the
mobility of labor and the ability of migration to equalize
real-wage rates, absorb local pools of unemployment, or
otherwise stabilize the regional development process.

If labor migration is unable to bring local labor supplies into balance with local labor demand, a second type
of market adjustment will occur. Market pressures will
cause permanent wage and other factor price differentials
to emerge. Wages will tend to rise in areas of strong
product demand and to fall in areas of weak demand and
excess labor supply. The prices of other fixed factors,
such as the capital embodied in buildings, will tend to
follow the same pattern. These adjustments in factor costs,
in turn, will reduce the costs of doing business in areas
suffering from soft demand, which will tend to divert to
them a greater share of production for national markets.
The size of the factor-cost adjustments that must occur
to absorb a given level of local unemployment will depend
upon the ease with which national product demand can be cap-
tured for local production through factor-cost reductions.[5]

[4]For evidence of high elasticity in regional capital supplies, see Engle (1974).

[5]The role of factor costs in location decisions of firms
is the subject of some controversy. Birch (1977) presents
evidence that the location of economic activity may not be
highly sensitive to differences in factor costs. However,
Carlton (1979) has found that when industries producing
for national markets are isolated, factor-cost differentials
play a clear and significant role in location decisions--

Only if both market-clearing mechanisms fail will there
appear permanent pockets of localized unemployment. Migration flows then will have been insufficient to move workers
to where the jobs are, and local cost adjustments will have
been insufficient to draw into production the region's unemployed resources.

Efforts to forge a national development policy or national urban policy in this country, like parallel efforts
to establish national settlement patterns in European countries, have been premised on the presumption that market
adjustments are inadequate (Sundquist 1975). Labor migration is thought to be insufficient to match fully jobs with
people, and institutional impediments (such as union wage
contracts and a national minimum wage) are thought to make
it impossible or undesirable for prices to fall far enough
in areas of weak demand to reestablish full employment.
If these presumptions are accurate, it may become efficient
for the government to subsidize job creation in areas of
excess labor supply. To the extent that the United States
has had a regional and local development policy in recent
years, it has consisted of federally subsidized job creation and capital investment in areas of high unemployment.
The 1978 renewal of the Comprehensive Employment and Training Act, for example, calls for the federal government to
create local public service jobs to absorb a minimum of 20
percent of local unemployment over 6 percent. The cornerstone of the Carter administration's urban policy, announced
in 1978, was a series of proposals for subsidizing capital
investment as a means of job creation in high-unemployment
areas. Conspicuously missing from government proposals
have been policies that would assist the private market
in its adjustments by facilitating labor migration or by
encouraging factor-cost reductions in areas of weak demand.

Migration

Although official U.S. development policies imply skepticism of migration as an equilibrating mechanism, most

---

though the factors whose prices and availability are most
important vary sharply by industrial classification. Note
that if a single factor is in excess local supply, price
adjustments will also lead to factor substitution in production, thus further tending to absorb the unemployed resources and equalize factor prices.

analytical studies suggest that migration has effectively performed its balancing role, at least for segments of the labor market.

Repeated research has demonstrated that labor migration responds to geographical differentials in earnings opportunities. Migration rates have been shown to be sensitive to regional differences in unemployment levels, rates of job growth, and wage rates or income levels (Alperovich et al. 1977, Greenwood and Gormeley 1971, Miller 1973, Morrison and Rellers 1975, Pack 1973, Rothenberg 1977). Longitudinal studies of individual migrants find that the income levels of those who migrate are improved as a result of their moves, suggesting that the expectations of greater economic achievement raised by regional differentials in earnings opportunities are, in general, satisfied for individual movers (Kiker and Traynham 1977, Lansing and Morgan 1967). The economic incentives for sustaining migration therefore appear to be present.

Studies of the effect of migration on the rates of return to schooling shed more light on the economics of the migration process. The differences in the level of skills and education among different regions of the United States have been long-standing; the portion of the labor force that possesses high occupational or educational skills is lower in the South than in the rest of the country. Southern-born men of both races, for example, have lower educational levels and lower occupational status than northern-born men. In a well-functioning market, the relative paucity of highly educated labor in the South should give rise to higher returns to education in that region and create special incentives for the migration of educated workers into the region.

Both of these expectations are borne out in practice. Studies of the rates of return to education reveal that the highly educated northern-born (white) worker who migrates to the South earns the greatest return on schooling (Featherman and Hauser 1978). Comparisons of interregional migration flows also show that this socioeconomic group has dominated North-South migration. To a considerable extent, as Featherman and Hauser (1978) note, the South has satisfied its need for highly skilled labor by attracting movers from the North who are able to earn higher returns on their educational training in the South than they can in the North.

Of course, the contribution that migration makes to regional skill equalization will depend upon the size of migration flows. The persistence of skill imbalances

throughout the 20th century indicates that migration has
not been quick to equalize the distribution of skills
among regions. However, the pace of skill equalization
has accelerated in recent years. Table 6 shows migration
patterns for the single year 1975-1976. It illustrates the
net out-migration of college-educated labor from the Northeast and North Central states, and its absorption in the
South and the West. The difference in skill mix between
migrants and native-born workers in the South is supported
by the fact that in 1970, 37 percent of people 25-64 years
old who migrated to the South Atlantic region had completed
4 or more years of college. Only 8.8 percent of nonmigrants in this region achieved this level of education
(Bouvier and Cahill 1975). A similar pattern emerges from
the breakdown of migration by occupation type. Net flows
of professional management workers to the South have been
far larger than those of service workers (see Table 6).

The ability of migration to alter skill distributions
can be seen from a comparison of the Houston and New York
metropolitan areas. In 1977, the Houston standard metropolitan statistical area (SMSA) had a higher proportion
of college graduates in the 30-34 age bracket than did
the New York SMSA, while in 1970, the New York SMSA had a
substantially higher proportion of such persons. The

TABLE 6   Net Migration Between Regions by Education and
Occupation 1975-1976 (in thousands)

| Region | Education Level | | | | | |
| | 4 or More Years of College | | | 0-8 Years of School | | |
	In-Migrants	Out-Migrants	Net Change	In-Migrants	Out-Migrants	Net Change
Northeast	70	-119	-49	24	-21	+3
North Central	74	-116	-42	31	-65	-34
South	124	-100	+24	63	-60	+3
West	118	-52	+68	58	-30	+28

| Region | Occupation Type | | | | | |
| | Professional-Management | | | Service | | |
	In-Migrants	Out-Migrants	Net Change	In-Migrants	Out-Migrants	Net Change
Northeast	55	-70	-15	21	-14	+7
North Central	43	-107	-64	11	-23	-12
South	107	-70	+37	29	-26	+3
West	88	-46	+42	23	-29	-6

SOURCE: U.S. Bureau of the Census (1977a).

change in skill mix is primarily attributable to net in-migration, although as job opportunities expand, the proportion of the native-born population receiving formal training also tends to rise.

Even if migration has succeeded in smoothing out some of the geographical imbalances in skill distributions and labor demand, there are groups of the population for which it has not functioned well as an equilibrating mechanism.

Interregional migration is far less feasible for low-educated, low-skilled workers than for the upper echelons of the work force. Highly skilled persons sell their labor to a national market and therefore are more aware of migration opportunities. Furthermore, the costs of interregional migration appear high to workers in relatively low-paying jobs. The costs of moving limit the ability of private markets to equilibrate wages or returns to education through migration.

Regional wage differentials are much greater for low-skilled jobs than for more highly skilled occupations, reflecting the fact that low-skilled jobs are insulated from the equilibrating force of migration. The difference between the South and the Northeast in average metropolitan wages for unskilled plant labor, for example, is more than 10 times as large as the difference for skilled maintenance workers (see Table 8). This wage difference is a result of numerous factors including the higher rate of union organization of low-skilled workers in the North. Nonetheless, the persistence and expansion of the low-skilled wage gap shows that migration has not caused wage equalization.

Labor migration within a metropolitan region also is limited as a stabilizing force. The dispersal of jobs and population throughout the metropolitan region has gone far to equalize suburban and central-city wage rates for given job titles.[6] But the concentration of low-paying jobs and low-earning households at the urban core has given rise to

[6]For example, in 1976 the construction wage index was 116 in New York City and 114 in Nassau and Suffolk counties, Long Island. (U.S. city average = 100). The wage structure of metropolitan areas formerly reflected the centralization of job opportunities. Suburban wages were lower than central-city wages in part because those who worked in the suburbs faced lower commuting costs. The decentralization of jobs has tended to equalize wages throughout the metropolitan region (Peterson 1979).

imbalances in local fiscal capacity. These imbalances
trigger inequalities in tax burdens and public-service
costs. Equalization of factor prices at the metropolitan
scale does not remove all the consequences of locational
clustering. Even where intrametropolitan migration is
successful in equalizing wage rates for given jobs, it may
create residential clusters of affluent and poor households,
leading to greater social segregation and concentration of
public-sector cost burdens (see section on fiscal impacts).

Unemployment Rates

Part of the equilibrating function of migration should be
to eliminate local pockets of unemployment or to spread
the long-term national unemployment rate more evenly among
geographical locations. Even the most cursory inspection
of unemployment data, however, reveals very strong geographical concentrations of unemployment. This raises the
question: Why has migration failed to smooth out the clustering of the unemployed? Has labor failed to respond in
adequate numbers and with adequate speed to local differences in earnings opportunities? Or have other factors
served to retain an excess supply of labor in some parts
of the country despite low employment demand?
     In an analysis of metropolitan unemployment rates,
Wheaton (1979) has sought to explain observed differences
in long-term rates over two periods: 1961-1967 and 1968-
1974. He finds that the bulk of systematic variation in
unemployment rates can be explained by what are called
structural factors. These include differences in the level
of unemployment compensation, differences in the industrial
composition of the labor force, and differences in the degree of union organization. In metropolitan areas where
unemployment benefits are more generous, unemployment is
higher. This suggests that at least part of local unemployment is voluntary. Unemployment rates also are higher
in metropolitan areas marked by a concentration of high-
wage, cyclical industries. The expectation of more frequent unemployment appears to be capitalized into the wage
structures of the construction industry and capital-goods
industries. High wages, in effect, compensate the worker
for the prospect of greater unemployment. Metropolitan
areas that concentrate in cyclical industrial activities
experience not only higher-than-average rates of unemployment, but also higher-than-average wages. Thus, there may

be no economic inducement to out-migration.[7] Finally, the positive relation between unemployment and the level of unionization of the labor force suggests that unions accept some additional unemployment as the price of sustaining higher wages or wages that can be maintained at fixed levels in the face of periodic slack demand.

Although not included in Wheaton's regression analysis, the unemployment data also point clearly to the conclusion that quality-of-life considerations play a role in unemployment differences. Metropolitan areas like San Diego persistently sustain above-average rates of unemployment, while metropolitan areas in the farm states, with their presumptively less congenial living environments, persistently have below-average rates of unemployment. Such findings are consistent with analyses of the reasons for household migration. Population movements are by no means motivated solely by earnings calculations. As long as people prefer to live in sunny climes and near large bodies of water, workers will tend to move to these areas, and unemployment rates will be higher than in areas with fewer environmental amenities. Workers' preferences for residing in certain parts of the country will also be reflected in their willingness to accept lower wages.[8] In both cases, households "pay" for superior living conditions through reduced earning power.

One of Wheaton's (1979) most interesting findings is that once structural variables are controlled, metropolitan differences in employment growth have no apparent effect on metropolitan unemployment rates; high-growth areas are as likely to suffer from high unemployment as low-growth areas. Wheaton interprets this as evidence that economically motivated migration successfully clears metropolitan labor markets, except to the extent that it is prevented from so doing by public policy and environmental features that make some areas more attractive residential locations than others.

Unfortunately, there are at present no reliable data on metropolitan rates of unemployment by industrial or skill classification. The crucial test of the ability of migration to clear labor markets would be its ability to break the relationship between job growth and unemployment, even for the low-skilled segment of the labor force. From the

[7]See also Vernez et al. (1977).
[8]For evidence on the relation between metropolitan wage levels and quality-of-life variables, see Hoch (1976).

direct evidence on migration patterns, it appears unlikely
that migration has smoothed out local unemployment rates
for unskilled labor. Elimination of local pockets of unemployment in this sector of the labor force thus becomes
the responsibility of public policy.

Unemployment rates for individual jurisdictions have
been estimated only since 1974, when they became an element
in federal-aid allocations. The procedures used to estimate
city unemployment have been subjected to well-deserved
criticism. The data do seem to establish, however, that
there is a strong negative connection, at least for large
cities, between local rates of unemployment and rates of
both population and job growth. Some simple associations
are shown in Table 7. Replication of Wheaton's estimating
equations at the local level confirms the importance of
structural factors in explaining variations in city unemployment rates. But it also indicates that at the city
level, laggard job growth systematically adds to the local
unemployment rate. The causes for the differences between
effects at the city level and effects at the metropolitan
level are currently unknown. These differences may be a
result of the concentration in the cities of lower-skilled
workers who cannot easily avail themselves of migration
opportunities or a consequence of the special time period
for which the city estimates were made,[9] or they may be
the result of other factors.

Conclusion: The Role of Migration

The general role of migration and factor movements in the
development process is one of the most controverted issues
of development policy.

Labor migration and capital movements are, beyond doubt,
largely responsible for the regional economic shifts that
have occurred in recent decades. One of the most frequent
policy responses to these development trends, especially

[9]Such estimates are possible only for the period 1974-
1977, which was a recession era. It is possible that migration responds with a lag to changes in economic conditions, and that several years would be required to adjust
to the sharply different job losses experienced in different cities during the recession. Alternatively, these
differential job losses might be viewed by workers as a
purely cyclical phenomenon and not a cause for migration.

TABLE 7   Population Change and Unemployment Rates, 1970–
1976, Cities over 100,000

Population Trend[a]	Unemployment Rate (%)		
	1970	1976	Growth 1970–76
Growing	4.4	7.6	72.7
Declining	4.7	8.8	86.9
Rapidly declining[b]	5.5	11.8	115.2
All cities	4.6	8.5	84.3

[a]1970–1975.
[b]More than 10 percent population loss.

SOURCES: Compiled from average unemployment estimates in
U.S. Bureau of Labor Statistics (1976a). Unemployment
data from *1970 Census of Population*.

in areas losing population and investment, has been to try
to impede factor movements. Almost all of the northern
states, for example, have pending legislation that would
restrict part of the investment assets of public pension
funds to local development purposes, regardless of the
need to accept lower rates of return. The public expenditures made on behalf of local public job creation are based
on the presumption that not only will labor migration not
suffice to clear local labor markets but also migration
of the scale necessary to do so would be injurious to local
economies and disruptive of national development policy.
The concept of development imbalance that underlies this
point of view might be labeled product-oriented. It is
concerned with total levels of economic production in different parts of the country and the rapidity of shifts in
levels of economic activity.
     The alternative concept of development imbalance focuses
on inequalities in factor earnings. If capital and labor
can earn the same return in different parts of the country,
there may be said to be development balance, despite the
fact that there are greatly different rates of total output growth in different regions. Both in principle and
in practice, migration remains a strong force in equalizing
factor earnings. The conflict between equal factor earnings and equal regional growth rates as objectives of
national development policy is frequently reflected in
legislation. For example, early versions of the proposed
national development bank argued that a national lending

and subsidy policy was necessary precisely because private
markets channel investment funds to where they can earn
the greatest return. If one looks at national development
from an equal earnings perspective, this fact is a strong
force tending to establish regional equilibrium. If, however, one looks at the objectives of "balanced growth" as
equal rates of product expansion in different parts of the
country, such movements of capital will tend to encourage
regional imbalance.

Even if equalization of factor earnings, especially
labor earnings, is accepted as an important goal of development policy, migration faces two serious limitations.
First, migration apparently does not serve to clear markets
in unskilled labor. Auxiliary measures are needed to protect this portion of the labor force from the impact of
local growth differentials. Second, by equalizing labor
earnings for particular jobs or particular skill levels,
migration may still produce a clustering of high-skilled,
high-earning households in one part of the country or in
one part of the metropolis and a clustering of low-skilled,
low-earning households elsewhere. Because of the nature
of local public-sector financing in the United States,
this geographical clustering is likely to give rise to
different tax and public service burdens.

FACTOR-COST ADJUSTMENTS

In a market economy, price adjustments are fundamental to
the establishment of equilibrium. Regional markets are
no exception to this rule. Market pressures in areas of
weak product demand will tend to depress factor prices.
These price signals will promote migration of labor and
other factors of production. If the migration response
is rapid, factor price differentials will then be eliminated. However, if migration is impeded, market forces
in areas of weak demand will cause factor prices to remain
depressed. Surplus factor supplies then must be absorbed
by lowering the costs of regional production by a sufficiently wide margin to divert production for national
markets into the region.

From a practical standpoint, the first question to ask in
deciding whether the market is assisting equilibrium adjustment is: Are factor prices adjusting to reflect regional and
other differences in product demand or factor availabilities?

That *some* regional factor-cost adjustments occur in
response to weak product demand is clear. Most obviously

affected are the prices of literally fixed factors of production, such as office and factory space. During the period 1972-1976, commercial rental costs in New York City office buildings, for example, fell by more than 25 percent at the same time costs per square foot were rising sharply in Houston, Dallas, and other growing markets. (New York City's rental costs, at least in Manhattan, recovered equally quickly with the revived demand during 1977-1979). Housing prices have responded with comparable sharpness to differences in demand as expressed by local population growth rates.

The factor of greatest importance in determining local production costs, however, is labor. It is far from clear whether wage costs have adjusted in a manner to restore cost competitiveness between regions. Resolution of this question is particularly difficult in view of the manner in which labor costs are commonly reported. Most regional comparisons of wage levels have run together wages for the entire nonagricultural or manufacturing sector. Comparisons spanning any length of time are therefore influenced to an unknown degree by the shifting composition of the regional labor force.[10] The Bureau of Labor Statistics does provide annual comparisons of wages for selected private-sector job titles. Table 8 summarizes relative wage indexes for three types of labor, by metropolitan area and region. The comparisons suggest that far from converging in response to labor demand imbalances, relative wage costs over the period 1967-1975 widened in the face of soft demand in the Northeast and some North Central states. Although relative wages in all three job groupings fell in the high-cost West region, they rose in the North Central region. For two of the three job groupings, relative wages rose in the Northeast. Despite strong employment growth in the South, wage increases there were below the average for large metropolitan areas. Only in the job class most exposed to interregional migration--skilled maintenance-- is there evidence of regional convergence in wage rates.

The localized nature of unskilled labor markets is emphasized by the sharp variations in wage trends for unskilled plant labor. In some markets, such as New York, Detroit, and San Francisco (all highly unionized), unskilled wage rates registered exceptionally large gains over the period 1967-1975. In other markets, such as San Antonio, unskilled wage levels remained depressed and even fell relative to other urban regions. This is explained by the

[10]See, for example, Mills (1978).

TABLE 8 Relative Wage Levels, by Metropolitan Area and Region
(U.S. metropolitan average = 100)

Metropolitan Area and Region	Job Class and Year					
	Office Clerical		Skilled Maintenance		Unskilled Plant	
	1967-68	1975	1967-68	1975	1967-68	1975
Northeast						
Boston	95	99	95	97	94	92
Buffalo	101	103	104	104	106	107
Newark	100	104	101	99	105	104
New York	103	108	101	100	108	121
Philadelphia	97	98	97	97	104	108
Pittsburgh	101	104	99	99	107	111
Average[a]	99.5	102.7	99.5	99.3	103.3	107.2
North Central						
Chicago	104	105	106	110	107	117
Cincinnati	97	97	98	99	102	102
Cleveland	102	101	102	105	108	113
Detroit	116	122	114	116	122	132
Kansas City	96	98	104	106	105	111
Milwaukee	99	99	106	106	111	110
Minneapolis-St. Paul	93	95	104	106	109	117
St. Louis	98	101	104	103	106	112
Average[a]	100.6	102.2	104.8	106.4	108.8	114.2

South						
Atlanta	100	103	95	100	79	70
Baltimore	94	99	99	101	91	90
Dallas	94	95	91	94	80	82
Houston	99	100	99	99	79	78
Memphis	88	92	93	94	81	81
Oklahoma City	91	89	90	94	84	78
San Antonio	85	81	88	—	71	66
Average[a]	93.4	94.1	93.6	97.0	80.7	80.7
West						
Denver	97	98	98	99	101	97
Los Angeles	112	107	105	103	114	115
Phoenix	96	90	101	99	87	85
San Diego	104	99	107	101	110	104
San Francisco	109	110	113	117	126	136
Seattle	106	102	104	108	120	120
Average[a]	104.0	101.0	104.7	104.5	111.3	109.5

[a]Average indexes are the simple average of the metropolitan areas subsumed under each regional heading.

SOURCES: U.S. Bureau of Labor Statistics (1969a,b, 1976b).

influx of Mexican workers, who have limited ability to
move to other, higher-paying labor markets. The inter-
metropolitan variation in unskilled wages far exceeds that
in the other labor categories, indicating that each local
labor market tends to respond to its own balance of supply
and demand for unskilled labor and to its own bargaining
situation.

Although Table 8 shows no signs of wage-rate convergence
over the period 1967-1975, more recent wage changes do suggest this possibility. Table 9 summarizes average wage
increases by region in 1975-1976 for the five job classes
now reported by the Bureau of Labor Statistics. The data
are too spotty to constitute a trend, but it is interesting
to note that between 1975 and 1976, wage adjustments in
the Northeast lagged behind the national average in all
five job classes.

Further signs of cost adjustments can be found in the
consumer price index. Since 1975, consumer costs in New
York, Boston, and other northern metropolitan areas have
increased at a rate much below the national average (see
Table 10). These regional cost differences have been led
by housing prices. In direct response to the pressure
population trends have placed on metropolitan housing markets, housing costs have climbed fastest in the South and
West and slowest in the northern SMSAs. Public-sector
tax burdens in northeastern SMSAs also have climbed more
slowly, as cities have limited their expenditure growth.[11]
If these regional variations in cost of living continue,
they eventually will be built into the regional wage structure. Thus, there are some signs that the recent divergence in regional growth rates has reduced differences in
the costs of living and doing business in different parts
of the country.

Labor Productivity

Wages alone provide an unreliable guide to labor costs.
Falling relative wages may be more than offset by declines
in labor productivity. Prices will then be forced to make
still larger adjustments if they are to reestablish regional cost competitiveness.

[11]For evidence of the year-to-year convergence in state-
local tax burdens on industrial produce in different metropolitan areas, see Hansen and Touhsaent (1978).

TABLE 9   Percent Increase in Average Hourly Earnings for
Selected Occupational Groups in All Metropolitan Areas,
1976-1977

Region	Work Classification				
	Office Clerical	Electronic Data Processing	Industrial Nurse	Skilled Maintenance	Skilled Plant
Northeast	7.2	6.6	7.8	8.5	8.7
North Central	7.8	7.1	8.3	8.4	8.8
South	7.2	7.0	8.2	8.9	9.0
West	7.6	7.1	7.9	8.7	10.0
United States	7.4	6.9	8.1	8.6	9.0

SOURCE: U.S. Bureau of Labor Statistics (1978b).

Table 11 compares for different parts of the country
value added per production worker in manufacturing. Because different industrial mixes are involved in the regional labor forces, comparisons of value added must be
made with caution. However, the data in the table suggest
that central cities as a group, especially the central
cities of New England and the Middle Atlantic states, lag
well behind the rest of the country in value added per
laborer. Productivity gains in these areas between 1970
and 1975 were also well below the national norm. At least
for the central cities, regional differences in value-added
growth were more pronounced than regional differences in
factor-cost adjustments. This suggests that manufacturing
is becoming less competitive in Northeast and Middle Atlantic cities--not because of widening wage differentials,
but because of comparatively low and slowly growing output
per employee. The productivity lag, in turn, could be attributed to changes in the industrial composition, to differences in the level of regional capital investment, or
to changes in the skill level of the labor force. Further
analysis would be required in order to identify the role
played by these factors, but each implies that recent regional income trends are likely to persist as the differences in labor productivity and productivity growth are
translated into household earnings.

Labor productivity growth in the South and West undoubtedly has benefited from the higher level of capital investment occurring in these regions. In recent years, regional
differences in private capital investment have exceeded

TABLE 10   Growth in Consumer Price Index, by Metropolitan
Area, 1976-1977, 1977-1978[a]

	1976-1977	1977-1978
Northeast		
Boston	5.6	3.3
Buffalo	7.2	5.7
New York	5.8	5.3
Philadelphia	6.9	6.7
Pittsburgh	6.9	6.7
Regional average[b]	6.1	6.1
North Central		
Chicago	6.2	7.7
Cincinnati	7.3	8.4
Cleveland	7.8	6.1
Detroit	7.7	8.7
Kansas City	7.7	7.5
Milwaukee	7.3	6.1
Minneapolis-St. Paul	6.4	8.5
St. Louis	7.4	7.1
Regional average[b]	7.2	7.7
South		
Atlanta	6.3	8.7
Baltimore	7.0	7.6
Dallas	7.9	7.4
Houston	8.4	7.6
Regional average[b]	6.8	7.9
West		
Los Angeles	7.5	7.6
San Diego	6.7	7.6
San Francisco	8.3	8.9
Seattle	8.4	9.4
Regional average[b]	7.8	8.6

[a]Covers period April to April, May to May, or June to June,
depending upon survey cycle.
[b]Average for entire region.

SOURCE: U.S. Bureau of Labor Statistics (1978a).

TABLE 11 Value Added Per Production Worker in Manufacturing--Central Cities and Inner Suburbs, by Region, 1970-1975

Region	Central City		Balance of Urban Community	
	Dollar Value Added Per Production Worker 1975 (in thousands)	Percent Change in Value Added Per Production Worker 1970-1975	Dollar Value Added Per Production Worker 1975 (in thousands)	Percent Change in Value Added Per Production Worker 1970-1975
New England	29	45	39	65
Middle Atlantic	34	47	56	75
East North Central	36	50	41	58
West North Central	40	54	45	73
South Atlantic	36	44	32	100
South East Central	38	65	39	63
South West Central	40	74	58	29
West	41	61	39	50
All cities	37	59	41	64

SOURCES: U.S. Bureau of the Census (1970, 1975).

regional differences in labor-force growth by a substantial margin, indicating that capital endowments per worker
are growing at a more rapid pace in growing regions than
in the older sections of the country.

Tables 12 and 13 provide partial measures of this trend.
Table 12 shows value per employee in industrial and commercial construction activities for selected metropolitan
areas in 1976. The advantage of western metropolitan regions is obvious. More detailed evidence on capital investment can be compiled for the manufacturing sector.
Between 1970 and 1975, capital investment per production
employee in the New England and Middle Atlantic states
trailed the national average by a wide margin, particularly
in central cities (see Table 13). Investment per manufacturing worker in the South Atlantic states and South Central states, for example, was more than twice that in the
New England and Middle Atlantic states. Average investment per employee in central cities ran well behind that
in the suburbs in all parts of the country. These differences in the capital endowments being provided to workers
threaten to widen the productivity gap between different regions of the country and between central city and suburb.[12]

Conclusion: Factor-Cost Adjustments

Until recently, price adjustments do not appear to have
worked to lower relative costs in the Northeast or in
northern cities generally. The failure of factor prices
to reflect trends in product demand has prevented market
forces from playing a more vigorous role in the restoration of regional equilibrium.

There are multiple signs that since 1975, factor costs
have begun to adjust in the manner predicted by market
theory. The severity of the 1974-1975 recession and the
accompanying local fiscal difficulties may have encouraged
the Northeast and large cities to realize that in the face

[12]The differences in manufacturing investment levels for
large metropolitan areas are still more striking. For
example, over the period 1970-1976, the Houston SMSA
benefited from $31,700 in capital investment per produc-
tion employee, compared to $16,000 of capital investment
per worker in New York, $7,700 in Philadelphia, and $6,400
in Pittsburgh.

TABLE 12   Industrial and Commercial Construction Activity
in Selected SMSAs, 1976

SMSA	Construction Value Per Employee ($)
Northeast	
New York	15
Philadelphia	36
Boston	62
Buffalo	92
West	
Los Angeles	140
Phoenix	137
Denver	175
San Diego	180

SOURCES: U.S. Bureau of Domestic Commerce (1976),
Bureau of Labor Statistics (1976a).

of weak product demand, their long-term interests are best
served by trimming their high costs of operation.

The difficulties of adjustment that confront the older
parts of the country should not be underestimated. Because
wide gaps in regional labor productivity have emerged, even
substantial price adjustments may be insufficient to restore
factor demand. If equilibrium were to be established solely

TABLE 13   Capital Investment Per Production Employee, by
Region, 1970-1975

Region	Central City ($)	Balance of Urban County ($)	Percent Difference
New England	5,467	6,952	27
Middle Atlantic	6,197	11,480	85
North Central	9,796	14,528	49
South Atlantic	11,626	9,594	-18
South Central	12,206	32,043	163
West	8,395	11,774	40
Average U.S.	8,910	12,064	35

SOURCE: Muller (1978).

through market adjustments, older parts of the country
would have to accept wage and other factor-cost adjustments
that probably would be socially intolerable. This provides
a rationale for direct government intervention in the development process. Because recent capital investment rates
could result in a cumulative divergence in regional and
local labor productivity, the federal government is provided with a special rationale for encouraging capital
investment in areas of laggard development. Private-
sector capital accumulation provides one of the best long-
term opportunities to stabilize the deteriorating competitive positions of older parts of the country.

FISCAL IMPACTS

During the late 1960s and the first half of the 1970s,
perhaps the most destabilizing impact of population change
was on the fiscal condition of local governments. The
fiscal dilemma posed by local population loss is that local
revenues have proved more elastic and more immediately sensitive to population decline than have local expenditures.
Many of the costs of operating the public sector are, under
normal conditions, "fixed" costs. It requires drastic
measures, such as large-scale employee layoffs and the
contraction of capital facilities, to trim public-sector
operating costs in line with population decline. Local
revenues, on the other hand, when measured in real terms,
tend to fall automatically and exponentially in response
to population loss. Under these conditions, population
decline magnifies the budgetary strain of cities; it de-
pletes taxable resources more quickly than it eases expenditure requirements.

Of course, rapid population growth can also pose financing problems. The bunching of public capital investment
requirements, in particular, can create the need for heavy
debt issuance. These debts, however, tend to be self-
liquidating because sustained economic growth usually gen-
erates more than adequate revenues for amortization. In
contrast, the fiscal difficulties of decline can easily
become cumulative. Tax rate hikes to balance public budgets may push firms and affluent citizens out of the city,
thereby further depleting the local taxable base. To the
extent that public-sector costs in declining cities are
deferred to the future, they become even more burdensome,
for tomorrow's taxpayers are likely to be fewer in number
and poorer in real wealth than today's taxpayers.

Because of the apparent importance of population trends for local fiscal conditions, population gains and losses have been included as criteria in several federal-aid formulas. The 1977 revisions of the Community Development Block Grant Program explicitly recognize local population shortfall (the difference between local and national population growth rates) as an element in determining the aid entitlements of cities. Below-average population growth has also been proposed as an element establishing eligibility or aid allocations for Supplemental Fiscal Assistance, National Development Bank subsidies, and other elements of the Carter administration's urban policy.

Population Change and the Local Tax Base[13]

Local population growth or decline alters the scale of almost all revenue sources. When population is climbing, earned and potentially taxable income, sales, and taxable property values tend to climb with it; when population is falling, revenue sources (measured in real terms) tend to decline as well. The importance of population change for the fiscal base does not lie in this magnification or reduction of scale alone, but in the imbalances it triggers. Different tax bases respond quite differently to population changes. As a result, the structure of the local tax system will tend to exaggerate or reduce the fiscal consequences of population change.

Of all local revenue sources, it is the property tax base that is most sensitive to local population shifts. Population growth adds directly to the stock of taxable residential property, just as population loss gradually tends to remove residential property from the tax rolls. More importantly, population shifts are reflected in the price of housing. A city's stock of housing is, in the short-to-intermediate term, relatively fixed in quantity. As with any commodity in relatively inelastic supply, shifts in demand will work large price changes. Between 1960 and 1973, Buffalo, Cleveland, Pittsburgh, and St. Louis sustained population losses of more than 20 percent. No city can withstand such losses without suffering a decline

[13]This section draws on material presented in Peterson et al. (1979) in which the impacts of population change, job growth, and employment rates on local fiscal conditions are examined in greater detail.

in the demand for housing. Between 1966 and 1971, the
average value of single-family houses sold in these four
cities increased by only 0.03 percent. During the same
period, in 13 large cities that gained population in the
1960s, the average sales price for single-family housing
increased by 48 percent. With residential housing accounting for the greatest share of taxable property values,
these divergent price trends are reflected directly in the
strength of the local tax base.

Table 14 compares the sensitivity of different local
tax bases to population change. The term "growth elasticity" in the table refers to the percentage gain (or loss)
registered by a particular tax base in response to a 1-
percent gain (or loss) in city population. For example,
the value of 2.7 for the property tax base elasticity over

TABLE 14   Local Tax Base Elasticities with Respect to
Population Change

Tax Base	Sample Size	Real Growth Elasticity 1960-1970	Real Growth Elasticity 1970-1975	R^2
Market value of taxable property	27 Central cities	2.1^a $(7.9)^b$		0.74
	23 Central cities		2.7^c $(4.8)^b$	0.59
Retail sales values	38 Central cities	0.8 (7.4)		0.69
	40 Central cities		1.6 (6.9)	0.67
Value of local income tax base	8 Central cities	NA	1.6 (1.9)	0.35

a 1961-1971.
b Numbers in parentheses are t statistics.
c 1971-1976.

SOURCES: Market values of property computed from Bureau of
the Census assessment data and aggregate assessment/sales
ratio, using preliminary data (Taxable Property Values,
Volume 2, Part 1). Retail sales values obtained from Sales
Management. Local income tax bases obtained from local
bond prospectuses and local financial offices. Data compiled for The Urban Institute.

the period 1971-1976 indicates that each 1-percent gain
in local population has on average been accompanied by a
2.7-percent gain in the value of taxable real property;
declines in local population are similarly magnified into
declines in taxing capacity. A growth elasticity value
of 1.0 would indicate that on a per-capita basis population growth or decline neither adds to nor detracts from
the tax base. Values greater than 1.0 imply that even on
a per-capita basis taxable resources grow and fall with
population growth and decline, respectively.

The elasticities in Table 14 were estimated from regression equations relating tax base growth in different cities
to population growth. The sample was comprised of the sub-
sets of the nation's 40 largest cities for which data were
available.[14] All tax base values have been deflated by
the GNP deflator to eliminate distortions due to general
price inflation.

The extent to which cities' tax bases respond to population change varies quite widely, although in all three
cases the elasticities are substantial. The property tax
base is the most sensitive to population trends. Table 14
suggests that heavy reliance on the property tax can have
highly disequlibrating effects on a locality that is suffering population loss because population decline is translated, with a multiplier effect, into a loss of taxable
resources. A shrinking tax base, of course, can be forced

---

[14]Estimates of the market value of taxable property are
not fully comparable across cities or time periods. Commercial and industrial property of high value is excluded
from the Bureau of the Census assessment-sales comparisons,
which are used to convert assessed valuations to market-
value equivalents. Thus market-value conversions implic-
itly assume that high-valued commercial and industrial
properties are assessed at the same proportion of market
value as residential and lesser-valued commercial and industrial properties. If this assumption is incorrect, a
bias is imparted to market-value calculations. Comparisons between 1961 and 1971 are further complicated by the
fact that sales ratios in the first year were computed for
"ordinary real estate," while in the final year they were
computed for "all types of real property." The extent of
distortion introduced by these inconsistencies in measuring
market values of real property is unknown, but felt by the
authors to be small relative to systematic variations across
cities.

TABLE 15 Per-Capita Expenditures by Large Cities for Common Functions[a]

Item	Growing Cities	Cities Growing in Population 1960–1970, Currently Declining	Declining Cities
Expenditures per capita, common functions			
1973[b]	$100	$139	$178
1976[c]	$158	$205	$247
Percent growth	+58%	+47%	+39%
Common function municipal workers, per 1,000 residents			
1974[b]	7.0	8.1	11.2
1977[c]	7.9	9.3	11.5
Percent growth	+28.6%	+14.8%	+2.7%
Average monthly wage, other than teachers			
1974	$908	$956	$973
1977	$1,065	$1,140	$1,199
Percent growth	+20.7%	+19.5%	+23.2%

[a]The cities covered in this table are all cities that reached a population of 500,000 at some point between 1960 and 1973.

[b]Per capita figures based on 1973 population estimates.

[c]Per capita figures based on 1975 population estimates.

SOURCES: U.S. Bureau of the Census (various years), *City Government Finances*, and *City Employment*.

to yield higher revenues through frequent increases in the local tax rate, but such actions may jeopardize a city's competitive position. Furthermore, such increases may be rejected by the voters or may be in violation of taxing limitations.

Locally imposed sales taxes and income taxes display less sensitivity to local population trends. These taxes tend to draw on resources held by the population throughout the metropolitan area, and thus are not so closely tied to trends in city population.

A second trend apparent from Table 14 is the greater sensitivity of both sales and property tax bases to population change in the most recent time period. The explanation of this phenomenon is not altogether clear; quite likely, however, it is attributable to a more pronounced distinction between growing and declining cities. Population loss, job loss, and real income loss are currently more closely intertwined than in the past; because each of these changes contributes to local tax base deterioration, a simple elasticity estimated with respect to any one of the variables is likely to be stronger than in the past. If the increasingly sharp distinction between growing and declining cities is a permanent development, ever greater redistributive efforts through state and federal-aid programs would be needed to stabilize local tax bases. It is likely, though, that this apparent distinction is partially a product of the period chosen for comparison. The period ends in 1975, at the bottom of the national recession that struck hardest at cities suffering long-term population losses.

Expenditure Elasticities

If local expenditures rose or fell with population in the same proportions as local tax revenues, population loss would pose no special financing problems for cities. In actuality, at least until very recently, city spending commitments tended to grow almost without relation to population growth or decline. As a consequence, per capita expenditures have been highest in those cities suffering population losses, creating a severe imbalance between spending trends and local tax base trends.

Table 15 compares per-capita expenditures as of 1973 for the same set of cities identified in Table 14. Expenditure totals have been drawn from the Bureau of the Census publication, *City Government Finances* (various years). The

common functions referred to in the table represent an
attempt to define a core of common services provided by
virtually all city governments. The per-capita spending
figures correspond to total current account spending on
highways, police protection, fire protection, sanitation,
parks and recreation, financial administration, general
control, and interest on debt. Other services, including
education, welfare payments, hospital services, and capital outlays, have been excluded because municipal responsibility for these functions varies greatly from city to
city. Also shown in Table 15 are the number of common-
function municipal employees per 1,000 residents and the
average monthly wage received by these employees.

Per-capita spending on common functions in 1973 can be
seen to have been almost 80 percent higher in large, declining cities than in large, growing cities. This result
was the product both of more municipal workers per 1,000
residents and of higher public-sector wages. Since 1973,
however, there has been a movement toward convergence of
city spending levels. Indeed, the convergence of public-
sector costs has exceeded the convergence of private-market
costs and prices, reviewed earlier in this chapter. Local
governments of all types have cut back on their historical
rates of spending growth. In the last 5 years public-
sector wages generally have failed to keep pace with inflation and have lagged behind private-sector wage increases.
However, the burden of convergence in city spending has
fallen almost entirely upon real-resource use. As Table
15 shows, the greater fiscal pressure on declining cities
so far has failed to have an impact on public wage adjustments in different cities. In contrast, different employment adjustments are readily apparent. In cities losing
population, public employment actually was reduced by almost the same proportion as the city population, despite
new federally sponsored job programs. The previous trends
toward larger public-sector work forces persisted in the
growing cities. Beyond common services, employment trends
have displayed still sharper divergence because older cities
have trimmed many of their optional service responsibilities
in response to fiscal pressure. Capital expenditures, too,
have been cut back more deeply in the older cities.

Table 16 compares the elasticity of total city spending
with respect to population growth and decline in different
periods. The expenditure elasticities have been estimated
in the same manner as the revenue elasticities in Table 14.
For the first two periods, the spending elasticities are
extremely low, indicating that in contrast to local tax

TABLE 16   Local Expenditure Elasticities with Respect to
Population Growth

Period	Sample Size	Elasticity of Real Expenditures
1960-1970	38 Central cities	0.35 (1.2)[a]
1970-1973	40 Central cities	0.49 (1.6)
1973-1976	40 Central cities	1.2 (3.8)

[a]Numbers in parentheses are *t* statistics.

SOURCE: The Urban Institute.

revenues, local spending levels in the past have been quite
insensitive to local population trends. Other studies have
reported the same result. Kasarda (1978), for example,
found that over the period 1950-1960 city spending growth
on most functions was actually negatively related to population change, i.e., total expenditures climbed more rapidly
in cities losing population than in cities gaining population. The period 1960-1970 is characterized by a slight,
positive relationship between city expenditure and population growth. These low or negative spending elasticities,
coupled with the high tax base elasticities reported earlier, imply that city population loss in the past has produced a budget squeeze for city governments. Cities with
declining populations have been forced to raise their tax
rates or receive more external aid in order to balance
their budgets in the face of spending commitments. In
actuality, most of the gap until recently was filled by
external assistance. Table 17 shows that state aid and
federal aid have greatly favored cities losing population.
Until recently, these levels of aid were an indirect consequence of the greater tax burdens, higher unemployment
rates, and other characteristics of such cities. Now,
however, population loss has become an element directly
determining aid entitlements under the Community Development Block Grant Program, and has been proposed as a basis
for aid allocation in other urban legislation. Growth in
external assistance was sufficient to insulate partially
city governments from the deterioration in locally taxable
resources.

TABLE 17 Revenue by Source, Fiscal 1970 and 1975, in Cities with 100,000 or More Residents

City Type	N	Local Revenue 1970 ($)	Local Revenue 1975 ($)	Local Revenue Percent Change	State Revenue 1970 ($)	State Revenue 1975 ($)	State Revenue Percent Change	Federal Revenue 1970 ($)	Federal Revenue 1975 ($)	Federal Revenue Percent Change
Growing	57	123	190	54.5	23	51	120.9	7	29	310.5
Declining	84	169	275	62.8	46	104	125.6	15	76	409.0
Rapidly declining[a]	11	199	298	49.5	47	153	225.8	13	89	582.5
Total	152	153	243	58.7	38	88	131.1	12	58	384.6

City Type	N	All Revenue 1970 ($)	All Revenue 1975 ($)	All Revenue Percent Change	Local Revenue as Percent of Total Revenue 1970 ($)	Local Revenue as Percent of Total Revenue 1975 ($)	Local Revenue as Percent of Total Revenue Percent Change
Growing	57	153	270	76.5	80.4	70.4	-12.5
Declining	84	230	455	97.8	73.5	60.4	-17.8
Rapidly declining[a]	11	259	540	108.4	76.8	55.2	-28.1
Total	152	203	389	91.6	75.4	62.4	-17.2

[a] Cities with population decline in excess of 10 percent between 1970 and 1975.

SOURCES: U.S. Bureau of the Census (1971, 1976).

The elasticity estimate for city spending in the 1973-1976 period stands out in sharp contrast to estimates for the earlier periods. The elasticity value of 1.2 implies that on a per-capita basis the expenditure levels of growing and declining cities are now converging toward each other. This convergence can be seen clearly in Table 15, in which the 1973-1976 changes can be seen to have served to narrow the per-capita spending differences that existed at the beginning of the period.

Even though city employment levels, wage rates, and capital operations have proved difficult to trim in response to population loss in the past, most public-sector costs are not literally fixed but merely difficult to reduce under normal conditions. The fiscal difficulties of 1974-1975 appear to have been severe enough to force many city governments to begin to cut back these costs. During this period, most of the declining cities finally began to catch up with past population declines through reductions in city employment. The result has been a much greater sensitivity of city spending trends to population change. It seems likely that future city spending will continue to be restrained by population and tax base trends, as cities tackle the difficult problem of bringing their budgets in line with their resources. This restraint is likely to be reinforced by a sharp decrease in the growth rate of federal aid to older cities. Federal support was sustained in 1977 and 1978 through the operation of temporary countercyclical programs, many of which were allowed to terminate during the period. The necessity of financing further expenditures from their own resources will be a major restraining influence on declining cities.

Finally, there are signs that the real costs of public service provision are experiencing convergence. Crime rates, for example, are rising much more rapidly in growing cities than in declining cities.[15] Construction and other capital costs are also moving toward equality. This

---

[15]Between 1970 and 1976, the crime rate per 1,000 residents in six representative declining cities (Detroit, Cleveland, St. Louis, Buffalo, Pittsburgh, and Newark) rose by 42 percent. The crime rate in six representative growing cities (San Diego, San Antonio, Phoenix, San Jose, Honolulu, and El Paso) rose 109 percent. This convergence eliminated the greater part of the crime rate difference between the two classes of cities.

convergence of selected private-market costs leaves its
imprint on public-sector spending patterns.

Conclusion

There can be little doubt that substantial population loss
compounds the fiscal pressure on city governments. Population decline tends to bring an automatic loss of tax-raising
capacity; corresponding economies in city expenditures are
much more difficult to achieve. Whether population shortfall is an appropriate basis for allocations of large
amounts of federal aid is less clear. Population loss
appears to create an adjustment problem, primarily because
of the amount of time needed for "fixed" costs to be rendered variable. Additional federal assistance, perhaps,
is in order during severe adjustment periods, but indefi-
nite scaling of grants to population decline would be inappropriate. Such assistance merely defers managerial
efforts to keep the size of the public sector roughly proportionate to total local economic activity. The evidence
available to date suggests that adjustments in public-sector
operating costs can be made, even in the face of local population decline. However, the adjustment process has been
rendered more difficult by the relative inflexibility of
wages and other prices paid by the public sector. As a
result, practically all of the burden of reducing local
government costs has been borne by real-resource cutbacks,
cushioned only by increases in state and federal aid to
the cities.

REFERENCES

Advisory Commission on Intergovernmental Relations (1978)
    Income Growth Differential Study. Washington, D.C.:
    U.S. Government Printing Office.
Alonso, W. (1978) The purposes of balanced growth. Pp.
    629-667 in *The White House Conference on Balanced Na-
    tional Growth and Economic Development*. Washington,
    D.C.: U.S. Government Printing Office.
Aperovich, G., Bergsman, J., and Ehemann, C. (1977) An
    econometric model of migration between U.S. metropoli-
    tan areas. *Urban Studies* 14:135-145.
Birch, D. (1977) Regional Differences in Factor Costs:
    Labor, Land, Capital and Transportation. Paper presented
    to the Conference on Alternatives to Confrontation: A
    National Policy Toward Regional Change, Austin, Tex.

Borts, G. (1960) The equalization of returns and regional growth. *American Economic Review* (June).

Bouvier, L., and Cahill, E. (1975) Demographic factors affecting the educational level of South Atlantic states. *The Review of Regional Studies* (fall).

Carlton, D. (1979) Why new firms locate where they do. In Committee on Urban Public Economics and the Urban Institute, *Papers in Public Economics: New Developments in Regional Economics* (June). Washington, D.C.: Urban Institute.

Engle, R. (1974) A disequilibrium model of regional investment. *Journal of Regional Science* 14:367-376.

Featherman, D., and Hauser, R. (1978) *Opportunity and Change*. New York: Academic Press.

Grasberger, F. (1978) Developing Tools to Improve Federal Grant-in-Aid Formulas. Formula Evaluation Project, Preliminary Report No. 3, Center for Governmental Research, Rochester, N.Y.

Greenwood, M., and Gormeley, P. (1971) A comparison of the determinants of white and nonwhite interstate migration. *Demography* 1971:141-144.

Hansen, E., and Touhsaent, S. (1978) *State-Local Taxation in 1977--A Comparative Analysis*. Rochester, N.Y.: Center for Governmental Research.

Hoch, I. (1976) City size effects, trends, and policies. *Science* (Sept.):856-863.

Kasarda, J. (1978) Industry, community, and the metropolitan problem. In D. Street, ed., *Handbook of Urban Life*. San Francisco, Calif.: Jossey-Bass.

Kiker, B., and Traynham, E. (1977) Earnings differentials among nonmigrants, return migrants, and nonreturn migrants. *Growth and Change* 8:1-7.

Lansing, J., and Morgan, J. (1967) The effect of geographical mobility on income. *Journal of Human Resources* 2:446-460.

Miller, E., (1973) Is outmigration affected by economic conditions? *Southern Economic Journal* 39:396-405.

Mills, D. (1978) The aging industrial legacy: labor force and wage rates. In G. Sternlieb and J. Hughes, eds., *Revitalizing the Northeast*. New Brunswick, N.J.: Center for Urban Policy Research, Rutgers University.

Morrison, P., and Rellers, D. (1975) *Recent Research Insights into Local Migration Flows*. RAND Paper Series. Santa Monica, Calif.: RAND.

Muller, T. (1978) Central City Business Retention: Jobs, Taxes, and Investment Trends. Report prepared for the U.S. Department of Commerce.

Pack J. (1973) Determinants of migration to central
   cities. *Journal of Regional Science* 13:249-260.
Peterson, G. (1979) *Urban Development Patterns.*
   Washington, D.C.: Urban Institute.
Peterson, G., Cooper, B., Dickson, E., Morhmer, H., and
   Reijeloth, G. (1979) *Urban Fiscal Monitoring.*
   Washington, D.C.: Urban Institute.
Rothenberg, J. (1977) On the microeconomics of internal
   migration. Pp. 183-205 in A. Brown and E. Neuberger,
   eds., *Internal Migration: A Comprehensive Process.*
   New York: Academic Press.
Sundquist, J. (1975) *Dispersing Population: What
   America Can Learn from Europe.* Washington, D.C.:
   Brookings Institution.
U.S. Bureau of Domestic Commerce (1976) *Construction
   Review* (various issues). Washington, D.C.: U.S.
   Department of Commerce.
U.S. Bureau of Economic Analysis (1978) *Survey of Current
   Business* (August and October). Washington, D.C.:
   U.S. Department of Commerce.
U.S. Bureau of Labor Statistics (1969a) *Regional Summaries,*
   1967-68. Washington, D.C.: U.S. Department of Labor.
U.S. Bureau of Labor Statistics (1969b) *Wage and Related
   Benefits. Part II: Metropolitan Areas, United States.*
   Washington, D.C.: U.S. Department of Labor.
U.S. Bureau of Labor Statistics (1976a) *Area Unemployment
   Statistics for CETA.* Washington, D.C.: U.S. Depart-
   ment of Labor.
U.S. Bureau of Labor Statistics (1976b) *Wage Differences
   Among Metropolitan Areas.* Washington, D.C.: U.S.
   Department of Labor.
U.S. Bureau of Labor Statistics (1978a) *CPI Detailed
   Report, June 1978 and June 1977.* Washington, D.C.:
   U.S. Department of Labor.
U.S. Bureau of Labor Statiscs (1978b) Occupational earn-
   ings and wage trends in metropolitan areas. In *Area
   Wage Surveys.* Washington, D.C.: U.S. Department of
   Labor.
U.S. Bureau of the Census (1970) *Census of Manufacturers.*
   Washington, D.C.: U.S. Department of Commerce.
U.S. Bureau of the Census (1971) *City Government Finances
   in 1969-1970.* Washington, D.C.: U.S. Department of
   Commerce.
U.S. Bureau of the Census (1975) *Census of Manufactures.*
   Washington, D.C.: U.S. Department of Commerce.
U.S. Bureau of the Census (1976) *City Government Finances i
   1975-1976.* Washington, D.C.: U.S. Department of Commerc

U.S. Bureau of the Census (1977a) *Geographic Mobility: March 1975 to March 1976.* In *Current Population Reports* (January). Washington, D.C.: U.S. Department of Commerce.

U.S. Bureau of the Census (1977b) *Money Income in 1976 of Households in the United States.* Washington, D.C.: U.S. Department of Commerce.

U.S. Bureau of the Census (1977c) Population estimates and projections. In *Current Population Reports* (various issues). Washington, D.C.: U.S. Department of Commerce.

U.S. Bureau of the Census (1978) *Money Income in 1877 of Households in the United States.* Washington, D.C.: U.S. Department of Commerce.

Vernez, G., Vaughan, R., Burright, B., and Coleman, S. (1977) *Regional Cycles of Employment Effects of Public Works Investments.* Santa Monica, Calif.: RAND.

Wheaton, W. (1979) Area wages, unemployment, and inter-regional factor mobility. In Committee on Urban Public Economics and Urban Institute, *Papers in Public Economics: New Developments in Regional Economics.* Washington, D.C.: Urban Institute.

POPULATION REDISTRIBUTION
AND EMPLOYMENT POLICY

Michael J. Greenwood

INTRODUCTION

Berry and Dahmann have identified a number of aspects of
population redistribution that may have serious implications for employment policy. After a number of decades
during which the West experienced the greatest volume of
net in-migration, the South, since 1970, has had a volume
of net in-migration roughly twice that of the West. Moreover, the historical trend of migration out of nonmetropolitan areas and into metropolitan areas has been reversed;
nonmetropolitan population is currently growing more rapidly
than metropolitan population. The absolute decline in the
population of some central cities, combined with a slackening of suburban growth, has contributed to the lower rate
of metropolitan growth.

Three questions arise regarding these findings. First,
to what extent do the observed changes in spatial population distribution reflect changes in the spatial distribution of economic activity? Second, what are the causative
factors in the relationship between population distribution
and the distribution of economic activity as measured by
employment distribution and composition? Third, what employment problems are caused or intensified by population
and employment redistribution, and do these problems war-
rant governmental action? Only after such problems have
been identified can appropriate policy solutions be developed and the appropriate level of government be selected
for administering the various policies.

Michael J. Greenwood is Professor of Economics, Arizona
State University.

The outline of this paper follows the order of the questions posed above. The first section is concerned with the identification of changes in the distribution of economic activity among Census regions and among central cities and suburbs.[1] Economic activity is defined in terms of employment. Changes that have occurred in recent years are placed in historical perspective to allow identification of trend reversal or continuation. The second part of the paper focuses on the causal relationships between population and employment change. Qualitative and, to a lesser extent, quantitative relationships are discussed. The term "qualitative relationship" refers to the direction of the causal linkage between two variables, while the term "quantitative relationship" refers to the magnitude of such a linkage. The third section deals with certain problems toward which employment policy might appropriately be directed.

THE SPATIAL DISTRIBUTION OF EMPLOYMENT

Area employment changes result from three basic forces. First, given labor supply and demand conditions, if labor markets are out of equilibrium, then wage changes that result from equilibrating market forces may result in employment changes. Second, given labor supply curves that are not perfectly inelastic, changes in labor demand can cause changes in employment. Changes in labor demand can be caused by a number of factors, such as changes in the state of the national economy, changes in area income, population changes brought on by natural increase or net migration, changes in population composition, and changes in consumer preferences. Third, given labor demand curves that are not perfectly inelastic, changes in labor supply can cause changes in employment. Changes in labor supply can also result from a number of factors, including changes in the working-aged population brought on by natural change or by net migration and changes in labor-force participation rates that are independent of wage levels. Although the three forces generally operate simultaneously in local

---

[1]The metropolitan-nonmetropolitan dichotomy is not discussed here because of the highly suspect quality of available 1970-1975 employment data that distinguish metropolitan status.

economies that are growing or declining, the latter two
are likely to be of primary importance.

Each of these forces, however, unfolds in the context
of the national economy, and therefore regional changes
in employment and population should not be viewed apart
from their national setting.

The National Setting

At the national level three factors distinguish the 1965-
1975 period from the earlier post World War II years:

1. The national rate of employment growth altered
sharply at about 1963, after which the annual average rate
doubled, and the rate of growth from 1963 to 1969 was particularly high relative to typical rates of earlier and
later periods.

2. The aging of the war-baby cohort brought an extremely
large number of young persons into the labor force, and
young persons tend to be quite mobile geographically.

3. Substantial changes in fertility patterns and
family composition, combined with a number of other factors, contributed to appreciable increases in labor-force
participation rates among young white women. These increased rates and the increased size of the young population cohort contributed greatly to increasing the size
of the labor force. Changes in fertility patterns, family
composition, and marriage rates also directly affected
migration rates.

These three factors are, of course, not independent of
one another or of other forces operating in the economy
and in society in general. Let us briefly consider the
relevance of each factor to changes in the spatial distribution of the population.

Rate of Employment Growth   Table 1 shows average annual
growth rates in national employment and civilian labor
force (CLF) for various periods during the postwar era.
The 30-year period 1947-1976 can conveniently be divided
into two subperiods: 1947-1963 and 1963-1976. During the
earlier period the average annual rate of employment growth
was 1.1 percent, but during the later period it was 2.0
percent. A further breakdown of the later period shows
that between 1963 and 1969 the average annual rate of

TABLE 1   Average Annual Rates of Growth in Employment and
Civilian Labor-Force Growth for Various Subperiods, 1947-1976

Period	Employment (%)	Civilian Labor Force (%)
1947-1948 to 1962-1963	1.1	1.2
1963-1964 to 1975-1976	2.0	2.2
1963-1964 to 1968-1969	2.4	2.0
1969-1970 to 1975-1976	1.7	2.3

SOURCE: Calculated from data presented in Tables A-1 and
A-3 of the *1977 Employment and Training Report of the
President* (U.S. Department of Health, Education, and Wel-
fare, and U.S. Department of Labor 1977).

employment growth was 2.4 percent, whereas between 1969
and 1976 the growth rate moderated considerably to an
average of 1.7 percent.

The high and sustained rate of employment growth between 1963 and 1969 was due in part to the effects of the
Vietnam War and to the sizeable increases in the labor
force.   Probably less important contributing factors were
the permanent tax cut of 1964 and the relative credit ease
beginning in late 1966.   The more moderate rate of growth
after 1970 was caused in part by dislocations and reallo-
cations brought on by post Vietnam War adjustments, by
the quadrupling of oil prices in 1973, and by deficient
aggregate demand.   The recession of 1974-1975 was the
most serious since 1950.   The national rate of unemployment averaged 8.5 percent during 1975 compared with 5.6
percent during 1974.

The differential behavior of the 1963-1969 period relative to the 1969-1975 period is emphasized by the behavior
of the manufacturing sector.   After increasing by 3,172,000
jobs between 1963 and 1969, or at an average annual rate
of 3.1 percent, manufacturing employment declined by
1,820,000 jobs between 1969 and 1975, amounting to a negative annual average rate of 1.5 percent.   Nationally only
285,000 more manufacturing jobs existed in 1975 than in
1965.[2]   The effects of the Vietnam War in the late 1960s

[2]The source of these figures is the *1977 Employment and
Training Report of the President,* U.S. Department of

and of the recessionary conditions of the early 1970s had
important implications for the manufacturing sector, which
in turn had important implications for the spatial distribution of employment. Moreover, since manufacturing is
the single most important source of urban employment, the
status of the manufacturing sector during the early 1970s
had obvious implications for urban growth and for the intraurban location of economic activity.

Vernez et al. (1977, p. x) summarize their findings regarding the regional employment impacts of national economic fluctuations:

> Areas that tend to be slow in recovery, with long
> cycles, are usually located in the North-East and
> North-Central census divisions and are character-
> ized by a slow rate of employment growth or a
> large labor force. Slow growth and large size
> also characterize areas with the largest cyclical
> amplitudes. They are typically located in the
> North-East and East-North-Central areas.
> . . . The severest cycles are more often found in
> areas of the North-East and North-West-Central
> census divisions and are characterized by slow
> employment growth.

Hence, according to the Vernez study, in terms of length,
amplitude, and severity of cycle impacts, the Northeast
and North Central regions tend to be the most seriously
affected by national economic conditions.

Health, Education, and Welfare, and U.S. Department of
Labor (Table C-1). Other sources yield slightly different
information. Data gathered from U.S. Department of Labor,
Bureau of Labor (1977), for example, indicate that manufacturing employment declined by 1,972,300 between 1969
and 1975 and that nationally only 182,700 more manufacturing jobs existed in 1975 than 1965. Note too that the
choice of 1975 as the end point of the series has special
implications for the manufacturing sector, which was especially impacted by the recession of 1974-1975, when manufacturing employment declined by 1,699,000 jobs or by 8.5
percent. These latter figures have been calculated from
data presented in the *1977 Employment and Training Report
of the President.*

Rate of Growth of the CLF   The period from approximately
1963 to and beyond 1975 is rather unusual in the recent
history of the American economy, because of the high rate
of labor-force increase brought on by the aging of the
war-baby cohort and by the increased labor-force participation rates of women. As indicated in Table 1, the civilian labor force increased at an average annual rate of 1.2
percent between 1947 and 1963. However, between 1963 and
1976 the CLF increased at an average annual rate of 2.2
percent. Again the periods 1963-1969 and 1969-1976 were
characterized by somewhat different rates of growth. During the former period the CLF grew at an average annual
rate of just less than 2.0 percent, while during the latter
period it grew at a rate of just over 2.3 percent. Note
also that between 1963 and 1969 the rate of employment
growth exceeded the rate of labor-force growth, but that
between 1969 and 1976 the rate of labor-force growth was
somewhat higher than the rate of employment growth.

Table 2 presents labor-force data by age, sex, and race
for 5-year periods beginning in 1950 and running to 1975.
Labor-force participation rates are shown for each sex-
age-race group at the various points in time. During the
1965-1975 period the labor force aged 16-24 increased by
8.1 million, which amounts to an annual average rate of
5.7 percent, compared with a 2.3-percent annual rate of
increase over the previous 15 years. The entry of women
25 and over into the labor force accounted for another
6.57 million workers between 1965 and 1975.

The 1965-1975 increase in the young labor force was due
not only to the larger number of persons aged 16-24 in the
population, but to the increased labor-force participation
rates of this group. Approximately 35.7 percent of the
increase in the labor force aged 16-24 can be attributed
to increased labor-force participation rates, with the
remainder due to increased size of the underlying population.[3] Between 1965 and 1975, participation rates increased
somewhat more for young women than for young men; rates for
women went from 44.0 to 57.1 percent and rates for men went
from 69.0 to 72.4 percent (see Table 2).

Table 3 reports labor-force participation rates of young
women by marital status. The largest increases in participation rates have clearly occurred among married women

---

[3]This estimate was derived by calculating the size of the
1975 labor force if 1965 participation rates had prevailed.

TABLE 2   Labor Force (numbers in thousands) and Labor-Force Participation Rates by Sex, Age, and Race, 1950-1975, with Projections to 1990[a]

	Males				Females			
	16 and Over		16-24		16 and Over		16-24	
Year	Wht	Nwht	Wht	Nwht	Wht	Nwht	Wht	Nwht
1950	43,819		7,136		18,389		4,387	
	[86.4]		[77.3]		[33.9]		[43.9]	
1955	40,196	4,279	4,857	732	17,886	2,663	3,679	489
	(85.4)	(85.0)	(72.0)	(74.5)	(34.5)	(46.1)	(43.5)	(40.3)
	[85.3]		[72.3]		[35.7]		[43.1]	
1960	41,742	4,645	5,992	917	20,171	3,069	4,071	565
	(83.4)	(83.0)	(71.3)	(74.0)	(36.5)	(48.2)	(43.1)	(41.2)
	[83.3]		[71.6]		[37.7]		[42.9]	
1965	43,400	4,855	7,277	1,012	22,736	3,464	5,177	700
	(80.8)	(79.6)	(68.9)	(69.3)	(38.1)	(48.6)	(44.3)	(42.3)
	[80.7]		[69.0]		[39.3]		[44.0]	
1970	46,013	5,182	8,533	1,180	27,505	4,015	7,135	979
	(80.0)	(76.5)	(70.2)	(64.4)	(42.6)	(49.5)	(52,1)	(46.2)
	[80.0]		[69.4]		[43.3]		[51.3]	
1975	49,881	5,734	10,795	1,363	32,203	4,795	8,890	1,216
	(78.7)	(71.5)	(74.3)	(60.1)	(45.9)	(49.2)	(59.0)	(46.4)
	[77.9]		[72.4]		[46.3]		[57.1]	

Projections

1980	60,000		12,974		41,673		11,292	
	[77.8]		[73.6]		[48.4]		[61.1]	
1985	62,903		11,976		45,699		11,091	
	[77.5]		[73.7]		[50.3]		[64.5]	
1990	65,220		10,647		48,619		10,305	
	[77.3]		[72.9]		[51.4]		[66.6]	

[a]Values in parentheses indicate sex, age, and race specific labor-force participation rate; values in brackets indicate sex and age specific labor-force participation rate.

SOURCES: Data for 1950-1975 are from or are calculated from the *1977 Employment and Training Report of the President* (U.S. Department of Health, Education and Welfare, and Department of Labor 1977, Tables A-3 and A-11). Projections are from Fullerton and Flaim (1976).

TABLE 3   Labor-Force Participation Rates of Young Women by
Marital Status, Various Years, 1950-1975

Year	Single 20-24	Single 25-34	Married, Spouse Present 20-24	Married, Spouse Present 25-34	Widowed, Divorced, Separated 20-24	Widowed, Divorced, Separated 25-34
1950	74.9	84.6	28.5	23.8	45.5	62.3
1955	69.6	80.9	29.4	26.0	55.1	60.5
1960	73.4	79.9	30.0	27.7	54.6	55.5
1965	72.3	83.4	35.6	32.1	58.6	62.8
1970	71.1	80.7	47.4	39.3	59.7	65.1
1975	69.3	80.0	57.1	48.3	67.6	67.4

SOURCE: *1977 Employment and Training Report of the President* (U.S. Department of Health, Education and Welfare, and Department of Labor 1977, Table B-2).

with spouse present.[4] Particularly since 1965, this group
has experienced an especially sharp rise in its participation rate. Between 1965 and 1975 the 20-24 age-group had a
21.5 percentage-point increase in its rate, while the 25-34
age-group had a 16.2 percentage-point increase. Approximately 4,612,000 more married women of all ages, with spouse
present, were in the labor force in 1975 than would have been
in the labor force if 1965 participation rates had prevailed.
     Changes of such magnitudes in the labor-force partici-
pation rates of married women with spouse present, and
especially of young married women, have potentially profound implications for geographic mobility. If the
4,612,000-person figure given above were doubled to reflect the fact that the affected households had a minimum
of two persons, the resulting 9,224,000 persons would be
a minimum estimate of the number of household members

[4]Married women with spouse present accounted for 59.8 percent of all women 16 years old and over in 1975. This
group also accounted for 57.8 percent of the female labor
force. Since married women with spouse present outnumber
both single women and women who are widowed, divorced, or
separated, and since the married group also experienced
the largest increases in labor-force participation rates,
we can conclude that married women with spouse present are
somewhat more responsible than the other groups for the
overall increase in female participation rates.

directly affected by the differential labor-force participation behavior of married women. This latter figure was
6.0 percent of the 1975 noninstitutional population of the
United States. If the spouses of these women are assumed
to be labor-force members, then these young women and their
spouses were 10.0 percent of the country's 1975 CLF.

Because many young couples that would previously have
had one wage earner now have two, their family income is
somewhat higher than it would otherwise have been. The
second salaries permit these families, at a relatively
young age, to purchase housing in locations that would
otherwise have been beyond their price range. These new
locations may be in the suburbs rather than in the central
city, in exurban or even rural areas, or in regions with
historically low wages but desirable amenities, such as
sunshine, mountains, or seashore.

As shown in Table 2, female labor-force participation
rates for the young are projected to continue their rise
through 1990, but male rates are projected to remain relatively constant. Overall, the rate of labor-force increase
is expected to moderate considerably during the 1980s, when
the projected average annual rate of increase will fall to
1.2 percent. The labor force aged 16-24 will decline in
absolute numbers; the decrease is expected to amount to
over 3.31 million.

The racial composition of the labor force has changed
relatively little in recent years. In 1965 blacks comprised 11.2 percent of the labor force, and in 1975, 11.4
percent. The most conspicuous change along racial lines
has been the appreciable decline in black male labor-force
participation rates, especially among the young. In 1960
black males, 16-24 years of age, had a participation rate
of 74.0 percent, compared with a corresponding rate of
71.3 percent for whites. In 1975 the participation rate
for black males in this age-group was 60.1 percent; the
corresponding rate for whites was 74.3 percent. If the
black participation rate in 1975 was what it had been in
1965, an additional 208,000 young black males would have
been in the labor force in 1975. Of course, if black rates
had risen along with the corresponding white rates, this
estimate would be somewhat higher. The 1975 unemployment
rate of black males, 16-24, was 27.4 percent. A conserva-
tive estimate of the unemployment and underemployment rate
among young black males is therefore 37.0 percent. Rates
such as these have important implications for employment
policy in the central cities of the nation's major metropolitan areas, where the unemployment and underemployment
rate is thought to exceed 37.0 percent.

These changes in the age composition of the labor force
have important consequences for interregional migration.
Lansing and Mueller (1967), using data from the *Current
Population Reports*, show that of all age-groups, the group
between 22 and 24 has the highest migration rate (17.8 percent). Migration rates decline rapidly with age; for the
30-34 and 35-44 age-groups the respective rates were 8.8
and 4.8 percent.[5]

Changes in Family Composition   Between 1960 and 1975 the
percentage of women, 20-24 years old, who had been or were
married but had not borne any children increased dramatically from 24.2 to 42.3. The percentage of whites in
this category increased from 25.0 to 44.7, but the percentage of blacks increased more slowly, from 17.0 to 20.2
(U.S. Bureau of the Census 1975a). Fertility and labor-
force participation behavior of women have been mutually
dependent and have together permitted or encouraged many
American families to move. However, the relatively small
percentage of black women in this category has served to
discourage black migration, both by reducing income per
family member and by increasing local community ties.
Black women tend to bear a higher cost of acquiring access
to the labor market (for example, the cost of day care),
which has important policy implications for central cities.
    Changes in female participation in the labor force and
in family composition have acted as permissive factors in
the population dispersion from the higher income areas of
the Northeast and North Central states. Information presented in *Current Population Reports* is consistent with
the claim that changes in family composition may have contributed to greater interstate migration rates. Of married
men 14-24 years old with wife present, 20.3 percent of
those with no children of their own changed their state of
residence between 1970 and 1975, compared with 17.2 percent of those with own children. Comparable percentages
for the 25-34 age-group are 25.4 percent for the group

---

[5]The data reported by Lansing and Mueller (1967) refer to
migration during the year ending in March 1965. Such rates
are somewhat sensitive to prevailing economic conditions,
but give a good indication of the order of magnitude of
the differences between age-groups. As reported in the
CPR, migration refers to anyone changing his county of
residence.

with no own children and 17.6 percent for the group with
own children.[6]

The influence of changes in fertility patterns on population movements from central cities to suburbs should not
be overlooked. Married couples with no children appear to
have higher rates of movement from central cities to suburbs than married couples with children. Of suburban married men 14-24 years old with wife present and no own
children as of 1975, 24.7 percent had moved to the suburbs
from the central city since 1970. The corresponding figure
for men with own children was 19.9 percent. For the 25-34
age-group, corresponding percentages for men with no own
children and with own children were, respectively, 35.6
and 26.4.[7]

A number of factors are responsible for higher rates
of movement from central cities to suburbs among married
couples with no children. One of the most important of
these is that couples with no children are more likely to
have two wage earners providing sufficient income to afford
housing in the suburbs. The mutual dependence of fertility
and labor-force participation behavior of young couples is
again evident.

Other societal trends have also been important in determining shifts in regional and urban location patterns,
although the quantitative relationship between these trends
and patterns has not been determined with any precision.
For example, marriage rates among the young have fallen
sharply. In 1975, 56.0 percent of the females aged 20-24
were married, compared with 61.4 percent in 1970 and 68.8
percent in 1962. Comparable percentages for males are

[6]These percentages were calculated from data presented by
U.S. Bureau of the Census (1975c, Table 23). The numbers
of persons abroad and for whom no information was available on mobility status were removed from the base population before the rates were calculated.
[7]The source of this information is U.S. Bureau of the
Census (1975c, Table 22). The number of relevant suburban persons abroad and for whom no information was
given on mobility status was removed from the denominator when these rates were calculated. The fractions of
relevant 1970 central-city married men who had moved
to the suburbs by 1975 would be more approriate, but
the data do not allow the computation of mobility rates
for the relevant base populations as defined in 1970.

38.6, 43.6, and 47.0 (U.S. Bureau cf the Census 1962, 1970, 1975b). This decline will probably act as a damper on both interstate and intrastate migration because there are significant differences in movement rates between the married and the unmarried segments of the population.[8] In itself, the drop in marriage rates should partially offset those factors contributing to increasing rates of movement.

As a result of the aging of the war-baby cohort and the high migration rates for the age categories through which the cohort has been passing since about 1965, the age composition of interregional migration streams has changed. As recently as 1965-1966, 40.9 percent of the interregional migrants were 18-34 years old; during the 1970-1975 period, 45.5 percent were in this age category (U.S. Bureau of the Census 1966, 1975c). In the absence of significant exogenous forces, such as severe energy shortages, interregional migration should decline after 1980, when the number of people in the most mobile age categories is expected to decrease.

Regional Changes in Employment and Population

Regional employment and population changes are positively correlated. Hence, at the regional level, the recent population changes depicted by Berry and Dahmann reflect

[8]The *Current Population Report* (No. 285, Table 20) indicates substantial differences in mobility rates between young married males with wife present and other young males. Of males aged 18-24 in 1975, 56.9 percent of those married with wife present had since 1970 changed houses within a given county, whereas only 21.8 percent of the remaining male population in this age-group had made a similar move. While married 18-24-year-old males with wife present had a 1970-1975 intercounty, intrastate migration rate of 20.0 precent, other males in this age class had a completely defined rate of 7.7 percent. The married group had a between-states migration rate of 18.7 percent, but the other group had a between-states rate of only 7.8 percent. In the calculation of the above rates, the number of persons abroad and the number for whom mobility status was not reported were excluded from the denominator.

corresponding employment changes, although the extent
to which population changes lead, lag, or occur simultaneously with employment changes is unknown. Moreover,
although a positive relationship exists between regional
employment and population changes, quantitative analysis of available data suggests an extremely unstable
relationship between the variables over time as well
as a relationship that differs considerably between
regions.

Table 4 shows for each Census region total nonagricultural employment and total population aged 5 years and
over for 5-year increments beginning in 1950 and running
to 1975. With the exception of the Northeast, which experienced slight declines in employment during the period
from 1970-1975, both population and employment increased
in each region during each period.[9] Moreover, during the
quarter of a century covered by the data, the four Census
regions ranked identically by percentage change in employment and by percentage change in population; the West,
experiencing the highest percentage changes (136.3 and
87.7, respectively), is followed by the South (110.4 and
44.2), the North Central region (51.0 and 29.6), and the
Northeast (30.6 and 25.3).

One consequence of interregional shifts of population
and employment has been a more equitable distribution of
employment opportunities relative to population. Table 5
indicates that in 1950 the Northeast held 31.6 percent of
the jobs and 26.1 percent of the population, whereas the
South held 24.8 percent of the jobs (the third-highest
share) and 31.2 percent of the population (the highest
share). By 1975 regional employment and population shares
ranked identically, with the Northeast containing 24.3
percent of the jobs and 23.2 percent of the population and
the South containing 30.7 percent of the jobs and 31.9 percent of the population.

---

[9]Note that the way in which the data are grouped in
Table 4 makes employment growth over the various periods
quite sensitive to conditions prevailing at the beginning and the end of each period. For example, if 1970-
1974 rather than 1970-1975 had been used to define the
latest period for the Northeast, nonagricultural employment there, instead of declining by 0.4 percent, would
have grown by 3.0 percent. Nevertheless, data so grouped
yield a reasonable indication of differences between
regions.

TABLE 4   Nonagricultural Employment, Population Aged 5
Years and Over (in thousands) and Their Percentage Changes,
by Region, 1950-1975

	Northeast		North Central		South		West[a]	
Year	Emp	Pop	Emp	Pop	Emp	Pop	Emp	Pop
1950	14,221	39,478	13,976	44,461	11,144	47,197	5,607	20,190
	(6.0)[b]	(5.4)	(10.5)	(8.5)	(15.1)	(5.5)	(22.4)	(12.2)
1955	15,079	41,610	15,447	48,243	32,826	49,808	6,864	22,646
	(3.5)	(7.4)	(2.5)	(7.0)	(11.1)	(10.4)	(17.9)	(23.9)
1960	15,610	44,678	15,837	51,619	14,243	54,973	8,091	28,053
	(6.9)	(6.2)	(10.5)	(5.1)	(17.4)	(8.4)	(17.1)	(14.8)
1965	16,693	47,451	17,502	54,225	16,725	59,579	9,477	32,205
	(11.8)	(3.3)	(14.0)	(4.3)	(21.8)	(5.4)	(20.3)	(8.1)
1970	18,654	49,000	19,953	56,577	20,377	62,798	11,400	34,809
	(-0.4)	(0.9)	(5.8)	(1.9)	(15.1)	(8.4)	(16.2)	(8.9)
1975	18,572	49,456	21,106	57,636	23,449	68,041	13,252	37,899

[a]Because data on Alaska and Hawaii are unavailable, for some years,
these two states have been excluded from the West, for the sake of
comparability. In 1975 Alaska and Hawaii together accounted for 3.6
percent of the West's nonagricultural employment.

[b]Values in parentheses indicate percentage changes between column
year under which they are listed and subsequent column year, thus
expressing changes over a 5-year period. For example, 6.0 percent
refers to the percentage change in nonagricultural employment in the
Northeast between 1950 and 1955.

SOURCES: Employment data are from U.S. Bureau of Labor Statistics
(1977). Population data are from U.S. Bureau of the Census *Current
Population Reports*, Series P-25, Nos. 147, 460, and 642.

Note that in the West and in the South the absolute difference between the rate of employment growth and the rate
of population growth is appreciable; and especially in the
South the relative difference is substantial. The data indicate that no obvious, generally applicable, quantitative
relationship exists between incremental population and

TABLE 5   Regional Employment and Population Shares, 1950
and 1975

| | 1950 | | 1975 | |
Region	Employment Share (%)	Population Share (%)	Employment Share (%)	Population Share (%)
Northeast	31.6	26.1	24.3	23.2
North Central	31.1	29.4	27.6	27.1
South	24.8	31.2	30.7	31.9
West	12.5	13.3	17.4	17.8
	100.0	100.0	100.0	100.0

SOURCE: Derived from Table 4.

incremental employment. Table 6 indicates the ratio of
incremental employment to incremental population, or
what might be interpreted as the extra employment
associated with one extra person. The most remarkable
characteristic of the data is the wide range of values
for each region. For example, the Northeast region
varies from a low of -0.180 extra jobs per extra person
(1970-1975) to a high of 1.266 extra jobs per extra
person (1965-1970).

These data strongly suggest that extra population, alone,
does not account for additional employment. Among the
other factors that contribute to regional employment growth
or that yield differentially high relationships between

TABLE 6   Ratio of Incremental Employment to Incremental
Population for 5-Year Periods by Region, 1950-1975

Period	Northeast	North Central	South	West
1950-1955	0.402	0.389	0.644	0.512
1955-1960	0.173	0.116	0.274	0.227
1960-1965	0.391	0.639	0.539	0.334
1965-1970	1.266	1.042	1.135	0.738
1970-1975	-0.180	1.089	0.586	0.599
1950-1975	0.436	0.541	0.590	0.432

SOURCE: Derived from Table 4.

extra population and extra employment are the demographic and socioeconomic composition of the population, the composition of employment, the labor-intensity of production processes, incremental regional income, technological factors, and the state of the national economy. Regarding the last point, note that the values for three of four regions are highest for the 1965-1970 period, which was a period of relative prosperity, while the values for three of four regions are lowest for the 1955-1960 period, which was characterized by recession and slow growth of gross national product.

When labor demand is high, considerable employment can be drawn from a region's indigenous population through some combination of reduced unemployment and increased labor-force participation. Note that four entries in Table 6 are in excess of unity. The responsiveness of labor-force participation rates to demand has, perhaps, been somewhat neglected relative to the responsiveness of population migration. Nevertheless, one of the most remarkable features of the 25-year period following 1950 is the regional equalization of the ratio of employment to population. In 1950 this ratio was quite dissimilar across Census regions: Northeast (0.360), North Central (0.313), West (0.278), and South (0.236). In 1975 the regions ranked in identical fashion, but the differences were narrowed considerably: Northeast (0.376), North Central (0.366), West (0.350), and South (0.345).[10]

A problem with examining 5-year increments in employment and population is that the corresponding percentage changes are extremely sensitive to conditions existing in the initial and final year of the interval, and these conditions are in turn dependent on the state of the macroeconomy. One means of partially avoiding this problem is to consider annual changes in employment by region. If the period 1947-1975 is examined, the annual data can again be grouped into fairly distinct periods that correspond to those defined in Table 1. As would be expected given the behavior of national employment, each region experienced

---

[10]Because the South historically has had a higher birth rate than other regions of the country, the employment-population ratio might be expected to be lower there. Southern birth rates have, however, been converging toward the national average, which would also tend to raise the employment-population ratio toward the national average, other things being equal.

somewhat higher average annual rates of employment growth
from about 1963 to 1975 than during the earlier post World
War II years.

The contrast between the 1947-1963 interval relative to
the 1963-1969 interval is readily apparent. Each region
experienced a substantially higher average rate of growth
from 1963 to 1969 than it experienced either before or
since. However, compared to its previous experience, the
Northeast fared particularly well during the late 1960s.
Average nonagricultural employment growth in the Northeast
was 3.5 times higher during the 1963-1969 period than during the 1947-1963 period. Nonagricultural employment
growth in the North Central states was 3.0 times higher
during the late 1960s, while in the South it was 1.9 times
higher, and in the West it was 1.4 times higher.[11]

The relative prosperity of the 1960s appears to have
temporarily concealed the longer-term adjustments being
experienced by the Northeast and North Central states.
The recessions of 1969 and 1974 had particularly severe
consequences in these regions, perhaps partially because
they coincided with the reemergence of the regions' long-
term relative decline. In the South and West, on the
other hand, secular growth appears to have absorbed some
of the impacts of recession, and these regions did not
suffer the relative employment setbacks experienced in
the Northeast and North Central states.

Shifts in Manufacturing Employment   Much has been written
about the relative decline of the manufacturing sector in
the Northeast and the rise of this sector in the South and
the West. This phenomenon has, however, not been limited
to the post World War II period. Fuchs (1962a) offers a
detailed description of changes in the location of manufacturing employment in the United States between 1929
and 1954. He summarizes his findings in the following
way (1962a, p. 9):

> The South and the West grew much more rapidly than
> the nation as a whole; the North Central region

[11]Average annual rates of growth of nonagricultural employment were as follows: 1947 to 1963--Northeast, 0.77%;
North Central, 1.22%; South, 2.43%; West, 3.15%; 1963 to
1975--Northeast, 1.34%; North Central, 2.24%; South, 3.64%;
West, 3.56%; 1963-1969--Northeast, 2.70%; North Central,
3.61%; South, 4.53%; West, 4.43%; and 1969-1975--Northeast,
-0.07%; North Central, 0.87%; South, 2.75%; West, 2.68%.

just held its share, and the Northeast showed a
large comparative loss. In 1929 the South and the
West together accounted for less than one out of
every four manufacturing jobs and for only one-
fifth of the value added by manufacture. By 1958
their share had increased to one-third, as measured by either variable. The direction of change
since 1947 was substantially the same as in the
longer period, but the comparative gains of the
West were conspicuously greater than those of the
South.

The trends distinguished by Fuchs actually began unfolding
somewhat earlier in the century than 1929.

As shown in Table 7, since 1958 the broad trends described by Fuchs have continued. The South and the West
have gained an increasing share of national manufacturing
employment--from about 33 percent in 1958 to almost 42
percent in 1975. The North Central region has held its
share, and the Northeast has experienced a large comparative loss. However, the pattern of manufacturing employment since 1958 differs in two ways from the period
described by Fuchs. First, between 1929 and 1958, although
the Northeast suffered a comparative loss of manufacturing
employment, this region gained 1,287,900 manufacturing
jobs, which amounted to more than a 23-percent increase.
Northeastern manufacturing employment continued to grow
until 1967, but between 1967 and 1975 manufacturing jobs
in this region decreased by 1,130,900. During the same
period the North Central region lost 527,500 manufacturing
jobs. Second, the locus of growth shifted from the West
to the South. Between 1958 and 1975 the West's share of
national manufacturing employment increased from 11.4 percent to 13.5 percent, while the South's share increased
from 21.6 percent to 28.3 percent.

Between 1969 and 1975, national manufacturing employment declined by 1,972,300 jobs. This decline occurred
in two steps, which are associated with the recessions of
1969-1970 and 1974-1975. By 1974 national manufacturing
employment was almost at its 1969 level, but between 1974
and 1975 alone, employment fell by 1,801,400 jobs. No
region was immune from the manufacturing employment declines of the 1974-1975 recession. The relative declines
in the North Central states (10.1 percent) and in the
Northeast (9.5 percent) were greater than in the West (6.1
percent) and in the South (8.5 percent). What made the decline in northeastern manufacturing employment particularly

TABLE 7 Regional Manufacturing Employment (in thousands) and Regional Shares of Manufacturing Employment, 1947-1975

Year	Northeast		North Central		South		West[a]		Total	
	Emp	Share	Emp	Share	Emp	Share	Emp	Share	Emp	Share
1947	5,429.0	(38.0)	5,109.0	(35.7)	2,710.1	(19.0)	1,054.2	(7.4)	14,302.3	(100.0)
1954	5,536.5	(35.3)	5,399.2	(34.4)	3,173.5	(20.2)	1,570.4	(10.0)	15,679.7	(100.0)
1958	5,512.5	(34.4)	5,225.3	(32.6)	3,459.5	(21.6)	1,823.7	(11.4)	16,021.0	(100.0)
1963	5,500.1	(32.4)	5,497.8	(32.4)	3,876.5	(22.9)	2,081.8	(12.3)	16,956.2	(100.0)
1965	5,623.0	(31.1)	5,979.0	(33.1)	4,340.7	(24.0)	2,118.1	(11.7)	18,060.8	(100.0)
1967	5,921.8	(30.7)	6,356.7	(32.9)	4,676.6	(24.2)	2,365.4	(12.2)	19,320.5	(100.0)
1969	5,887.5	(29.1)	6,612.9	(32.7)	5,200.2	(25.7)	2,515.2	(12.4)	20,215.8	(100.0)
1970	5,602.6	(28.9)	6,258.3	(32.3)	5,139.2	(26.5)	2,368.7	(12.2)	19,368.8	(100.0)
1972	5,295.3	(27.8)	6,134.4	(32.2)	5,227.2	(27.5)	2,370.4	(12.5)	19,027.3	(100.0)
1974	5,295.1	(26.4)	6,484.9	(32.4)	5,646.5	(28.2)	2,618.4	(13.1)	20,044.9	(100.0)
1975	4,790.9	(26.3)	5,829.2	(32.0)	5,165.1	(28.3)	2,458.3	(13.5)	18,243.5	(100.0)

[a] Alaska and Hawaii have been excluded from the West to maintain comparability for years when data are unavailable for these states.

SOURCES: Census of Manufacturers (U.S. Bureau of the Census 1947, 1954, 1958, 1963, 1967, 1972); and Employment and Earnings (U.S. Bureau of Labor Statistics 1965, 1969, 1970, 1974, 1975).

severe was that this sector never fully recovered from
the recession of 1969-1970 and, moreover, had been declining rather steadily since approximately 1967.

These data suggest two conclusions. First, the increases in manufacturing employment during the 1960s that
resulted in part from the Vietnam War served to mask the
longer-term plight of this sector in the Northeast and
North Central regions. Second, the general state of the
economy has much to do with the performance of the manufacturing sector, as indicated by the 1975 decline even
in the South and the West.

The long-term trends in the locus of manufacturing employment have been attributed to a number of factors:
the growth of markets, the lack of unionization, relatively
low wages, and the availability of sunshine in the South
and the West. Burrows et al. (1971), Thompson and Mattila
(1959), and Wheat (1973), for example, place particular
emphasis on the growth of markets, whereas Fuchs (1962b)
argues that the lack of unionization and relatively low
wages, in combination with climatic factors, have attracted
manufacturing employment to the South and the West. Others,
such as Vaughan (1977), place more emphasis on technological
change. They attribute the southward and westward shifts
of the manufacturing sector to factors such as the decreasing raw material content of manufacturing output, the
rising importance of truck transportation, and the general
availability of air conditioning.

Moreover, it is argued that because the manufacturing
capital stock in the Northeast and North Central regions
is old, the manufacturing sector of these regions is at a
competitive disadvantage that is particularly severe in
light of the strong and growing foreign competition. Finally, the growth of manufacturing employment in the South
and West is sometimes seen as a cumulative phenomenon,
since manufacturing firms have a tendency to cluster in
order to enjoy agglomeration economies.

Shifts in Agricultural Employment   Because of the historical concentration of black workers in southern agriculture,
brief recognition of regional trends in agricultural employment is pertinent. Table 8 reports agricultural employment by region in 1950, 1960, and 1970. While agricultural employment declined in each region during each decade,
the relative declines were somewhat greater in the South
than in the other regions. These declines in the South
were in part the cause and in part the effect of the exodus
of black workers from southern agriculture. As described

TABLE 8   Regional Levels of and Percentage Changes in
Agricultural Employment, 1950-1970

Region	Employment Level 1950	1960	1970	Percentage Change 1950-1960	1960-1970
Northeast	549,748	384,157	277,674	-30.1	-27.7
North Central	2,433,415	1,625,366	1,064,595	-33.2	-34.5
South	3,386,186	1,853,663	1,037,095	-45.3	-44.1
West	825,161	661,688	537,066	-19.8	-18.8

SOURCE: U.S. Bureau of Economic Analysis (1975).

by Kain and Persky (1971), the migration of blacks from
southern rural areas to large northern urban areas has
brought large concentrations of people with relatively
little education to these urban areas. Moreover, white
migrants from southern rural areas to the smaller metropolitan areas of the North also had comparatively little
education. The consequence has been that the urban North
must now confront the problems that derive from inadequate
education.

*Changes in Central-City and Suburban Population and Employ-
ment*   Central-city decay in the major metropolitan areas
of the country is a well-known phenomenon. One frequent
explanation for the plight of central cities is that both
workers and jobs have been involved in a self-reinforcing
movement to the suburbs. Moreover, by eroding the central-
city tax base and thus shifting the burden of local taxes
to employers and to relatively high-income residents remaining behind, this movement is thought to have encouraged
further flight from the central city.
     Several studies dealing with the cumulative flight phe-
nomenon have focused more or less specifically on the
causal relationships between the movement of jobs and the
movement of workers. Do jobs follow workers to the suburbs,
or do workers follow jobs? Partially because manufacturing
has traditionally been the single most important source of
urban employment and partially because more and better data
are available on manufacturing, the manufacturing sector
has received particular attention. Kain (1968b, p. 17),

for example, argues that "manufacturing determines the
locational decisions of urban households, not vice versa."
Mills (1970, p. 12), on the other hand, tentatively concludes that "the movement of people to the suburbs has
attracted manufacturing employment rather than vice versa."
In a more recent study, Steinnes (1977, p. 78) concludes
that "people do not follow manufacturing and services, but
retail trade." He argues further that while manufacturing
jobs follow people, people may actually be moving away
from manufacturing jobs.

The direction of the causal relationship between the
intrametropolitan movements of workers and jobs cannot be
resolved in this paper. However, recent changes in the
location of workers and jobs can be described and placed
in historical perspective. The best data sources for iden-
tifying central-city and suburban employment growth (as
distinguished from the residence of employed persons) are
the *Census of Manufactures* and the *Census of Business* (U.S.
Bureau of the Census, various years). These sources allow
the description of four types of employment change: manufacturing, retail, wholesale, and selected services.

Table 9 indicates central-city and suburban employment
for the major metropolitan areas of each Census region.
Central-city manufacturing employment has declined in the
Northeast in each year for which data are available. The
decline between 1963 and 1967 was, however, by far the
smallest recorded. Similar declines in the central cities
of the North Central region are also evident, except that
an increase occurred between 1963 and 1967. Probably due
mainly to the Vietnam War, 1967 was an unusually good year
for the manufacturing sector, and again served to mask the
longer-term plight of the sector in the central cities of
the older industrial areas. By 1975, the long-term trend
had reestablished itself, and the added effects of a serious recession could also be seen. Even the central cities
of the major metropolitan areas of the South suffered manufacturing employment declines between 1967 and 1972. Moreover, suburban manufacturing employment declined in the
Northeast and in the West.

The argument has been made that during recessions the
least productive capital is removed first from the production process. The least productive capital is typically
the oldest capital, which consequently embodies the least
recent technology. Since the oldest plants and equipment
are found in central cities, especially in the central
cities of older industrial areas of the Northeast and North
Central regions, central cities tend to be most seriously

TABLE 9 Central-City and Suburban Civilian Labor Force and Employment for Various Years (in thousands)

Northeast / North Central

Year	Civilian Labor Force CC[b]	SR[c]	Manufacturing[a] Employment CC	SR	Other Measured[a] Employment CC	SR	North Central Civilian Labor Force CC	SR	Manufacturing[a] Employment CC	SR	Other Measured[a] Employment CC	SR
1947			2,162.9	1,343.8					2,326.9	975.6		
1948					1,900.7[d]	567.3					1,647.5	372.0
1950	6,547.6		2,129.4[d]		1,856.8[d]		5,502.2		2,272.7[d]		1,629.3[d]	
1954			2,084.7	1,539.2	1,769.1	697.5			2,200.5	1,115.9	1,592.8	495.6
1958			1,964.4[d]	1,594.7	1,896.9[d]	870.0[d]			2,009.2	1,255.1[d]	1,652.5[d]	610.9[d]
1960	6,287.9	5,728.1	1,941.4[d]	1,623.9[d]	1,873.8[d]	959.1[d]	5,412.0	4,487.5	1,974.3[d]	1,325.8[d]	1,604.1[d]	698.5[d]
1963			1,907.0	1,667.6	1,839.1	1,092.7			1,922.0	1,431.8	1,531.4	830.0
1967			1,906.2[d]	1,871.6[d]	1,902.8[d]	1,299.0[d]			1,937.0[d]	1,503.2[d]	1,639.6[d]	1,061.5[d]
1970	5,903.4	7,227.9	1,699.0[d]	1,817.4[d]	1,863.7[d]	1,532.9[d]	4,996.3	6,611.3	1,799.7[d]	1,721.8[d]	1,619.0[d]	1,357.0[d]
1972			1,560.8	1,781.2	1,837.7	1,688.9			1,708.1	1,867.6	1,605.3	1,554.0

South / West

Year	Civilian Labor Force CC	SR	Manufacturing[a] Employment CC	SR	Other Measured[a] Employment CC	SR	West Civilian Labor Force CC	SR	Manufacturing[a] Employment CC	SR	Other Measured[a] Employment CC	SR
1947			588.5	210.7					438.5	318.0		
1948					976.4[d]	166.3					756.4[d]	271.3
1950	3,277.1		640.5[d]		996.0[d]		2,261.6		513.5[d]		775.0[d]	
1954			709.9	294.4	1,035.2	216.5			613.4	549.7	812.3	367.6
1958			775.0[d]	359.3[d]	1,209.4[d]	319.3			722.8[d]	648.7[d]	932.5	510.0[d]
1960	4,047.2	2,581.6	785.3[d]	381.0[d]	1,219.3[d]	369.7[d]	3,058.7	3,103.1	733.8[d]	725.5[d]	967.7[d]	596.8[d]
1963			800.7	413.5	1,234.1	445.2			750.3	845.7	1,020.5	727.1
1967			889.7[d]	561.6[d]	1,402.4[d]	667.0[d]			761.7[d]	1,077.3[d]	1,135.8	861.2[d]
1970	4,363.1	4,617.6	879.9[d]	650.8[d]	1,545.0[d]	927.6[d]	3,446.1	4,779.1	770.1[d]	1,024.5[d]	1,230.2[d]	1,072.6[d]
1972			873.3	710.2	1,640.0	1,101.3			775.7	990.0	1,293.2	1,213.5

[a] All data are based on 1970 SMSA definitions. No adjustments have been made for central-city annexations of outlying areas.

[b] CC refers to central cities.

[c] SR refers to suburban rings.

[d] Value has been enterpolated.

NOTE: In 1970, 64 of 242 SMSAs in the continental U.S. had a population in excess of 500,000. With the exclusion of Jacksonville, which in 1970 is defined in such a way as to have no suburban ring, these SMSAs constitute the data base. All data have been adjusted to correspond with 1970 SMSA definitions. However, no attempt has been made to adjust central-city and suburban data for central-city annexations of outlying territory. If the data were adjusted for these annexations, based on 1970 central-city definitions, central-city data entries back through time would generally have higher values while suburban entries would have lower values.

SOURCES: Civilian labor-force data are from U.S. Bureau of the Census, *U.S. Census of Population* (1950, 1960, 1970); manufacturing data are from U.S. Bureau of the Census, *U.S. Census of Manufactures* (various years). Other measured employment data consists of retail, selected services, and wholesale, and are from U.S. Bureau of the Census, *U.S. Census of Business* (various years).

affected by national recessions. If this argument is
valid, the central cities of the Northeast and North Central regions are particularly susceptible to recessions
such as that of 1974-1975.

Other measurable sources of central-city employment
have performed somewhat better than manufacturing. In
both the Northeast and North Central regions, modest declines have occurred in retail, wholesale, and selected
service employment between 1948 and 1972 (3.3 percent and
2.6 percent, respectively), but these declines have not
been steady. Over both the 1950-1960 and 1960-1970 decades, central-city manufacturing employment declined somewhat more rapidly than the central-city civilian labor
force (CLF), but CLF declined more rapidly than other
sources of employment. These changes suggest that as far
as employment is concerned, the decline of the manufacturing sector is a critical component of central-city problems. It contributes not only to a decline in jobs but
also to a decline in the central-city tax base.

During the decade of the 1960s, the suburban CLF of
major metropolitan areas grew at dramatic rates. As calculated from Table 9, it grew by 26.2 percent in the Northeast and by 78.9 percent in the South. Although suburban
manufacturing employment did not grow as rapidly as either
suburban CLF or other measurable sources of suburban employment, manufacturing employment grew quite rapidly in
the suburbs, and certainly grew far more rapidly than in
the central cities. In the South, suburban manufacturing
grew by 70.8 percent, while in the West it grew by 41.2
percent. Suburban retail, wholesale, and selected service
employment grew at roughly twice the rate of suburban CLF
in the Northeast, the North Central, and the South regions.

A number of scholars have specifically addressed the
question of the match (or mismatch) of central-city job
requirements to the skills possessed by central-city residents (Harrison 1974, Kain 1968a, Mooney 1969). For many
reasons, including overt discrimination against blacks in
the housing market and the location of affordable housing,
blacks are largely restricted to urban cores. Although
certain types of central-city employment have grown, it
is argued that black central-city residents are not
equipped to fill these jobs. Black central-city residents
are better suited for the jobs that are growing in the
suburbs, but because intraurban transportation networks
between central cities and the suburbs are inadequate and
because discrimination in hiring takes place, blacks are
unable to gain suburban employment in significant numbers.

Conclusions

A number of conclusions can be drawn from the foregoing
discussion. Regional population changes and employment
changes are positively correlated, although perhaps not
as highly as might be expected. Changes in labor-force
participation rates appear to be an important source of
increased employment. Regional employment shifts since
1970 are consistent with post World War II trends. However, the long-term decline of the manufacturing sector
in the Northeast was temporarily reversed in the late
1960s, probably due in large part to the Vietnam War.
When the long-term trend was reestablished in the early
1970s, the Northeast faced particularly severe adjustments
that resulted in a sizeable absolute decline in manufacturing employment. Although the rate of southern population
growth approached that of the West during the 1970-1975
period, the rate of southern employment growth has been
approximately equal to that of the West since 1960. Finally, regional employment growth is sensitive to the condition of the national economy, and national conditions
were so depressed in 1975 that their regional impacts cannot be ignored.

Moreover, the trend of central-city employment during
the 1970-1975 period was consistent with that of earlier
periods, as was the trend of suburban employment. However,
since approximately 1967 central-city manufacturing employment in the Northeast and North Central regions has declined somewhat more precipitously than in earlier periods.
Again, this decline appears to have been amplified by the
discrepancy between national economic conditions prevailing
during the late 1960s and the early 1970s. These conditions have particularly severe consequences in the central
cities of older industrial metropolitan areas. Furthermore, to the extent that blacks are "last hired, first
fired," the concentration of blacks in central cities makes
these areas all the more susceptible to high unemployment
during recessionary periods.

While the severity of the employment effects is transi-
tory in the sense that the effects will be somewhat alle-
viated with a return to fuller employment, no apparent
reason exists to suppose that the effects will not return
with future recessionary conditions. Hopefully, the severity of the 1974-1975 recession will not be repeated.

During the post World War II period, a number of important national forces contributed to the changing spatial
distribution of population and economic activity. The

years from approximately 1965 to 1975 stand distinctly
apart from the earlier postwar years as a period during
which conditions encouraged a disproportionate amount of
spatial redistribution. The aging of the war-baby cohort
brought an extremely large number of young persons into
the labor force, and young persons tend to be quite mobile
geographically. Furthermore, economic conditions offered
the inducement for movement. Moreover, as a result of the
increased labor-force participation rates of young married
white women, young couples had two salaries, which permitted them to locate in areas that might otherwise have
been beyond their means at that stage of their life.

THE RELATIONSHIP BETWEEN POPULATION SHIFTS AND EMPLOYMENT
CHANGE

The Conceptual Underpinnings

Of the sources of spatial population change, migration is
likely to have the most immediate implications for employment. Therefore, the primary focus of this section is
on the relationship between migration and employment
growth. At the extremes, two theoretical approaches
have been developed to characterize the relationship
between migration and employment change. One approach
hypothesizes a one-way causation running from employment
change to migration (Blanco 1963), while the other hypothesizes a one-way causation running from migration to
employment change (Borts and Stein 1964). Empirical support has been found for each position. More recently,
however, migration and employment change have been treated
as jointly dependent, and each variable has been found to
influence the other (Greenwood 1975a, 1975b; Muth 1971).
    The basic idea behind the simultaneous-equations models
is that the migration of labor-force members is responsive
to job opportunities. Areas with the highest rate of employment growth, and hence presumably the highest rate of
growth in job opportunities, are those that will experience
the highest rates of in-migration and the lowest rates of
out-migration. Furthermore, the migrants themselves influence both the supply of and demand for local labor.
Employment should grow most rapidly in those areas that
are attractive to migrants and least rapidly in those areas
that are suffering losses in population and labor force due
to migration.
    It is important to recognize that the effects of migration

on labor supply are dependent not only on the numbers of
persons migrating, but also on the characteristics of the
migrants. This subject has received inadequate attention
in migration literature. Clearly, in-migration and out-
migration of labor-force members have immediate impacts
on local labor supply. As long as local labor demand is
not perfectly inelastic, employment will tend to grow in
areas of in-migration and decline in areas of out-migration.
Moreover, labor-force participation rates differ between
age, racial, education, and earnings classes. Bowen and
Finegan (1969) demonstrate a strong tendency for participation rates of prime-age (25-54) males to rise with education. Table 2 shows that such rates are higher for
white males than for black males. Because prime-age population groups, whites, and the better-educated tend to
have higher labor-force participation rates, migration
streams composed of relatively large numbers of persons
in these categories tend to have greater impacts on labor
supply in sending and receiving areas. Other things being
equal, employment should grow most rapidly in localities
experiencing relatively high rates of (net) in-migration,
as well as relatively high rates of in-migration of prime-
age, white, and well-educated persons.

The labor-demand effects of migration are similarly
dependent on both the numbers and the characteristics of
the migrants. Two types of labor demand that are affected
by migration should be distinguished: the demand for labor
in the production of private goods and the demand for labor
in the production of public goods. The demand for locally
produced and consumed commodities will tend to rise with
the population increase resulting from in-migration. Furthermore, other things being equal, the higher the income
or wealth of the migrants and the better their education,
the greater will be the increase in the derived demand for
local labor.

Another factor that may be important is the entrepreneurial ability of the migrants. Allaman and Birch (1975)
argue that the interstate migration rate of firms is relatively low. What distinguishes states and regions with
rapidly growing employment from other states and regions
is the rate at which new firms are established. They conclude by emphasizing the role of entrepreneurial activity
in encouraging employment expansion and by suggesting that
the locational choices of persons with entrepreneurial
ability are critical for differential employment growth,
such as has recently occurred in the South.

Net in-migration of retired persons is concentrated in

TABLE 10 Gross In-Migration and Out-Migration and Net Migration of the Population by Region, 1940-1975 (in thousands)

Year	Northeast			North Central			South			West		
	In	Out	Net	In	Out	Net	In	Out	Net	In	Out	Net
1940-1947	819	1,084	-265	1,817	2,099	-282	1,280	2,803	-1,523	2,767	697	2,070
1949-1950	256	391	-135	515	569	-54	688	574	114	470	395	75
1953-1954	364	408	-44	827	654	173	682	1,083	-401	671	399	272
1954-1955	360	439	-79	724	683	41	814	993	-179	752	535	217
1955-1956	398	418	-20	778	651	127	811	1,091	-280	687	514	173
1956-1957	388	445	-57	575	968	-393	961	821	140	734	424	310
1957-1958	551	465	86	672	944	-272	984	1,003	-19	738	533	205
1958-1959	419	522	-103	748	719	29	759	985	-226	739	439	300
1959-1960	466	463	3	662	797	-135	867	1,078	-211	877	534	343
1960-1961	433	524	-91	677	994	-317	1,088	1,027	-19	979	552	427
1961-1962	479	493	-14	723	874	-151	806	1,089	-283	969	521	448
1962-1963	451	594	-143	962	1,170	-208	1,002	1,216	-214	1,163	598	565
1963-1964	517	611	-94	671	985	-314	1,036	1,143	-107	1,101	586	515
1964-1965	582	623	-41	687	854	-167	1,115	1,082	33	998	823	175
1965-1966	569	509	60	838	860	-22	1,036	1,214	-178	905	765	140
1966-1967	514	652	-138	943	919	24	1,056	1,307	-251	1,022	657	365
1967-1968	545	717	-172	1,038	1,055	-17	1,283	1,311	-28	944	777	217
1968-1969	557	594	-37	887	899	-12	1,079	1,313	-234	961	678	283
1969-1970	521	827	-306	868	1,007	-139	1,279	1,247	50	1,085	690	395
1970-1971	609	804	-195	870	1,183	-311	1,425	1,171	254	1,032	780	252
1970-1975	1,057	2,399	-1,342	1,731	2,926	-1,195	4,082	2,253	1,829	2,347	1,639	708

SOURCES: U.S. Bureau of the Census, *Current Population Reports*, Series P-20, *Mobility of the Population of the United States, 1948-1976*.

a few states, such as Florida and Arizona. Although the
destinations of retired persons are largely chosen for
reasons other than job opportunities, retirement migration
has important implications for employment growth and subsequently induced labor-force migration. The in-migration
of retired persons increases local labor demand without
coincidentally increasing labor supply. The increased demand for local labor may be satisfied in part by increased
local labor-force participation, but immediate local demands, such as in the construction industry, are unlikely
to be completely satisfied by local sources. In-migration
of labor-force members is, therefore, likely to occur, further fueling the growth of the area.

Thus, other things being equal, greater excess labor
demand is created by the retired migrant than by the labor-
force migrant. This factor may help explain the observation that areas of retirement in-migration also experience
appreciable nonretirement migration. Much of the nonretirement migration may be caused by the same amenities
that cause retirement migration, but a great deal of nonretirement migration also appears to be responsive to
growing job opportunities.

Migrant numbers and characteristics influence the demand
for public services and the revenues that support their
provision. The extra local revenues provided by many low-
income migrants are likely to fall short of the extra
costs of the public services they consume. The opposite
is true for many high-income migrants. Fiscal plight is
likely when a locality simultaneously experiences net in-
migration of low-income persons and out-migration of high-
income persons. This situation is typical of many of the
central cities of the nation's major metropolitan areas.

Interregional Migrants: Their Numbers and Characteristics

As indicated in Table 10, during the years between 1940
and 1969, the Northeast, the North Central, and the South
regions generally experienced net out-migration, while the
West experienced net in-migration. Note that in most years
net migration is a small fraction of gross migration, and
thus that relatively small changes in gross in-migration
or out-migration, or in both, can cause relatively large
year-to-year changes in regional net migration. Especially
for the regions experiencing net out-migration, substantial
year-to-year fluctuations are evident in the volume of net
migration. However, as noted in Table 4, regional population

has continued to rise in spite of the net out-migration
from the Northeast, North Central, and South regions.
These population increases are, of course, due to natural
increase and to net immigration (from abroad).

The observation has frequently been made that migration
rates rise with education (Lansing and Morgan 1967). From
the point of view of regions of net out-migration, this
observation has relevance because it may mean that these
regions suffer disproportionately heavy losses of their
best educated manpower. Similarly, regions of net in-
migration may experience disproportionately heavy gains
of such persons. Present value estimates of the returns
to better educated people who migrate are higher than estimates of the returns to less educated people who migrate;
this fact has important implications for regional development (Wertheimer 1970). Important spillover benefits accrue to areas in which the better educated reside. Among
other factors, the educated may contribute to technological
change and may breed entrepreneurship, both of which would
tend to foster more rapid employment growth.

For each of the nine Census divisions, Table 11 shows
1965-1970 interdivisional net migration rates of nonnative
college graduates. With the exception of New England,
each division that experienced net out-migration had a
substantially higher rate of out-migration of college
graduates than the overall rate of out-migration. Furthermore, again with the exception of New England, each
division that experienced net out-migration had a considerably higher rate for out-migration of college graduates
between the ages of 25 and 34 than for college graduates
as a whole. Similarly, the three divisions (South Atlantic,
Mountain, and Pacific) that experienced net in-migration
enjoyed especially high in-migration rates of college
graduates. This pattern suggests a "brain drain" from
the Middle Atlantic, East and West North Central, and East
South Central divisions to the South Atlantic, Mountain,
and Pacific divisions.[12]

The South Atlantic division is particularly noteworthy
in this respect. The rate of 1965-1970 net in-migration

---

[12]The brain-drain argument is typically focused on the
drain of talent from less developed or less prosperous
areas to developed or more prosperous areas. In this
context, the net migration of the better educated from
more prosperous to less prosperous regions does not fit
the conditions established for the brain-drain argument.

TABLE 11   Interdivisional Net Migration Rates of College
Graduates, 1965-1970[a] (as percentage of division population)

Census Division	All Persons 25-64	College Graduates 25-64	College Graduates 25-34
New England	-0.34	1.00	0.61
Middle Atlantic	-1.96	-3.91	-5.14
East North Central	-0.89	-3.57	-5.37
West North Central	-2.27	-5.34	-9.41
South Atlantic	2.47	6.10	8.72
East South Central	-2.34	-3.72	-9.90
West South Central	-0.54	-1.18	-2.07
Mountain	2.95	3.24	4.20
Pacific	3.39	5.87	11.12

[a]Refers to persons who were residing in one Census division
in 1965 and in another in 1970 and who were not returning
to the division of their birth. Rates are expressed relative to the relevant 1970 Census division population.
"College graduates" refers to persons with 4 or more years
of college in 1970.

SOURCE: U.S. Bureau of the Census (1973a).

was 2.47 percent, while the rate for college graduates was
6.10 percent and the rate for young college graduates was
8.72 percent. Net in-migration of college graduates to
the South Atlantic Census division is not a recent phenomenon. Between 1965 and 1970, this division experienced a
net migration gain of 93,680 nonnative college graduates;
between 1955 and 1960, when the South in general had reasonably heavy out-migration (see Table 10), it experienced
a net gain of 43,203 such persons. Note that the Pacific
division also had a substantial net gain of nonnative college graduates and especially of young college graduates.
   Despite relatively heavy net out-migration during the
years between 1940 and 1969, the South enjoyed sizeable
increases in employment. Over the past 15 years, these
increases have not only kept pace with those of the West
but have frequently exceeded them, despite the fact that
the West experienced considerable in-migration during the
period. In the past, labor-force participation rates were
low in the South and hence a portion of the southern employment increase can be attributed to the rising labor-force

participation of indigenous residents. Moreover, gross in-migration to the South was substantial during the entire period--so substantial, in fact, that in most years the volume of southern in-migration exceeded that of the other regions. Given the favorable balance of migration of the best educated, these observations suggest (although do not prove) that migration may have contributed to changing the South's population composition in a fashion conducive to employment growth.

Kain and Persky (1971) go a step further in arguing that South-to-North migration has, historically, contributed to the problems of the metropolitan North. Rural areas of the South have underinvested in human capital, and when persons raised in the rural South migrate to the urban North, they are ill-equipped to compete effectively for the available jobs.

Intraurban Movers and Their Characteristics

For individual standard metropolitan statistical areas (SMSAs) that had a 1970 population in excess of 500,000, the 1970 Census reports fairly detailed characteristics of those who moved to central cities between 1965 and 1970, and those who moved between central cities and suburban rings during the same time period. These data contribute to an understanding of why the central cities of the major metropolitan areas of the Northeast and, to a lesser extent, those of the North Central states have experienced critical fiscal and economic problems.

Table 12 indicates that relative to their suburbs, the central cities of the major metropolitan areas of the Northeast have difficulty in attracting CLF in-migrants: for every CLF member who migrates to the central city, there are 1.9 who migrate to the suburbs. In other regions, the suburbs also attract absolutely more migrant CLF members than the central cities, but the ratios are somewhat smaller. In the South, for example, for every CLF member who migrates to the central city, only 1.3 migrate to the suburbs.

Relative to the CLF of the central cities and of the suburbs, the movement of CLF members from central cities to suburbs is quite low in the Northeast and North Central states compared with the South and the West. However, in the Northeast and North Central regions, CLF migration to the central cities fails to replace the CLF members who move to the suburbs, while in the South and the West, CLF

TABLE 12   Suburban In-Migration Relative to Central-City
In-Migration and Intraurban Relocation of Civilian Labor-
Force Members for Major Metropolitan Areas, 1965-1970[a]

	Northeast	North Central	South	West
$\dfrac{\text{IMR}^b}{\text{IMCC}^c}$	1.9	1.6	1.3	1.5
$\dfrac{\text{CC} \rightarrow \text{R}^d}{\text{R} \rightarrow \text{CC}^e}$	3.0	2.5	2.6	1.7
$\dfrac{\text{CC} \rightarrow \text{R}}{\text{CLFCC}^f}$	7.2%	12.0%	10.4%	11.7%
$\dfrac{\text{CC} \rightarrow \text{R}}{\text{CLFR}^g}$	5.8%	9.1%	9.8%	8.4%
$\dfrac{\text{IMCC}}{\text{CLFCC}}$	5.6%	9.1%	14.5%	16.2%
$\dfrac{\text{IMR}}{\text{CLFR}}$	8.7%	10.8%	18.2%	18.0%

[a]All mobility data refer to place of residence in 1965 and
place of residence in 1970 of persons defined as civilian
labor-force members in 1970.
[b]Suburban-ring in-migration.
[c]Central-city in-migration.
[d]Migration from central city to suburban ring.
[e]Migration from suburban ring to central city.
[f]1970 Civilian labor force of central city.
[g]1970 Civilian labor force of suburban ring.

SOURCE: Calculated from data presented in U.S. Bureau of
the Census (1973b).

migration to the central cities is considerably greater
than central-city losses of CLF members to the suburbs.
The major impetus for CLF growth in the suburbs of the
South and West is the migration from other regions rather
than the movement from central cities, although such movement is of some consequence.   In the Northeast and North
Central regions, migration from other regions and from
central cities contributes more equally to suburban CLF
growth.
   As indicated in Table 13, the central cities of the

TABLE 13   Suburban In-Migration Relative to Central-City
In-Migration and Intraurban Relocation for Major Metropolitan Areas, by Income Class, 1965-1970[a]

Region (SMSAs)	$\dfrac{\text{IMR}[b]}{\text{IMCC}[c]}$	$\dfrac{\text{CC}\rightarrow\text{R}[d]}{\text{R}\rightarrow\text{CC}[e]}$
Northeast (15)		
Income $25,000+	5.6	5.8
Less than $25,000	2.9	4.2
North Central (17)		
Income $25,000+	4.4	2.1
Less than $25,000	5.2	2.9
South (19)		
Income $25,000+	1.9	1.7
Less than $25,000	3.2	3.1
West (12)		
Income $25,000+	2.4	1.9
Less than $25,000	2.0	2.1

[a] All mobility data refer to persons in families with 1969
family income as indicated.
[b] Suburban-ring in-migration.
[c] Central-city in-migration.
[d] Migration from central cities to suburban rings.
[e] Migration from suburban rings to central cities.

SOURCE: See Table 12.

Northeast, relative to their suburbs, have had an especially
difficult time attracting and retaining high-income residents.   Between 1965 and 1970 northeastern central cities
attracted one high-income ($25,000+) migrant for every 5.6
that the suburbs attracted.   For every one high-income
mover from the suburbs to the central city, 5.8 moved in
the opposite direction.   By contrast, the central cities
of the South attracted one high-income migrant for every
1.9 who located in the suburbs, and for every high-income
mover from suburbs to central city, 1.7 such persons moved
from central city to suburbs.
     When the data of Tables 12 and 13 are compared, it is
apparent that in the South and the West the metropolitan
location patterns of both in-migrants and intraurban movers
are fairly similar for CLF members as a whole and for high-
income persons.   High-income persons do have a greater tendency than CLF members as a whole to locate in the suburbs,

but this tendency is nowhere near as pronounced as in the
Northeast.

Conclusions

Population growth and employment growth are mutually dependent. Each variable reinforces the other, with migration and labor-force participation rates forming the major
linkages between the two. Local employment growth is dependent not only upon the number of persons migrating, but
also upon the characteristics of the migrants. Among migrants that have particularly great impacts on local employment are the young, the well-educated, the high-income,
whites, and retirees. Such persons influence, to varying
degrees, local labor demand, local labor supply, or both.
   A pattern of self-perpetuating decline has frequently
characterized the nation's depressed regions. The better
educated, more highly skilled, younger, and higher income
residents, all of whom tend to be the most mobile groups
in society, have migrated out of depreseed areas, thus
depriving the local economies of human resources that are
essential for sustained development. As conditions further deteriorate, other residents are induced to follow.
This pattern has been true in movement from the farm, in
earlier migration out of the South, and in the exodus from
the central cities of the nation's major metropolitan areas.
An opposite set of forces appears to be operating in the
nation's expanding areas.

THE EMPLOYMENT POLICY IMPLICATIONS OF POPULATION
REDISTRIBUTION

The long-term trends in the regional distribution of population and employment are the result of powerful economic
and social forces. Technological change, combined with
rising incomes and different life-style expectations, have
facilitated and encouraged the westward and southward movements of population and employment. Although these broad
movements of population and employment have been somewhat
influenced by federal action, they have largely been determined by the major economic and social forces discussed in
this paper.

The Rationale for Public Intervention

Various regions of the country cannot reasonably be expected
to experience the same rates of employment and population

growth. In a market economy, spatial differentials in
real-wage rates and in employment opportunities provide
signals to workers that encourage spatial mobility. This
mobility not only increases the well-being of the migrants
themselves, but also results in improved resource allocation. As Kuznets (1964) emphasizes, migration is not only
a consequence of economic growth, but also an indispensable
cause of such growth.

Productive resources are, however, not perfectly adaptable to new uses that arise in the natural course of
economic growth and change, and, therefore, adjustments in
the allocation of resources require time. In certain instances, without public intervention the labor adjustment
process would require indefinitely long periods during
which socially unacceptable hardships would be borne by
the less adaptable (i.e., less mobile) persons in society.
Some form of public intervention is appropriate.

What is frequently not recognized is that any migration
results in redistributions of income in both the place of
origin and the place of destination as well as between the
two places. In other words, in both sending and receiving
areas, migration benefits certain individuals and groups
and has negative effects on others. Broadly speaking,
four groups can be distinguished (although in practice the
individual members of each group may not easily be identified): the migrants themselves, the employers of the
migrants, the consumers affected by the migrants, and the
workers affected by the migrants. Let us briefly consider
how income redistribution caused by migration might affect
each of these groups.[13]

The migrants, as a group, clearly benefit from the migration. After presumably deciding that the expected benefits of their migration outweigh the expected costs, they
relocate. A number of factors might underlie the migration
decision, such as job and earnings opportunities and location amenities. Several studies have specifically focused
on the monetary returns to migration. Generally, the findings have been that the monetary returns are positive for
all, but are greatest for the young, the better educated,
and whites (Wertheimer 1970). If we are going to have policy concerns about migrants, we should base our concern not
on the fact that these people have migrated, but rather on t

[13]For a more detailed discussion of the income redistributions associated with migration, see Gerking and Greenwood
(1977) and Romans (1974).

fact that certain of them are poor, old, unemployed, poorly
housed, or whatever, despite their migration.

Much interregional and intraurban mobility is a consequence of spatial employment disparities, and such mobility
generally tends to alleviate these disparities. However,
the migrant, in making the decision to move, takes into
account only the private costs and benefits of the move.
To the extent that the social costs associated with migration are not internalized by the individual, private migration decisions can result in nonoptimal consequences for
society and these may justify public intervention. An obvious example of these social costs is the increased congestion and pollution that result from migration from less
densely populated areas to crowded cities.

Thurow (1970, p. 33) describes the problems that derive
from migration-induced income transfers between consumers
of public goods:

> Private incomes may increase enough to more than make
> up for the costs of moving, but the social costs of
> accommodating people in a crowded urban area may ex-
> ceed the net private gain. More public services must
> be provided, and congestion may increase. Excess
> capacity, and hence waste, may develop in the produc-
> tion of socal services (schools, etc.) in areas from
> which people are moving, and new investment in social
> services may be needed in areas to which they are moving.

Whether consumers of public goods benefit from the presence or absence of migrants is a complex question. The
answer is dependent upon many factors: the number of migrants, the migrants' demand for public goods, the magnitude of the migrants' tax bill, the costs of producing
public goods, etc.

Public goods are typically priced at average costs.
When a public good like education or police protection is
provided in a large or moderately large city under conditions of rising average cost, a migrant who consumes an
average quantity of the public good and pays an average tax
bill will impose a burden on the indigenous residents because their tax bills will rise. If the migrants tend to
be lower-income individuals and/or to consume disproportionately much of the good, the burden on the indigenous
residents will be particularly great. Even if the nominal
price of the public good remains unchanged after the influx
of the migrants, the real price could still rise because
of quality deterioration resulting from congestion.

Based on the increasing number of communities that are adopting "local growth management" policies, we might conclude that more and more localities are interested in protecting their indigenous residents from the social costs of in-migration. Local growth management policies include public acquisition of land, public improvements, environmental controls, zoning techniques, subdivision techniques, tax and fee systems, and restrictive covenants. Although these policies can be extremely effective in controlling local growth, they are likely to affect neighboring communities and to impact relatively heavily on particular groups. The next decade is likely to see a number of legal battles fought over local growth management policies, which are now being implemented in communities across the country.[14]

The effects of migration need not be symmetrical in sending and receiving localities. For example, if the migrants were to come from rural communities where certain public goods are produced under conditions of decreasing cost, the individuals left behind in these localities could also experience an increase in their tax bills. Or if the migrants had relatively high incomes, such as those who leave central cities to move to the suburbs, the burden of local taxes could fall more heavily on those left behind—perhaps on individuals who are least able to bear such increased burdens.

With the reversal of the historical trend of net migration out of nonmetropolitan and into metropolitan areas, the social costs of increased congestion, pollution, and provision of public services in large cities should cause relatively less concern. More concern will now be directed at the social costs of increased population densities in nonmetropolitan areas. To the extent that in-migration to nonmetropolitan areas is motivated by the availability of natural resources, such as clean air and water, scenery, recreational amenities, etc., the environmental costs of migration will receive added attention in years to come.

Selected Employment Policy Options

The policy discussion has thus far focused more directly on population than on employment, because, in the interregional

[14]For a detailed discussion of the economic and legal issues associated with local growth management, see Evans and Vestal (1977).

and the intraurban contexts, the distinction between population policy and employment policy becomes blurred. The blurring is due to the interdependency between population growth and employment growth. In many instances the best way to influence employment growth is to influence population growth. A number of previously cited papers suggest that the primary cause of spatial employment redistribution had been spatial redistribution of market demand resulting from population redistribution. Reasons for this may be that higher income, better educated, and younger persons tend to have greater migration rates and that the local employment effects of migration tend to be especially sensitive to persons with these characteristics.

Employment redistribution also causes population redistribution. The earlier sections of this paper have emphasized that the state of the national economy largely determines interregional and intraurban employment-growth differentials. Particularly during periods of high national unemployment and slow growth of gross national product, employment growth in the Northeast and North Central regions and in the central cities of the major metropolitan areas appears to be adversely affected relative to employment growth in other regions or in the suburbs. Thus, the use of fiscal and monetary policies to maintain full employment must stand as the cornerstone of any regional or urban employment policy.

Even during periods of full employment, however, the incidence of unemployment falls unevenly on various localities, and within localities on various population groups, and growth in employment and earnings proceeds at differential rates that encourage migration. Employment policy concern need not be directly focused on the migrants. Rather, the most immediate concern should be with the less mobile elements in society, who have difficulty engaging in the mainstream of economic activity.

A number of factors are responsible for lack of mobility, including personal and labor market characteristics. The goal of public policies intended to influence geographic mobility must be to alter the costs and/or benefits of migration as perceived by the less mobile segments of society. A similar goal would be applicable to situations in which the net social costs of migration exceed the net private gain. The means by which private perceptions of the benefits and costs of migration might be altered can be broadly grouped into two categories: direct and indirect.

The following is a partial list of the alternatives included under each category:[15]

I. Policies operating *directly* on individual incentives:
    1. subsidized moving costs,
    2. subsidized housing,
    3. public employment,
    4. tax incentives,
    5. manpower training programs,
    6. employment information,
    7. changes in minimum wages, and
    8. changes in welfare requirements.

II. Policies operating *indirectly* on individual incen-
    tives:
    1. encouragement of private-sector employment growth
        through
        a. investments in public infrastructure,
        b. tax or subsidy incentives to firms,
        c. government procurement policies, and
        d. credit institutions;
    2. encouragement of planning for growth or decline;
    3. reducing local disamenities, including pollution,
        congestion, and crime; and
    4. influencing aggregate labor supply by means of
        immigration policy.

Some degree of arbitrariness is inherent in this classification scheme. For example, alternative II.3 could be
regarded as direct, and alternative I.7 could be regarded
as indirect. The distinction is that certain policies
operate immediately on the individuals involved, whereas
others operate in such a way as to affect the environment
in which they live and work or the markets in which they
supply their labor services. Clearly, many of the policies
that directly influence individuals or families also influence the environment in which they live and the markets in
which they participate.

Of the above alternatives, the following can be characterized as employment policy options: I.3, I.5, I.6, I.7,
II.1, II.2, and II.4. Let us consider each of these options.

A sound case can be made for developing local institutional planning capabilities. Planning activities should
be directed not only at facilitating growth in expanding

[15]For a discussion of policies adopted in various European
countries, see DeJong (1975) and Sundquist (1975).

local economies, but also at accommodating lagging local
economies to lower levels of economic activity. One of
the most important aspects of the planning process is forecasting local labor demand by detailed occupational category. This type of information should contribute to the
efficiency of the migration mechanism and to the functioning
of the local labor market by allowing better informed decisions regarding the occupation and location in which an
individual will render his labor services.

Manpower-training programs have a primary objective of
overcoming personal characteristics that limit employment
alternatives and consequently reduce occupational and geographic mobility. Such programs have traditionally been
directed at minority and low-income populations, and hence
have had a high degree of geographic specificity (namely,
in areas where minorities and the poor reside). Because
manpower programs have not in themselves been an unquali-
fied success, as evidenced by the high unemployment and
underemployment rates of blacks, an argument can be made
for instituting complementary programs that affect labor
demand in areas with high concentrations of less mobile
persons.

A number of market imperfections prevent local and national labor markets from functioning more efficiently.
Many workers and potential workers either do not have
access to information regarding job and earnings opportunities in alternative locations and occupations, or they
are unable to decipher the complex information that is
available. Public intervention to provide information to
people who potentially might move and/or change their
occupations is appropriate.

For some individuals who receive manpower training, the
probability of migrating out of an area rises. This tendency is not undesirable, except inasmuch as the loss of
a potential complementary input affects the employment of
others in the locality. Policy makers recognize that manpower programs should be coordinated with the planning
process if the programs are to achieve a reasonable degree
of success. Information generated through the planning
process and by other means should be made available to
recipients of manpower training so that they can make
better informed choices regarding occupation and migration.
The combination of planning, training, and dissemination
of information is likely to have some impact on migration,
but the impacts cannot be assessed at this time.

Immigration policy is an aspect of public intervention
that has potentially dramatic effects on labor supply.

Recently illegal aliens have come under special scrutiny
because of their apparently large and growing numbers.
Various reports in the popular press and by government
agencies have placed the number of illegal U.S. residents
at between 4 and 12 million persons. In fiscal 1975,
766,000 deportable aliens were apprehended in this country,
of which 89 percent were Mexicans. This percentage over-
states the percentage of illegal Mexican aliens relative
to the total number of illegal aliens, but it does indicate that Mexico is an extremely important source of illegal alien labor.[16] Available information indicates that
illegal aliens tend to be young and to have a high degree
of labor-force attachment. Moreover, they are concentrated
along the southwestern border and in the central cities of
the nation's major metropolitan areas. New York City alone
is estimated to have over 1 million illegal aliens.

Table 2 indicates that between 1980 and 1985 the expected
increase in the labor force is slightly less than 7 million.
If the illegal alien labor force increases by 250,000 persons per year, then this increase would be 18 percent of
the increase in the domestic labor force. Since projected
increases in the male labor force are somewhat smaller
than projected increases in the female labor force, and
since the preponderance of illegal aliens, at least of
Mexican aliens (Dagodag 1975), are young males seeking
work, the relative impact on the male labor force would
be considerably greater. The influx of illegal aliens
could cause the size of the young labor force to increase,
rather than decline absolutely as is now projected. Finally, the relative impacts on the civilian labor forces
of the Southwest and West, and of the central cities of
the major metropolitan areas, would also be great.

Two hypotheses have been advanced regarding the employment effects of illegal alien labor. One hypothesis, referred to as the "segmentation hypothesis," states that
labor markets are sufficiently segmented that illegal alien
workers do not take jobs that would otherwise be taken by

[16]Mexicans are overrepresented in apprehensions because
the United States and Mexico have a common border across
which Mexicans enter the United States and along which
the U.S. Border Patrol can be deployed to apprehend those
entering illegally. Furthermore, Mexicans can more easily
be distinguished by their physical appearance than many
other nationalities that contribute to the illegal alien
population.

American workers (Abrams and Abrams 1975 and Nafziger 1975).
Illegal alien workers are presumed to occupy low-wage jobs
that would not interest American workers. The other hypothesis, called the "replacement hypothesis," states that
illegal alien workers do displace American workers (Briggs
1975). It can easily be demonstrated that illegal aliens
must displace American workers, although counteracting
effects do occur due to the complimentarity of illegal and
American workers and due to the effects of illegal workers
on local demand. Because illegal aliens generally tend
to be unskilled, they compete in the labor market with
low-wage American workers, principally blacks, Mexican
Americans, and teenagers.

The measurement of the net effects of the presence of
illegal alien workers must await a detailed empirical
analysis of the problem. However, immigration policy directed at greatly reducing the flow of illegal alien labor
into this country will have dramatic labor-force effects,
and many of these effects will be localized.

Three aspects of policy on the demand-side of the labor
market seem particularly relevant: economic development
programs, alterations in minimum-wage laws, and public
service employment.

Whether inadequate aggregate demand or structural factors play a greater role in causing unemployment has been
debated for some time. The Economic Development Administration (1976) financed a study that used National Planning
Association state employment projections to estimate the
number of state-specific jobs required in 1980 and in 1985
to reduce state-specific unemployment rates alternatively
to 6 percent, 5 percent, and 4 percent. If we assume that
macroeconomic policies will reduce the unemployment rate
of each state to 6 percent in 1985, we may, using these
estimates, calculate the number of additional jobs that
would be needed between 1980 and 1985 in each region to
reduce the region's unemployment rate to 4 percent. This
2-percentage-point reduction would presumably have to be
accomplished through structural economic policies.

The estimates indicate that the following number of
jobs would be required to reduce unemployment rates from
6 percent to 4 percent in each region for the period 1980
to 1985: Northeast, 978,000; North Central, 1,224,000;
South, 1,454,000; and West, 824,000. Nationally, 4,480,000
additional jobs would be required. If we assume an average
annual cost of $10,000 per job, which is a rough estimate
of the present average cost of a public service job, almost
$45 billion would be necessary in 1985 alone (assuming no

secondary effects, which is probably unrealistic given magnitudes of this kind) to reduce the unemployment rate by 2 percentage points. Although a number of criticisms can be made of the employment estimates and of the technique used to derive the $45 billion figure, the expenditures required to achieve even modest increases in employment and decreases in unemployment are tremendous. A similar estimate of the cost of reducing the unemployemnt and underemployment rate of black males, 16-24 years old, from the current 37.0 percent to 10 percent is $4.24 billion.

Because programs such as public service employment would require ongoing expenditures of tremendous magnitudes. manpower programs, in combination with economic development programs, are more likely to be used to deal with long-term problems of local distress. The magnitudes so far discussed are slight relative to those that would be required in the unfortunate instance that an attempt were made to reverse the major spatial employment trends discussed herein.

In a recent discussion paper prepared by the Economic Development Administration (1977, p. II-4), economic development programs are defined as "the planned investment of public resources to attract private investment to specific areas and communities in order to create permanent private sector jobs and strengthen local private economies." A distinction is made between "general development programs, which are parts of various federal activities that have primary objectives other than subnational economic development but nevertheless have local economic development consequence as by-products, and "economic development programs," whose primary objective is local economic development. Federal economic development programs are shown to be a relatively small fraction of federal development programs--about 13 percent, as indicated in Table 14.

The Economic Development Administration paper sensibly argues that economic development financing is currently and probably will remain sufficiently low such that when spread across many areas and communities, it produces only minimal effects in any given locality. However, if economic development programs are coordinated with the more sizeable general development programs, such as those indicated in Table 14, significant beneficial effects may be forthcoming. For example, by coordinating economic development programs, manpower programs, and housing programs, the federal government might contribute meaningful relief to central-city minorities.

Harrison (1974) and others have made strong cases for ghetto or for central-city economic development programs

to assist the immobile, or at least the less mobile,
central-city minorities. Such programs would probably
have the greatest success if they were coordinated with
general development programs, as recommended by the Economic Development Administration. The employment impacts
of these programs cannot easily be forecast because the
impacts differ greatly by specific type of program. Moreover, much uncertainty exists regarding the average cost
of job creation through economic development programs.
If the average cost were $10,000 per job, then approximately
446,000 permanent jobs could be created via economic development programs, given the estimated fiscal 1978 expenditures. This average cost must be unrealistically low, for
if $10,000 were a reasonable estimate, Congress would have
learned long ago that economic development programs are
too good to disregard as a means of relieving unemployment.

Because the decline of the manufacturing sector in the
central cities of the major metropolitan areas of the
Northeast and North Central regions has contributed appreciably to central-city problems, one is tempted to conclude
that central-city economic development programs should be
oriented toward manufacturing employment. However, if
Steinnes (1977) is correct that people are moving away from
manufacturing employment, programs to encourage manufacturing employment growth in central cities could be partially
self-defeating.

Finally, alterations in the minimum-wage legislation
could have appreciable effects on employment, particularly
on teenage employment. Ragan (1977) has concluded that
federal minimum-wage legislation significantly reduces
youth (16-19 years old) employment and raises youth unemployment rates. Nonwhite males are particularly affected.
He estimates that if the 1966 minimum-wage amendments had
not been implemented, youth employment would have been
225,000 persons higher in 1972. However, it should be
recognized that many illegal alien workers now satisfy
the demand for subminimum wage labor. The implications
of youth employment for interregional migration are not
great. However, the implications for employment of black
young people in central cities are potentially great, and
thus the issue seems relevant.

Several of the policy alternatives mentioned above would
have greater effect on the migration decisions of persons
with low incomes than on the decisions of persons with
higher incomes. Policies that operate directly on individual incentives frequently are of this type, whereas policies
that operate indirectly on incentives generally influence

TABLE 14 Federal Development Assistance: Fiscal 1978 Estimates (in millions of dollars)

Department/Agency	General Development Amount	%	Economic Development Amount	%
HUD	3,600	12.0	550[a]	12.3
USDA	5,780	19.4	927[b]	20.8
DOC				
EDA			400	9.0
OMBE			11	.3
NOAA/OCZM	27	.1		
DOL (CETA)			1,880[c]	42.2
DOD				
Economic Adjustment			NA	
Corps of Engineers	50	.2		
DOT (FHA, UMTA)	10,500	35.2		
ARC			300	6.7
Title V Regional Commissions			100[d]	2.2
BIA	650	2.2	150[e]	3.4
CSA	358	1.2	42	.9
EPA (Sewers)	4,500	15.1		
SBA	3,100	10.4	100[f]	2.2
FAA	550	1.8		
TVA	45	.2		
GSA	12	.0		
HEW	650	2.2		
Total	29,867	100.0	4,459	100.0

[a] Assumes that 10 percent of the Community Development Block Grant ($4 billion) is used for economic development purposes. Also includes $150 million of federal disaster assistance. Does not include proposed funding for the Urban Development Action Grant.

[b] Includes emergency adjustment, aid to Indian areas and Community Facilities Loans which include activities not necessarily directed at economic development.

[c] Excludes funding for Public Services Employment in Titles II and VI. Includes only Title I which provides funding for job training in the private sector.

[d] Includes only Industrial/Business Development Grant and Loan Program and Disaster Relief Programs.

[e] Includes only the Community Economic Development Program, Emergency Energy Conservation Program, and grants for State Economic Opportunity Centers.

[f] Includes only disaster relief funding and aid to minority/disadvantaged small businessmen.

SOURCE: Economic Development Administration (1977).

the migration decisions of a broad spectrum of society. Subsidized moving costs, subsidized housing, public employment, manpower programs, changes in minimum-wage requirements, and changes in welfare requirements are all likely to have their greatest impacts on the low-income population. The availability of tax incentives and of information would presumably be of some importance to all potential migrants, regardless of income level. Similarly, economic development programs, planning programs, and reductions in local disamenities should benefit both low-income and high-income persons. The labor-supply effects of more restrictive enforcement of immigration laws would be most beneficial for workers in occupations with lower wages, but in a broader sense much of society would be affected, either positively or negatively, by more restrictive enforcement.

Although economic development programs do not directly influence the low-income and disadvantaged populations, such programs do have "trickle down" effects on the target populations. Chinitz (1971, p. 25) makes the case for economic development programs by arguing that the "welfare of an individual...depends on the environment in which he lives as well as his own attributes, assets, and skills." Economic development programs and other programs that yield potential benefits to a broad spectrum of society, if used in conjunction with programs that impact more directly on the disadvantaged population, would result in a more "normal" population composition in the various localities because the programs would appeal to a wide variety of persons.

Localized programs that tend to benefit only the disadvantaged population can have the undesirable side effect of encouraging the disadvantaged to concentrate in specific localities, such as in the central cities of the major metropolitan areas. Such concentrations of low-income persons can spur high-income persons to leave in order to avoid the effects of various local programs on income redistribution. As a consequence, the local public sector is placed under considerable strain. Hence, a balanced policy approach seems essential. This balance must be struck not only within the framework of employment policy, but also between employment policy and other forms of policy.

SUMMARY

The regional changes in population and employment that occurred between 1970 and 1975 are generally consistent

with those that have occurred during the post World War II
era. The rates of population and employment growth have
been highest in the West and the South and lowest in the
Northeast and North Central regions.

However, during the 1965-1975 period, young people and
women entered the labor force in far greater numbers than
they had in the past. Because there are absolutely and
relatively more young CLF members and because migration
rates are especially high among the young, during the past
10 years interregional migration streams have been more
heavily weighted with young labor-force members. This
phenomenon should moderate after 1980.

The recession of 1974-1975 had particularly severe consequences in the older industrial areas of the Northeast
and, to a lesser extent, in those of the North Central region. After experiencing unusually rapid employment growth
between 1965 and 1969, the Northeast suffered an absolute
decline in employment between 1969 and 1975. The large,
young, and mobile age cohort in the Northeast thus had the
added migration incentive of fewer employment opportuniiites.
Furthermore, migration of southern blacks to the Northeast
decreased while migration of northeastern blacks to the
South increased. Perhaps partially as a result of employment conditions in the Northeast, the historical net flow
of blacks from the South to the Northeast reversed over
the 1970-1975 period. It is unclear whether this reversal
will continue when more "normal" employment conditions are
established in the Northeast.

Differentials in the interregional and intraurban impacts
of national recessions emphasize the importance of macroeconomic policies to achieve and maintain full employment.
Public policy should not be directed at the reversal of
major trends in the interregional or intraurban distribution of employment and population. Not only would such
attempts be inordinately costly, but to the extent that
they were successful, serious distortions in resource allocation and social well-being could result.

There is, however, justification for public intervention in local or regional economies in order to deal with
mobility-related problems. Intervention might appropriately
be directed at correcting or preventing externalities that
result from migration, at alleviating distress among the
less mobile persons in society, and at improving the efficiency of local and regional labor markets and of the
migration mechanism. Alterations in minimum-wage legislation have potentially sizeable effects on black teenage
employment. More restrictive immigration laws would

probably have important effects on minority employment in
the Southwest and the West and in the central cities of
major metropolitan areas, such as New York, Chicago, and
Los Angeles; but whether more restrictive policies are
beneficial for society as a whole is unclear. A combination of employment and other policies that encourages population growth that is demographically and economically
balanced seems appropriate.

REFERENCES

Abrams, E., and Abrams, F. S. (1975) Immigration policy--
    who gets in and why? *The Public Interest* (Winter):3-29.
Allaman, P. M., Birch, D. L. (1975) Components of
    Employment Change for States by Industry Group, 1970-
    1972. Working Paper No. 5, Joint Center for Urban
    Studies.
Blanco, C. (1963) The determinants of interstate popula-
    tion movements. *Journal of Regional Science* 5(Summer):
    77-84.
Borts, G. H., and Stein, J. L. (1964) *Economic Growth in
    a Free Market*. New York: Columbia University Press.
Bowen, W. G., and Finegan, T. A. (1969) *The Economics of
    Labor Force Participation*. Princeton, N.J.: Princeton
    University Press.
Briggs, V. M., Jr. (1975) Illegal aliens: the need for
    a more restrictive border policy. *Social Science Quar-
    terly* 56(December):477-484.
Burrows, J. C., Metcalf, C. E., and Kaler, J. B. (1971)
    Industrial Location in the United States. Lexington,
    Mass.: Heath Lexington Books.
Chinitz, B. (1971) National policy for regional develop-
    ment. Pp. 21-39 in J. F. Kain and J. R. Meyer, eds.,
    Essays in Regional Economics. Cambridge, Mass.: Harvard
    University Press.
Dagodag, T. W. (1975) Source regions and composition of
    illegal Mexican immigration to California. *Interna-
    tional Migration Review* 9(Winter):499-511.
DeJong, G. F. (1975) Population redistribution policies:
    alternatives from the Netherlands, Great Britain, and
    Israel. *Social Science Quarterly* 56(September):262-273.
Economic Development Administration (1976) *Estimated Em-
    ployment Expansion Required for Full Employment, 1976,
    1980, and 1985 - by State*.
Economic Development Administration (1977) The Development
    of a Subnational Economic Development Policy. Unpub-
    lished staff paper. Washington, D.C.

1977 Employment and Training Report of the President (1977)
U.S. Department of Health, Education, and Welfare, and
U.S. Department of Labor. Washington, D.C.: U.S.
Government Printing Office.

Evans, V. J., and Vestal, B. (1977) Local growth management: a demographic perspective. *North Carolina Law
Review* 55(March):421-460.

Fuchs, V. R. (1962a) *Changes in the Location of Manufacturing in the United States Since 1929.* New Haven:
Yale University Press.

Fuchs, V. R. (1962b) Statistical explanations of the rela-
tive shift of manufacturing among regions of the United
States. *Papers and Proceedings of the Regional Science
Association* 8:106-126.

Fullerton, H. N., Jr., and Flaim, P. O. (1976) New labor
force projections to 1990. *Monthly Labor Review* 99
(December):3-13.

Gerking, S. D., and Greenwood, M. J. (1977) Illegal Aliens
in the United States: Who enjoys the Benefits and Who
Bears the Costs? Paper presented at the NIH-INS Belmont
Conference on Illegal Aliens, Belmont, Md.

Greenston, P., and Snead, C. E. (1976) A Selected Review
of Urban Economic Developments. Report prepared for
the Economic Development Administration by The Urban
Institute.

Greenwood, M. J. (1975a) A simultaneous equations model
of urban growth and migration. *Journal of the American
Statistical Association* 70 (December):797-810.

Greenwood, M. J. (1975b) Research on internal migration
in the United States: a survey. *Journal of Economic
Literature* 13(June):397-433.

Harrison, B. (1974) *Urban Economic Development.* Washington, D.C.: The Urban Institute.

Jackson, J. E., and Solomon, A. P. (no date) Urban and
Regional Development: A Critical Review of the Litera-
ture. Report prepared for the Economic Development
Administration.

Kain, J. F. (1968a) Housing segregation, Negro employment,
and metropolitan decentralization. *Quarterly Journal
of Economics* 82(May):175-197.

Kain, J. F. (1968b) The distribution and movement of jobs
and industry. Pp. 2-39 in J. Wilson, ed., *The Metropolitan Enigma.* Cambridge, Mass.: Harvard University
Press.

Kain, J. F., and Persky, J. L. (1971) The North's stake
in southern rural poverty. Pp. 243-278 in J. F. Kain
and J. R. Meyer, eds., *Essays in Regional Economics.*
Cambridge, Mass.: Harvard University Press.

Kuznets, S. (1964) Introduction: population redistribution, migration, and economic growth. In H. T. Eldridge and D. S. Thomas, eds., *Population Redistribution and Economic Growth: United States, 1870-1950.* Vol. III, *Demographic Analysis and Interrelations.* Philadelphia, Pa.: The American Philosophical Society.

Lansing, J. B., and Mueller, E. (1967) *The Geographic Mobility of Labor.* Ann Arbor, Mich.: Institute for Social Research, University of Michigan.

Lansing, J. B., and Morgan, J. N. (1967) The effect of geographical mobility on income. *Journal of Human Resources* 2(Fall):449-460.

Mills, E. S. (1970) Urban density functions. *Urban Studies* 7(February):5-20.

Mooney, J. D. (1969) Housing segregation, Negro Employment and metropolitan decentralization: an alternative perspective. *Quarterly Journal of Economics* 83(May):299-311.

Muth, R. F. (1971) Migration: chicken or egg. *Southern Economic Journal* 37(January):295-306.

Nafziger, J. A. R. (1975) Undocumented Aliens. Paper presented at the Regional Meeting of the International Association of Law.

Ragan, J. F., Jr. (1977) Minimum wages and the youth labor market. *Review of Economics and Statistics* 59(May):129-136.

Romans, J. T. (1974) Benefits and burdens of migration (with specific reference to the brain drain). *Southern Economic Journal* 40(January):447-455.

Steinnes, D. N. (1977) Causality and intraurban location. *Journal of Urban Economics* 4(January):69-79

Sternlieb, G., and Hughes, J. W. (1977) New regional and metropolitan realities of America. *Journal of the American Institute of Planners* 43(July):227-241.

Sundquist, J. L. (1975) *Dispersing Population: What America Can Learn from Europe.* Washington, D.C.: The Brookings Institution.

Thompson, W. R., and Mattila, J. M. (1959) *An Econometric Model of Postwar State Industrial Development.* Detroit, Mich.: Wayne State University Press.

Thurow, L. (1970) *Investment in Human Capital.* Belmont, Calif.: Wadsworth Publishing Company, Inc.

U.S. Bureau of Economic Analysis (1975) *Regional Employment by Industry, 1940-70.* Washington, D.C.: U.S. Department of Commerce.

U.S. Bureau of Labor Statistics (1977) *Employment and Earnings: States and Areas 1939-1975.* Washington, D.C.: U.S. Department of Labor.

U.S. Bureau of Labor Statistics (various years) *Employment and Earnings*. Washington, D.C.: U.S. Department of Labor.

U.S. Bureau of the Census (1962) Marital status and living arrangements, March 1962. Series P-20, No. 122 in *Current Population Reports*. Washington, D.C.: U.S. Department of Commerce.

U.S. Bureau of the Census (1966) Mobility of the population of the United States, March 1965 to March 1966. Series, P-20, No. 156 in *Current Population Reports*. Washington, D.C.: U.S. Department of Commerce.

U.S. Bureau of the Census (1970) Marital status and living arrangements, March 1970. Series P-20, No. 212 in *Current Population Reports*. Washington, D.C.: U.S. Department of Commerce.

U.S. Bureau of the Census (1973a) Lifetime and recent migration. Subject reports PC(2)-2D in *Census of Population: 1970*. Washington, D.C.: U.S. Department of Commerce.

U.S. Bureau of the Census (1973b) Mobility for metropolitan areas. Subject reports PC(2)-2C in *Census of Population: 1970*. Washington, D.C.: U.S. Department of Commerce.

U.S. Bureau of the Census (1975a) Fertility of American women, 1975. Series P-20, No. 301 in *Current Population Reports*. Washington, D.C.: U.S. Department of Commerce.

U.S. Bureau of the Census (1975b) Marital status and living arrangements, March 1975. Series P-20, No. 287 in *Current Population Reports*. Washington, D.C.: U.S. Department of Commerce.

U.S. Bureau of the Census (1975c) Mobility of the population of the United States, March 1970 to March 1975. Series P-20, No. 285 in *Current Population Reports*. Washington, D.C.: U.S. Department of Commerce.

U.S. Bureau of the Census (various years) Estimates of the population of states. Series P-25 in *Current Population Reports*. Washington, D.C.: U.S. Department of Commerce.

U.S. Bureau of the Census (various years) *U.S. Census of Business*. Washington, D.C.: U.S. Department of Commerce.

U.S. Bureau of the Census (various years) *U.S. Census of Manufactures*. Washington, D.C.: U.S. Department of Commerce.

U.S. Bureau of the Census (various years) *U.S. Census of Population*. Washington, D.C.: U.S. Department of Commerce.

U.S. Department of Housing and Urban Development (1976)
   1976 Report on National Growth and Development. Wash-
   ington, D.C.: U.S. Department of Housing and Urban
   Development.
Vaughan, R. J. (1977) *The Urban Impacts of Federal Policies*
   Vol. 2. *Economic Development.* Report R-2028-KF/RC.
   Santa Monica, Calif.: RAND.
Vernez, G., Vaughan, R., Burright, B., and Coleman, S.
   (1977) *Regional Cycles and Employment Effects on Public
   Works Investments.* Report prepared by the RAND Corp.
   for the Economic Development Administration. Santa
   Monica, Calif.: RAND.
Wertheimer, R. F., III (1970) *The Monetary Rewards of
   Migration Within the U.S.* Washington, D.C.: The Urban
   Institute.
Wheat, L. F. (1973) *Regional Growth and Industrial Loca-
   tion.* Lexington, Mass.: Lexington Books.

DEMOGRAPHIC CHANGE, NEW LOCATION PATTERNS, AND TRANSPORTATION POLICY

Gary R. Fauth and *Jose A. Gomez-Ibanez*

INTRODUCTION

Location and demographic changes may have a substantial
effect on federal policy formulation over the next 10-20
years. Geographic shifts of jobs and residences from the
central cities to the suburbs, from larger to smaller metropolitan areas, and from the Northeast to the Sun Belt cities
of the West and South are expected to continue. Important
demographic changes anticipated include declining average
household size, due to higher divorce rates, lower fertility, and other factors; increasing average age of household members due to the passing of the postwar-baby boom
and to declining fertility; and increasing labor-force
participation, particularly of women.

These expected changes have two potential implications
for U.S. transportation policy. First, the changes might
aggravate or mitigate particular U.S. transportation problems and thus influence the policies designed to solve them.
Second, U.S. transportation policies might be called upon
to arrest or slow the shifts in population between central
cities and suburbs and among regions because such shifts
are viewed by many analysts as having undesirable consequences.

We expect neither of these potential impacts to be realized. In brief, we argue that the effect of expected geographic and location changes on transportation problems
in the near future is likely to be relatively modest and
that the response of transportation policy should be

Gary R. Fauth and Jose A. Gomez-Ibanez are both Associate
Professors, Department of City and Regional Planning,
Harvard University.

169

correspondingly small. Future transportation policy will
be molded principally in reaction to other developments,
such as rising per capita incomes. We also argue that
transportation policy should not be used to control or
arrest these new location trends. Whether such control
is socially desirable, it cannot be effectively established
through transportation policy, which has very limited leverage over decisions governing residential and business locations.

These arguments are developed in the following two
sections. The first section assesses how the demographic
and location changes will affect the basic transportation
trends or problems and thus the transportation policies
designed to solve these problems. Because urban transportation, intercity freight, and intercity passenger sectors
each have distinct trends that require different policies,
each will be considered separately here. The second section critically examines the reasons for using transportation policy to control or reduce the expected shifts in
population location.

THE IMPACT OF DEMOGRAPHIC AND LOCATION PATTERNS ON URBAN
PASSENGER TRANSPORTATION

Recent Urban Travel Trends and Policy Reactions

Two important travel trends have influenced postwar urban
transportation policy: (1) the rise in automobile ownership and use, and (2) the decline in patronage of public
transit systems. As Figure 1 shows, the number of automobiles registered in the United States grew from 25.7
million to 106.1 million between 1945 and 1975. The rate
of growth in registration was highest in the late 1940s and
early 1950s, when it averaged 7.3 percent per year. But
even in the 1960s and 1970s automobile ownership was increasing at the rapid pace of about 3.7 percent per year.
The number of vehicle-miles of automobile travel has kept
pace with automobile registrations, growing (as Figure 1
illustrates) from 250 billion in the 1940s to 1,028 billion
in 1975.

The decline in urban mass transit patronage has mirrored
the rise in automobile use. Between 1946, when patronage
was at its postwar high, and 1975, annual transit ridership
fell from 19 billion revenue passengers to 5.6 billion
revenue passengers. As Figure 2 shows, the sharpest declines in transit patronage occurred before 1955. In the

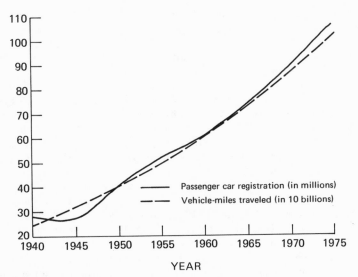

FIGURE 1   Passenger car registration and passenger-car-miles of travel in the United States, 1940-1975.

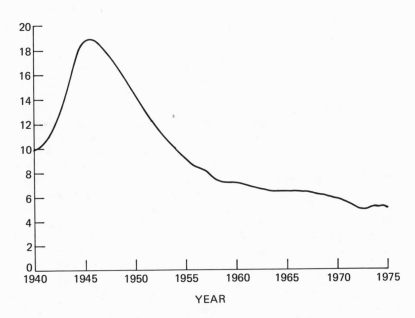

FIGURE 2   Transit revenue passengers carried (in billions), 1940-1975   (American Public Transit Association, various years).

1960s ridership declined at an average annual rate of 2.2
percent per year and since 1973 patronage has been holding
roughly stable.

As a result of these trends, the automobile has come to
dominate urban passenger travel. The automobile is by far
the most popular mode for the journey to work: in 1970,
82 percent of all work trips were made by automobile while
only 14 percent were made by public transit. (The remaining 4 percent of commuters walked or used other modes of
travel) (U.S. Bureau of the Census 1972). Automobiles are
used for an even higher percentage of urban trips that are
not related to work.

Government policies pertaining to increased automobile
use and declining transit ridership have evolved over the
postwar period. In the 1940s and 1950s, the principal
policy for ameliorating growing traffic congestion was expansion of the highway system. Disenchantment with this
approach spread in the late 1950s, largely because highway
construction often involved the destruction of urban neighborhoods and because the new highways still suffered from
congestion (although they also carried much higher volumes
of traffic). The early 1960s saw increased efforts to
support urban mass transit, with the initiation of federal
assistance for transit and the planning and construction
of new rail transit systems in several metropolitan areas.
The emphasis on mass transit was reinforced when automobile
air pollution and energy consumption were identified as
problems in the late 1960s and early 1970s. Recently, however, there has been growing skepticism about relying on
transit to solve urban transportation problems, largely
because of the failure of transit subsidies and new transit
systems to attract appreciable numbers of automobile users
from their vehicles. Current urban transportation policy
incorporates an increasingly sophisticated blend of pre-
scriptions to ameliorate the problems of increased automobile use, including support for modest improvements to
highways, aid to mass transit, and direct regulation of
new car pollutant emissions and energy efficiency.

The federal government still provides substantial assistance for urban highway construction but now requires that
states and cities show they are efficiently using and man-
aging their existing facilities before they receive aid
for new construction. Management techniques encouraged
by the federal government include reserved bus and car-pool
lanes and other techniques to give high-occupancy vehicles
priority in traffic, metering the ramps of limited-access
highways to prevent the development of stop-and-go-traffic,

and higher parking charges or other restraint measures in
severely congested downtown areas.

To assist the declining transit industry, the federal
government currently has two major grant programs: one for
capital expenses and the other for operating expenses.
Capital grants are distributed on a project basis and pay
up to 80 percent of the cost of transit capital improvements. Local governments applying for capital grants to
fund expensive new rail transit systems or extensions must
show that they have adequately examined less costly alternatives, such as bus transit systems. Operating grants are
distributed among metropolitan areas according to a con-
gressionally mandated formula and require at least 50 percent matching assistance from local governments. The
federal government also sponsors demonstrations of innova-
tive services, such as demand-responsive transit (dial-a-
ride), to explore new methods of competing with the automobile in low-density areas.

Among the most significant recent urban transportation
policies are federal regulations governing the emissions
and energy consumption of new cars. The federal government began regulating pollution emissions in 1965, when
Congress passed legislation requiring that 1970 model-year
cars emit only 50 percent of the HC and CO per mile emitted
by 1957-1967 uncontrolled models. The Clean Air Act of 1970
set a staged timetable for further pollution reductions,
with a 90-percent reduction in 1970 model-year emissions of
HC, CO, and NO_x to be achieved by 1976. Congress has extended the deadlines of the 1970 Clean Air Act several times,
but substantial progress has been made. The 1977 cars emit
only 17 percent of the HC and CO and 57 percent of the NO_x
of 1957-1967 model-year vehicles.

In 1975 Congress passed mandatory average fuel-efficiency
standards for each manufacturer's new-car fleets, which would
raise average new car fuel economy by 80 percent in 10 years
--from about 15 miles per gallon (mpg) in 1975 to 27.5 mpg
in 1985. Debate about the practicality of the congressional
timetable has been heated but there is mounting evidence
that by 1985 significant gains in new-car fuel economy will
be feasible through reduction in the weight of standard and
large cars, improvement in drivetrains and gearboxes, and
some substitution of smaller automobiles for larger ones.

Future Urban Travel Trends

Both the increase in overall urban travel and the shift
from public transit to automobile are likely to

continue at about the same rates as in the recent past
because the underlying factors that caused these travel
trends are long-standing and likely to be present in the
future.

Two important factors that will continue to encourage
overall growth in urban travel are population expansion
and increases in real income per household. Although the
growth in the number of households residing in urban areas
is expected to be slower than the 2-percent average annual
gains experienced in the 1950s and 1960s, some growth is
still expected. Most forecasts assume that the number of
urban households will increase at a rate of around 1.7 percent per year in the future. Households with higher real
incomes, all other things being equal, travel more frequently
within metropolitan areas. Although the future rate of
growth in household real income is uncertain, gains over
the long term are likely to be similar to those experienced
in the past. Therefore, real income per household will
probably grow at an average annual rate of 2-3 percent.

This increase in real income, along with shifts in the
locations of residences and employment, will continue to
encourage growth of automobile travel rather than growth
of mass transit. The steady increase in real incomes over
the postwar period is considered the most important cause
of the decline of public transit and the rise of the
automobile. Between 1947 and 1975, real incomes per household grew by a remarkable 88 percent. As incomes grow,
people are willing and able to pay for the amenities more
commonly associated with the automobile than with public
transportation. Especially important are door-to-door
convenience, instant availability, and faster speeds that
conserve on traveler time. Moreover, rising incomes affect
public transportation operators adversely by increasing the
wages necessary to attract drivers and other qualified
personnel. Public transportation costs are more sensitive
to wage increases than are the costs of automobile use,
because public transportation drivers must be paid.

The second cause of the shift from mass transit to automobiles has been the shift in the location of residences and
employment: population and employment are growing more
rapidly in the suburbs than in the central cities, in smaller
metropolitan areas than in larger ones, and in the South
and Southwest than in the Northeast. These shifts in
population are caused by a variety of complex factors:
growth in real income, which encourages the purchase of
larger and newer homes, particularly in the suburbs;
changes in production technology, such as the one-story

plant; and transportation developments, such as widespread use of the truck and the postwar construction of highways. The shift of residences and jobs from the central cities to the suburbs has contributed to the shift from public transportation to the automobile because conventional mass transit is not well suited for serving families that live and work in dispersed locations. In addition, the suburbs, smaller metropolitan areas, and the cities of the Sun Belt generally have newer and more extensive highway systems with lower levels of congestion, which encourage automobile use.

Some analysts have argued that future increases in energy prices and government regulations governing the emissions, energy consumption, and safety of new cars may increase the cost of automobile use and thereby slow the growth in urban travel in general and the shift from mass public transit to auto in particular. The role of energy, air pollution, and safety problems in determining automobile ownership and use has probably been exaggerated, especially for the near future. The cost of owning and operating an automobile may be only slightly increased, and the fundamental attractions of the automobile, such as shorter travel time, door-to-door service, instant availability, and privacy, will remain unchanged. Energy problems are likely to have a greater impact on urban passenger travel patterns in the long run; even then, however, improved energy sources and propulsion technologies may make continued dominance of some auto-like transportation mode possible.[1]

---

[1]Energy problems may not have a large impact on car sales for the next 10 years. It appears that new-car fuel economy will be greatly improved over the next decade, as a result of the law passed by Congress in 1975. Because the fuel economy improvements add relatively little to the purchase price of the car and because reduced gasoline consumption will at least partially offset expected increases in fuel prices, the cost of owning and operating an automobile may be only slightly increased.

Air-pollution and safety regulations may have a similarly modest effect on automobile ownership in the near future, although it is difficult to be sure because of uncertainties about the exact policies that the government will pursue, the technologies that will be available, and their costs. The only major pending pollution regulation change is

The Role of Expected Demographic and Location Changes

Although population and income growth will have major effect
on automobile and mass public transit use, expected demographic changes will have only minor impacts. Demographic
changes may contribute to small increases in urban travel
and may slightly offset the general shift from automobile
to mass public transit. The declining average household
size, the increasing average age of households, and the
increased rates of labor-force participation all cause
increases in the number of trips made per capita. Increasing numbers of elderly households and increased labor-force
participation may shift travelers away from automobile use
because many members of elderly households are too old to
drive and because the second worker in a two-worker household often uses mass public transit instead of buying a
second car.

A recent study for the U.S. Department of Transportation
confirms our conclusion that anticipated location and demographic changes will be relatively unimportant, compared
with income and population growth, in determining future
urban passenger travel (Kain et al. 1977). A sample of
307,000 households in the 125 largest U.S. standard metropolitan statistical areas (SMSAs) was analyzed to determine
the extent to which particular variables influence the number of cars a household owns and the mode of transportation that household workers use for commuting. The variable
examined in the study are: real household income; family
structure (such as household size, the age, race, and sex
of the head of household, and the numbers of workers and
driving-age adults; the location of residence and employment (central city or other); and the amount of highway
and transit service in the metropolitan area. Results

----

imposition of a stricter NO_x standard, which has already
been delayed several times and is now scheduled for the
1981 model year. The costs of meeting the new standard
will probably not exceed several hundred dollars per new
car. The only major new automotive safety requirement
being contemplated for the near term is the airbag, which,
according to current timetables, will be required in all
new models by 1984. The auto industry and the government
differ in their estimates of airbag costs, but it is likely
to be only $200. (Federal Task Force on Motor Vehicle
Goals Beyond 1980, 1976, Wildhorn et al. 1975).

from this analysis were used to forecast the number of cars per household and the number of workers commuting by automobile between 1970 and 1990.

The forecasts, shown in Table 1, indicate that between 1970 and 1990, location shifts will cause slight increases in the average number of cars per household and the percentage of persons commuting by automobile, while demographic changes will decrease automobile dependence, although by a smaller amount. As a result of both location and demographic changes, the number of automobiles per household can be expected to increase by 1 percent (from 1.24 to 1.25), and the proportion of workers commuting by automobile can be expected to increase by 1 percent (from 78.6 to 79.5).

The estimated effects of the demographic and location shifts on automobile use are relatively small when compared with the effects caused by increases in income. Growth in real household income, assumed to be 3 percent per year, will cause the number of cars per household to increase by 13 percent (from 1.24 to 1.42).

The calculations in Table 1 are averages for a typical household. If the number of households increases at an annual rate of 1.7 percent per year, as anticipated, then increases in the numbers of households alone should cause

TABLE 1 Projected 1970-1990 Changes in Household Automobile Ownership and Percentage of Workers Commuting by Automobile

	Average Number of Autos Owned per Household	Percentage of Workers Commuting by Auto
1970	1.24	78.6
1990 Change caused by location shifts	+.03	+1.4
1990 Change caused by demographic factors	-.02	-0.5
1990 Change caused by income gains[a]	+.165	+3.4
1990 With all changes	1.42	82.9

[a]Growth in real household income was assumed to be 3 percent per year.

SOURCE: Kain et al. (1977).

automobile ownership to rise by 40 percent from 1970 to
1990.

Policy Implications

The anticipated demographic and location trends will have
some impact on urban transportation policy, since they will
affect the urban travel patterns that condition that policy.
However, since the demographic and location changes are not
the prime determinants of urban transportation patterns,
they should not play a primary role in determining transportation policy.

The current population trend toward less centralized
living patterns will reduce transit ridership, and probably
increase transit operating deficits. As a result, pressure
will be directed at federal, state, and local governments
to provide additional operating subsidies. Public policy
should respond to this pressure cautiously, because there
is increasing evidence that transit operating subsidies
are not effective means to reduce pollution and congestion,
conserve energy, or generate other claimed social benefits
(Hilton 1974, Ingram and Fauth 1974).

Government should respond to pressure for added transit
subsidies with programs that encourage operators to improve
productivity and control costs. Numerous opportunities to
improve the productivity of urban mass transit can be identified and could be facilitated by appropriate federal
responses (Gomez-Ibanez and Meyer 1978). For example,
benefits might be derived from increased federal support
for bus priority measures that permit more express operations.

Trends toward more dispersed residential locations may
decrease pressures on federal and local governments to
construct new rail transit systems or extend old systems
in larger metropolitan areas. If there is little or no
growth in the population and, especially, in the number of
downtown jobs in larger metropolitan areas, then the potential ridership on rail systems is likely to be small and,
as a result of income gains, ridership may possibly decline.
The lower the projected ridership, the more difficult it
will be to justify the massive investments required by
rail transit and the more likely it will be that a bus
system will be able to provide comparable or better transit service at lower cost.

Growth in population in smaller metropolitan areas, many
of which currently have little or no public transportation

service other than taxi, may also increase pressure for
transit service in these areas, particularly in the form
of dial-a-ride or demand-responsive services. Like taxis,
dial-a-ride vehicles usually provide door-to-door transportation in response to telephoned requests, but like buses
and rail transit, they also carry different passengers to
different destinations on the same trip. Proponents of
dial-a-ride argue that the mode may be able to compete
effectively with the automobile in low-density areas. However, experience with existing demand-responsive systems
needs to be carefully examined to determine if this promise
can be realized. Frequently, these systems have cost more
than private taxi service even though they have provided
lower levels of service.

Although the shift of population to the suburbs and
smaller metropolitan areas will increase automobile use, it
may also, paradoxically, decrease some of the pressures on
federal and local governments to regulate the impact of the
automobile. For example, if, as newer cars are introduced
into the U.S. urban automobile fleet, the populations of
large metropolitan areas and the numbers of persons traveling to downtown grow only slowly, automobile air-pollution
concentrations should decrease, thereby reducing pressure
for tighter emission standards on new vehicles. Evidence
suggests such a move may be socially desirable (Harrison
1975). Present national targets for mobile sources, especially for NO_x, could be relaxed if stationary sources were
more stringently regulated or if a national two-car strategy
were adopted. Such a strategy would require tight emissions
control only on that portion of the total automobile fleet
that operates in the most polluted air-quality control regions.

Future trends may also result in lower levels of traffic
congestion in large, older metropolitan areas. Such a
change might reduce demands for more intensive use of existing facilities, such as priority for buses and car pools in
street and expressway traffic (Interplan Corp. 1976). U.S.
policy, however, should continue to pursue more efficient
facility management since capacity problems may begin to
appear in smaller metropolitan areas, and since appropriate
prices for use of central-area streets encourage commuters
and shoppers to organize their travel patterns.

THE IMPACT OF DEMOGRAPHIC AND LOCATION PATTERNS ON
INTERCITY FREIGHT TRANSPORTATION

Recent Freight Trends and Policy

Like current urban transporation policy, policy toward intercity freight can be seen largely as a reaction to a few impor
tant trends in intercity freight transporation. Specifically, postwar intercity freight policy has been preoccupied
with the poor financial performance of the railroad industry.
During the postwar period, the rate of return on capital
earned by the railroad industry has been lower than that
earned by most other industries. In recent years, the industry's return has been below 3 percent, less than one-third
the average for all private industry (Meyer and Morton 1974).
    A major part of the railroad industry's problem is that
rail traffic has been growing relatively slowly and that the
growth that has occurred has been profitless. Between 1950
and 1975, revenue ton-miles carried by class I railroads
increased by 32 percent, but operating revenue in real terms
increased by 8 percent and railway operating income (operating revenue less operating expenses) declined in real terms
by 56 percent.
    The slow growth in rail traffic is due partly to slow
growth in freight traffic carried by all modes. Between 1950
and 1975, freight traffic has grown more slowly than the
gross national product (GNP). The number of ton-miles shippe
increased by only 102 percent (from about 1,084 billion to
2,213 billion), while the real GNP increased by 123 percent
(from $533 billion to $1,192 billion in 1972 dollars).
    Nonetheless, as Table 2 shows, the railroads have failed
to maintain their share of intercity freight traffic, particularly of shipments of highly valued commodities for which
profit has traditionally been highest. Although railroad
traffic increased from 597 billion ton-miles in 1950 to 858
billion ton-miles in 1973, the railroads' share of total
intercity freight traffic dropped from 56 percent to 38 percent. During the same period, the portion of intercity
freight ton-miles carried by trucks increased from 16 percent to 23 percent, and the portion carried by pipelines
increased from 12 percent to 23 percent.
    The government, concerned that the declining role of
the railroads may not be socially desirable, has become

[2]For an excellent discussion of the problems of the railroads
and the underlying freight trends, see Morton (1973) and
Task Force on Railroad Productivity (1973).

increasingly involved in helping the railroads. Railroads
may be at a disadvantage in competing with trucks for freight,
because truck operators may not pay the full social costs
of the highways and energy they use or the pollution they
produce. Moreover, the Interstate Commerce Commission's
regulation of railroad and truck tariffs and operating
rights are thought by some to have unduly crippled the railroads' ability to compete with other modes. Finally, even
if some contraction of railroad shipments and services is
desirable, the burdens of the transition, particularly the
loss of rail freight service in small communities, may require some government involvement.

Over the past 20 years, the federal government has assist-
ed the railroads primarily by relaxing government regulatory
restrictions that might hamper the railroads' ability to
compete with other modes. The Transportation Act of 1958,
for example, limited the power of state regulatory authorities to require the continuation of passenger service,
which, according to the railroads, lost money and acted as
a drain on freight operations. The "3Rs" and "4Rs" Rail
Regulatory Reform Acts of the 1970s simplified the procedures
under which railroads can abandon unprofitable branch lines
and slightly reduced the Interstate Commerce Commission's
authority to dictate rail rates.

More recently, the federal government has become directly
involved in subsidizing some rail operations. The federal
government's initial capitalization and subsequent subsi-
dization of Amtrak, the quasi-government corporation now
responsible for operating almost all intercity rail-passenger
service, was the first form of direct government subsidies.
Since then a second government-created and -subsidized corporation, Conrail, has been established to take over the
operations of the Penn Central and several other bankrupt
railroads in the Northeast. The "3Rs" Act also established
a program of grants to allow local governments to subsidize
the continued operation of branch lines that the railroads
wish to abandon.

Although federal government has been concerned with assisting the railroads, it has also continued to provide substantial assistance to competing modes, especially trucks and
barges. During the postwar years, annual expenditures by
federal, state, and local governments for highway construction and maintenance grew from less than $10 billion to
more than $20 billion. Over that same period the Army Corps
of Engineers has spent an average of approximately $650
million per year in constructing and maintaining the
inland waterway system, which is used mainly for freight

TABLE 2 U.S. Intercity Freight Traffic: 1940-1973

Mode	Billions Ton-Miles					Modal Share of Traffic				
	1940	1950	1960	1970	1973	1940	1950	1960	1970	1973
Railroads	379	597	579	771	858	61.3	56.2	44.1	38.7	38.5
Motor trucks	62	173	285	412[a]	505	10.0	16.3	21.8	21.3	20.6
Great Lakes	36	112	99	114[a]	126	15.5	10.5	7.5	6.9	6.6
Inland waterways	22	52	121	205[a]	232	3.6	4.9	9.2	10.6	10.4
Pipelines	49	129	229	431	507	9.5	12.1	17.4	22.3	22.7
Airways	nil	nil	1	3	4	nil	nil	.1	.2	.2

[a]Excludes traffic moving on these waters in ocean-going vessels when part of domestic deep-sea movements.

SOURCE: Transportation Association of America: *Transportation Facts and Trends*, December 1974, p. 3 (as cited in U.S. Department of Transportation 1974, p. 33).

transportation.[3] Barge operators pay no special user fees or taxes to help for the costs of the inland waterway system.

There have been some signs, however, that support for federal programs that assist the intercity trucking and barge industries may be weakening. Over the past decade or more, there has been increasing pressure to assess whether intercity truckers are paying (through license fees and gas and excise taxes) their fair share of the costs of constructing and operating the interstate highway system. Perhaps more significantly, Congress recently refused to authorize an Army Corps of Engineers' proposal to expand a major lock facility on the Mississippi River at Alton, Illinois; and many observers believe that this project will never be authorized unless the barge operators agree to pay fees to help defray some of the costs of constructing and operating the inland waterway system.[4]

Future Freight Trends

Rising per-capita income has been, and probably will continue to be, the major reason that growth in intercity freight has been modest. As per-capita incomes rise, freight grows more slowly than the GNP because a declining share of total income pays for goods with high raw-material inputs, such as agricultural commodities, construction materials, and durable manufactured goods. An increasing proportion of the GNP is used for services that require few material inputs. Furthermore, the weight and raw-material inputs per dollar value of manufactured goods declines, because rising per-capita incomes generate improvements in the quality, design, and variety of such goods but generally do not generate weight.

Rising per-capita incomes and the resulting changes in the types of commodities produced and shipped have also contributed to the decline in the railroads' share of the intercity freight market. Railroads are at a disadvantage in competing with trucks for manufactured goods that have undergone high levels of processing because shippers of such high-value goods generally require frequent, fast, and reliable service that is more commonly associated with trucks. Moreover,

[3]The inland waterway system is also used for recreation; see U.S. Department of Transportation (1977).
[4]After this paper was written, Congress enacted legislation approving the Alton locks and imposing for the first time a system of waterway user charges to help finance the construction and maintenance of waterway systems.

the railroads have had a difficult time competing for bulk
commodities because the major growth in bulk-commodity movements in the postwar period has been in petroleum shipments;
and pipelines are often better suited for transporting
petroleum.

The movement of manufacturing and other plants from central-city to suburban locations has also contributed to the
railroads' declining share of traffic. This trend, which
is expected to continue, is caused by a variety of factors,
including the shift of residences from the central city to
the suburbs; the increases in wage rates that encourage
substitution of floor space for labor; and highway construction that makes suburban locations accessible to trucks
Suburban plants tend to use trucks rather than railroads
because suburban highways tend to be less congested and the
plants are usually far from major rail yards, which tend to
be located in the inner city.

Although the primary causes of slow traffic growth in
the railroad industry are likely to remain, several secondary factors that have slowed railroad traffic growth in the
past may be operating with less force in the near future.
One such factor is the trend toward dispersal of manufacturing plants. As plants become more dispersed, the distance
that final goods must be shipped decreases. (These freight
losses are, however, at least partially offset by longer
raw-material hauls.) The reasons for the dispersal of manufacturing plants are only poorly understood, but some analys
speculate that demographic trends may have been one of many
contributing factors. In particular, the increasing size of
the population and its concentration in urban areas may have
encouraged dispersal by increasing the number of metropolita
areas that are sufficiently large to be profitable as plant
locations. To the extent that concentration of population
and population growth encouraged dispersal of plants in the
past, the anticipated shift of population to smaller metropolitan areas may, in the near future, slow dispersal and
slightly encourage freight traffic. Railroads, however, are
not likely to attract more than a small portion of the added
traffic because the smaller metropolitan areas are probably
well served by highways and trucks.

Another factor that contributed to the past difficulties
of the railroads, but may be slightly less important in the
future, is government assistance for the construction of
highways and inland waterways. As noted earlier, there is
some pressure to reduce government expenditures in this area
or to make increased expenditures contingent on higher user
fees. Whether this pressure will result in any substantial
change in government policy is problematic. It is unlikely

that over the next 10 years public policy will change to
such an extent that the competitive advantages of truckers
or barges will be strongly affected.

In the future, rising energy prices may help the railroads somewhat, but the effect is likely to be small. For
many types of shipments, railroads use somewhat less energy
per ton-mile than trucks. However, increasing energy prices
probably will be of little aid to the railroads in attracting manufactured goods because energy costs are only a small
fraction of total transportation costs for these goods.
Rising energy prices are not likely to help the railroads
attract bulk commodities either because, for many of these
commodities, railroads compete with relatively energy-
intensive modes, notably barges and pipelines. Furthermore,
increases in the price of energy may be sufficient to encourage alternatives to transportation, such as processing
at the mine mouth.

Thus, freight movements will probably continue to grow
slowly and the share of freight carried by the railroads
will probably continue to decline in the near future. Although several factors may encourage somewhat higher freight
growth and a slightly more competitive position for the
railroads, the underlying causes for the decline--especially
rising incomes--are likely to continue into the future.

The Influence of Expected Location and Demographic Changes

Although it is unlikely that expected demographic trends
will have much influence on freight patterns, expected
locational changes may have significant effects, particularly on the railroads. The greatest damage will probably
come from the most long-standing of the location shifts--
the movement of manufacturing and other types of plants
from central-city to suburban locations. The suburbanization of employment will further diminish the ability of
the railroads to attract freight because suburban plants
generally are served by less congested highways and are
located further from rail lines and rail yards.

The movement of population away from the Northeast and
to the West and the South may reduce the volume of bulk-
commodity shipments on which the railroads are increasingly
dependent. Since the postwar period, the West and South
have become the principal sources of raw materials used
for manufacturers. The movement of population to these
regions will probably be accompanied by a shift of manufacturing and a resulting reduction in the distances that
bulk commodities are hauled.

Finally, the shift of population to smaller metropolitan
areas may slightly increase not only total freight shipments
but also the share of freight that goes to trucks. If, in
the past, the concentration of population in large metropolitan areas contributed to the dispersal of manufacturing
and the decrease in shipping, in the future the growth of
smaller population areas may, to some degree, concentrate
manufacturing and increase the amount of manufactured goods
that are transported. However, because these goods have
high values and because these shipments are destined for
areas served by relatively uncongested highways, the railroads are unlikely to capture this new traffic.

Because location changes will have only modest effect on
the railroad industry, they are unlikely to alter intercity
freight policy significantly. To the extent that the new
location trends increase the difficulties of the railroads
and improve the prospects for trucks, they have two possible
implications for current public policy. First, they slightly
diminish the chances for success of recent government attempts to improve the financial position of the railroads.
Conrail, in particular, may be hindered if a reduction in
raw-material shipments into the Northeast accompanies the
shift in population to the West and South. Second, the increase in truck traffic that may result from greater dispersal of population and manufacturing may strengthen the
pressure to spend substantial sums on highway improvements,
particularly in smaller metropolitan centers and nonmetropolitan areas.

THE IMPACT OF LOCATION AND DEMOGRAPHIC CHANGES ON INTERCITY
PASSENGER TRAVEL

Recent Travel Trends and Policies

The postwar trends in intercity passenger travel that have
received the most attention from the federal transportation
policy makers are the steady increase in the total volume of
intercity travel and the changes in the distribution of
passengers among the principal intercity modes. In the postwar period, total domestic intercity passenger-miles grew at
an average annual rate of 4.1 percent: from approximately
508 billion in 1950 to 1,357 billion in 1973. The automobile
continued to be the dominant intercity passenger mode (especially for shorter-length trips): between 1950 and 1973
the automobile's share of intercity passenger-miles remained
reasonably steady at about 87 percent. During the same

period, the airlines' share of passenger-miles grew from
2.0 percent to 10.2 percent while the railroads' share
dropped sharply from 6.4 percent to 0.7 percent and the
bus companies' share fell from 5.2 percent to 2.0 percent
(U.S. Bureau of the Census 1976).

Recent public policy toward intercity passenger travel
has been concerned with preserving a minimum level of railroad passenger service and controlling some of the congestion
and noise pollution caused by the rapid growth of air travel.

Pressure to preserve railroad service is based partly on
the premise that the competing intercity passenger modes,
especially automobiles and airlines, pay only a small share
of the costs of the facilities they use (e.g., the highway,
airports, and airway systems) and the social, environmental,
and energy problems they cause.

Initially, federal and state regulating agencies attempted
to maintain passenger service by denying railroad petitions
to abandon service and by forcing the railroads to cross-
subsidize passenger losses with profits from freight. The
limitations of forced cross-subsidization became apparent
in the 1950s as the railroads' position in the freight market
weakened. In 1972, the federal government created the National Railroad Passenger Corporation, known as Amtrak, to
take over the remaining rail passenger service. Although
Amtrak was expected to break even in a few years, operating
deficits have increased.

The federal government has been active in reducing both
airport congestion and noise. Federal agencies operate the
airport and airways navigation systems and regulate safety,
fares, and other conditions of airline service. Airport
congestion has been abated somewhat through government
grants for airport and landing-system improvements (although
greater improvements resulted from reduced traffic during
the recent recession and the introduction of wide-bodied
jets). Airport noise is being reduced by government regulations that set noise standards for new aircraft and, to a
lesser extent, by newly required procedures for landings and
approaches.

Although federal, state, and local governments all encourage intercity automobile travel through the construction
and upgrading of intercity highways, the federal government
has recently made efforts to reduce some of the social costs
of intercity automobile use. The federal standards governing
air-pollutant emissions and energy conservation for new cars
along with the 55 mph speed limit on the interstate highway
system are the principal policy initiatives in this area.

Future Trends in Intercity Passenger Travel

Many of the factors that caused the recent rapid growth in
intercity passenger travel are long-standing and likely to
continue. The single most important factor accounting for
the rapid postwar growth in passenger travel has been the
growth in per capita income. Households with higher incomes
tend to make many more person-trips, as the figures in
Table 3 show. Population growth has also played an important role in travel growth, accounting for perhaps one-
seventh of the total postwar increase in travel.[5] Substantial reductions in intercity travel times and travel costs
have also contributed to the increase in travel. As Table
4 shows, time and cost reductions were particularly large
for airlines, automobiles, and buses. These reductions
were due primarily to postwar highway construction and technological developments in aircraft, such as the introduction
of pressurized cabins and jets.

TABLE 3   Intercity Passenger Travel by Family Income Level

Family In-come ($)	Percent of All Fami-lies in 1965	Percentage of All Intercity Per-son-Trips in 1967	Relative Trip-Making Rates (less than $4,000 = 100.0)
Less than 4,000	23.8	11.7	100
4,000-5,999	17.2	15.9	188
6,000-7,499 } 7,500-9,999 }	33.7	16.2 } 21.4 }	227
10,000-14,999	17.7	22.3	256
15,000 or more	7.6	12.5	335

SOURCE: Calculated from data in U.S. Bureau of the Census
(1970, pp. 19,20).

[5]Between 1950 and 1973 the U.S. population increased by 38
percent while intercity passenger-miles increased by 267
percent. If population growth causes a proportionate growth
in intercity passenger travel, then population increases
would account for 14 percent of the gain in intercity travel
during postwar years.

TABLE 4   Time Series Characteristics of Automobile, Bus,
Rail, and Air Travel, 1950-1970

Characteristic and Year	Auto	Bus	Rail	Air
Average price per passenger-mile in current cents[a]				
1950	NA	1.89	2.74	5.56
1955	NA	2.05	2.70	5.36
1960	9.76	2.71	3.03	6.09
1965	11.02[b]	2.88	3.14	6.06
1970	11.89	3.60	4.02	5.96
Average speed (mph)				
1950	48.7	49.8	37.4	180
1955	52.0	52.3	39.8	208
1960	53.8	55.5	40.7	235
1965	57.8	57.4	41.3	314
1970	60.6	58.8	40.3	350

[a] Auto entries are not in current (1972) cents.
[b] The 1965 automobile entry is based on a report for 1968.

SOURCES: U.S. Bureau of the Census (1972, p. 548), and U.S.
Department of Transportation (1972) as cited in Miller (1975).

Rising per-capita income also is probably the most important factor in the automobile's continued dominance of
intercity travel. Another factor has been the improvements
in intercity highways, which resulted in increased speeds
for intercity trips. The growth of suburban areas has also
been a factor, because as the result of such growth, the
origins and destinations of increasing numbers of intercity
trips are distant from center-city train and bus stations.

The recent rapid growth in airline travel is also due in
large part to postwar increases in per-capita income. These
increases have permitted more people to take advantage of
the higher speed and convenience offered by air service,
especially for longer trips. Technological improvements
that have greatly improved travel speeds and reduced capital
and operating expenses for airlines have also made significant contributions.

Because of rising incomes and other factors, railroad
passenger service has become unprofitable in all but a few
markets. The most important of these potentially profitable
markets is the Boston-New York-Washington corridor, in which

central cities are large and close to each other. Railroad
service remains competitive in that corridor because the
high volumes of traffic allow convenient, frequent train
service, and because the short distances and congested highways make airlines and automobiles less attractive alternatives, especially for trips between central cities.

In the near future, intercity passenger travel is likely
to continue to grow although the rate of growth may decrease,
and automobiles and airlines are likely to continue to be
the dominant modes. Continued gains in per capita income
will favor automobiles and airplanes. Growth of airline
and automobile use may be slowed somewhat by reduced rates
of technological improvement, higher energy prices, and perhaps lower rates of intercity highway investment, but these
impacts will not be sufficient to offset the growth that
will result from rising real income.

Implications of Expected Location and Demographic Trends

Recent location and demographic trends are unlikely to affect
significantly the growth in intercity travel and the dominance of auto and air. Moreover, any small effect such
trends may have will reinforce existing travel trends.

The dispersal of population to smaller metropolitan areas
may well require persons to make more intercity trips for
business, shopping, and recreational purposes. In 1967, for
example, residents of metropolitan areas averaged only 1.7
person-trips and 1,440 person-miles of intercity travel per
year while residents of nonmetropolitan areas averaged 1.9
person-trips and 1,738 person-miles.[6] Although part of this
difference is probably accounted for by factors other than
location of residence, some small increase in intercity
travel would probably accompany a shift of population out
of larger metropolitan areas. Most of this new traffic
would likely be carried by automobiles or airlines, rather
than by the railroads.

The movement of population to the West and the South
might also slightly decrease intercity travel in the Northeast corridor and thus result in a small decrease in railroad passenger traffic and a slower growth of airline
traffic in Northeast airports, where congestion and noise
problems are generally greater.

[6]Intercity trips are defined as trips of more than 100 miles
that include one or more nights spent away from home. The
data were calculated from U.S. Bureau of the Census (1970).

Demographic changes probably have very minor effects.
Slower population growth due to reduced fertility may reduce intercity travel growth somewhat. However, the effects
of slower population growth may be offset by the expected
increase in the number of people between the ages of 30
and 65 because this age-group shows a greater propensity
toward travel.

The new location patterns and demographic changes are
unlikely to affect intercity passenger policy in any significant way, because their effects on travel are probably
minor and reinforce the travel trends that policy currently
addresses. These changes conceivably have two implications
for policy: if the relatively more isolated and modern
Sun Belt airports are used more intensively than congested
northeastern facilities, noise and congestion at airports
may be slightly easier to control; and demands for highway
and airport expansion may increase in smaller metropolitan
areas.

TRANSPORTATION POLICY AS A MEANS FOR AFFECTING LOCATION
TRENDS

In the past, transporation policy has been viewed largely
as a means of solving problems within the transporation
sector. Increasingly, however, policy makers have been
tempted to use transporation policy to try to correct
other problems, including some that have been created by
recent location trends. The particular location trends
that are most often suggested as appropriate targets for
transportation policy are the migration of people and jobs
from larger metropolitan areas to smaller ones and the migration from central cities to suburbs. Public investments
in new rail transit systems, operating subsidies for bus or
rail transit, and higher tolls or other restraints on automobile use are examples of transportation policies that
are sometimes advocated as means to reduce or reverse migration from larger metropolitan areas and from central
cities.

The use of transportation policy to encourage growth of
large metropolitan areas and central cities is probably
undesirable, if only because the current range of transportation policies appears to be relatively ineffective in
determining the actual rates of city and suburban growth.
Many policy analysts find this hard to believe, because
transportation changes are thought to have been the single

most important factor in shaping the general patterns of
metropolitan development and regional growth. In the past
2 centuries, transportation facilities, such as ports, navigable waterways, and railroads were often decisive determinants of the location of major cities and the rates of
regional growth. The spread of horse and electric street
railways between 1870 and 1910 is credited with being the
first stimulant to extensive suburbanization, because it
allowed workers to travel greater distances to jobs at the
center of the city. The automobile was also an important
stimulant to residential suburbanization, and the truck
enabled businesses to locate farther from railroad and
port facilities, which tended to be in the city center.[7]

It is important to keep in mind that these past transportation developments, widely credited with shaping central-
city and suburban growth, represented, in their time, enormous changes in transportation technologies, costs, and
accessibility. Because of these changes, accessibility is
extremely high in major metropolitan areas: one can travel
very rapidly between any two points in most metropolitan
areas--often within 20-30 minutes, even in the rush hour.
However, the transportation policies currently being contemplated by U.S. policy makers would not change the general
levels of accessibility and transportation costs nearly
as much as past developments did. Many current transportation policies, such as the regulation of new-car emissions,
fuel economy, and safety standards, change the out-of-pocket
costs of travel only modestly and leave travel speeds unaffected. Even public policies or projects that are widely
regarded as having major effects on accessibility, such as
the construction of a new freeway or a new rail transit line
usually alter travel costs and times for only a fraction of
the metropolitan population--those who live or work close to
the facility and choose to use it. And even for those persons, the new facility often reduces travel times by only
20-40 percent during the rush hour and by less, or not at
all, during the remainder of the day (Weber 1976). Because
the effect of current transportation policies on accessibility will be much smaller than that of past transportation
developments, the impact of current policies on the shape
of metropolitan development should be proportionately less.

Furthermore, the effects of changes in accessibility on
central-city and suburban growth rates are likely to be

---

[7]The history of technology is summarized from Harrison
(1976).

mitigated by a number of factors. Changes in the costs
and time of travel encourage households and businesses to
relocate their residences, offices, and plants. However,
in the short term, the possibilities for relocation are
severely limited because houses and commercial buildings
are extremely durable and expensive to move or replace.
The enormous expense of moving, demolishing, or abandoning
an existing building is reflected in the fact that a high
percentage of the buildings standing today are the first
and only structures that ever stood on their sites.

The high costs of moving or abandoning and replacing
existing structures might not impede location changes if
some households and businesses could respond to transportation policy changes by moving from their present buildings
to other existing structures in different locations.
Substantial changes in residential and business
location patterns might be possible using the existing
building stock if some occupants of existing structures
could exchange positions instead of moving or abandoning
the structures. However, the possibilities for such ex-
changes are limited by the fact that the existing stock
of buildings is composed of distinct types that are expensive to alter. The buildings vary in important structural
characteristics and these characteristics are difficult to
change; for example, in residential buildings it is costly
to alter the number of units per building, the number of
rooms per unit, and the sizes of the rooms and lots. The
characteristics of neighborhoods, such as crime rates, racial
composition, and quality of public services, are also often
important to potential occupants and difficult to alter.
Because of the heterogeneity of the existing stock of buildings and the expense of altering their critical structural
or neighborhood characteristics, households and businesses
have difficulty responding to transportation policy changes
by relocating within the current stock of buildings.

The ability of transportation policy to shape central-city
and suburban growth rates is weakened by the importance of
considerations other than those of transportation in determining household and business location decisions. The
effects of these other factors may more than offset the
effects of transportation policy. The steady postwar growth
in real per capita income is thought to have played an especially significant role in encouraging residential suburbanization. As per-capita incomes grow, households usually
purchase more and better quality housing. Because large
lots are frequently considered an important quality of
housing, many households locate in the suburbs where land

prices are lower. Furthermore, new housing is often considered more desirable than older housing, and most new
housing is located in the suburbs. Thus, the effects of
a future transportation policy designed to discourage residential suburbanization would be offset in part, if not entirely, by the continued rise in real per capita incomes.

The factors other than transportation that influence
business locations decisions are probably more numerous
(and more poorly understood) than those that influence
residential changes (Straszheim 1977). Rising wage rates
and consequent changes in production technologies, for
example, are thought to have been important factors in sub-
urbanizing the location of businesses. As per-capita income and wage rates increased, it became profitable for
manufacturers to substitute capital for labor by using production lines and one-story plants; since these new plants
were space extensive, surburban locations, where land was
cheap, proved to be advantageous. Improvements in communi-
cations technologies,which made it more possible to locate
central office, clerical, manufacturing, and other functions
of a single firm on separate sites, may have also encouraged
suburbanization of employment.

Whereas transportation policy may be a relatively ineffective means of increasing growth of central cities and
slowing suburbanization, there may be other much more effective means of achieving these goals. Development of central
cities is seldom seen as an end in itself, but rather as a
means toward some other end. Many of those promoting growth
of central cities are really concerned about improving the
welfare of poor and minority persons who are trapped in the
central city because of racial discrimination in surburban
housing markets or the lack of affordable suburban housing
due to restrictive zoning. Growth of central cities, it is
hoped, would help these populations by bringing additional
jobs into the city and by expanding the tax base available
to support social services. Promoting central-city growth
through altered transportation policies would seem an un-
necessarily indirect and cumbersome means of helping low-
income and minority central-city residents. Other more
direct mechanisms deserve serious consideration. These
alternatives include more direct attacks on the institutions
that trap poor people in cities, such as racial discrimination in housing or restrictive zoning. More feasible and
effective, perhaps, would be measures to help poor persons
who remain trapped in cities. Such measures might include
job training or wage subsidies to help long-term unemployed
persons find jobs. An additional consideration might be

an increase in federal revenue sharing to central cities
to provide the expanded tax base needed to support public
services.

SUMMARY

Transportation policy has traditionally been conditioned by
a few major transportation trends and problems: urban transportation policy has been largely shaped by the growth in
automobile use and the decline of mass transit; intercity
freight policy has been shaped by the relative decline of
the railroads; and intercity passenger policy has been
shaped by increases in travel by airline and automobile
and decreases in travel by railroad and bus. Although expected demographic and locational developments will have a
modest effect on major transportation trends, other factors,
particularly rising real incomes, will be far more important determinants.

There is increasing pressure to use transportation policy
to alleviate the effects of anticipated locational changes,
largely because transportation changes are thought to have
greatly shaped location patterns in the past. However, the
leverage of transportation policy over future location
decisions is likely to be small, partly because past transportation developments have already made transportation costs
so low. In addition, there are more appropriate policy tools
that could be used if development control seems warranted.

REFERENCES

American Public Transit Association (various years) *Transit
    Fact Book*. Washington, D.C.: American Public Transit
    Association.
Federal Task Force on Motor Vehicle Goals Beyond 1980 (1976)
    Draft Report of the Federal Task Force on Motor Vehicle
    Goals Beyond 1980. Washington, D.C.
Gomez-Ibanez, J., and Meyer, J. (1978) Productivity growth
    and labor relations in urban mass transit. Pp. 147-156
    in *Urban Transportation Economics*. National Research
    Council, TRB Special Report no. 181. Washington, D.C.:
    Transportation Research Board.
Harrison, D. (1975) *Who Pays for Clean Air*. Cambridge,
    Mass.: Ballinger.

Harrison, D. (1976)   Transportation Technology and Urban
     Land Use Patterns.   Harvard University, Department of
     City and Regional Planning Research Report R 76-2, July.
Hilton, G. (1974)   *Federal Transit Subsidies: The Urban
     Mass Transportation Assistance Program.*   Washington, D.C.
     American Enterprise Institute for Public Policy Research.
Ingram, G., and Fauth, G. (1974)   *TASSIM: A Transportation
     and Air Shed Simulation Model.*   Vol. 1.   *Case Study of
     the Boston Region.*   Prepared for the U.S. Department of
     Transportation.
Interplan Corporation (1976)   Transportation Systems Manage-
     ment, State of the Art.   Report prepared for the U.S. Urb.
     Mass Transit Administration.
Kain, J., Fauth, G., and Zax, J. (1977)   Forecasting Auto
     Ownership and Mode Choice for U.S. Metropolitan Areas.
     Report prepared for the U.S. Department of Transportation,
     Office of University Research, Washington, D.C.
Meyer, J., and Morton, A. (1974)   The U.S. railroad industry
     in the postwar period: a profile.   *Explorations in Econor
     Research* 2(Fall):453.
Miller, J. C., III (1975)   An economic analysis of the
     Amtrak program.   In James C. Miller, ed., *Perspectives
     on Federal Transporation Policy.*   Washington, D.C.:
     American Enterprise Institute for Public Policy Research.
Morton, A. (1973)   Freight Demand.   Unpublished Ph.D.
     dissertation, Harvard University.
Motor Vehicle Manufacturers Association (1977)   *Motor
     Vehicle Facts and Figures '77.*   Detroit: Motor Vehicle
     Manufacturers Association.
Straszheim, M. (1977)   Researching the role of transporta-
     tion in regional development.   *Land Economics* 48.
Task Force on Railroad Productivity (1973)   *Improving Rail-
     road Productivity.*   Report to the National Commission
     on Productivity and the Council of Economic Advisors.
     Washington, D.C.:   U.S. Government Printing Office.
U.S. Bureau of the Census (1970)   *National Travel Survey.*
     Pp. 20 and 38 in vol. 1 of *1967 Census of Transportation.*
     Washington, D.C.:   U.S. Department of Commerce.
U.S. Bureau of the Census (1972)   *U.S. Census of Population,
     1970.*   Washington, D.C.:   U.S. Department of Commerce.
U.S. Bureau of the Census (1976)   *Statistical Abstract of
     the United States,* p. 583.   Washington, D.C.:   U.S.
     Department of Commerce.
U.S. Department of Transporation (1972)   *National Trans-
     portation Report,* p. 75.   Washington, D.C.:   U.S.
     Department of Transportation.

U.S. Department of Transportation (1974)   *The Replacement of Locks and Dam 26.*   An advisory report of the Department of Transportation to the Senate Commerce Committee. Cited in Transportation Association of America (1974) *Transportation Facts and Trends,*   December, p. 3.

U.S. Department of Transportation (1977)   *National Transportation Trends and Choices (to the Year 2000),* p. 278. Washington, D.C.:   U.S. Department of Transportation.

Webber, M. (1976)   The BART experience--what have we learned. *The Public Interest* 45:78-108.

Wildhorn, S., Burright, B., Enns, J., and Kirkwood, T. (1975) *How to Save Gasoline: Public Policy Alternatives for the Automobile.*   Prepared for the RAND Corp. Cambridge, Mass.: Ballinger.

POPULATION REDISTRIBUTION:
IMPLICATIONS FOR ENVIRONMENTAL
QUALITY AND NATURAL
RESOURCE CONSUMPTION

Dale L. Keyes

INTRODUCTION

Historically, patterns of human settlement have mirrored
the spatial distribution of nature's bounty. Fertile land,
clean water, navigable rivers, accessible mineral deposits,
and abundant forest resources have worked singly or in con-
cert to define those sites best suited for habitation.
Though where we choose to reside is now less a function of
resource location, we are no less dependent on our natural
resource base.

The magnitude of population redistribution in this country has been amply documented. A major shift in settlement
patterns both within and among regions is surely under way.
In the main, considerations other than the availability of
natural resources are fueling these movements. But the impact on the supply and quality of these resources may well
act as a servomechanism reinforcing certain shifts and
throttling others.

Organization

For purposes of exposition, it is expedient to treat the
spatial redistributional trends occurring at the metropolitan scale separately from those that are taking place
among regions, although the two scales of migration are
surely interrelated; a move from New York to Tucson probably
entails a concomitant move from city to suburb. Where these

Dale L. Keyes is Project Manager and Senior Policy Analyst
at Energy and Environmental Analysis, Inc., Arlington,
Virginia.

interrelationships appear important, the distinction between interregional and intraregional population shifts will be blurred. For the most part, however, the scale of the observed relocation pattern will serve to organize the discussion.

In exploring the environmental implications of population redistribution, three types of scarce natural resources are featured: energy (in its various forms), clean water, and clean air. We will look at the stress that this redistribution places on the provision of these resources, either by increasing demand or by decreasing quality. Alternatively, population movements may spatially separate the demand from the scarcity. Both resource stress and relief will be considered. Finally, the ways in which environmental or resource allocation policy may impact on migration patterns will be explored.

New Terms

Many of the terms used elsewhere in this volume appear in this paper as well. New terms that may be unfamiliar to the reader appear below.

Energy
Btu   British thermal unit, a unit measure of energy in the
      form of heat (therm = 100,000 Btus)
VMT   Vehicle-miles traveled

Air Pollution
SO_2 Sulfur dioxide
TSP   Total suspended particulates

REDISTRIBUTION AT THE METROPOLITAN LEVEL

Berry and Dahmann have already identified the major dimensions of population redistribution observed at the metropolitan scale during this decade. The major thrust continues to be from central-city to suburban areas, although significant movement to settlements outside standard metropolitan statistical areas (SMSAs) is also apparent. This centrifugal dynamic may carry with it important ramifications for natural resource consumption and environmental quality.

Evidence is now accumulating that ties together levels
of resource use and the spatial patterning of development
within (and, by extension, outside) metropolitan areas.
Because population decentralization suggests profound
changes in the mosaic of metropolitan-wide development,
changes in the availability and demand for natural resources
are inferred.

Mills discusses in this volume the changes in population
density that have accompanied redistribution. Density is a
useful statistic for describing development patterns. It
conveys a sense of the propinquity of people and the clustering of urban activities. However, it can obscure the uneven-
ness of development in any spatial direction and does not
necessarily reflect the accessibility of people to activity
centers.

Other commentaries on metropolitan development patterns,
although often qualitative and limited in the number of
metropolitan areas discussed, give a fuller sense of changes
in the urban development fabric (Mayer 1969, Ward and Paulhaus 1974). Suburbanization frequently brings with it a
proliferation of metropolitan subcenters as well as dispersion of the population. Commercial and employment centers
evolve at points with access to principal transportation
arterials and they spawn secondary development around these
nuclei. Movement to areas outside SMSA boundaries frequently
leads to development of new metropolitan subcenters, or to
growth in older, pre-existing satellite towns. The degree of
suburban multinucleation varies among SMSAs, and the evolving
development patterns are far from homogeneous within SMSAs.

Energy for Transportation

Shifts in development patterns may bring about significant
changes in metropolitan travel patterns and thus alter the
demand for gasoline and other transport fuels. First, because population decentralization has historically preceded
employment decentralization, commuting trips have been significantly lengthened. In SMSAs with mass transit systems
that primarily serve the inner city (typically the larger,
older ones), suburbanization has frequently siphoned commuting trips from transit to the less efficient automobile.
Shopping and other discretionary travel may also increase,
especially where circumferential highways facilitate trips
among clusters of retail activity.

The magnitude of these changes can be seen in the travel
patterns of households living at various distances from

the urban core. A recent study by The Urban Institute
(Neels et al. 1977) found considerable variation among
sample households from six SMSAs. Using both population
density and distance from the urban core as classifiers
of neighborhoods, the authors found that in any SMSA, people living in low-density fringe neighborhoods took about
1.5 times as many trips and traveled about twice as many
miles as their counterparts in high-density inner neighborhoods. These trends apply to both work and nonwork
trips, although the differentials for work trips were
more pronounced. Transit use also dropped off with distance from the core, although transit failed to account
for more than 5 percent of the travel in any neighborhood.

Variations in travel suggest similar differences in
gasoline consumption, even though travel at more efficient
speeds in suburban and exurban areas may narrow the gap
somewhat. George Peterson and I have investigated variations in gasoline consumption among 50 SMSAs, and related
these variations to differences in development characteristics (Keyes and Peterson 1977). After controlling for
gasoline price and household income, we found a significant relationship between the amount of gasoline consumed
per person and various development and transport system
characteristics of the SMSAs sampled. Large metropolitan
areas with low population densities, relatively high levels
of employment in the central business district (implying
long commuting distances), and extensive highway networks
produce higher levels of per-capita gasoline consumption.
In magnitude, the differences are quite impressive. SMSAs
that score in the top 16 percent on each of these variables
(one standard deviation above the mean) show per-capita
consumption levels of 65-80 gallons (20-25 percent) above
the average. Because these are metropolitan-wide averages,
the consumption differentials between individual households
living at the SMSA fringe and those at more central, higher
density locations must be even larger.

These findings accord with the mainstream of evidence
in the transportation literature. They tend to be somewhat lower than energy consumption levels predicted by
simulations of future growth in specific metropolitan
areas (Edwards and Shofer 1975, Roberts 1975), but the
latter often assume worst-case conditions rarely observed
in U.S. SMSAs (such as the most extreme separation of new
residences from new employment opportunities).

Based on these observations, it is possible to
conclude that metropolitan population redistribution
poses a threat to scarce energy resources, specifically

petroleum-based fuels. But the seriousness of this threat
should be judged in terms of the likely increase in demand
relative to national consumption levels as a whole, and
against possible ameliorating factors. If current low-
density settlement patterns were replaced by high-density
ones, I have estimated that energy savings could eventually
exceed 2 quadrillion Btus per year, or less than 2 percent
of the estimated yearly U.S. consumption by the end of the
century (Keyes and Peterson 1977, U.S. Bureau of Mines
1975). However, gasoline consumption is clearly sensitive
to the efficiency of automobiles and the price of gasoline.
Acting alone, either one of these factors would deflate
gasoline consumption and thus reduce the differences between decentralized metropolitan areas and more compact,
higher density ones. The Federal Energy Administration
(1974), now part of the Department of Energy, has estimated
that achieving a sales-weighted 20 miles per gallon fuel
efficiency by 1980 would result in an annual savings of
approximately 0.4 quads by 1985, whereas doubling the real
price of gasoline may reduce gasoline consumption by over
50 percent in the long run (4 quads or more).[1] Cast in
this light, the impact of population redistribution trends
at the metropolitan level are significant but not alarming.

Energy for Space Heating and Cooling

The amount of energy needed to heat and cool our homes is
determined in large part by the size of the dwelling and
the insulating characteristics of the outer shell. Both
factors typically come into play when central-city residents
move to suburban or nonmetropolitan locations. First, such
moves are often associated with the purchase of more living
space. And secondly, these moves may be from townhouses or
apartments, where shared walls minimize heat loss to the
outside, to detached dwelling units, with six exterior surfaces. Of course, not all decentralization moves entail
such changes. Single-family detached units can still be

[1]This is based on estimated long-run price elasticities
of gasoline demand of -0.5 to -0.9. (Chase Econometric
Associates 1974, Wildhorn et al. 1975). These elasticities account for the purchase of more efficient automobiles as one strategy consumers would use to offset higher
gasoline prices. The estimates incorporate the effect of
improvements in automobile efficiency cited above.

found in built-up central-city areas, and duplexes, town-houses, and multifamily structures appear with some regularity in suburban locations. But as Table 1 demonstrates, dwellings with at least one shared wall are found much more frequently in central cities.

Whether the movement toward single-family detached homes is significant for energy use depends above all on the relative efficiency of the alternative structural types. Simulations of heat loss from prototypical and real dwellings (Anderson 1973, Tokmanhekin and Harvey 1974), cross-sectional comparisons of jurisdictions with different housing inventories (Keyes and Peterson 1977, Regional Plan Association, Inc., and Resources for the Future 1974), and surveys of individual households (Keyes and Peterson 1977, Response Analysis Corporation 1974) consistently show the superior energy efficiencies of units with shared walls. The only exceptions are extremely tall buildings for which the energy requirements to light and heat common areas and to operate common facilities outstrip the gains from thermal insulating characteristics of the individual units (Sweet 1974).

TABLE 1   Percent of Housing Types Within and Outside SMSAs by Age of Structure

| | Housing Type (Units per Structure) | | | |
| | 1 Unit | | 2-4 Units | 5 or More |
	Detached	Attached		
Existing (1970)				
Central cities	45.0	5.6	21.0	27.6
Suburbs	72.6	2.3	10.3	11.5
Non-SMSAs	81.3	0.8	8.5	4.1
New (1970-1976)				
Central cities	36.0		11.8	49.2
Suburbs	56.2		6.7	26.4
Non-SMSAs	62.1		5.3	7.1

SOURCES: U.S. Bureau of the Census and U.S. Department of Housing and Urban Development (1978); U.S. Bureau of the Census (1972).

Figure 1 summarizes the results of four key studies. Although the absolute values of energy consumed for heating and cooling similar types of structures vary among the four studies (due primarily to climatic variations and differences in insulation properties of the individual buildings), a similarity in the trend lines is observed. Single-family detached dwellings are about 1.5 times less energy-efficient than units of the same size in small to medium multi-family structures. When typical size differences are considered, single-family units would be expected to consume at least twice as much energy as units in apartment buildings.

As impressive as these differences in efficiency may be, the significance of the implied increase in energy demand remains to be established. In doing so, the amount of new residential construction over the next several decades must be considered. If it is assumed that 1.35 million units will be built annually in metropolitan areas,[2] and (unrealistically) that all these units could be small multi-family structures as contrasted with the current mix of about 50 percent single-family detached dwellings, 20 percent townhouses, 30 percent mid-rise units, and 1 percent high-rise units,[3] then the increase due to current patterns in annual energy consumption by 1985 (using 1975 as the base year) would be about 0.5 quadrillion Btus. By the year 2000, the increase would be about 1.2 quadrillion Btus per year.[4] When these increases are viewed in the context of total annual energy demand, the first equals about 0.5 percent of estimated energy consumption in 1985, and the second equals about 1.0 percent of estimated energy consumption in the year 2000 (Federal Energy Administration 1974, U.S. Department of Energy 1979).

This "excess" demand can be cut by energy price increases or by improvements in end-use efficiencies, such as more

[2]During the period 1970-1973, when housing construction rates were high, 1.51 million new units were added each year (U.S. Bureau of the Census 1975).
[3]This is the distribution estimated for the period 1973-1975 by the National Association of Homebuilders (1974).
[4]These calculations further assume that the average annual fuel consumption is 1,600 therms for single-family detached units, 1,200 therms for townhouse units, and 960 therms for small multi-family units.

liberal application of wall insulation or energy-saving
design features. Savings of 0.8 quads per year by the
year 2000 have been estimated for the implementation of
upgraded insulation standards (this assumes application to
all new dwellings but is especially effective for single-
family detached units). Annual savings that could result
from substantial increases in the price of natural gas,
electricity, and fuel oil have been estimated at 4 quads
or more per year by the year 2000 (Hirst 1978).[5]

Because of these counterbalancing factors and the increase in two-person households, many of which favor small
townhouses or apartments, increases in energy demand accompanying the outward movement of metropolitan populations
will be less substantial than they first appear to be.

Water Consumption

The lower population densities characteristic of current
settlement patterns portend upward shifts in the demand
for another increasingly scarce resource--water. Low residential densities are created by large lots supporting
thirsty lawns. Sprinkling requirements together with other
outdoor water uses account for substantial portions (up to
60 percent) of many household water bills. Conceivably,
population movements from residences with small lots or
shared lawns (common areas) to homes with extensive private
yards could create an expanded demand for water.

However, evidence pointing to the highly discretionary nature of outdoor water use has been accumulating
for many years. As far back as the early 1950s, studies
of homes with and without metering indicated differences
in water use of from 25 to 50 percent (Hanke and Flack
1968, Porges 1957). As a further indication of how
sensitive this portion of household water use is to
price level, price elasticities of demand have been
estimated to range from -0.7 to -1.6. Thus, an increase
in the price of water could give rise to a more proportional decrease in consumption.

Suburbanization and exurbanization of metropolitan populations will likely lead to some increase in water use. But

[5]Hirst simulated rapid increases in fuel prices between
1975 and 1990, with less rapid increases thereafter. The
ratios of 2000 to 1975 prices (in 1975 dollars) were: 1.9
for gas, 1.2 for electricity, and 1.4 for oil.

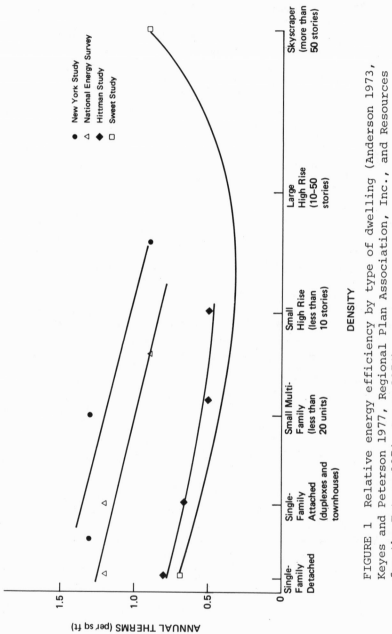

FIGURE 1 Relative energy efficiency by type of dwelling (Anderson 1973, Keyes and Peterson 1977, Regional Plan Association, Inc., and Resources for the Future 1974, Sweet 1974).

the increment is not likely to be large once water is
priced at its scarcity value.

Water Quality

If migration to the suburbs or beyond entails an increase
in a household's demand for selected economic goods, it is
not difficult to envisage a similar rise in the volume of
waste material generated as a result of this inflated consumption. Where these wastes are waterborne, further degradation
of local water resources may result. However, only small
differentials in domestic wastewater production are observed
between central-city and surburban households (probably due
to income differences). Instead, whatever impact on water
quality may result from metropolitan decentralization will
arise from differences in the quantity and waste content of
stormwater runoff.

Research has shown that stormwater runoff from developed
areas is highly polluted, and, in some cases, can seriously
degrade the quality of local surface water (Hydroscience,
Inc. 1975). Moreover, the extent of paved surfaces in an
urban area is believed to affect the volume and perhaps
pollutant strength of the runoff (i.e., more pavement, more
pollution). Since dispersed, low-density urban areas have
more paved surface per capita than compact SMSAs, one can
argue that decentralization increases runoff and reduces
water quality. Unfortunately, the evidence is less than
definitive (Keyes 1977b). In general, the data on rates at
which waste materials accumulate in urban areas (and are
thus available for washoff during storms) are unreliable or
have been collected with little documentation of the relevant environmental conditions.

However, even if waste materials were deposited at
higher rates per capita in low-density, dispersed settlements, it does not necessarily follow that these areas
would discharge greater quantities of pollutants. The lower
density of paved areas in dispersed settlements often makes
feasible the use of natural drainage networks instead of
storm sewers to convey runoff to receiving waterways. As
the runoff passes over fields and other vegetated land, the
flow of water is slowed, debris settles out, and water
begins to percolate through the soil. These natural processes provide a degree of pollutant removal that may compensate for whatever greater initial pollutant loadings may
be caused by dispersed development. Thus, clear differences
among types of development patterns should not be expected.

The findings of a recent water-quality study in Sonoma County, California bear this out (Association of Bay Area Governments 1976). The study found that metropolitan-wide variations in land-use intensities and arrangements have little effect on water quality. Thus, water-quality dis-benefits are likely to be conferred equally on all development patterns.

Air Quality

It could also be argued that air quality should deteriorate as a result of population redistribution at the metropolitan level. Again, the argument centers on travel behavior; as automobile trips become longer and more frequent, total emissions of air pollutants rise. However, air quality is not necessarily a simple function of air-pollutant emission levels. The spatial distribution of sources, characteristics of the terrain, and meteorological factors such as predominant wind directions interact to determine the concentration of pollutants in the atmosphere. Moreover, the space between residential and employment centers, on one hand, and sources of air pollutants, on the other, will affect the ambient pollutant levels to which people are exposed.

Harvard researchers who simulated the effect of various land-use patterns on auto-related air pollution in the Boston region (Ingram and Fauth 1974, Ingram and Pellechio 1976) found that decreasing population densities by dispersing people and jobs from the urban core decreases the atmospheric concentration of automobile-related pollutants (specifically carbon monoxide) throughout the core, despite the fact that SMSA-wide emissions of automobile pollutants are increased. Although more automobile trips are taken and the average trip is longer, the trips are more highly dispersed spatially. This allows for greater atmospheric dilution of pollutants and lower population exposure levels.

I have extended this line of analysis to cover emissions from stationary sources, using an air-quality simulation of alternative development patterns in a hypothetical metropolitan area (Keyes 1977a). In general, the results are strikingly similar to the findings of the Boston study: the air is less polluted, as measured by levels of population exposure, where sources and people are dispersed throughout the region or where sources or people are isolated at remote locations. And in the case of stationary sources, population dispersal

does not result in increased emission levels that partially
offset the dilution factor.

These findings lead inexorably to the conclusion that
dispersed, not compact, land-use arrangements are more desirable from an air-quality perspective. But a cautionary
flag must be raised. This conclusion seems obvious for
pollutants that are relatively inert (i.e., carbon monoxide
from mobile sources, particulates and sulfur dioxide from
stationary sources). For pollutants such as photochemical
oxidants (the constituents of smog) that are formed in the
atmosphere as a result of chemical reactions among other
pollutants, the situation is far more complex. Ambient concentrations of photochemical oxidants arise following the
emissions of precursors (from both mobile and stationary
sources) in ways that are imperfectly understood at the present time. Some experts believe that the level of photochemical oxidants observed at any location within an urban
region is most closely associated with area-wide levels of
precursor emissions. Others believe that the spatial pattern
of emissions is also important. This uncertainty prevents
us from drawing firm conclusions about the effect of settlement patterns on air pollution caused by photochemical oxidants. However, only in the case of photochemical oxidants
could metropolitan decentralization possibly lead to lower
levels of air quality.

Continued decentralization of congested urban cores
would appear to be an effective goal for air-quality stra-
tegists. Even though the implementation of mobile and stationary source emission standards as mandated by the 1977
amendments to the Clean Air Act (Public Law 95-95) will
reduce the size of the net air-quality benefit from population dispersal, previous analysis has demonstrated that this
approach to achieving clean air may prove to be a useful
adjunct to direct emission control of stationary sources,
especially, for those pollutants for which source controls
alone may be insufficient to attain the National Ambient
Air Quality Standards (Keyes 1977a).

Summary and Policy Implications

Whether the trends in population redistribution on the metropolitan scale signal an ominous upswing in resource demands
remains unclear. On one hand, a more widely distributed
population base implies greater water consumption and greater
energy consumption for both personal travel and residential
space conditioning. However, the extent of these increases

is uncertain. On the other hand, the net effects of lower
density, metropolitan (and nonmetropolitan) development are
beneficial to air quality and, at worst, are not detrimental
to water quality.

Even for energy and water supplies, alternative means to
mitigate the effects of population redistribution are available. Increases in the prices of fuel and water could
effect large and rapid decreases in the demand for these
resources. Regulations on end-use efficiencies or, in the
extreme, bans on particular activities, such as lawn
sprinkling or outdoor lighting, are other alternatives.

Whether any environmental, energy, or water-use policy
currently in effect influences the pattern of metropolitan-
scale migration is highly questionable. These policies
would affect migration patterns only if environmental and
natural resource considerations are important to migrating
households, and if public policies in these areas create
differentials among central cities, suburbs, and nonmetropolitan jurisdictions. Neither seems probable.

INTERREGIONAL MIGRATION

Although the trend toward metropolitan decentralization
promises to occupy the attention of urban scholars, the impact of regional migration patterns may well prove to be
more significant. Berry and Dahmann have documented the
major feature of these patterns--a shifting of the population to the South and the West. The South Atlantic, East
South Central, West South Central, and Mountain regions
all have experienced a recent spurt in population growth,
largely at the expense of the North Central and Northeast
regions. As a result of interregional migration alone, the
South has experienced a net population gain of 1.8 million
from 1970 to 1975. Moreover, this shift has altered the
stress on clean air and water resources, relaxing demands
in some areas, and heightening them in others.

Energy

A net flow of households to warmer climes should result in
a reduction in the total energy used for space heating and
cooling. Reduced heating expenditures have, in fact, been
proffered as a key motivational factor for migrants to the
South and the Southwest. But these interregional shifts in
population also hold importance for the mix of fuels employed to satisfy national energy demand.

Energy Demand   Roughly two-thirds of the average American household's residential energy bill results from heating and cooling. Of this, heating costs far outpace cooling costs. In the far South cooling demands rise somewhat, but the savings in space heating are substantial enough to lower the total energy bill.

Table 2 shows regional variations in average per capita energy consumption for on-site uses in 1972. Climatic effects are clearly evident; a typical home in New England requires about twice as much energy to heat and cool as one in the South Atlantic region. These numbers may also reflect regional variations in income levels, energy prices, housing characteristics, and other factors related to residential energy consumption. But the energy differentials do not appear to diminish when standardized housing units (and, implicity, similar households) are compared. Arthur D. Little, Inc. (1974) has estimated that a gas-fueled single-family detached home in Detroit would require about twice

TABLE 2   Net Population Change (1970-1975) and Regional Variations in On-Site Household Energy Use (1972)

Region		Net Population Change, 1970-1975 (millions of people)	On-Site Energy Use (millions of Btus per capita)	
North-east	New England	-1.34	75.0	69.3[a]
	Middle Atlantic		67.5	
North Central	East North Central	-1.20	70.7	65.9[a]
	West North Central		63.9	
South	South Atlantic	+1.83	38.5	41.6[a]
	East South Central		44.2	
	West South Central		45.0	
West	Rocky Mountain	+0.71	53.9	47.6[a]
	Pacific		45.4	

[a]Population weighted averages.

SOURCES: Berry and Dahmann (this volume); Hoch (1977); Murray and Reeves (1975).

as many Btus per square foot to heat and cool as would an identical home in Pine Bluff, Arkansas.

From the data presented in Table 2, we can derive a rough approximation of the residential energy savings created by interregional migration between 1970 and 1975. Assuming that the in-migrants and out-migrants did not differ appreciably from the average residents of the appropriate regions, the net flux of population southward and westward probably saved approximately 60 trillion Btus per year. These savings are small by national standards (less than 0.1 percent of the national total in 1975), and they will be eroded by improvements in both the efficiency of heating and cooling equipment and the insulation of new homes. Even with accelerated migration to the South and the West and without improvements in end-use efficiencies, the savings in residential energy probably will not be much above 0.5 percent per year by the end of the century. For comparison, Hirst (1978) estimates that a 0.8 percent reduction could be effected through upgraded building standards by the year 2000.

Energy used for personal travel is even less affected by interregional migration patterns. Table 3 shows per-capita expenditures for gasoline and lubricating oil taken from recent household surveys conducted by the Bureau of the Census. The greatest variation among regions is about 20 percent, and, more importantly, variations are even smaller when the two regions of net in-migration are compared with the two regions of net out-migration. The travel-economizing effect of population clustering in the East is apparently offset by the region-wide dispersal of population in the North Central region. This is not to diminish the importance of energy savings to individual households. But on a national scale, the economies are not large.

TABLE 3   Regional Differences in Expenditures for Gasoline per Household

Region	1972 (1972 dollars)	1973 (1973 dollars)
Northeast	303	332
North Central	336	402
South	345	386
West	346	378
Average	333	376

SOURCE: U.S. Bureau of the Census (1976b).

Energy Supply   A full accounting of energy implications associated with national patterns of population redistribution should include the availability of different forms of energy as well as changes in aggregate energy demand. Table 4 displays patterns of energy use in the residential sector (and thus, indirectly, the availability of energy supplies) by fuel type for the nine Census regions. Although the percentages refer only to energy used in single-family detached dwellings, they illustrate the general trends in the entire residential sector. The variations are striking. Distillate fuel oil supplies over half of the household energy used in the East while gas predominates in the other regions, especially in the West and the West South Central regions. Except for the East South Central region, electricity supplies only a small fraction of total household energy consumption.

TABLE 4   The Distribution of Residential Energy Consumption by Fuel Type and Region, 1970   (single-family detached homes)

Region		Percentage Distribution of Fuel Use			
		Gas	Oil	Electric	Coal & Wood
North-east	New England	20	76	3	1
	Middle Atlantic	46	45	3	6
North Central	East North Central	71	23	2	4
	West North Central	76	20	2	2
South	South Atlantic	41	39	13	7
	East South Central	60	4	20	16
	West South Central	93	--	4	3
West	Rocky Mountain	81	8	5	6
	Pacific	76	12	10	2

SOURCE: Oak Ridge National Laboratory (1975, Figure 11).

TABLE 5   Percentage Distribution of New Homes by the Fuels
Used for Heating and Cooling, 1975

Region	Gas	Electric	Oil	Other
Northeast	27	37	46	--
North Central	49	38	9	4
South	29	66	4	1
West	59	39	--	2

SOURCE: U.S. Bureau of the Census and U.S. Department of
Housing and Urban Development (1976).

As shown in Table 5, fuel shares for new homes differ
considerably from these patterns. Shortages of natural
gas and uncertainties about future oil supplies have given
a large boost to all-electric homes. Still, the greater
reliance of eastern households on oil continues to hold.

These patterns are largely the result of local fuel availability. Natural gas is abundant in the Gulf Coast area and
in the Southwest. And despite the concomitant availability
of petroleum, the lower price of gas ($1.40 per million Btu
for gas and $3.25 per million Btu for oil in 1974) makes it
the number-one choice for residential uses. Northeasterners
are simply unable to obtain sufficient quantities of gas;
oil is selected over electricity, again on the basis or relative cost ($3.10 per million Btus for oil and $11.10 per
million Btus for electricity).[6]

If prices were held constant and new demands went unchecked, a new movement of people to the Southwest would
result in increased use of gas relative to oil. Neither
condition is probable, however. Moratoria on new gas con-
nections are a reality and a schedule for natural gas price
increases was recently passed by Congress. Moreover, if
the President's original energy proposals were to be adopted,

[6]These prices are approximate averages for the states in
the regions indicated. The data are taken from Edison Electric Institute (1975) and American Gas Association (1975,
1977), as reported in Energy and Environmental Analysis
(1977). Prices are expressed in terms of usable Btus, taking typical efficiencies of furnaces and heaters and, in the
case of electricity, generation and transmission losses,
into account.

alternative fuels would eventually reach the same price level
on an equivalent Btu basis. As a result, the demand for increasingly scarce supplies of natural gas would ease somewhat, although only total deregulation of market prices
would allow gas to be priced at its scarcity value. The
net effect of recent legislation and the relative availability of fuel stocks should be to lessen the disparities
in fuel shares among regions.

But the major energy impact of growth in the South and
the West may be totally obscured by the information in
Table 5. As important as the distribution of total demand
among alternative fossil fuels may be in the near term,
satisfaction of consumer demand in the long term clearly
depends on the development of alternative forms of energy.
The South and especially the Southwest, blessed with abundant supplies of solar energy, stand ready for application
of emerging solar technologies. Figure 2 quantifies the
relative advantage of a southern climate in this respect.

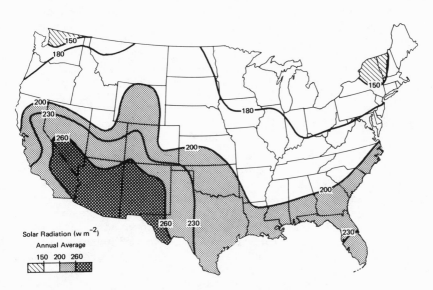

FIGURE 2   Annual levels of solar insolation in the United
States (watts per square meter)(Calvin 1974, Figure 1).

Regardless of whether the technological breakthroughs
needed for large-scale application of solar energy in all
economic sectors occur soon, the potential for extensive
use of currently available technologies in the residential
sector is considerable from now until the end of the century. The physical requirements (i.e., space for collectors
and storage facilities) are satisfied by almost all newly
constructed single-family detached units (Office of Technology Assessment 1977). Currently, initial costs may pre-
clude large-scale application. However, when the price of
fossil fuel increases to such a degree that a consumer could
install solar facilities, knowing that in a period of perhaps 5 years the amount he would save in fossil-fuel costs
would equal the cost of installation, the use of solar
energy should increase dramatically. The Sun Belt stands
to benefit above all other regions once this occurs.

If it is assumed that the rate of migration from the
North and the East will continue at the current level, that
a solar option will be only available to homes in the South
and the West, and that every migrating household will eventually install a solar heating and cooling unit, the savings
in fossil-fuel consumption due to interregional migration
between now and the end of the century could reach over
1 quadrillion Btus per year (about 0.9 percent of total
projected annual consumption for the entire nation and
more than 2.0 percent of projected fossil fuel use). Given
the anticipated increase in the price of fossil fuels,
savings of this magnitude may be feasible.

Water Use

In stark contrast to the solar abundance and associated
temperate winters of the South and the West, water scarcity
looms ever larger as a threat to continued growth. Arizona
has already tapped all but a small fraction of the surface
water available in the state and annually pumps about three
times as much groundwater as is recharged naturally (Kelso
et al. 1973). In Florida, excessive groundwater withdrawal
has led to seawater intrusion of coastal aquifers, steadily
decreasing water levels in the Everglades, and a total ban
on new construction in the Keys. Even though these trends
cannot be extended to all southern and western areas, they
are alarming enough that the wisdom of permitting unbridled
growth in these regions should be seriously questioned. The
drought of 1977 served to sharpen the horns of the apparent
dilemma.

TABLE 6   Water Withdrawn by Type of Use (in millions of gallons per day)[a] and Land Use (in square miles) for Three Sun Belt States, 1975.

| | Water Withdrawn | | |
	Arizona	California	Florida
Residential (mgd)	372	3,129	1,130
Public supply	340	3,000	930
Self-supply	32	129	200
Industrial and commercial (mgd)	410	2,620	2,810
Public supply	60	720	210
Self-supply	350	1,900	2,600
Agricultural (mgd)	7,043	35,100	2,963
Livestock	43	100	63
Irrigation	7,000	35,000	2,900
	Land Use		
Irrigated area (sm)	2,200	14,000	3,100
Developed area (sm)[b]	859	5,863	4,330

[a]Withdrawals include water consumed and water returned to bodies of surface water or groundwater in usable form.
[b]Urban area.

SOURCE: Murray and Reeves (1975, Table 10).

A review of current patterns of water use can bring the problem into better focus. Table 6 shows the amount of water withdrawn in 1975 for three Sun Belt states disaggregated by economic sector. Water demand is clearly dominated in both Arizona and California by the agricultural sector, specifically by irrigation uses. On a per-acre basis, crop irrigation far outstrips residential, commercial, and industrial uses of water--2.59 million gallons per day (mgd) per acre compared with 0.95. In Florida, however, the uses per acre are about equal, with urban uses averaging 0.91 and agricultural uses 1.02 mgd per acre. These differences are apparently due to variations in precipitation levels between Arizona and California, on one hand, and Florida, on the other.

These patterns of water use suggest that population
growth should have quite disparate effects on water demand.
In California and Arizona, the displacement of farmers by
urban development should create net reductions in overall
demand, but in Florida, urban growth that pre-empts agricultural land uses will have little impact on the demand
for fresh water.[7] In either case, however, shrinking water
supplies are likely to favor urban over agricultural uses,
since the former usually can outbid the latter.

Kelso et al. (1973) have gauged the economic impact on
Arizona of rising water prices created by increased pump-
ing costs as groundwater levels fall. They conclude that
water withdrawal will closely approach replenishment by
the end of the century even with a continued growth in population of over 2 percent per year: the least valuable
crops per gallon of water required for plant growth will
be replaced by more valuable, less water-demanding ones.
Increased urbanization should also contribute to balancing
the water budget, although Kelso et al. did not include
this effect in their calculations.

Where more rapid movement toward depressing water demand
is deemed necessary, the various policy tools discussed in
the previous section can be employed. Increases in water
utility prices or bans on particular uses have proven effective tools for curbing consumption during drought conditions.
A pricing approach may be useful in a state like Florida,
where urban uses account for a large percentage of total
demand. In most southwestern states, however, use curtail-
ments in the agricultural sector will have to be effected.
Unfortunately, direct price control is typically infeasible
for the vast majority of self-supplied farm users. Instead, public authorities must rely on increasingly diffi-
cult-to-reach sources of water or resort to land-use pre-
emptions to throttle demand. In any case, there is no
reason to believe that urban growth is primarily responsible
for water shortages or that it should be necessarily inhib-
ited by concern for future availability of supplies in
water-short regions.

[7]Arizona law allows municipalities to secure water supplies
by eminent domain. Thus, the tools to implement an urban
growth strategy are already in hand, even though they have
seldom been used.

Air and Water Quality

The movement from North and East to South and West, from
old, heavily industrialized metropolitan centers to
smaller, less concentrated urban areas, suggests a major
shift in environmental stresses. At a minimum, air and
water pollution will be more evenly distributed geographically. To the degree that a redistribution of people
also signals the development of a new, less polluting industrial base or the replacement of old capital stock with
new and better controlled facilities, net improvements in
air and water quality should be experienced nationwide.
And to the extent that growth regions are better able to
assimilate or dissipate waste loadings, ambient levels of
air and water pollutants to which many people are exposed
will be lowered even further.

As a test of the deductions articulated above, we can
examine the current status of localities with respect to
recorded levels of three air pollutants--sulfur dioxide,
particulate matter, and photochemical oxidants--for each
county in which valid measurements were made between 1974 and
1976. (See U.S. Environmental Protection Agency 1977, Figures
4-1, 4-2, and 4-3.) Although air quality in more than half
of all counties is not monitored, most of the unmonitored
counties are sparsely populated. Such an examination shows,
first, that pollution from sulfur dioxide is not as geographically pervasive as pollution from photochemical oxidants or particulates. Less than 10 percent of all counties
monitoring SO_2 reported violations of the national standard,[8]
and those that do show that violations are fairly evenly
distributed among the four major Census regions.[9]

Violations of total suspended particulates, on the other
hand, are recorded in almost 30 percent of all counties
monitoring air quality (U.S. Environmental Protection Agency

---

[8]Updated lists of areas not attaining the National Ambient
Air Quality Standards are now available (U.S. Environmental
Protection Agency 1977). However, the geographic unit used
to designate nonattainment areas varies among the states;
some used subcounty areas as the minimum unit, others used
entire counties, and still others, the entire state. Regional comparisons based on these nonuniform definitions
have little meaning.
[9]The greater coverage of nonattainment areas in the South
west is due to the large size of the counties in this
region, not to a greater number of reported violations.

1977, Figure 4-2). Again, violations are found in each
region, although some increased incidence of nonattainment
may be observed in arid climates where windblown dust raise
background levels. Conversely, when wind speeds are low,
visibility in the West is far greater than in the East.
Finally, a study of photochemical oxidants reveals a serious
problem in almost all counties where data are available
(U.S. Environmental Protection Agency 1977, Figure 4-3).
Even a few rural counties record high concentrations, indicating that oxidants can be formed and transported over
large areas.

    A similar lack of regional distinction emerges when in-
dividual cities are compared. Major growth centers such as
Los Angeles, Denver, Phoenix, Houston, Atlanta, and Miami
have all recorded violations of the particulate or oxidant
standard, or both, in recent years. Declining urban areas
such as New York, Boston, Buffalo, Chicago, and Detroit
have also been unable to attain the standards. The examples
cited here are all fairly large urban complexes, each with
an array of major emissions sources. Other cities, such as
Phoenix and Tucson, suffer the burden of one particular heavy
industry--copper smelting in this case. Still others, such
as Los Angeles and Denver, are dominated by emissions from
automobile travel.

    It would appear that very little in the way of net air
quality improvement can be realized from population shifts
among metropolitan areas, even if such shifts are from one
region to another. Only when migrations are from large to
small SMSAs or, better yet, to nonmetropolitan areas will
appreciable air-quality benefits accrue to the migrants.

    In large part, geographic patterns of water quality are
similarly undifferentiated among the four major Census regions. The annual report of the U.S. Council on Environmental Quality (1976) shows a broad distribution of high
levels of several water pollutants or water-quality indicators. Some predominance of water pollution in "middle
America" is apparent, but low-quality streams and lakes
are abundant in every region. Some correlation between
urban size and water quality is observable, as was the case
for air quality. But examples of seriously degraded bodies
of surface- and groundwater can be found in sparsely populated areas as well, due in large part to agricultural and
feedlot activities. There is simply no guarantee that moving
from one region to another or from SMSAs to nonmetropolitan
areas will improve access to clean water.

    For most of us, however, access to any water body,
whether clean or polluted, is limited. On the other hand,

we all must share the cost of removing sewage and other
contaminants before wastewater is discharged into receiving
water bodies. The Environmental Protection Agency (EPA)
is currently moving toward a third level of wastewater
treatment as a means of achieving the level of water quality
mandated in the Clean Water Act (Public Law 92-500, 1972).
One promising approach to tertiary treatment is a technique
known as land application, by which effluent from treatment
plants is sprayed or allowed to flow over cropland (Hall
1975, Stewart 1973). As the wastewater percolates downward,
soil particles trap bacteria and nutrients contained in the
effluent, destroying the former and making the latter available to cultivated crops.

This technique is ideally suited for arid climates; the
lack of waterlogged soils and a long growing season allow
for continuous application of sewage plant effluent. Based
on EPA's avid interest in land application, it is reasonable
to speculate that additional funds for sewage treatment may
soon be available to communities in arid regions--primarily
the Southwest. To the extent that increased funding levels
materialize, the southwestern states (primarily Texas, New
Mexico, Oklahoma, Arizona, Nevada, Utah, and California)
stand to benefit.

Summary and Policy Implications

That millions of families continue to move southward and
westward within the United States is undeniable. Why they
move is more problematic. Whereas environmental considerations probably are not major motivational factors, a desire
for more temperate winter seasons and fresh air and clean
skies may be important for some migrants. Presumably, concerns about water shortages may discourage others. Whatever
the causes for the observed migrational patterns may be, it
is the environmental and resource consumption effects of
migration that concern us here.

Of the three major effects examined, the impact on fossil-
fuel consumption appears to hold the largest payoff for
society. Even though some lowering of per capita energy-use
levels can be anticipated as the result of regional migration, the impact will be modest. But the opportunity to
tap direct solar radiation for a substantial portion of
residential energy use promises to lessen the national demand for fossil fuels.

The impact of interregional migration on scarce water
supplies would appear, initially, to cancel whatever energy

benefits may be reaped. For states such as Florida, where
farming and nonagricultural activities are about equally
water-intensive, continued development may lead to overuse
of available supplies, the destruction of valuable wetland
areas, and eventual water rationing. However, in some area
where water supplies serve mainly to support agricultural
activities, urban development can actually lead to reductions in water demand. This will be the case if the
effect of urban growth is to replace crop irrigation with
urban land uses that consume less water on a per-acre basis
A second effect that may be experienced where water supplie
are shared between urban and nonurban users is an economic
one: because water is valued more highly by most urban
users, the price of available water supplies will be bid
upwards, causing farmers to switch to less water-intensive
crops and thereby reduce their consumption.

Finally, the effects of migration among metropolitan
areas in different regions on the quality of air and water
resources is probably negligible. Relocating in some parts
of the West will provide more opportunities to enjoy clean
air, especially as measured by visibility criteria, but
households can experience the greatest improvement in air
quality by moving from urban areas to nonmetropolitan sites
within any region, or from SMSAs in one region to nonmetropolitan areas in another.

Regional differences in water quality, if they do exist,
are even less obvious. Evidence of water pollution can be
found throughout the country. Future improvements in water
quality will depend on the application of more advanced
(tertiary) levels of wastewater treatment. Herein may lie
the basis for distinguishing among regions. Arid climates
are believed to offer the best opportunity to use land-
application techniques for tertiary treatment. Full exploitation of these techniques could be a cost-effective means
for improving the quality of surface- and groundwater while
simultaneously augmenting water supplies for irrigation
purposes.

On balance, then, the present patterns of interregional
migration confer an environmental and natural resource benefit to society as a whole. However, conclusion is not drawn
from a detailed review of development pressures on sensitive
environmental areas in any of the regions. Nor have the
growing environmental and resource (especially water) demands of fuel extraction in the West been considered (Harte
and El-Gossier 1978). Measures taken to protect areas of
environmental or cultural value in the South and West combined with competition for scarce resources due to coal

mining, oil-shale extraction, and the like may work to limit urban growth in these regions. The "prevention of significant deterioration" provisions of the Clean Air Act (1977 amendments), for example, place severe limitations on new sources of air emissions in the vicinity of wilderness areas, national monuments, and other classified areas. Several proposed power plants in the West may be adversely affected by these requirements. Conceivably, some restraint on urban growth could result if utilities and industrial corporations are unable to find a sufficient number of suitable sites. It is more likely, however, that these amendments and similar protective measures will serve to channel growth within western states rather than to restrict it.

Other environmental and natural resource policies may bear either directly or indirectly on the current trends in population redistribution. Policies that affect the price of fossil fuels (taxes or price deregulation) or the economics of harnessing solar energy will influence migrating households in proportion to the importance that such households place on energy expenditures. Water resource development projects, such as the Central Arizona Project, will subsidize additional growth in the Southwest. At the local level, successful use of eminent domain to wrest water supplies from nonurban users may ease the concern of some who contemplate a move to the South or the West.

Air- and water-quality policies enacted at the federal level seem fairly evenhanded with respect to their geographic application. For example, all new sources of air and water emissions covered in the Clean Air Act and the Clean Water Act must meet the same emissions standards. But recent policy interpretations and emphases promise to produce subtle distinctions among regions.

The Environmental Protection Agency's nonattainment policy is illustrative. It requires all new sources of air emissions wishing to locate in areas currently violating the air-quality standards to buy emissions offsets or credits from existing sources (Public Law 95-95, Clean Air Act Amendments of August 7, 1977). However, President Carter's proposed urban policy would relax these rules for older urban areas by allowing local governments to accumulate offset credits as old sources are closed down and to offer them as inducements to new sources at a later date. If enacted, this would put declining urban areas at a decided advantage in bidding for new industrial growth.

Water-quality policy remains geographically neutral in

its application. The one exception could be EPA's emphasis
on a thorough investigation of land application for tertiary
wastewater treatment. To the extent that EPA's interest in
this method of treating liquid wastes is translated into
preferential funding of wastewater projects, southwestern
states, where an arid climate provides optimal conditions
for land application of wastewater, would stand to benefit.
    State and local environmental laws may also create in-
centives or barriers to growth. California, for example,
has enacted more restrictive automobile emissions standards than those imposed by the federal government.
Colorado may follow suit. These regulations increase
the price and operating costs of automobiles. How
onerous these costs may be to prospective in-migrants
is difficult to judge, but for most households, they are
unlikely to be a critical element in the decision to
migrate.

SUMMARY

We have seen that population redistribution at the metropolitan level is fairly neutral, on balance, with respect
to environmental and resource consumption effects. Current
redistribution patterns at the regional level, however,
appear to convey a net social benefit, defined largely in
terms of fossil-fuel savings. Selected environmental and
resource policies at federal, state, and local levels may
exert some influence on current redistributional patterns,
but the impact is not likely to be major. Possible exceptions are policies that affect the price of energy. If
prices are deregulated or if substantial energy taxes are
enacted, the pace of migration to the South and West is
likely to quicken.

REFERENCES

American Gas Association (1975) *1974 Gas Facts*. Arlington,
    Va.: American Gas Association.
American Gas Association (1977) 27th Annual Household
    Heating Survey, Gas Utility Industry, U.S., 1973-1977.
    American Gas Association, Arlington, Va.
Anderson, R. (1973) *Residential Energy Consumption, Single
    Family Housing*. Columbia, Md.: Hittman Associates, Inc.
Arthur D. Little, Inc. (1974) *Residential and Commercial
    Energy Use Patterns 1970-90*. *Project Independence*.
    Cambridge, Mass.: Arthur D. Little, Inc.

Association of Bay Area Governments (1976) *Integrated Land Use/Air Quality/Water Quality Control Study for Sonoma County, California.* San Francisco, Calif.: Association of Bay Area Governments.
Calvin, M. (1974) Solar energy by photosynthesis. *Science* 184:375-381.
Chase Econometric Associates (1974) *Report to the Council on Environmental Quality.* No. 2. New York: Chase Econometric Associates.
Edison Electric Institute (1975) *EEI Statistical Yearbook.* New York: Edison Electric Institute.
Edwards, J., and Schofer, J. (1975) Relationships between Transportation Energy Consumption and Urban Structure: Results of Simulation Studies. Department of Civil Engineering, Northwestern University.
Energy and Environmental Analysis (1977) *Energy Consumption Data Base.* Vol. III. Ch. 7, Final Report. Washington, D.C.
Federal Energy Administration (1974) *Project Independence Report.* Washington, D.C.: U.S. Government Printing Office.
Hall, J. (1975) *Land Application of Wastewater.* Philadelphia: U.S. Environmental Protection Agency, Region III.
Hanke, S., and Flack, J. (1968) Effects of metering urban water. *American Water Works Journal* 60(December):677-681.
Harte, J., and El-Gossier, M. (1978) Energy and water. *Science* 199:623-634.
Hirst, E. (1978) Effects of federal residential energy conservation programs. *Science* 199:845-851.
Hoch, I. (1977) The Role of Energy in the Regional Distribution of Economic Activity. Paper presented at the Conference on Balanced National Growth and Regional Change, September 24, Austin, Texas.
Hydroscience, Inc. (1975) *An Overview of Waste Loads and Urban-Suburban Stream Quality Response.* Westwood, N.J.: Hydroscience, Inc.
Ingram, G., and Fauth, G. (1974) *TASSIM: A Transportation and Air Shed Simulation Model.* Vol. 1. Prepared for the U.S. Department of Transportation, Washington, D.C.
Ingram, G., and Pellechio, A. (1976) Air Quality Impacts of Land Use Patterns: Some Simulation Results for Mobile Source Pollutants. Department of City Planning, Harvard University.
Kelso, M., Martin, W., and Mack, L. (1973) *Water Supplies and Economic Growth in an Arid Environment.* Tucson: University of Arizona Press.

Keyes, D. (1977a) Metropolitan Development and Air Quality.
  Working paper 5049-16. The Urban Institute, Washington, [
Keyes, D. (1977b) Metropolitan Development and Water Qual-
  ity. Working paper 5049-11. The Urban Institute, Wash-
  ington, D.C.
Keyes, D., and Peterson, G. (1977) Metropolitan Develop-
  ment and Energy Consumption. Working paper 5049-15.
  The Urban Institute, Washington, D.C.
Mayer, H. (1969) The Spatial Expression of Urban Growth.
  Resource paper no. 7. Association of American Geo-
  graphers, Commission on College Geography, Washington,
  D.C.
Murray, C., and Reeves, E. (1975) Estimated use of water
  in the United States in 1975. Table 10 in *Geological
  Survey Circular 765*. Washington, D.C.: U.S. Geological
  Survey.
National Association of Homebuilders (1974) *Economic News
  Notes* XX(1).
Neels, K., Cheslow, M., Kirby, R., and Peterson, G. (1977)
  An Empirical Investigation of the Effects of Land Use
  on Urban Travel. Working paper 5049-17-1. The Urban
  Institute, Washington, D.C.
Oak Ridge National Laboratory (1975) *Fuel Use by Single
  Family Homes*, Figure 11. Oak Ridge, Tenn.: Oak Ridge
  National Laboratory.
Office of Technology Assessment (1977) Application of
  Solar Technology to Today's Energy Needs. Draft docu-
  ment. Washington, D.C.
Porges, R. (1957) Factors influencing per capita water
  consumption. *Water & Sewage Works* 104:199-204.
Regional Plan Association, Inc., and Resources for the
  Future (1974) *Regional Energy Consumption*. RPA bulle-
  tin 121. New York: Regional Plan Association.
Response Analysis Corporation (1974) *Lifestyles and Energy:
  1973 National Survey*. Report prepared for the Washing-
  ton Center for Metropolitan Studies, Washington, D.C.
Roberts, J. (1975) *Energy Land Use and Growth Policy:
  Implications for Metropolitan Washington*. Washington,
  D.C.: Metropolitan Washington Council of Governments.
Stewart, J., ed. (1973) *Proceedings of a Workshop on Land
  Disposal of Wastewaters*. Raleigh, N.C.: Water Resources
  Research Institute, North Carolina State University.
Sweet, A. (1974) Effects of residential building type on
  energy consumption. *Building Research* April/June:18-24.
Tokmanhekin, M., and Harvey, D. (1974) *Residential Energy
  Consumption, Multi-Family Housing Final Report*. Colum-
  bia, Md.: Hittman Associates, Inc.

U.S. Bureau of the Census (1972) *1970 Census of Housing: Housing Characteristics for States, Cities, and Counties.* Vol. 1, Part 1. Washington, D.C.: U.S. Department of Commerce.

U.S. Bureau of the Census (1975) *Annual Housing Survey: 1973 Part A, General Housing Characteristics.* Washington, D.C.: U.S. Department of Commerce.

U.S. Bureau of the Census (1976a) *Characteristics of New Housing Construction Reports.* Washington, D.C.: U.S. Department of Commerce.

U.S. Bureau of the Census (1976b) *Consumer Expenditure Survey Series.* Washington, D.C.: U.S. Department of Commerce.

U.S. Bureau of the Census and U.S. Department of Housing and Urban Development (1976) *Construction Report: Characteristics of New One-Family Homes: 1975.* Washington, D.C.: U.S. Government Printing Office.

U.S. Bureau of the Census and U.S. Department of Housing and Urban Development (1978) *Annual Housing Survey: 1976, Current Housing Reports.* Washington, D.C.: U.S. Government Printing Office.

U.S. Council on Environmental Quality (1976) *Environmental Quality, the Seventh Annual Report of CEQ.* Washington, D.C.: U.S. Government Printing Office.

U.S. Department of Energy (1979) *National Energy Plan II.* Washington, D.C.: U.S. Department of Energy.

U.S. Environmental Protection Agency (1977) National Air Quality and Emissions Trends Report 1976. EPA-450/1-77-002. Research Triangle Park, N.C.

Ward, J., and Paulhaus, N., Jr. (1974) Suburbanization and Its Implications for Urban Transporation Systems. Study prepared for the U.S. Department of Transportation, Systems Development and Technology, Washington, D.C.

Wildhorn, S., Burright, B., Enns, J., and Kirkwood, T., eds. (1975) *How to Save Gasoline: Public Policy Alternatives for the Automobile.* Prepared for the RAND Corp. Cambridge, Mass.: Ballinger.

SOCIAL SERVICES AND
POPULATION REDISTRIBUTION

Robert Perlman

INTRODUCTION

In view of the significant place that the social services
occupy in the lives of Americans and in the politics and
economics of the country, it is remarkable that so little
study has been devoted to the relationship between social
services and the distribution and movement of population.
Health and welfare programs now account for one-fifth of
all goods and services produced in the United States and
expenditures in this field exceed 40 percent of all funds
spent by federal, state, and local governments.

This paper seeks to relate social services to the population movements of the 1970s. It focuses mainly on
vulnerable populations, such as the elderly or the poor,
on the assumption that these groups generate the heaviest
demands for health and welfare services. As background
the paper notes briefly the constraints within which
policy makers typically respond to changes in the demand
for services. It describes the present geographic
distribution of services and the extent to which it coincides with the distribution of vulnerable populations.
The population movements of this decade are then considered
and the paper concludes with a discussion of social service
policies in this context.

It should be noted at the outset that policies governing
the allocation of social service resources apparently have
had little impact on the movements of people in this country. The critical issues revolve instead around the ways

Robert Perlman is Professor of Social Welfare, Florence
Heller Graduate School for Advanced Studies in Social
Welfare, Brandeis University.

228

in which social welfare policies will respond to the population redistribution that is taking place in the 1970s.

There is no generally accepted definition of what constitutes the "social services." This term will be used here to refer to programs concerned with health, income maintenance, and personal care.[1] These programs cover a large and varied field and it becomes hazardous to make generalizations about programs as disparate as retirement benefits, general hospital services, public assistance, and rehabilitative services for the disabled.

Notwithstanding the differences in purpose, target population, organization, and financing, all the services have one characteristic in common that is especially relevant to this inquiry: the social services are usually directed at categories of people with a particular condition or status related to their age, income, physical or mental state, employment, or family situation. These conditions provide the legal basis for eligibility for most benefits; they generate the demand for others. Frequently the conditions overlap in the same individual, family, or geographic area. The most important instance of this overlap is the combination of deprivations and needs that are characteristic of many blacks, Hispanics, and other minorities.

This link between demographic characteristics and the demand for social services provides the main tool for analysis in this paper. We shall assume that the demands for services vary directly with the proportion of the old, the very young, the physically and mentally impaired, and the poor in a population.

[1]The major programs in each of the three areas are:

Health services. Medical, dental, hospital, and nursing services provided or paid for by private insurance, consumers, the Veterans Administration, the Public Health Service, and the Social Security Administration, which administers Medicare and Medicaid.

Income maintenance. The social insurances (primarily old age, survivors, disability, and health insurance; and unemployment compensation) and the income-tested programs (Aid to Families with Dependent Children, Supplemental Security Income, food stamps, etc.).

Personal care services. Supportive and rehabilitative programs for children, the aged, families; group services; and information and access services.

Sometimes the demand for services by a vulnerable group
is almost automatically translated into use or consumption
of social service benefits, as in the case of elderly
individuals receiving social security retirement benefits.
At other times, the demand is present but is not met and
continues as an unfulfilled need, as when many poor preg-
nant women do not receive adequate prenatal care. For the
purposes of this paper, we shall assume that as families
and individuals who are vulnerable move from place to place,
they bring about increases and decreases in the demand for
services, whether or not their needs are in fact met.

The connection between membership in a vulnerable population and the demand for services can be illustrated by
reference to the elderly. They are heavy consumers of
retirement benefits and Medicare. Because there is a high
proportion of low-income people among the aged and because
health and physical needs generally increase with age, the
elderly consume large amounts of subsidized nursing, medical,
and hospital care.

The responses of policy makers to shifts in the demand
for social services will be shaped by the dynamics of
decision making and financing in the health and welfare
systems. In recent decades tremendous expansion has taken
place in the social services. Between 1950 and 1975, public
support alone increased tenfold. Significant elements in
American society are now balking at the continued growth
of social programs and are pressing to reduce some of them
from their present levels. Other forces are working for
further development of programs, such as national health
insurance. Which programs will be cut, which will be
frozen, and which will be expanded in the next decade or
so will significantly affect the extent to which the distribution of services coincides with the geographic distribution of vulnerable populations.

Which programs and target populations will gain or lose
support will depend, in part, on who pays the bill. The
financial resources of states and localities, together with
the willingness of voters to support services, account for
great variation. Thus, as Orr (1976) points out: "public
assistance (welfare) benefits in the most generous states
are over six times as large as those in the least generous
states." The main thrust in recent years has been for
localities to shift the cost of social services upward to
state governments, who in turn press Washington to assume
more and more of the financial burden.

It should be noted that "politically unattractive"
groups, such as poor female-headed families, generally fare

better under federal financing and federal minimum standards
than they do under state funding. Other groups, such as
those with physical disabilities, have been more successful
in exerting pressures on state legislatures and governors.
The formulas by which costs are divided among levels of
government have become major political issues, calling
into being coalitions along both interest and geographic
lines and producing profound impacts on the distribution
of social service resources among areas of the country and
among consumers of the services.

A few other characteristics of the social services require
brief comment. Except for cash transfers, most social
services are delivered from physical facilities by specialized personnel. Location, access, and transportation,
therefore, become important considerations, especially for
people in areas of low population density and for the aged,
the sick, and the disabled. These considerations raise a
number of questions: To what extent will the population
movements of the 1970s require new locations for service?
Will professional personnel move to areas of population
growth? Will the rising cost of energy inhibit travel to
centrally located facilities?

Changes in the technology and organization of services
affect the siting of facilities, the location decisions of
professionals, and patterns of use. One example is the
recent movement to deinstitutionalize the mentally ill,
the retarded, and other groups and to relocate them in
their homes or in facilities within the community. Other
examples are the new communication technology for the
diagnosis and treatment of illness and the reassignment of
tasks to health professionals with less training than that
of a physician; these open up possibilities for decentral-
izing health services and serving populations over larger
areas.

However, institutional rigidities and political resistance often retard the adoption of new organizational and
technical developments. In the first example, deinstitu-
tionalization has led to severe difficulties because
communities receiving people from institutions were not
prepared to provide essential services. In the other
examples, the flow of Medicare and Medicaid funds, training
policies, and the personal preferences of physicians may
inhibit the decentralization of health and hospital services.

The choice of target populations and of goals for the
social services is essentially a political process, resting
ultimately on collective evaluations of what is desirable
and possible. Two primary and recurring issues concern the

respective roles of the family and the state and the determination of those conditions and problems that are morally
"worthy" of public intervention. Fundamentally, however,
decisions about the purpose, quality, quantity, and location
of social services in American society are very much inter-
laced with choices concerning racial and ethnic matters,
income redistribution, economic development, and social
control. Political decisions about these issues will
largely determine which people and which geographic areas
will be given priority in the social services.

SPATIAL DISTRIBUTION OF SERVICES

Social services in the United States were first developed
in densely populated urban centers where there were greater
needs and a stronger economic base to support these services
than in rural areas. As a consequence, the North, the
East, and metropolitan areas in general have provided more
services and better benefits--in terms of gross and per-
capita expenditures--than the West, the South, and nonmetropolitan areas. It should be kept in mind that almost
half the residents of the South live in nonmetropolitan
areas, but almost 8 out of 10 persons in the Northeast and
the West live in metropolitan areas. The North Central
area population is two-thirds metropolitan.[2]

The long-standing pattern of stronger services and
higher benefits in the Northeast and in urban areas is
illustrated in Table 1 in terms of payments in Aid to
Families with Dependent Children (AFDC), preventive medical
care, hospital beds, and the availability of physicians.
Comparisons of the Northeast with the South and the West
reveal the sharpest contrasts.

Since World War II, shifts have been taking place in
the distribution of services in response to a combination
of forces: the movement of population, changes in per-
capita income and tax revenues, federal intervention and
support, and the personal preferences of professional
personnel. In some instances, court decisions concerning
"the right to service" have accelerated the development of
services in states that were previously poorly served.

One illustration of the redistribution of services is

[2]The percentage of the population living in metropolitan
areas in 1974 was 79.2 in the Northeast, 66.5 in the North
Central region, 56.4 in the South, and 77.9 in the West.

TABLE 1   Availability of Selected Resources by Region and
Metropolitan and Nonmetropolitan Areas

	Average AFDC Payment per Recipient ($)[a]	Percent of Population under 17 Years with Routine Physical Exam. in Past 2 Years	Nonfederal Hospital Beds per 1,000 Population[b]	Nonfederal Patient-Care Physicians per 100,000
Northeast	74-111	72.6	7.9-8.2	--
North Central	39-86	62.3	6.5-7.3	--
West	36-76	60.5	4.7-5.1	--
South	14-61	56.4	5.8-6.5	--
Metropolitan	--	66.7		149
Nonmetropolitan	--	53.3		68

[a] In part, these payments reflect differences in the cost
of living. Only three states fall outside these ranges:
Maine's average payment was $50, Hawaii's was $93, and
California's was $94.

[b] The ranges represent the divisions within each region,
e.g., the Pacific and Mountain divisions in the West.

SOURCES: Column 1--Social Security Administration (1976);
Columns 2 and 3--National Center for Health Statistics
(1976); Column 4--Kindig (1976).

the trend toward more equal distribution of hospital beds.
Since 1948, when the Hill-Burton program became operational,
"the distribution over the country of hospital beds has
become more nearly balanced. States such as Mississippi,
Alabama, Arkansas, Georgia, and Tennessee, which had the
lowest bed-population ratios in 1948, now are at the
national average or above it. Some of the states with
particularly high bed-population ratios in 1948 have actually experienced a decrease. Within states there is also
evidence of an improved balance in hospital facilities
between the less and more affluent areas" (U.S. Bureau of
Health Resources Development 1975).
   Another example of the shifting of resources is the

TABLE 2 Selected Characteristics of Population by Region and Metropolitan and Nonmetropolitan Areas

	Year	North-east	North Central	West	South	Metro-politan Areas	Nonmetro-politan Areas
1. Infant mortality rate (per 1,000 live births)[a]	1975	15.5	15.8	14.1	17.8	--	--
2. Percent of population 65 years and over	1975	11.2%	10.6%	9.5%	10.5%	9.2%	11.4%
3. Percent of population below poverty line	1975	10.2%	9.7%	11.7%	16.2%	9.7%	14.0%
4. Percent of families headed by females	1970	11.8%	9.3%	10.3%	12.0%	11.5%	9.3%
5. Average number of days of disability	1973	13.9	15.5	18.1	18.4	16.3	16.9
6. Incidence of acute conditions[b]	1973	153.3	185.4	192.3	171.7	177.4	170.1

[a]Deaths of infants under 1 year.
[b]Rate per 100 persons of all ages.

SOURCES: Item 1--National Center for Health Statistics (1977, p. 6). Item 2--U.S. Bureau of the Census (1975, 1976). Item 3--U.S. Bureau of the Census (1977, pp. 23, 38-40). Item 4-- U.S. Bureau of the Census (1973, pp. 1-312, 1-413). Items 5 and 6--National Center for Health Statistics (1976).

movement of physicians to the suburbs. In 1943, the
physician/population ratio for America's inner cities was
1 to 500 and for suburban areas it was 1 to 2,000. Twenty-
five years later, in 1968, the inner cities had a ratio of
1 to 10,000 and the suburbs had a ratio of 1 to 500
(National Center for Health Statistics 1976).

Notwithstanding these trends, the more heavily populated
North and East continue to have a proportionately larger
share of health and welfare resources than the South and
West. The share for metropolitan areas is greater than
for nonmetropolitan areas. However, it would be erroneous
to consider all deviations from an equal per capita distribution of resources as "maldistribution" because the
need for services is not equally or randomly distributed
in the general population. We pointed out earlier that
virtually all social services are delivered to categories
of people distinguished by income, age, health condition,
and family status and that the characteristics that are
critical in terms of need for services are concentrated
in certain areas.

This distribution of needs must be taken into account
before we can evaluate the distribution of services. In
Table 2, we have selected six indicators of need and shown
their distribution by region and by metropolitan/nonmetro-
politan areas. These indicators are infant mortality, the
percentage of the population 65 and over, the percentage
of the population living below the poverty line, the percentage of households headed by females, the number of
days of disability, and the incidence of acute conditions.[3]

These indicators are ranked by area in Table 3. What do
they suggest about the distribution of vulnerable populations?
The South evidences the greatest needs in terms of infant
mortality, poverty, female-headed familites, and disability.
The rankings in each of the other three regions are mixed.

On three of five measures, nonmetropolitan areas reveal
greater potential need for services; only in terms of

[3]Acute illnesses are of relatively short duration, although
they account for about 60 percent of all bed disability days.
The definition of acute illness is an illness that "must
have caused the person to seek medical attention or to miss
work or school, go to bed or cut down on other activity"
National Center for Health Statistics 1976, p. 239.

The data in Table 2 refer to the number of incidents of
acute illness in a year, presented as the rate per 100
persons of all ages.

TABLE 3   Ranking of Areas by Vulnerable Populations

Indicators	North-east	North Central	West	South	Metro-politan	Non-metro-politan
Infant mortality	3	2	4	1	--	--
Percentage elderly	1	2	4	3	2	1
Percentage in poverty	3	4	2	1	2	1
Percentage female-headed families	2	4	3	1	1	2
Days of disability	4	3	2	1	2	1
Acute conditions	4	2	1	3	1	2

SOURCE: Based on Table 2.

female-headed households and the incidence of acute conditions do the metropolitan areas exceed the nonmetropolitan
areas.   However, data on central cities and areas outside
central cities must be added to give a more complete picture of metropolitan areas.   Within metropolitan areas,
central cities rank significantly higher than the outlying
areas with respect to the percentages of the population
over 65 years of age, people living in poverty, and female-
headed families.

A comparison of services and population, as shown in
Tables 1-3, shows that the South has the greatest extent
of poverty but the lowest AFDC payment levels, the highest
infant mortality rate, and the lowest proportion of population under 17 years of age who had been given a physical
examination in the past 2 years.   The Northeast rated
highest in benefits and next to lowest on two indicators
of need--poverty and infant mortality.   Similarly, metropolitan areas are currently endowed with more plentiful
health resources than nonmetropolitan areas but are
apparently less in need of them on a per capita basis,
although differences between inner-city areas and suburbs
should be kept in mind.

The data suggest that there is a mismatch between the distribution of social services and populations that are vulnerable. Moreover, the areas that are least able financially to support services need them the most. Of course, the situation is not static--both people and services move--and, as we noted above, shifts in health and welfare resources are evident. Some of these shifts, such as the building of hospitals in underserved areas, tend to diminish the inequalities; some, such as the movement of physicians out of the central cities to the suburbs, exacerbate the imbalance between human needs and available resources.

RECENT DEMOGRAPHIC AND ECONOMIC CHANGES

Before considering the population movements of the 1970s, we must take note of changes in the demographic profile of the United States that have a direct bearing on the size of vulnerable populations and therefore on the level of demand for social services. We touch only briefly on a few aspects here.

The number and proportion of the elderly have been rising steadily. Between 1950 and 1974, for example, the number of persons 65 years of age and over almost doubled-- from 12.3 million to 21.8 million. In 1950, they were 8.1 percent of the total population; by 1974, they had become 10.3 percent of the population. The demand for social services has been increasing among the elderly not only because their numbers have increased but also because they are living longer and a greater percentage of them use these services. Nursing homes offer a good illustration. There were approximately 500,000 people 65 years and over in nursing homes in 1964, constituting 3 percent of the elderly population. Ten years later the number had increased to 1,000,000, constituting 5 percent of the elderly (U.S. Bureau of the Census 1976, p. 204).

The birthrate has been declining for some time. Between 1950 and 1974 it dropped from 24.1 per 1,000 population to 15.0, so that the increase in the number of children has been declining. Children 0 to 14 years of age increased by 3.2 percent between 1950 and 1960 but by only 0.4 percent between 1960 and 1970.

The number of children who live in families with only one parent or with both parents working has been increasing rapidly and, as a result, the demand for day care and other services has presumably increased. Between 1954 and 1975,

the number of female workers who had ever been married and
who had one or more children under 6 years of age rose from
2.2 million to 5.4 million. The proportion of these women
who are working rose dramatically from 17.0 percent in 1954
to 38.9 percent in 1975 (U.S. Bureau of the Census 1976,
p. 375). The estimated number of children involved in
divorces and annulments more than tripled between 1953,
when it was 330,000, and 1974, when it reached 1,099,000.
Similarly the proportion of children living with only one
parent has grown from 9.3 percent in 1960 to 17.1 percent
in 1975 (U.S. Bureau of the Census 1976, p. 67).

A combination of factors may be contributing to increased
economic independence among women and thereby to their
mobility. Greater participation in the labor force by
women, the continuing rise in the divorce rate, and the
redefinition of sex roles may lead to greater mobility of
women, including those with children.

There have been some fluctuations in the number and
percentage of persons living below the government's estimate
of a poverty level, with the number falling from 28.5 million (14.7 percent of total population) in 1966 to 25.9
million (12.3 percent of total population) in 1975. For
the population over 44 years of age, the proportion of
people living below the poverty level decreased during
this period. However, it remained stable for those under
14 years (18%) and those between the ages of 14 and 21
(14%) (U.S. Bureau of the Census 1976, p. 467).

Thus, although it is true that the birthrate is declining and children comprise a smaller part of the population,
currently, nearly one child in five lives with only one
parent and one child in five lives in poverty. The distribution of these children and their families has weighty
implications for the demand for social services.

The implications of demographic trends for the AFDC
program have been explored by Wertheimer and Zedlewski
(1976), who point out:

> that the growth in the AFDC caseload will be greatly
> affected by the birth rate, the marriage rate, and
> the divorce rate prevailing during the next ten
> years. If society moves toward greater family
> stability and AFDC benefits are increased only at
> the same rate as the cost of living, the AFDC
> caseload may not increase at all. If society moves
> toward less stability, the AFDC caseload may grow
> by more than 50 percent even if AFDC benefits in-
> crease only at the same rate as the cost of living.

The number of families headed by women is likely to
grow under a wide range of demographic assumptions.
. . . The number of families with low incomes is
highly sensitive to the divorce rate.

In our discussion of population redistribution in the
1970s we assume that the demographic trends noted above
will continue. In addition, we assume that economic conditions generally will remain at roughly the 1976-1977
level and that regional trends will continue, directly
affecting both the need for services and the financial
resources to support them. The tendency toward some
equalization among regions, already noted with regard to
services, is closely related to economic changes. From
1969 to 1976, per capita income in the South Atlantic and
Rocky Mountain areas rose 20 percent faster than per capita
income in New England and the Middle Atlantic states. Over
that period, more than one-third of the differential in
per-capita income between those two regions of the country
was eliminated. These economic changes are directly reflected in programs of income support in the various regions.
Writing about regional patterns in the 1965-1975 period,
Renshaw and Friedenberg (1977) note that in the Northeast
and Great Lakes regions:

a long-term reduction in job opportunities, aggravated
by the cyclical downswings in 1970 and 1974-75,
accelerated in the seventies. The redistribution
of manufacturing and related activities away from
these highly industrialized regions led to the rapid
growth of public assistance and unemployment compensation payments. The transfers contributed to
financial difficulties, because they increased faster
than the State and local tax base. In contrast, in
the southern and western regions . . . economic activi-
ity grew rapidly and was relatively unaffected by
recessions. Therefore personal income required
relatively little supplementation by transfers.

Another variable, energy, must be taken into account
among our assumptions. It is assumed here that in the
short term energy will continue to be available at approximately current levels, but it is recognized that both short-
term and long-term changes in the energy situation can
affect the distribution and use of social services. It was
found in the 1973-1974 energy crisis that serious difficulties arose for small numbers of people who had to travel

long distances for highly specialized services. For example, instances were reported in Connecticut of a leukemic
child who needed to be taken regularly by car to a hospital
in New York and of a Vietnam War amputee who had to travel
weekly to rehabilitation services in another city. In
both situations the inability to buy gasoline created
problems that could magnify in number and severity in a
more prolonged energy shortage (Perlman and Warren 1977).

Population Redistribution in the 1970s

Between 1970 and 1975, approximately 9 million people
moved from one region of the country to another and 12
million moved between metropolitan and nonmetropolitan
areas. (These groups are not mutually exclusive.) Little
information is available on the characteristics of the
interregional migrants. The data in Table 4 below have
two limitations: they are based on only 1 year's experience and they pertain to only small percentages of the
total populations of the regions. Nevertheless, they
provide an indication of net changes in the numbers of
persons who are vulnerable within each region as well as
shifts in the number of persons financially capable of
supporting social services.

TABLE 4   Net Regional In-Migration and Out-Migration by
Selected Characteristics 1975-1976 (in thousands)

	North-east	North Central	South	West
Under 5 years of age	−29	−16	+21	+22
65 Years or over	−18	−18	+27	+8
Below poverty level	−40	−100	+78	+63
Unemployed				
Male	+1	−7	−20	+30
Female	−13	−10	+19	+4
4 College years	−42	−18	+17	+41
Professional, technical workers				
Male	−7	−34	+16	+25
Female	−4	−15	+7	+13

SOURCE: U.S. Bureau of the Census (1977, p. 108).

The general pattern is consistent except for unemployed
men. With respect to such vulnerable groups as the old,
the young, the poor, and unemployed women, the Northeast
and North Central regions have experienced net decreases
and the South and the West have experienced net increases.
This is most striking in terms of the number of persons
living below the poverty line.

The net changes in the movement of poor people suggested
by the data above are confirmed in a recent study in which
Long (1978) concludes:

> the most important empirical result was to detect
> the southern region's shift from annual net out-
> migration to net immigration of the poor between
> 1967 and 1977. Concomitantly, the Northeast, where
> many migrants from the South had gone in previous
> decades, came to have a small annual net outmigra-
> tion of persons below the poverty level. The West
> and North Central regions appear to be continuing
> patterns in existence in the late 1960's, with the
> West having net immigration and the North Central
> region net outmigration of persons below the poverty
> level.

The growing tendency of men to leave the labor force not
only at age 65 but also between the ages of 55 and 64 can be
expected to increase the number of retirees moving to the
warmer states of the South and the Southwest. By comparison, labor-force participation rates for females over 65
years of age have remained quite stable since the mid-
1950s and have increased for women between the ages of
55 and 64 (U.S. Bureau of the Census 1976, p. 373).

The tendencies cited above must be seen in juxtaposition
with indications that while the South and the West showed
a net increase in the number of more educated, highly
skilled, and higher income adults, the North and the East
showed a decline in groups that strengthen the capacity
of an area to provide services to vulnerable and dependent
populations. It would appear, therefore, that although
the burdens of providing services may have declined somewhat in the Northeast--at least in terms of population
movements--and increased in the South and West, the latter
regions may be acquiring more resources for assuming those
burdens.

Available information concerning the influx of undocumented or illegal aliens into the United States is extremely
inadequate. The number of illegal Mexican aliens in the

Southwest is estimated in the millions. It can be safely
assumed that a large part of the illegal immigration consists of a low-income, high-need population. However, no
systematic effort has been made to assess the actual or
potential impact on health and welfare services.

The character of the movements in and out of metropolitan
areas, central cities, and suburbs has been documented in
the paper by Berry and Dahmann in this volume. The metropolitan areas have been growing more slowly than the nonmetropolitan areas and have been losing migrants to the
areas outside the standard metropolitan statistical areas
(SMSAs), especially those with manufacturing, higher education institutions, and retirement centers. However, the
movements to cities and to suburbs continue. According
to Berry and Dahmann: "More blacks, more poor, and greater
numbers of young persons are moving to, rather than from,
central cities. The suburbs receive proportionately more
whites, the more affluent, and families rather than single
persons." Additional data appear in Table 5.

Clearly, in 1974, central cities and nonmetropolitan
areas had the highest proportions of the elderly, the
poor, and female-headed families. The changes that took
place in the preceding 4 years reveal a mixed picture. The
percentage of older people and female-headed households
increased most rapidly outside the central cities in the

TABLE 5   Selected Characteristics of Population in Metropolitan and Nonmetropolitan Areas in 1974 (in percent)[a]

	Nonmetro- politan Areas	Metro- politan Areas	Central Cities	Outside Central Cities
Population 65 years and over	11.4 (+8.1)	9.2 (+5.8)	10.8 (+0.2)	8.0 (+11.6)
Population below poverty line	14.0 (-30.0)	9.7 (-11.7)	14.0 (-9.0)	6.4 (-16.3)
Families receiv- ing public aid	0.7	0.9	1.7	0.5
Female-headed families	7.8 (+12.9)	10.4 (+23.9)	13.5 (+22.4)	7.7 (+26.1)

[a]Figures in parentheses represent percentage changes
between 1970 and 1974.

SOURCE: U.S. Bureau of the Census (1975).

suburbs and outlying towns and cities. Increased demand
for services in outlying areas could, therefore, be expected.
Some of the pressure on income programs may be lessened in
the nonmetropolitan areas, which registered the largest
drop in the proportion of people living below the poverty
level. Poverty declined least in the inner cities.

Another way of gauging the impact of recent movements
in and out of metropolitan areas is to compare two populations: the almost 7 million people who moved from SMSAs
to nonmetropolitan areas between 1970 and 1974 and the 5
million people who moved in the opposite direction. Unfortunately, data are available only on the ages of the two
populations. The nonmetropolitan areas received a higher
proportion of the old and the young in these shifts than
did the metropolitan areas. Between 1970 and 1975, of the
6,721,000 persons moving from SMSAs to locations outside
SMSAs, 23.2 percent were 5-14 years of age and 7.3 percent
were 65 or older. Of the 5,127,000 in-migrants to SMSAs,
19.2 percent were 5-14 years old and 3.9 percent were 65
or older (U.S. Bureau of the Census 1975).

Because nonmetropolitan areas and the South are receiving
larger numbers of the old and the young, pressures on
services related to these age-groups are increasing. Early
warnings of inadequacies can be seen in retirement communities. Elderly but healthy populations have moved into
retirement communities that provide only a minimum of
social services for the aging. As these people grow older
and require considerably more health and social services
(for example, nusing care, meals on wheels, hospitalization,
etc.), current service provisions will prove to be seriously
inadequate both in quantity and type of program.

The need for income-related programs will likely increase
in the South and the West, but will continue to be keenly
felt in all urban areas of the country, particularly in
the cities of the North and the East that continue to
receive black migrants from the South whose incomes are
only half as large as the incomes of blacks already living
in the cities.

The demand for the full range of health and welfare services in the cities of the Northeast will increase if current unemployment rates among blacks and Hispanics persist,
if substantial numbers of old people and poor people remain
in these cities, and if the number of one-parent families
increases in these cities. As a side effect, a strong
demand for urban social services (for example, greater use
of city hospitals) provides an opportunity for employment
of low-income residents of the city.

The movement of moderate- and middle-income families to the suburbs will probably be accompanied by a shift of service resources. The suburbs, having the strongest political and economic position, are likely to get the services they feel they need from both public and private sources and through direct consumer purchases. In this context, sectarian service organizations, primarily Catholic and Jewish, will continue to face choices between their responsibilities in the cities and their growing constituencies in the suburbs. The latter are not likely to suffer in the process.

In the absence of policy changes or major shifts in economic development, there will be a tendency toward equalization of particular benefits between regions. The improvement in economic conditions in the South and the West and the erosion of tax resources in the North will particularly contribute to equalization of public assistance and related benefits, because much of the recent growth in these expenditures has been financed by state and local governments (Friedman and Hausman 1977). This has intensified pressures on some of the northern, industrialized states to reduce their welfare costs. Because per-capita income is one of the principal determinants of the level of welfare benefits, rising income levels in states with traditionally low benefits can be expected to result in higher welfare benefits (Orr 1976).

We should note that mobility itself may generate demands for social services because it involves uprooting, strains, and readjustments for most people who migrate from one area to another. Although there is evidence that people with incipient or active mental disorders are overrepresented in the group that migrates, Berliner (1977) finds support for the assertion that "migration does contribute in some measure to mental illness."

Nonetheless, the vast body of evidence shows that migration is "an important vehicle of social mobility. . . . The generally positive experience of blacks who left the rural South, and of ethnic groups that left city ghettos, confirms the value of geographic mobility as a means of access to conditions that foster improvements in personal status" (Morrison 1977).

SOCIAL SERVICE POLICIES AND POPULATION REDISTRIBUTION

How can policy changes in the health and welfare field affect population movements in the 1970s and the years

beyond? The question rests on the debatable assumption
that these policies influence population distribution.
They do not seem to. Nor is there evidence that they
have been designed in the past to play a part in influencing population movements.

Research on these issues is meager. The literature on
mobility and motivations for moving reports that most
people move from one area to another primarily to improve
their incomes or jobs. Housing, schools, and environmental
amenities are secondary considerations. The quality of
health and welfare resources in a particular area does
not seem to be an important factor, even where services
and benefits vary widely. In many programs, such as
services to veterans, federal financing and adminstration
have largely eliminated regional and local differences.

The belief that higher public welfare benefits attract
low-income people to certain cities and states is not
supported by the evidence. Morrison (1977) indicates that
people who have migrated to New York "start using the
welfare system only gradually, not immediately; the delay
is more easily interpreted as due to discouragement in
finding work after the migrant arrives than to prior motivation for moving to New York deliberately to claim benefits."
Morrison also points out, however, that high benefits may
retard out-migration, causing welfare recipients "to pile
up" in such areas.

Deliberate efforts to shape the distribution of population are not characteristic of the social services. One
of the few studies, conducted for the Department of Commerce,
that touches on this subject, found that the following
programs had no impact on population movement or economic
growth: Head Start, Comprehensive Health Planning, Health
Facilities Construction, Medicaid, and Vocational Rehabilitation Services (Center for Political Research 1970).

This subject leads logically to a basic policy issue that
has recently surfaced with renewed urgency: Should public
policies be addressed to "places" or to "people"? Should
social-service resources be allocated, for example, to
economically declining areas with abandoned, aging populations or to growing areas with young families? Should
facilities and personnel be directed, through administrative
decision or incentives, to people in economically backward,
low-density rural areas? It seems to this observer that
a stronger case can be made for directing social resources
to vulnerable populations than to geographic areas as such.
To favor "places" over "people" is to put vulnerable groups
in double jeopardy; they will have been bypassed by the

workings of the market economy and then subjected to deliberate neglect by public policy.

There are, of course, political constraints on the use of policy to promote specific population goals. Muller (1975) argues:

> The older metropolis cannot reverse most of the conditions causing its fiscal problems, although some adverse effects can be mitigated. To attract middle-income families, socially controversial positions would have to be adopted, such as reversing long-standing public education policies and curtailing programs aimed at redistributing income. The political feasibility of either action is questionable, as their implementation would project an image of cities turning their backs on minorities and low income households.

In short, it is questionable whether public policies in the social services can or do influence population movements, but it is clear that policy affects the geographic distribution of health and welfare resources. The distribution of these resources depends greatly on the answers to the following questions:

1. Given the strained finances of localities and states and the greater taxing ability of the federal government, how will financial responsibilities for the services be divided between the federal government and the states?

2. Will the authority to set standards be exercised to ensure minimum, if not uniform, benefits across localities and states?

3. To what extent will services be organized and delivered on a categorical basis (for example, by age-group, income, type of disability, veteran status, etc.)? The influence of interest groups representing these consumer categories can affect the quality and the distribution of services.

4. How will policies concerning the social services be shaped by fundamental value choices in American society concerning racial and ethnic discrimination, income redistribution, economic development, and social control?

5. Will public policy be used explicitly to direct health and welfare resources to geographic areas with needs that are not being met?

We can hardly deal adequately in this paper with these issues. Most of our comments will be addressed to the first area--the locus and level of financial support--but we pause to take brief notice of the effort to use public policy to steer resources to areas of special need.

In terms of research and policy initiatives, far more work has been done on the distribution of health manpower than on the distribution of other social services. Attention has been largely focused on that costly and most independent of health resources, the private physician. Efforts have been directed toward encouraging doctors and other health personnel to practice in inner-city neighborhoods and rural areas. Federal support for professional education has been used toward this end, as have experiments and demonstrations in new forms of organizing services and reallocating tasks among professionals. The literature abounds with recommendations for policies to equalize the distribution of physicians and other health professionals.[4]

This example stands out as one of the few instances for which policy has been deliberately geared to improving the fit between human needs and the geographic distribution of social welfare resources. Resource distribution is generally far more influenced by the political decisions that are made about the financing of social services.

IMPLICATIONS OF ALTERNATIVE POLICIES

It is clearly impossible to weigh the implications of the thousands of policy choices in the social services that might affect their location, quantity, and quality. We shall concentrate here on the federal financing of services. Cities, counties, states, and regions continually compete for federal funds for health and welfare in order to lighten their own financial responsibilities and, at the same time, secure better services and benefits for their residents.

Practically every important decision in Washington about the support of social services calls into play coalitions of cities or states, increasingly banded together on a regional basis, to protect their interests in the shaping and implementation of social programs. An example is provided by the Northeastern-Midwest Coalition, a bipartisan group of 204 members of Congress from 16 states, who

[4]See, for example, U.S. Bureau of Health Resources Development (1975) and National Center for Health Statistics (1975).

commissioned a study of the food-stamp program and in May
1977 mounted an offensive to modify the Carter administration's proposals to reform that program so that their
areas would not lose funds to the South, which they thought
was favored by the proposed modifications.

In order to illustrate the implications that federal
financing has for the distribution of social services,
we shall examine three policy alternatives. The first
assumes a major extension of federal responsibilities
and an expansion of services. The second assumes a contraction of both the federal role and the scope and level
of social services. The third assumes only small, incremental changes in federal participation.

Under the first alternative, the federal government
would take over the financing of public assistance in all
its forms, would institute a national health program, and
would further develop supportive and rehabilitative services for vulnerable populations. This would entail the
infusion of large resources into the health and welfare
system. Of equal importance to the concerns of this paper,
this policy would minimize intrastate, interstate, and
interregional differences in benefit levels and quality of
services.

Under these circumstances, the social services might
have a greater impact on population redistribution than
they have had in the past, but would still not approach
the attraction power of local economic conditions as
reflected in job opportunities and income levels. Health
and welfare services are currently becoming more important
in the lives of Americans and may figure more prominently
in decisions to move, particularly if resources are increased and geographic differences are more nearly equalized. This will be the case particularly for those families
and individuals with clearly established needs for social
services. The relevance for the elderly has already been
noted. Because greater emphasis will be placed on noninstitutional, community-based care for the retarded, the
mentally ill, and other individuals who were formerly
institutionalized, their families will be even more sensitive to the availability of services in the areas in which
they live or to which they plan to move.

This alternative would primarily help those cities,
counties, and states that now have minimum resources for
social services. It would provide the greatest benefits
to the most socially and economically disadvantaged groups.
It could be expected to reinforce the slowdown in the
migration of blacks from South to North because income

support programs and other social services in the South
would provide greater benefits than they have in the past.

Indeed, these conditions might increase the flow of
migration to the South, the West, and to nonmetropolitan
areas because people with low or moderate incomes might
take greater risks in seeking better jobs and living conditions if they knew that their income maintenance, health,
and other needs would be met more fully than in the past.
The effects on mobility of greater assumption of responsibility by the federal government for functions and burdens
now primarily carried by the family, such as the cost of
health care, are unclear.

The second alternative presupposes that it is impossible
to maintain social services at their current levels or to
redistribute the financial costs upward to the federal
government. This would tend to further depress social
services in the areas that traditionally provide low
benefits. However, the improving economic situation in
the South and West would partly offset this effect. States
in those regions are already better positioned then they
have been, in comparison with the North and the East, to
meet the costs of health and welfare programs.

The northern and eastern states, with further weakening
of their economies and the diminution of federal support
for health and welfare, would have difficulty in maintaining the higher benefits they currently provide. The effects
would again be felt most keenly by the most dependent
population groups, certainly the minority groups in urban
centers. If the expansion of services might be expected
to facilitate population mobility, the contraction implied
in the second alternative would be likely to impede mobility
among vulnerable populations.

Realistically, the probable course of events would include neither of these extreme scenarios, but most likely
would result in a series of small, incremental changes.
These would include a modest welfare reform that would
reduce differences in benefits among states and regions
and the beginnings of a national health insurance program
that would deal with the most pressing problems, such as
the cost of catastrophic illnesses. At the same time, many
states would probably trim some of their social service
programs in order to reduce rising costs, although they
would also be pressed by well-organized interest groups
to maintain and expand other programs. The net effects
on population mobility would be minimal.

The policy alternatives discussed here are highly specu-
lative because there are large gaps in our understanding

of the relationship between the social services and population redistribution. The most basic kind of research
on these alternatives is needed.

SUMMARY

Historically, programs concerned with health, income
supports, and personal care have been heavily concentrated
in the North and the East and in urban areas with the
greatest population density. However, needs for these
social services are generated not by the population at
large, but by specific groups that are vulnerable: the
very young, the old, the poor, the sick, the disabled,
the unemployed. These groups are not evenly distributed
on a geographic basis.

Viewed in this light, the distribution of health and
welfare programs and benefits has not coincided with the
needs of geographic areas, especially the South and rural
places. This is due largely to the weaker economic base
in those areas, which accounts for both the higher level
of need and the lower capacity to support social services.

Recently, the relationship between services provided
and the needs of geographic areas has changed. There has
been a trend toward equalization of services and benefit
levels among the regions of the country. This trend is
related to shifts in population, improved economic conditions in the South and the West, a declining tax base to
finance services in the North and the East, and greater
participation by the federal government. Simultaneously,
health and welfare resources have been moving from central
cities to suburbs.

Although the data are limited, there are indications
that in the early 1970s the numbers of potentially dependent
persons, such as the aged and the poor, were increasing in
the South and the West and decreasing in the North and the
East. However, it must be emphasized that inner cities,
particularly in the North and the East, continue to have
tremendous needs for social services.

Policies governing the social services apparently have
not significantly affected population movements. However,
this may change as health and welfare services become more
important in the lives of all Americans--as they already
have for the aged.

Decisions that will be made in the next decade or so
about the financing, organization, and delivery of social
services will substantially determine their geographic
distribution and, in turn, the extent to which this distri-

bution will coincide with the distribution of vulnerable populations. Probably the most critical element in these decisions will be the extent to which the federal government assumes greater responsibility for supporting the services and the degree to which federal standards move toward equalization of benefits.

What those decisions will be and how they will affect the people who depend most heavily on the social services will be closely intertwined with the ways in which this country confronts issues of racial and ethnic discrimination, income redistribution, economic development, and unemployment. Those decisions will also reflect implicit national goals concerning the minimum conditions of life that the nation wants to ensure for all of its people.

REFERENCES

Berliner, J. (1977) Internal migration: a comparative disciplinary view. In *Internal Migration: A Comparative Perspective*. New York: Academic Press.

Center for Political Research (1970) Federal Activities Affecting Location of Economic Development. Vol. I. Report prepared for the U.S. Department of Commerce.

Friedman, B., and Hausman, L. (1977) Welfare in retreat: a dilemma for the federal system. *Public Policy* (July).

Kindig, D. (1976) *Health Manpower Issues*. HRA 76-40. Bureau of Health Manpower. Rockville, Md.: U.S. Department of Health, Education, and Welfare.

Long, L. H. (1978) Interregional migration of the poor: some recent changes. Series P-23, No. 73 in U.S. Bureau of the Census, *Current Population Reports*. Washington, D.C.: U.S. Department of Commerce.

Morrison, P. (1977) *New York State's Transition to Stability: The Demographic Outlook*. Santa Monica, Calif.: RAND.

Muller, T. (1975) Fiscal Issues in the Aging Metropolis. Prepared for the Conference on the Aging Metropolis. Center for Urban Policy, Rutgers University.

National Center for Health Statistics (1975) *Decennial Census Data for Selected Health Occupations: United States, 1970*. HRA 75-1231. Rockville, Md.: U.S. Department of Health, Education and Welfare.

National Center for Health Statistics (1976) *Health United States, 1975*. HRA 76-1232. Rockville, Md.: U.S. Department of Health, Education and Welfare.

National Center for Health Statistics (1977) *Monthly Vital Statistics Report, Advance Report, Final Mortality Statistics, 1975*. HRA 77-1120. Vol. 25, no. 11.

Rockville, Md.: U.S. Department of Health, Education
and Welfare.

Orr, L. (1976) Statement at the Workshop on the Implications of Population Redistribution, National Research
Council, Washington, D.C.

Perlman, R., and Warren, R. (1977) *Families in the Energy
Crisis*. Cambridge, Mass.: Ballinger.

Renshaw, V., and Friedenberg, H. (1977) Transfer payments:
regional patterns 1965-75. *Survey of Current Business* 57

U.S. Bureau of Health Resources Development (1975) *Factors
Influencing Practice Location of Health Manpower--
Review of the Literature*. Washington, D.C.: U.S.
Department of Health, Education and Welfare.

U.S. Bureau of the Census (1973) Characteristics of the
population, United States summary. In *1970 Census of
the Population*. Vol. 1. Washington, D.C.: U.S.
Department of Commerce.

U.S. Bureau of the Census (1975a) Mobility of the popula-
tion of the United States, March 1970 to March 1975.
Series P-20, No. 285 in *Current Population Reports*.
Washington, D.C.: U.S. Department of Commerce.

U.S. Bureau of the Census (1975b) Social and economic
characteristics of the metropolitan and nonmetropolitan
population, 1974 and 1970. Series P-23, No. 55 in
Current Population Reports. Washington, D.C.: U.S.
Department of Commerce.

U.S. Bureau of the Census (1976) Demographic aspects of
aging and the older population in the United States.
Series P-23, No. 59 in *Current Population Reports*.
Washington, D.C.: U.S. Department of Commerce.

U.S. Bureau of the Census (1977a) Characteristics of the
population below the poverty level, 1975. Series P-60,
No. 106 in *Current Population Reports*. Washington,
D.C.: U.S. Department of Commerce.

U.S. Bureau of the Census (1977b) Geographic mobility,
March 1975 to March 1976. Series P-20, No. 305 in
Current Population Reports. Washington, D.C.: U.S.
Department of Commerce.

U.S. Bureau of the Census (1977c) *Social Indicators 1976*.
Washington, D.C.: U.S. Department of Commerce.

U.S. Social Security Administration (1976) *Social Security
Bulletin Annual Statistical Supplement, 1974*. SSA
76-11700. Washington, D.C.: U.S. Department of Health,
Education and Welfare.

Wertheimer, R., and Zedlewski, S. (1976) *The Impact of
Demographic Change on the Distribution of Earned Income
and the AFDC Program: 1975-1985*. Washington, D.C.: The
Urban Institute.

IMPLICATIONS OF POPULATION
REDISTRIBUTION FOR EDUCATION

Martin T. Katzman

OVERVIEW

Population redistribution has always been with us. Many
of the trends observed today have their roots in the 19th
century or earlier. The westward movement and relative
decline of the Northeast began before the first Census in
1970 fixed the center of population slightly west of
Baltimore. As soon as significant urbanization commenced,
suburbs were linked to the downtown by horse-drawn street-
cars (Warner 1962). The 1970s, however, have brought two
related and unprecedented phenomena: an end to metropoli-
tanization in many parts of the country and a turnabout
in the chronic decline of many rural areas. Although many
central cities lost population in the 1960s, entire metropolitan areas appeared to lose population in the 1970s.
Although most of the metropolitan decline occurred in the
largest cities and in the Northeast, a slowdown in metropolitan growth is apparent throughout the nation (Berry
and Dahmann in this volume).

It is impossible to understand the implications of
population redistribution without taking account of the
decline in fertility to replacement levels. Population
redistribution during periods of aggregate population
growth results in more rapid growth for some areas than
for others. In the slow-growing areas, newspaper circu-
lation, bank deposits, and utility consumption may not
expand as fast as in the boom areas and land values may
not increase as much; nevertheless, all areas share in the
expansion that American society associates with progress.

Martin T. Katzman is Professor of Political Economy, School
of Social Sciences, University of Texas at Dallas.

253

When aggregate population growth approaches a standstill, population redistribution is a zero-sum game; growth in one area is an inevitable concomitant of decline in another

In general, American society has not yet learned to cope, either psychologically or politically, with decline. While there have been pockets of poverty left by declining sectors, such as textiles and coal mining, decline is largely beyond the American experience.

If decline were symmetric to growth, then public policy makers could simply replace a strategy of more building and more hiring with one of less. Because there are major irreversibilities in the behavior of the public sector, particularly in the disposal of public buildings and in firing personnel, a mere shifting of gears from forward to reverse is insufficient. Decline demands innovation because it is a new phenomenon, whereas the problems of growth have been confronted since the birth of the nation.

EFFECTS OF DEMOGRAPHIC CHANGES ON PUBLIC SERVICES, INSTITUTIONS, AND POLICIES

The demographic changes of the 1970s have aggregate, distributional, and compositional dimensions of relevance to the educational sector. The aggregate dimension reflects the absolute number of children of various ages in primary- and secondary-school systems; the distribution reflects their spatial location; and the composition reflects their racial and class attributes.

The Recent Trends

Aggregate Effects   Anticipating the impact of aggregate demographic trends is, in principle, easier for education than for other sectors. The reason is that the number of children entering, for example, kindergarten in 5 years can be ascertained by applying mortality tables to the number o 1-year-old children living today. Surprisingly, recent demographic changes and the problems they entail were not widely anticipated by educators and were experienced for several years before they were generally acknowledged.

Aggregate enrollments in primary and secondary schools had increased continuously until 1970. Since then, elementary enrollments have declined at a rate of more than 0.5 percent per year and will continue to decline into the early 1980s and at an even faster rate. If current patterns

TABLE 1   School-Age Population, 1950-1990

| | School-Age Population, Age 5-17 (thousands) | | |
| | Elementary | Secondary | |
	Age 5-13	Age 14-17	Total
1950	22,423	8,444	30,867
1960	32,985	11,219	44,204
1970	36,836	15,910	52,746
1974	34,002	16,878	50,880
1980	30,246	15,753	45,999
1985	30,380[a]	14,388	44,768
1990	34,643[a]	12,941	47,584

[a]Projected from Series II.

SOURCE: U.S. Bureau of the Census. Series P-25, No. 601, in *Current Population Reports*, Tables E, 6 and 8 [as reported in Davis and Lewis (1976, Table 3)].

of fertility persist, these declines will persist through 1990 or beyond. Because of the inertia of the age profile, secondary-school enrollments will continue to decline at least through the late 1980s regardless of any changes in fertility in the next 10 years (see Table 1).

Distributional Effects   Because of population redistribution, some school systems have faced or are likely to face more rapid enrollment declines than others. Between 1970 and 1975, enrollments grew between 5 and 8 percent in Arizona, Florida, Alaska, Nevada, and New Hampshire (a state experiencing exurban growth from Boston). While enrollments grew by less than 5 percent in Colorado, Idaho, Virginia, and the remaining northern New England states, they declined in every other southern and western state (Davis and Lewis 1976; National Association of State Boards of Education 1976, Table 2). In Texas, the decline was 1 percent; in California, it was 5 percent.

Within all states, of course, there are growing and declining school systems. Paralleling the overall patterns of population redistribution, net migration of elementary-school-age children (5-14 years old) tends to flow from the central cities to the suburbs and nonmetropolitan areas (Davis and Lewis 1976, Table 6). In the central cities, net out-migration reinforces the change in the age structure and accelerates decline; however, even in suburban

school systems in the aggregate, net in-migration was
insufficient to forestall decline. Enrollments declined
in 73 of the largest urban districts in the nation from
fall 1971 to fall 1975, a phenomenon that affected such
Sun Belt cities as Houston and Dallas (National Association
of State Boards of Education 1976, p. 5). Because of
the preponderance of individuals of child-bearing age
among interregional migrants, schools in metropolitan
areas with stable or declining populations are likely to
decline in enrollments for some time to come (Morrison
1976).

Compositional Effects   Declining fertility alters the age
distribution of the population. In 1950, only 18 percent
of the population was of school age (5-17 years). This
percentage continually increased until 1970, when a peak
of 26 percent was reached. This percentage will almost
certainly decline to 21 by 1980 and if current patterns
of fertility persist, the proportion will fall to the
level of the 1950s sometime during the 1980s (see Table 2).
     Although the trends in age composition among whites
and nonwhites are similar, the percentage of the nonwhite
population between 5 and 17 years of age is greater. In

TABLE 2   Age Structure of Population, 1950-1990

	Percent Population, Age 5-17			Percent Nonwhite of Total Population, Age 5-17
	White[b]	Nonwhite[c]	Total	
1950			18	
1960	24	28	24	13
1970	25	31	26	15
1974	23	29	24	16
1977	22	28	23	16
1980	20	26	21	17
1985[a]	18	24	19	18
1990[a]	19	23	19	18

[a]Projected from Series II.
[b]As percent of total white population.
[c]As percent of total nonwhite population.

SOURCES: Davis and Lewis (1976, Tables 3,5), U.S. Bureau
of the Census (1978).

1960, 24 percent of the whites were of school age; 28 percent of the nonwhites were in this age bracket. This suggests that communities with higher proportions of nonwhites are likely to have relatively greater educational burdens due to demographic factors alone. More important, the relative share of the nonwhite school-age population has been increasing since 1960 due to differential rates of fertility decline for whites and nonwhites. In 1960, before significant desegregation occurred in either the North or South, nonwhites comprised only 13 percent of the school-age population. In 1970, when massive desegregation began in the South, blacks comprised 15 percent; in 1974, when major desegregation began in northern big cities, nonwhites comprised 16 percent. This percentage is likely to be 17 in 1980 and 18 by 1990 (Davis and Lewis 1976).

The differential migration trends of blacks and whites indicate that between 1970 and 1977, the proportion of blacks has been increasing in metropolitan areas, while remaining stable in nonmetropolitan areas. Within metropolitan areas, the proportion of blacks rose in the central cities and their suburbs. In all regions except the Northeast, the black population in central cities increased absolutely, while in all regions but the West the white population declined. In all regions, the black population in the suburbs is growing faster than the white population (U.S. Bureau of the Census 1978).

The U.S. Commission on Population Growth and the American Future extrapolated these trends to the year 2000 (Morrison 1976, Table 6). In the cities, the percentage of population under age 15 is expected to drop from 26.4 percent to 23.2 percent in the period 1970-2000, while the percentage of nonwhite children is projected to rise from 29 percent to over 43 percent in the same period. In the suburbs, the percentage of population under age 15 is expected to fall from 29.7 to 22.7. In other words, suburbs are expected to become less child-centered than before and in fact less different from the central cities in this respect. The percentage of suburban children who are nonwhite is expected to rise slightly from about 7 percent to about 9 percent.

The observed trends of the 1970s and their extrapolation to the year 2000 suggest that central-city school systems are likely to become overwhelmingly black. To the extent that suburban school systems remain immune from pressures to integrate and that whites resist sending their children to schools with near black majorities, the likelihood of stable integrated central-city school systems remains dim.

IMPLICATIONS OF DEMOGRAPHIC CHANGE

For the educational sector, the distributional dimension
of demographic change--whether one area is growing faster
than another--is of less importance than the aggregate and
compositional dimensions. The aggregate dimension refers
to the relative and absolute decline in the number of
school-age children in the population; the compositional
dimension refers to the changing location of class, race,
income, and subcultural groups.

Changing Age Composition

The changing composition of family types and age-groups
in American society may have a great impact, not yet
totally discernible, on support for public schooling. The
decline in fertility, the protracted period of childless-
ness among the married, and the general aging of the population affect both the supply and demand for educational
funds. In terms of demand, the obvious implication is
that the number of children requiring elementary and
secondary education is declining as a proportion of the
population. In terms of supply, the effects of these
trends on electoral support for public education are much
more difficult to fathom. Perhaps the recent elimination
of the mandatory retirement age and refinancing of the
social security system portends greater concern with
senior citizens' issues and less concern with youth-oriented
issues.

Clearly, families with school-age children derive much
greater benefit from well-funded school systems than households without children. Nonetheless, a relative increase
in the share of households without children need not
necessarily result in a reduction in electoral support for
public education on a per-pupil basis, because, as the number
of school-age children decreases, the tax rate necessary
to raise a given level spending per pupil also falls.

It is useful to distinguish between households whose
members have not yet borne children, primarily comprised
of young adults that are unmarried or married, and households past the childbearing age. Young, childless households are generally highly mobile both economically and
geographically. As a consequence, they tend to rent rather
than to own housing and concomitantly tend to have relatively low voting turnout. Older couples, with or without
children, have a high propensity for owning their own homes
and voting.

Housing tenure has an enormous impact on the support for
public expenditures, as indicated by results of referenda
and actual community expenditures. Apparently because
renters perceive the property tax to be borne largely by
the landlord, they are considerably more likely than homeowners to favor local expenditures for education (Bloom
1976, Davis and Haines 1966, Kee 1965, Peterson 1975,
Wilson and Banfield 1964). The increasing proportion of
younger, childless households, therefore, has offsetting
effects on electoral support for public schooling: some
households may react with indifference or hostility as a
result of receiving no direct benefit, whereas others may
demonstrate support as a result of perceiving no direct
cost. The increasing proportion of older, childless households, however, would appear to lessen support for public
education because among this group are many homeowners who
would perceive both the lack of direct benefit and the
incidence of the costs.

If all voters in a metropolitan area were collectively
to vote on school expenditures, the changing age composition
and concomitant tenure composition might or might not
result in a decline in support per school child. The nature
of school finance and organization in most American metropolitan areas adds a dimension of complexity. The differ-
ing interests of each age-group create an incentive for
residential segregation. Young households may locate with
little attention to public spending; families with children
may seek education-oriented suburbs, just as they do today;
and older families may seek communities that spend little
per pupil but devote taxes to public services of greater
interest to their own age cohort.

Support per pupil in the long run does not necessarily
diminish, so long as financing is largely local. To the
extent that broad-based, statewide taxes are relied upon,
the macro-demographic changes may result in reduced support;
younger households are probably aware of the impact of
school spending on their own sales tax and income tax
payments. These results are not inevitable; they can, to
some degree, be manipulated by tax policy. For example,
property-tax circuit breakers for citizens over 65 may
reduce antipathy to educational expenditures.

Surprisingly, there is little definitive evidence that
the age composition of a community affects its support for
public schooling. Studies on this subject rarely produce
significant or easily interpretable results. For example,
in a cross-sectional analysis of states, McMahon (1970)
finds that for every 1-percent increase in the share of

school-age population, the share of state income spent on
schooling, which includes both state and local funds,
increases 0.15 percent; time series produce comparable
results. In other words, support per pupil appears to
fall as the percentages of students in the population
rises. One would have expected that opinion in states
with a high proportion of families with children would
favor greater expenditures per student, but that such
preference might be offset by the taxes necessary to
support higher costs. In a study of local support for
schooling in suburban Boston, Bloom et al. (1975) find
that the change in the number of children per household
over a 10-year period results in a proportional change in
school expenditures per household. This means that school
support per child is similar in communities with widely
varying shares of school children, when other factors are
held constant. Attitudinal surveys by Bloom (1976), however, produce results that contradict the observed patterns
he finds that the elderly, as compared with younger child-
bearing households, are much less willing to support public
school expenditures.

Needless to say, more research is required into patterns
of preference for public expenditures by people at differen
stages in the life-cycle. It is becoming apparent, for
example, that the elderly, despite their greater likelihood
of home ownership, support higher local public expenditures
than do younger groups; however, they are more interested
in police protection and recreation than in education
(Bergstrom and Goodman 1973). Nevertheless, voting decisions are not always based on narrow self-interest and
preferences are not polarized along the life-cycle. The
elderly often provide *some* electoral support for educationa
expenditures, from which they derive no conceivable direct
benefits, whereas all childbearing families are not invariably staunch supporters of high expenditures (Barzel 1973)

Implications of Enrollment Growth and Decline

Because the phenomenon of enrollment decline is new and
psychologically unsettling to Americans, dealing with
decline demands greater managerial capacity than dealing
with growth.

Anticipated Growth   When growth in enrollments is anticipated, educators have the opportunity to set aside land
for future school construction, or at least to take an

option on such land. Actual construction can be phased
with attention to the overall capital budget of the
municipality. Not only can recruitment be orderly, but
the continual hiring of young teachers (at the low end of
the salary scale) ensures that average salaries per teacher
remain low. With expansion of the school system, opportunities for upward mobility are high among the teaching
staff, and administrative promotions attainable.

Unanticipated Growth   When growth has not been fully
anticipated, new students begin to crowd the existing
classrooms, which may in fact result in decreasing costs
per student. The schools facing these growing pains may
shift to double sessions until new classroom space can be
completed. While school taxes may rise to meet these
capital expenditures, the tax base may also rise in proportion, thus maintaining the historical tax rate. The
problems of growth are transitional; moreover, educational
managers have a whole body of experience to draw upon, as
growth has been common to most school systems in the recent
past. Planning for growth may ease the transition, but
the outcome--more teachers and increased facilities--will
be the same regardless of whether planning occurs.

Unanticipated Decline   Although a growing school system
can expand the teaching staff by hiring, a declining school
system cannot so easily contract because of the institution
of tenure. Teacher-pupil ratios and hence costs per pupil
are likely to rise even though hiring ceases.

In a school system that has ceased hiring, the average
age and experience of teachers is likely to rise. On
one hand, some evidence suggests that experience can generate substantial pedagogical benefits for students in
certain circumstances (Katzman 1971, Murnane 1977). On
the other hand, average nominal salaries will rise because
teacher salary schedules are stepped. It is not clear on
balance whether costs rise faster than benefits.

Confronted with the per-student cost increases created
by declining enrollment and an aging faculty of fairly
constant size, a school board might foster attrition by
freezing the salary schedule. In the face of inflation,
a nominally fixed salary schedule suffers a real decline.
To the extent that a school board wished to foster attrition among the more experienced teachers, it might freeze
salaries at the more senior end of the scale while granting
increases to the more junior teachers. What effect such
a policy would have on faculty morale is unclear.

Even if teacher attrition keeps pace with the decline
in enrollment, there may be pension expenses that cannot
be reduced. Because few teacher pension systems have
been fully funded, school systems must annually appropriate
funds for past teaching service (Tilove 1976). In a growing system, the burden of pensions may not prove excessive,
especially because the hiring of new faculty keeps the
average teacher age low, but declining systems face a
proportionately higher burden of pension payments per
active teacher.

In addition to pensions, school plant and equipment are
overhead items that are difficult to reduce in the face of
enrollment declines. The debt service and maintenance
cost of school buildings are more difficult to reduce in
the public sector than are similar costs in the private
sector. When a national chain wishes to close a branch
supermarket, it attempts to find a willing buyer for its
building, without regard for the loss or inconvenience to
its customers. In contrast, when a school board wishes
to close a building, a small group of parents who face
severe inconvenience can influence the decision, often
outweighing the larger number of parents for whom the
benefits are more diffuse.

Anticipated Decline   Had school systems correctly anticipated decline, they might have altered their administrative
practices by employing more temporary teachers or including
severance-pay clauses in contracts, by leasing rather than
purchasing school buildings, and by fully funding their
pension plans. Because they failed to alter their practices,
school systems face higher per-pupil costs, which require
higher taxes and in turn dissuade parents from moving into
the school district.

It is difficult to assess the relevance of the above
theoretical arguments. Several studies attempt to relate
costs per pupil to levels or rates of growth in school
enrollment or population. These studies are somewhat
difficult to interpret because the quality of service is
rarely held constant. For example, a large number of
studies purporting to test for economies of scale relate
costs to community characteristics, but rarely to the
quality of education (Katzman 1971, Ch. 4). These limitations aside, none of these studies identify major economies
or diseconomies of school systems.

Sternlieb (1974) reviews several studies of small towns
that relate costs to rates of growth of enrollment. These
studies as well as his own analysis of New Jersey communities

identify no consistent effect of growth or decline on costs of schooling per capita. Using a somewhat different approach, Muller (1975) examines the costs of providing public services in growing and declining large cities. Growing cities tended to have lower costs per capita than declining cities. There is some difficulty, however, in interpreting these results: Does population decline cause high service costs, or do high service costs result in decline?

A study of migration among 75 standard metropolitan statistical areas (SMSAs) by Liu (1977) indicates that almost no inferences can be drawn from Muller's data. He finds that the rate of state-local taxation in a metropolitan area does not affect net migration, the major contributor to differential growth. Conversely, the rate of net migration has no effect on the level of local taxation.

Because the relative stagnation of productivity in the public sector is projected to continue into the near future, the costs of providing a given level of services in any category will increase. The nature of the educational category will tend to change and become more costly, as busing becomes more widespread, and as more and more "special-needs" groups, ranging from linguistic minorities to the physically handicapped, are identified. To the extent that the federal government assumes many of these costs, the effects may not differ among regions or between cities and suburbs. To the extent that these costs are borne locally, as are special-needs programs in Massachusetts, the programs may hit the central cities hardest. Per-student costs are apparently affected less by growth and decline in enrollments than by these other factors, although the evidence is somewhat tenuous.

Subcultural Conflicts

Prior to the Korean War, when net migration was in a rural-urban and south-nonsouth direction, people moved from areas of low educational standards to areas of higher standards. By most objective measures, such as school enrollments, physical facilities, teacher training and verbal skill, and student reading scores, the Southeast and Southwest have caught up to the rest of the nation (Armor 1972, McKinney and Bourque 1971). Except for the southern regions, indicators show that the quality of metropolitan and nonmetropolitan schools is quite similar. Because of the homogenization of schools, migrating

TABLE 3   Indicators of School Quality, Whites in White Schools, 1965

	School Facilities		Teacher Background		Teacher Verbal Score		6th Grade Verbal		1st Grade Verbal	
	Metro	Non-metro	Metro	Non-metro	Metro	Non-metro	Metro	Non-metro	Metro	Non-metro
Middle										
Atlantic	15.5	13.2	2.8	2.7	25	25	37	36	19	19
Great Lakes	13.9	10.6	2.8	2.7	25	25	37	36	19	20
South	11.2	9.8	2.7	2.7	24	23	36	33	19	18
Southwest	11.3	10.6	2.8	2.8	25	24	35	36	19	19
Pacific	15.7	12.7	3.3	2.9	25	25	36	38	19	19

SOURCE: Armor (1972, Ch. 6).

families will not find schools at their destination
markedly different from schools at their origin, at least
with respect to school facilities and student basic skills
(Table 3).

However, population redistribution is likely to bring
into contact families with radically different perceptions
and expectations concerning the role of education. In one
of the few studies that documents conflict over "cultural"
or "social" issues, Gans (1967) vividly describes culture
conflict emerging as upper-middle-class urbanites, with
an "expansive" or tolerant subculture, moved into tract
homes in a formerly rural county dominated by families of
strikingly different values. This upper-middle-class
group was succeeded by an "invasion" of lower-middle-class
urbanites of a different ethnic composition, with a "restrictive" subculture. The conflicts centered not only on
fiscal issues--how high should school taxes be?--but also
on social issues of discipline versus permissiveness, lock-
step versus individualized instruction, emphasis on basics
versus frills, etc. Countless such conflicts have occurred
and will continue to occur as the rural fringe becomes
urbanized and as subcultural groups succeed each other in
metropolitan neighborhoods. As northeastern, urban, upper-
middle-class households move into small towns of the South,
one can expect continual conflict over such social issues
as discipline, sex education, and the covert practice of
religion in the schools.

Because school districts in the growing areas of the
Southeast and Southwest are so large, cultural dissidents
are less able to form educational enclaves by moving to
the suburbs. Instead, they might be expected to sustain
private schools that have become a permanent fixture in the
region.

Selectivity of Metropolitan Movers

The relative and absolute decrease of the white and middle-
class population in the central city results in several
changes that affect the remaining population. The tax
base, the mix of potential peers in the classroom, the
political ethos of the city, the willingness to tax, and
the effective school resources per child can all be expected
to change as a result of out-migration.

Changes in the Tax Base per Student   The value of real
property per student in central cities may be greater or

less than in their corresponding suburbs. In metropolitan
areas like Boston, Cleveland, Baltimore, and Milwaukee,
real property wealth per pupil was higher in the suburbs
in 1969-1970. In others, like New York, Minneapolis, San
Francisco, and Denver, real property wealth per pupil was
higher in the central city. In still others, like Philadelphia, Detroit, Chicago, and St. Louis, there was little
difference between the cities and the suburbs (Reischauer
and Hartman 1973).

Although there have been few longitudinal studies of
property wealth disparities between city and suburb, there
are theoretical reasons to expect continuing disparities
that favor the suburbs. First, the process of suburbanization has been associated with a flattening of the gradient
of land values emanating from the central business district. In other words, land values have grown faster in
sites farther from the central city (Edel and Sclar 1975,
Mills 1969, Yeates 1965). While in some cities, like
Boston, downtown land values have continued to rise absolutely, in others, like Chicago, land values peaked in
the first half of this century. While land represents
only about one-fourth of real property values, its variation over space approximates that of the whole. In the
1960s, median housing in the major cities of all regions
increased only two-thirds as fast as in their suburbs
(Advisory Commission on Intergovernmental Relations 1973,
Table B-11).

In the past the migratory patterns of families at
different stages in the life-cycle resulted in the suburbs
being heavily endowed with school-age children, as compared
with the cities. However, the size of the school-age
population and property values tended to vary proportionately, thus accounting for the similarity of property wealth
per pupil between many cities and their suburbs. The
expected change in the age composition of the suburbs,
alluded to earlier, provides the second reason that population changes are likely to raise the relative suburban
wealth per pupil. The number of school-age children may
begin to fall faster in the suburbs than in the cities,
while property values may rise faster in the suburbs than
in the cities.

These expected adverse consequences of population redistribution on the relative tax base of central-city school
systems will be somewhat assuaged by trends in school
finance reform, which is discussed below.

Change in Peer Mix   To the extent that whites view black
schools as inferior--regardless of whether a particular

case warrants such a view--increasing the percentage of
blacks in central-city school systems has complex, and
largely deleterious, effects on the quality of the peer
environment. Where the social class and ethnic composition
of a school is largely determined by that of the surrounding neighborhood, schools are likely to vary significantly
in the mix of students (Duncan and Duncan 1955, Farley and
Taeuber 1973, Kantrowitz 1973, Rhodes et al. 1965). As
suggested by a wealth of educational research largely
initiated by the *Equality of Educational Opportunity Survey*
(Coleman et al. 1966, Mosteller and Moynihan 1972) lower-
class students are likely to benefit educationally from
attending largely middle-class schools, regardless of
race. While middle-class peers were not widely available
to lower-class students because of housing segregation,
some lower-class students have had these advantages. Moreover, some middle-class blacks have been able to move into
white middle-class school attendance zones.

The differential mobility of the white middle class
out of the central-city school system reduces the potential
of providing a rich peer environment for some lower-class
students, reduces the chances of black middle-class children
having white middle-class peers, and tends to "tip" the
expectations of educators away from goals of achievement
toward tasks of order maintenance.

The process of white flight from the central-city schools
reflects a divergence between individual values and aggregate behavior. In an ingenious analysis of segregation,
Schelling (1971, 1972) noted that the stability of integration depended upon the relative size of the black and
white groups and the distribution of preference for contact
with members of the other group. Ranking whites from most
to least prejudiced, one can draw a cumulative curve of
the percentage of whites willing to remain in a school or
neighborhood with a given percentage of blacks. If one
assumes that blacks move into a school district only by
replacing whites, and that in a particular case 20 black
families move into a neighborhood of 100 houses, then
stability would be achieved if at least 80 percent of the
white population would remain in an environment that is
20 percent black. If one assumes that normal turnover
would result in an additional 20 percent of the houses
being vacated by whites and occupied by blacks, then
stability would be achieved if at least 60 percent of the
original white families would remain in an environment
that is 40 percent black. However, the 60 to 40 ratio
rarely results in stability. Whites begin to move out in

response to the black presence, thereby increasing the percentage of blacks, which encourages additional whites to leave the school. The system tips in a cumulative and circular manner until it is almost entirely black.

In terms of integration, the remaining whites and blacks would have been better off if they could have induced the second 20 percent to stay or could have sought other white occupants and established a benign quota. However, resegregation can occur by such a process even when blacks constitute a small percentage of the total school population if the blacks are concentrated in a few white schools. Were the movement of blacks dispersed into all of the white schools, thereby reflecting the proportion of blacks in the metropolitan area, the situation would be stable.

Political Ethos   Some scholars attribute to the middle class an abiding concern with efficiency, impartiality, and "public-regardingness" in municipal government; and to the working class, a concern with jobs, favors, protection, and class or ethnic recognition (Katzman 1971, Ch. 4; Wilson and Banfield 1964). Although other scholars have challenged the linkage between ethnicity and "public regardingness" (Wolfinger and Field 1966), the link between class and reform is widely recognized. Therefore, in areas where the proportion of middle-class families is declining, the share of the electorate concerned with maximizing educational outputs is probably also declining. However, if cities, in the future, attract sufficient numbers of middle-class young singles and "empty nesters" to replace the middle-class families with children who are departing, these new middle-class populations may be more concerned with cost cutting than with maximizing educational output.

Willingness to Tax   The benefits that a household receives from a big city school system are distributed roughly in proportion to the number of its children, while the costs are paid roughly in proportion to income and wealth. Consequently, big city school systems tend to redistribute income from childless families, usually of higher-than-average income, to families with many children, usually of lower-than-average income (Grubb 1971). The polarization of the big city population between relatively affluent households (both young and elderly) without children and relatively poor households with many children suggests that the asymmetry between benefits and costs will increase.

Under these circumstances, the willingness of the electorate to tax itself is likely to decrease. In South Carolina, there was little relationship between county expenditures per student and the racial composition of the schools in the late 1960s. After desegregation in the 1970-1971 school year, white private-school enrollments increased in proportion to the percentage of blacks in the school-age population. The process of flight left some districts overwhelmingly black, others with a large majority of blacks, and still others, in which blacks were a small proportion of the population, overwhelmingly white. In the 1970s, growth in tax rates and expenditures per pupil was slowest in districts with the highest percentages of blacks, even when such districts ranked relatively high in wealth per student. In other words, districts in which whites had little interest gained relatively little in financial support (Sherman 1977).

Effective School Resources   White flight and enrollment decline may not have totally pernicious consequences for poor and minority students. Murnane (1977) has found that in one large northeastern city, the average experience of teachers in minority schools is increasing. The explanation is that freedom of choice in teaching assignments is a privilege associated with seniority in most school systems. In growing or stable systems, lower-class and minority children are usually taught by inexperienced teachers with little choice (Katzman 1971, Ch. 5). As enrollment declines and the teaching force ages, there are fewer escape valves for the more experienced teachers within the school system. To the extent that teaching quality improves with experience (Katzman 1971, Ch. 2), the quality of teaching may improve for the remaining youngsters.

Summary   The set of consequences outlined here is most likely to occur in metropolitan areas with relatively small central cities, surrounded by numerous independent suburbs. While the declining metropolitan areas of the Northeast and Midwest have these characteristics, most of the growing metropolitan areas contain relatively larger central cities, with greater powers of annexation (Norton 1977). Suburbanization or a flattening population density gradient in the growing regions of the nation is less likely to be associated with a weakened fiscal base or with middle-class out-migration.

Intermetropolitan/Interregional Migration

Migration is a mechanism of transferring human capital from one location to another. Because of current institutions for financing education in the United States, individual migrants are financed at the expense of taxpayers in one location but enjoy the fruits of their education in another. The shibboleth "brain drain" suggests that there is something inequitable about such a situation (Greenwood 1975, Grubel and Scott 1966).

The normative implications of the migration of skilled and educated workers depend upon whether the family or the individual is considered obligated to pay the costs of education. If the family is taken as the responsible unit, the process of schooling involves an intergenerational transfer of resources, generally unrequited, and the families through taxes pay the costs of schooling. All families in a declining area might educate their children to obtain better opportunities in a growing area, and no inequity would necessarily result from the migration process. If the individual is considered as the responsible party, then the area that financed the education would not receive future tax benefits in return. It should be noted that if the potential migrant remained in the region, the taxes he would pay should be diminished by the public services he would consume in order to derive the net fiscal benefit to the rest of the community. While state and local governments do tend to extract more in taxes than they deliver in benefits to high-income people, the magnitude of income redistribution is minimal (Pechman and Okner 1974).

There is some evidence that the electorate tends to view emigrants as losses to the community, for in areas of high out-migration, the level of support for public schooling tends to be lower even when there is no weakening of the tax base (Weisbrod 1964). High rates of area emigration, then, can result in an inefficiently low level of schooling from the national point of view. With the increasing role of states in the financing of schooling, and the convergence in school quality among regions, the quantitative importance of these inefficiencies is likely to diminish.

THE IMPACT OF PUBLIC POLICY ON POPULATION REDISTRIBUTION

The concept of public policy in the field of education is at best an abstraction. The educational system in the

United States has evolved as a cumulation of decisions made by all branches of government at all levels of the federal system, by religious organizations, and by parents who express their choices among the public and private schools available to them. Several dramatic judicial decisions in the 1960s made the evolution of educational policy prior to that time appear almost glacial. These actions reflect concerns with increasing equality between black and white and between rich and poor.

The Thrust Toward Desegregation

The most viable change in educational policy has been the wholesale attack on de jure segregation and a somewhat more halting attack on de facto segregation in the public schools. The landmark *Brown* v. *Board of Education* decision of 1954, which declared de jure segregation unconstitutional, was followed by a decade of pitched battles over token desegregation and considerable confusion on the parts of lower courts over standards and methods of implementation (Read 1975). The inaction and even obstructionism of Congress were swept aside by the moving events of a march on Washington and the murder of a president committed to civil rights. These events culminated in the passage of the Civil Rights Act of 1964, which empowered the Department of Health, Education, and Welfare (HEW) to provide technical assistance to communities planning desegregation, to set guidelines for integration, and to withhold federal funds from districts practicing racial discrimination. This latter authorization translated into considerable leverage for HEW after the passage of the Elementary and Secondary Education Act of 1965, which provided the first major injection of federal funds into local school systems. In the period 1968-1972, the courts and HEW effectively eliminated dual school systems in the South. In the early 1970s attention was shifted to the North and West, where de facto segregation occurred as a result of residential patterns and intentional gerrymandering of school districts.

Interestingly, the burdens for remedying school desegregation rest upon the school district rather than on any larger sociopolitical unit of which the school district is a part. Suburban districts with few blacks have been almost uniformly excused from sharing this burden. In the few cases in which the courts have imposed metropolitan solutions, such as Charlotte, North Carolina, Louisville, Kentucky, Wilmington, Delaware, and Indianapolis, Indiana,

the suburban areas had been historically joined to county-
wide school districts or prevented from doing so with
segregative intent (*Swann* v. *Charlotte-Mecklenburg;
Newburg* v. *Board of Education; Evans* v. *Buchanan; U.S.* v.
Board; compare *Bradley* v. *School Board of Richmond*). In
most metropolitan areas, especially in the North and West,
where housing discrimination as well as market forces have
excluded blacks from the suburbs, suburban districts have
not been held responsible for de facto segregation. In
the landmark Detroit decision, *Milliken* v. *Bradley,* the
Supreme Court overturned a city-suburban school consolida-
tion ruling of the district court, but raised the possibility of considering arguments based upon housing
discrimination.

Although a case could be made that government-supported
housing discrimination in the suburbs has been historically
responsible for the heavy concentration of blacks in the
central city (Orfield 1975), it is likely that *Milliken* v.
Bradley will prove a watershed. Through the *Keyes v. School
Board No. 1, Denver* decision of 1975, the court ruled that
discriminatory action in any part of the school system was
presumptive of discrimination everywhere. The Supreme
Court's *Dayton* v. *Brinkman* decision in essence reverses
the recent precedents by ruling that the remedy is to be
proportionate to the wrong. In other words, excluded from
the remedy are not only ostensibly innocent suburbs but
also those parts of central-city school districts in which
no overt segregative acts were perpetrated.

The *Milliken* and *Dayton* decisions, if indicative of
future policy, are likely to have a profound effect on the
spatial structure of metropolitan areas. In terms of
distorting the housing choices of blacks and whites, the
situation after *Milliken* but before *Dayton* could be viewed
as reflecting the worst of all possible worlds. The racial
composition of big city schools would have been determined
by city-wide racial proportions. In cities with a high
proportion of school-age blacks, the propensity of whites
to suburbanize would have been reinforced. As blacks
entered inner suburbs in increasing numbers, de facto
segregation there would have required cross-busing, encouraging entire suburbs to tip from white to black.[1]

After *Dayton*, the courts are likely to be more tolerant
of de facto school segregation created by residential

---

[1]The most perceptive analysis of the residential choice of
whites with and without children is Clotfelter (1974, Ch. 4).

patterns. This might stabilize white enclaves in predominantly black cities. To the extent that suburbs or
central cities tip to overwhelmingly black, the courts
may follow the precedent of the recent Inglewood case
(*New York Times*, May 11, 1975, p. 26, col. 1). This Los
Angeles suburb was originally ordered to integrate its
schools at a time when the majority of students were
white; subsequently, however, the school system underwent
a major transition and became predominantly black. The
State Superior Court's lifting of the integration order
means that the remaining whites may be able to attend
public schools in which they are not a decided minority.
The following of such a precedent may help stabilize
affluent enclaves in cities with black majorities.

   If current policy is maintained, the effects of school
integration will have worked themselves out by the end of
the decade. In cities such as Washington, D.C., and
Atlanta, the working out of school integration policy has
been associated with a nearly complete abandonment of the
central-city public school system by white students, with
the exception of a few enclaves. Depending upon the racial
proportions of the school-age population, similar results
may follow in other big cities with predominantly black
enrollment, such as Chicago, Philadelphia, and Baltimore
(Farley 1975).

Impacts of Desegregation on Population Redistribution

Thus far, results of current desegregation pressures
appear dramatic. In the mid-1960s, indexes of segregation
in the public schools were high, on the order of 80.[2]
Across cities, these indexes were highly correlated with
residential segregation. By the early 1970s, school segregation decreased in big city systems in all regions of
the nation, and especially in the South. The desegregation
of big city systems is only part of the picture. With the

---

[2]An index of segregation or dissimilarity can vary theore-
tically from 0 to 1. Intuitively, the value of the
index represents the share of one group that would have to
be redistributed in order to conform to the spatial distribution of another group. A value of 80 means that 80 percent of the blacks (or whites) would have to be redistributed
geographically to conform to the spatial distribution of
whites (or blacks).

disproportional suburbanization of white youngsters, interdistrict segregation increased. In most of the large city
school systems, whites have become relatively dispersed
among blacks, but the number of whites per black pupil
has decreased concomitantly (Coleman et al. 1975, Farley
and Taeuber 1973).

Whether desegregation has precipitated white flight or
middle-class flight from the public school has stimulated
considerable research in various social science disciplines
(Katzman 1978). Without question, factors like population
growth, income gains, and job redistribution have encouraged suburbanization long before courts moved into the
arena. The existing literature indicates that almost all
central cities, with the exception of a few booming cities
of the Southeast and Southwest, have been experiencing
enrollment decline since the late 1960s because of declining birthrates and continued suburbanization. The rate
of white enrollment decline is greater in cities with
(1) higher proportions of blacks in the public schools,
(2) greater total enrollment, and (3) numerous suburbs
that serve as escape valves. As indicated by cross-
sectional and time-series comparisons of enrollment changes,
housing prices, and mover behavior, there is indeed evidence
that the integration of blacks into exclusively white
schools stimulates white flight. Desegregation tends to
increase the rate of white enrollment decline in proportion
to (1) the percentage of blacks in the public schools,
(2) the total enrollment, and (3) the urban-suburban differentials in racial proportions. The evidence for "threshold" or "tipping" effects is mixed: the fragmentary
evidence suggests that when blacks comprise less than 25
percent of district enrollment, whites are insensitive to
small changes in black enrollment, but when blacks comprise
more than 50 percent, white enrollment decline is precipi-
tous. When these characteristics are taken into account,
federal actions--in either the executive or judicial branch-
have had similar affects on integration in the North and
South. Furthermore, the instruments of integration--
redistricting or busing--make little difference in the
outcome.

Migration to the suburbs has quantitatively contributed
much more to white enrollment declines than has private
education. Where school systems are county-wide and where
suburbs do not offer an escape, approximately 5-10 percent
of the white school-age population uses private schools,
even when the black proportion is below the 25-percent
threshold. As the black proportion rises, the likelihood

of white students shifting to private education is proportional to family income. Consequently white enrollment decline in response to integration results in a downgrading of the social-class composition of the remaining white school population (Clotfelter 1975, Giles et al. 1976, Katzman 1978, Ch. 3).

Changes in the composition of the white population, however, may create pressures countering white flight. The increasing number of families without children, particularly with two wage earners, may translate into increasing demand for central-city residences. These families, caring little about the quality of public schools, may be attracted to locations more accessible to jobs and big-city amenities, and particularly to neighborhoods of historic value. The big city of the future might be comprised of young and affluent whites without children, working-class blacks, and destitute lower-class individuals of all ethnic groups.

Equalizing School Finance

A second set of equality issues focuses upon school finance. Here the initiative for new policies has been largely at the state level, the Supreme Court having indicated no federal interest in *San Antonio* v. *Rodriguez*. In the late 1960s and early 1970s, there was a flurry of academic proposals to reform educational finance and increase school expenditures in poor districts (Coons et al. 1970, Reischauer and Hartman 1973, Wise 1968). Paradoxically, at the same time a series of major studies came to the disheartening conclusion that additional expenditures yielded little benefit as measured by cognitive scores (Coleman et al. 1966, Katzman 1971, Jencks et al. 1972, Mosteller and Moynihan 1972). Thus, the intellectual underpinning of an argument linking school-expenditure equalization to equality of opportunity and hence equality of results was challenged at the very time courts appeared most interested in school finance reform.

In the early 1970s, academic arguments notwithstanding, landmark decisions in California (*Serrano* v. *Priest*) and New Jersey (*Robinson* v. *Cahill*) found that disparities in real property values per pupil resulted in unconstitutional inequalities in school spending and that new systems of financing were required. State legislatures have been slow to implement court orders; in the early 1970s there were only weak trends toward increasing state support for elementary and secondary education, and there was little evidence that interdistrict inequality was decreasing. While the level of state support climbed from about 20 percent to 40 percent from 1920 to 1950, it remained almost invariant until 1975. The Elementary and Secondary Education Act of 1965 (ESEA) raised the federal share of school financing from 3 percent of the total to 8 percent in 1968; the 1972 federal share was only 7 percent (Reischauer and Hartman 1973).

Judicial initiatives in school finance reform came to fruition in 1975 when the New Jersey Supreme Court threatened to close schools unless the legislature implemented a satisfactory financing plan. Courts in California and nearly 2 dozen other states followed (Lawyers' Committee for Civil Rights Under Law 1978). Among these states that underwent school finance reform, the state share of funding rose from 39 percent to 52 percent (Odden et al. 1976). Whether intrastate inequalities in expenditures have correspondingly decreased in school-reform states has not been well researched, although cross-sectional analysis indicates that equality among districts varies directly with the share of state support (Katzman 1971, Ch. 4).

It is conceivable that in the next decade, all states will increase levels of support, thereby encouraging intrastate equalization. Central cities may be increasingly successful in tapping state coffers to serve an expanding circle of "special need" students. While these policies may raise expenditures and lower taxes in the cities relative to the suburbs, they are unlikely to make the central city significantly more attractive to families with children. Parents are more sensitive to peer achievement than to school expenditures as an indicator of school quality. Because peer achievement is so highly related to social class, which is highly related to race (Mosteller and Moynihan 1972), an improved fiscal picture for the central city is unlikely to offset a deteriorating social-class composition in attracting white families with school-age children.

Ironically, school finance reform may have a greater effect on the mobility of whites without children than on those with children. An influx of state aid based upon fiscal capacity per pupil will permit a greater reduction (or slower increase) in property taxes in school districts with relatively low real property wealth per student. As noted above, some cities are relatively wealthier than their suburbs; others are less wealthy. The general conclusions that can be drawn are that the implementation of

state-aid formulas based upon fiscal capacity will lower
the tax price of dwellings in some jurisdictions in a metropolitan area more than others, and that housing demand will
increase disproportionately in such jurisdictions. In
some cases, this will favor the cities; in others, the
suburbs.

MAJOR POLICY ALTERNATIVES

Desegregation Policy

The Options   With regard to racial integration policy,
there would seem to be little that any level of government
could undertake to alter interregional flows. On the
intrametropolitan level, there are two very different
policies of dubious feasibility that could substantially
reduce the flight of white, middle-class families with
children.

Metropolitan integration plans that would equalize racial
proportions in all schools would lessen the attractiveness
of suburbanization as a mode of escaping integration. Evidence from metropolitan school systems in the South suggests
that private schools are also used as a means of escaping
integration by some white families, particularly the affluent. Although metropolitan integration might encourage
some suburban whites to choose this option, it would offer
central-city families whose schools were about to tip more
acceptable racial proportions. For example, in a metropolitan area where half the whites and all the blacks lived
in the central city and the blacks comprised half the
central-city population, central-city schools would be 50
percent black. Experience suggests that tipping is likely
to occur at these proportions; however, under metropolitan
integration, central-city schools would be only 33 percent
black. Because suburban schools would also be 33 percent
black under a metropolitan plan, central-city schools would
be relatively more attractive to the remaining whites.

An alternative solution could be based on tuition vouchers,
which parents could spend at any school, public or private.
To prevent the establishment of "segregation academies,"
admissions would have to be color-blind; however, a wide
number of schools catering to parents with different lifestyles and subcultural values would emerge, thus encouraging
self-segregation. On the assumption that much of racial
prejudice is class prejudice, the establishment of schools

of homogeneous social class might make central-city schooling more appealing to the white middle class.

The Squeeze on Middle-Class Blacks   An emerging phenomenon
that appears ripe for study is the reaction of blacks to
white flight (Katzman 1979). Rather than treating blacks
as a monolithic community, researchers should distinguish
between those who have largely middle-class orientations
and the remainder of the population. The aspirations and
perceptions of middle-class blacks concerning school
quality are similar to those of whites, although blacks
are perhaps more perceptive of class and subcultural differences within the black population and hence are less
likely to engage in "statistical discrimination"--that is,
assume that a school is lower class simply because it is
overwhelmingly black. Nevertheless, the reduction in the
number of middle-class whites in a big-city school system
is likely to have two deleterious effects on black middle-
class children: (a) the tone of the school system may
shift from an emphasis on achievement and mobility to an
emphasis on maintaining order and discipline; and (b) middl
class students, who are a minority among blacks in most big
city schools, may be victimized by their lower-class peers,
who are hostile to middle-class behavior. [This latter
effect may be a reason why some middle-class blacks have
difficulty in transmitting their status to their own
children (Duncan 1967)]. Middle-class blacks thus may
feel increased pressures to extract their children from
lower class public school environments.
    Three options for middle-class black parents are self-
segregation within big-city school districts, movement to
inner suburbs, and use of private education. In attempting
to segregate themselves from working-class and lower-class
households, middle-class blacks may find themselves in
increasing competition for well-situated and bascially
sound housing in neighborhoods being rehabilitated by
affluent white families without children. Although discrimination has hindered black migration to the suburbs
in the past, decline of the white population in the aging
inner suburbs, combined with the intense demand for housing
on the part of blacks, is likely to result in a major
influx of blacks to suburban areas in the next decade. In
metropolitan areas where the possibilities for self-
segregation and suburbanization are inadequate, middle-
class black parents will probably turn to private education

School Finance

Reforms in school finance undertaken at the state level
are unlikely to have any interregional consequences. The
effects on intrastate and particularly urban-suburban population distributions depend upon the type of formula
enacted by a state. Most of the proposed aid formulas
include "power equalizing" provisions, which permit localities, regardless of their own tax bases, to use a given
tax rate to raise similar amounts of revenue per pupil at
similar tax rates. Formulas that link "fiscal capacity"
to property tax base per pupil are likely to channel aid
into jurisdications with relatively low property tax bases.
These jurisdications, however, are no more likely to be
high income than low income or urban rather than suburban
(Alexander 1975, Callahan et al. 1973). If the definition
of fiscal capacity is expanded to include measures of current income, then aid obviously goes disproportionately to
poorer districts. These, however, are not invariably more
urban.

An alternative formula bases aid upon need, perhaps
measured by the percentage of poor in the population,
following Title I of the Elementary and Secondary Education
Act. Although central-city school districts contain a
disproportionate number of poor, differences between cities,
suburbs, and rural areas are smaller than one might imagine
(Callahan et al. 1973). State-aid formulas based upon need
may be more favorable to central cities than those based
upon fiscal capacity, but the differences between central
cities and rural areas are so small that any differential
reductions of urban property taxes are likely to be incon-
sequential. Although school finance reform may enable
particular jurisdictions to reduce significantly their
property taxes and hence their housing costs, the central
city is not inevitably favored by such reform.

Although interregional migration will not be affected by
state funding reforms, it could be significantly affected
by large increases in federal funding. Federal aid might
be based on three principles: (1) financing for programs
that meet special needs, such as bilingual education; (2)
compensatory financing for high-cost school systems; and
(3) compensatory financing for areas with low fiscal
capacity. Federal financing for such special needs as
bilingual education would be particularly favorable to
states in the Industrial Belt, but would also benefit states
on the Pacific Coast and in the Southwest. If special needs
were defined broadly--as they probably will be--to include

general categories, such as the handicapped, then it is not
clear what interstate biases might result from the distribution of aid. Whether Alabama or New York has more than
its share of exceptional children or learning disabilities
cannot be ascertained at this time. If federal aid for
these categories is forthcoming, the definitions and
standards for admission into these categories would probabl
be shaped by political competition for these funds.

Compensatory aid for high-cost school systems would
clearly benefit the Northeastern and Industrial Belt states
particularly their central cities, where nominal salaries
are high. Bailing out high-cost systems may reinforce
inefficient administration or encourage less stalwart
collective-bargaining postures on the part of school system
The pressures for such a bailout, however, must be recognized.

Compensatory aid for districts with low fiscal capacity
are likely to favor the southeastern states and rural areas
where nominal salaries are low. A bias in favor of such
areas is inherent in any federal program that distributes
aid with reference to nominal income, uncorrected for cost-
of-living differentials.

The effects of federal financial aid on interstate migra
tion depend, of course, on the magnitude of this aid. Sinc
the late 1960s, federal aid has been declining and it is
unlikely that this trend will be reversed. As was noted
previously, the changing age structure of American society
is likely to shift political concerns away from children's
issues toward issues of the middle-aged and elderly. Although the trends toward equalization of school finance see
firmly established, the level at which expenditures are to
be equalized is likely to be lower than in the past.

CONCLUSION

The redistribution of population in the United States from
the Northeast to the Southwest, and from the central cities
to the suburbs and rural areas, poses important short-term
management problems for school systems. The most difficult
problems will confront school systems with declining en--
rollments. These systems will be forced to make unpleasant
choices concerning fiscal and employment policies, unless
they can diversify their product in the same way that
baby-food manufacturers have entered the gerontological
market. School systems that shift to the product diversi-
fication strategy--utilizing their facilities and personnel

for new functions, such as day care, youth vocational training, mid-career porgrams, and continuing education--will
require administrators with entrepreneurial skills. If
this shift in orientation cannot be made successfully,
declining school systems will confront an era of turmoil
in which the interests of taxpayers, children, and teachers
will clash. These problems probably will have worked
themselves out by the mid-1980s, but the interim will be
painful.

The consequences of selective migration to and from the
central city will be largely determined by the socioeconomic
characteristics of the migrants. To the extent that middle-
class parents are highly sensitive to peer environments in
schools, the increasing lower-class central-city schools
will be less and less attractive. Countervailing forces
such as less expensive housing in the city, increasing
gasoline prices, and urban cultural amenities may draw
childless, white middle-class households, an increasing
proportion of the population, back to the central city
or slow their exodus. Although the influx or reduced
outflow of childless middle-class families will not improve
the peer environment for poor and minority school children
in the central city, it can improve the tax base of the
central city. This improvement can be negated, however,
by school finance reform that divorces local school expenditures from local fiscal capacity.

The major change in educational policy in the last 10
years--the thrust toward racial desegregation--was initiated
by the federal courts and supported strongly by the Department of Health, Education, and Welfare. Although these
policies apparently have had little effect on population
redistribution in county-wide school districts in the South,
they probably have exacerbated white flight from central
cities that have high percentages of blacks and numerous
suburbs offering escape from integration. Although the
courts currently appear to be retreating from their earlier
rulings on integration, many cities with large black populations have already felt their impact. In most of the
big cities of the North, Midwest, and West the flight of
white students from the public school appears to have an
irreversible momentum. Even the rescinding of integration
orders in these cities is unlikely to change the trend.
By the mid-1980s, the full results of federal policy on
school integration will be apparent, and school systems in
most big cities will be comprised almost entirely of minorities. For administrators in big cities, the challenge
will be making the best of a student population unleavened
by the middle class.

Middle-class black families in the central cities,
finding themselves surrounded largely by the working class
and the lower class, are likely to enter the inner suburbs
in great numbers within the next decade. Since black
suburbanization in the 1970s is apparently more rapid than
white suburbanization, a conference on population redistribution in the 1980s might well focus upon this remarkable
and hitherto unnoticed phenomenon.

REFERENCES

Advisory Commission on Intergovernmental Relations (1973)
    *City Financial Emergencies: The Intergovernmental
    Dimension.* Commission Report A-42. Washington, D.C.:
    U.S. Government Printing Office.
Alexander, A. (1975) *Inequality in California School
    Finance: Dimensions, Sources, Remedies.* RAND R-1440-FF.
    Santa Monica, Calif.: RAND.
Alonso, W. (1973) Urban zero population growth. *Daedalus*
    102(Fall):191-206.
Armor, D. (1972) School and family effects, on black and
    white achievement: a reexamination of the USOE data.
    In F. Mosteller and D. Moynihan, eds., *On Equality of
    Educational Opportunity.* New York: Random House.
Barzel, Y. (1973) Private schools and public school
    finance. *Journal of Political Economy* 81(January):
    174-186.
Bergstrom, T., and Goodman, R. (1973) Private demands for
    public goods. *American Economic Review* 63 (June):280-296
Bloom, H. (1976) The Determination and Expression of Demand
    for Public Services: The Case of Local Public Schools.
    Unpublished Ph.D. dissertation, Harvard University.
Bloom, H., Brown, H., and Jackson, J. (1975) Residen-
    tial location and local public schools. Pp. 73-98
    in John Jackson, ed., *Public Needs and Private Beha-
    vior in Metropolitan Areas.* Cambridge, Mass.:
    Ballinger.
Callahan, J., Wilken, W., and Sillerman, M. (1973). *Urban
    Schools and School Finance Reform: Promise and Reality.*
    Washington, D.C.: National Urban Coalition.
Clotfelter, C. (1974) An Economic Analysis of the Effect
    of School Desegregation on Residential Location and
    Private School Enrollment. Unpublished Ph.D. dissertatio
    Harvard University.
Clotfelter, C. (1975) School desegregation, "tipping,"
    and private school enrollment. *The Journal of Human
    Resources* XI(December):28-50.

Coleman, J., Campbell, E., Hobson, C., McPartland, J., Mood, A., Weinfeld, F., and York, R. (1966) *Equality of Educational Opportunity* (2 volumes). Washington, D.C.: U.S. Office of Education.

Coleman, J., Kelley, S., and Moore, J. (1975) Trends in School Desegregation, 1968-73. Urban Institute Paper 722-03-01, Washington, D.C.

Coons, J., Clune, W., and Sugarman, S. (1970) *Private Wealth and Public Education*. Cambridge, Mass.: Harvard University Press.

Davis, O., and Haines, G. (1966) A political approach to a theory of public expenditure: the case of municipalities. *National Tax Journal* 19(September):259-275.

Davis, R., and Lewis, G. (1976) The Demographic Background to Changing Enrollments and School Needs. Center for the Study of Public Policy, Cambridge, Mass.

Duncan, O. (1967) Discrimination against Negroes. *Annals of the American Academy of Political and Social Science* 371(May):85-103.

Duncan, O., and Duncan, B. (1955) Residential distribution and occupational stratification. *American Journal of Sociology* 60(March):493-503.

Edel, M., and Sclar, E. (1975) The distribution of real estate value changes: metropolitan Boston, 1870-1970. *Journal of Urban Economics* 2(Fall):366-387.

Farley, R. (1975) Residential segregation and its implication for school integration. *Law and Contemporary Problems* 39(Winter):164-193.

Farley, R., and Taeuber, A. (1973) Racial segregation in the public schools. *American Journal of Sociology* 79 (January):888-905.

Gans, H. (1967) *The Levittowners: Ways of Life and Policies in a New Suburban Community*. New York: Random House.

Giles, M., Gatlin, D., and Cataldo, E. (1976) *Determinants of Resegregation*. Report No. NSF/RA-760179. Washington, D.C.: National Science Foundation.

Greenwood, M. (1975) Research on internal migration in the United States: a survey. *Journal of Economic Literature* 13(June):397-433.

Grubb, M. (1971) The distribution of costs and benefits in an urban public school system. *National Tax Journal* 24(March):1-12.

Grubel, H., and Scott, A. (1966) The international flow of human capital. *American Economic Review* 56(May): 268-274

Jencks, C., Smith, M., Acland, H., Bane, M., Cohen, D., Gintis, H., Heyns, B., and Michaelson, S. (1972)

Inequality: A Reassessment of the Effects of Family and Schooling in America. New York: Basic Books.

Kantrowitz, N. (1973) *Ethnic and Racial Segregation in the New York Metropolis.* New York: Praeger.

Katzman, M. (1971) *The Political Economy of Urban Schools.* Cambridge, Mass.: Harvard University Press.

Katzman, M. (1978) The Quality of Municipal Services, Central City Decline, and Middle-Class Flight. Department of City and Regional Planning, Harvard University.

Katzman, M. (1979) Black Flight: The Middle Class Black Reaction to School Integration and Metropolitan Change. Discussion Paper No. 17. Southwest Center for Economic and Community Development, University of Texas at Dallas.

Kee, W. (1965) Central city expenditures and metropolitan areas. *National Tax Journal* 18(December):337-353.

Lawyers' Committee for Civil Rights Under Law (1978) Update on State-Wide School Finance Cases. Washington, D.C.

Leppert, J., and Routh, D. (1976) An Analysis of State School Finance Systems as Related to Declining Enrollments. A report prepared under contract with the National Institute of Education.

Liu, B. (1977) Local government finance and metropolitan employment growth: a simultaneous-equation model. *Southern Economic Journal* 43(January):1379-1385.

McKinney, J., and Bourque, L. (1971) The changing South: national incorporation of a region. *American Sociological Review* 36(June):399-412.

McMahon, W. (1970) An economic analysis of major determinants of expenditures on public education. *Review of Economics and Statistics* 52(August):242-252.

Mills, E. (1969) The value of urban land. Pp. 231-256 in Harvey S. Perloff, ed., *The Quality of the Urban Environment.* Baltimore, Md.: Johns Hopkins.

Morrison, P. (1975) *The Current Demographic Context of National Growth and Development.* RAND Paper Series. Santa Monica, Calif.: RAND.

Morrison, P. (1976) *The Demographic Context of Educational Policymaking.* RAND Corporation Paper P-5592. Santa Monica, Calif.: RAND.

Mosteller, F., and Moynihan, D., eds. (1972) *On Equality of Educational Opportunity.* New York: Random House.

Muller, T. (1975) *Growing and Declining Urban Areas: A Fiscal Comparison.* Working Paper 0001-02. Washington, D.C.: The Urban Institute.

Murnane, R. (1977) The Impact of Changing Student Enrollment Patterns on the Distribution of Teachers in an Urban School District. National Insitute of Education, Finance and Productivity Group, Washington, D.C.

National Association of State Boards of Education (1976)
A Report on Declining Enrollments. Imperative of
Leadership Series, Vol. II, No. 1. Denver, Colo.:
NASBE.

Norton, R. (1977) City Life Cycles. Unpublished Ph.D.
dissertation, Princeton University.

Odden, A., Augenblick, J., and Vincent, P. (1976) *School
Finance Reform in the States, 1976-77.* Denver, Colo.:
Education Commission of the States.

Orfield, G. (1975) Federal policy, local power, and metropolitan segregation. *Political Science Quarterly* 89
(Winter):777-802.

Pechman, J., and Okner, B. (1974) *Who Bears the Tax
Burden?* Washington, D.C.: Brookings Institution.

Peterson, G. (1975) Voter demand for public school
expenditures. Pp. 99-120 in J. Jackson, ed., *Public
Needs and Private Behavior in Metropolitan Areas.*
Cambridge, Mass.: Ballinger.

Read, F. (1975) Judicial evolution of the law of school
integration since *Brown* v. *Board of Education. Law
and Contemporary Problems* 39(Winter):7-49.

Reischauer, R., and Hartman, R. (1973) *Reforming School
Finance.* Washington, D.C.: Brookings Institution.

Rhodes, A., Reiss, A., and Duncan, O. (1965) Occupational
segregation in a metropolitan school system. *American
Journal of Sociology* 70(May):682-694.

Schelling, T. (1971) Dynamic models of segregation.
Journal of Mathematical Sociology 1(July):143-186.

Schelling, T. (1972) Neighborhood tipping. Pp. 157-184.
in Anthony H. Pascal, ed., *Racial Discrimination in
Economic Life.* Lexington, Mass.: Lexington Books.

Sherman, J. (1977) *Underfunding of Majority-Black School
Districts in South Carolina.* Washington, D.C.: Lawyers'
Committee for Civil Rights Under Law.

Sternlieb, G. (1974) *Housing Development and Municipal
Costs.* Chs. 4-6. New Brunswick, N.J.: Rutgers
University Press.

Tilove, R. (1976) *Public Employee Pension Funds.* A
Twentieth Century Fund Report. New York: Columbia
University Press.

U.S. Bureau of the Census (1978) *Social and Economic
Characteristics of the Metropolitan and Nonmetropolitan
Population: 1977 and 1970.* Series P-23, No. 75 in *Current
Population Reports.* Washington, D.C.: U.S. Department
of Commerce.

Warner, S. (1962) *Streetcar Suburbs: The Process of Growth
in Boston,* 1870-1900. Cambridge, Mass.: Harvard University Press.

Weisbrod, B. (1964) *External Benefits of Public Education.* Princeton, N.J.: Princeton University Press.

Wilson, J., and Banfield, E. (1964) Public-regardingness as a value premise in voting behavior. *American Politic Science Review* 58(December):876-887.

Wise, A. (1968) *Rich Schools, Poor Schools.* Chicago: University of Chicago Press.

Wolfinger, R., and Field, J. (1966) Political ethos and the structure of city government. *American Political Science Review* 60(June).

Yeates, M. (1965) Some factors affecting the spatial distribution of Chicago land values, 1910-1960. *Economic Geography* 41:57-70.

POPULATION REDISTRIBUTION AND THE CRIMINAL JUSTICE SYSTEM[1]

Colin Loftin

INTRODUCTION

A theory would be useful that would allow us systematically to link changes in population distribution to changes in community structure and to link these, in turn, to changes in crime and crime control. With such a theory we could project the impact of changes in population distribution and community structure on levels of crime and on crime-control institutions. Unfortunately, only the meager beginnings of such a theory exist. In spite of the fact that quantitative studies of relationships between community structure, population distribution, and crime are among the oldest scientific studies in criminology (Guerry 1833, Quetelet 1842), negligible progress was made on the development of systematic theories until the late 1960s. Since that time, the situation has been changing rapidly as criminologists and other analysts have again become interested in these problems. The discussion that follows draws some of these materials together in order to explore the implications for crime and crime control of current trends in the spatial distribution of population in the United States.

One obstacle to the development of a theory of crime and crime control is that criminal statistics suffer from several well-known and frequently discussed biases that have discouraged analysts from using them extensively in

Colin Loftin is Assistant Professor, Department of Sociology and Center for Research on Social Organization, University of Michigan.

[1]The author wishes to acknowledge the assistance of Frank Zimring, who provided many ideas during the initial phase of work on this paper.

287

theory-building efforts. We make no attempt here to
justify or evaluate the accuracy of criminal statistics;
but before beginning the discussion I wish to note some
possible sources of bias and warn the reader that all of
the inferences that I make in the paper crucially depend
on the assumption that crime statistics are reasonably
accurate and representative of the patterns of crime. I
make this assumption not because I wish to argue that it
is true, but because it provides a convenient point of
departure for the development of relatively simple theoretical models. More sophisticated models that consider the
structure of errors in crime statistics are needed but are
not yet avaiable.

The first bias in crime statistics is that they refer
to only a limited subset of the concept of illegal activity
or even serious illegal activity. Almost all the research
referred to in this paper is based on the crime index of
the *Uniform Crime Reports (UCR)*, which is a tabulation of
seven selected offenses: criminal homicide, forcible rape,
robbery, aggravated assault, burglary, larceny-theft, and
motor-vehicle theft (Federal Bureau of Investigation 1976).
The offenses are reported by local law-enforcement agencies
to the Federal Bureau of Investigation, which tabulates the
and issues annual reports. While some authors argue that
the bias in the index toward street crimes is an advantage
because the crimes represented are those that concern most
citizens, that is, "predatory crimes against innocent victims" (Wilson and Boland 1976, p. 183), most agree that
the exclusion of other types of illegal activity is a
serious limitation. The point I wish to emphasize is that
if we think of "crime" as a violation of the criminal law
and we measure it with the *UCR* indexes, we are working
with a biased sample of the relevant conceptual domain.
Like any biased sample, it can be misleading. The reader
should keep in mind that all of our generalizations are
conditioned by the assumption that we are referring to the
types of offenses that are covered in available sources of
data.

The second bias arises from the inaccuracy of the counts
of crime incidents. The most negative assessment of the
value of the *UCR* data is undoubtedly Robinson's (1966,
p. 1061) well-known statement that "the F.B.I.'s figures
are not worth the paper they are printed on." At the other
extreme, however, even the most optimistic, positive
assessment of the *UCR* data has a hesitant, almost apologeti
tone that is characteristic of the writing of most users
of the data (Hindelang 1974, p. 14):

It should be reemphasized here, however, that it is decidedly not being suggested that the *UCR* are without shortcomings--there is, in fact, agreement here that the shortcomings are numerous, severe, and varied, and are in drastic need of attention--but rather that in spite of these problems the *UCR* *seem to have at least some applicability as crude* *approximations which are of utility for some* *purposes.* [Emphasis added.]

No evaluation of the problem is presented here. There are several good (though incomplete) discussions available (Wolfgang 1963, Zeisel 1971). However, our inferences about the distribution of crime must be treated as problematic because of a lack of knowledge concerning the structure of reporting error in the data.

With respect to the implications of population redistribution for crime and crime control, the discussion is organized into two major sections. First, crime as a cause of population redistribution is considered. Crime is widely believed to be a major factor driving current patterns of migration, especially the flight of the white middle class from central cities. The discussion examines whether changes in the level or distribution of crime affect patterns of migration or residential choice. Existing evidence suggests that intuitive estimates of the impact of crime on residential choice are biased upward, and that economic and ecological factors dominate these decisions, leaving little room for consideration of crime.

Second, attention is turned to the consequences of population redistribution patterns for crime and crime control. What are the consequences of declining population and the associated changes in social organization for levels of crime and for law enforcement (police, courts, and correctional systems)? Similarly, what are the implications of population increases and concomitant organizational changes in growing areas?

DEFENSIVE SETTLEMENT PATTERNS: CRIME AS A CAUSE OF MIGRATION

An examination of when and where crime occurs reveals several patterns that suggest that the fear of victimization may be a major factor contributing to the selective migration of the middle class from central cities into suburban areas and, more recently, into nonmetropolitan areas.   Crime

TABLE 1 Selected Crime Rates (per 100,000 residents) and Percentage Change in Crime Rates by Community Size or Community Type, 1965, 1970, and 1975

Community Size/ Community Type	Year	Murder Rate	Percent Change	Robbery Rate	Percent Change	Burglary Rate	Percent Change
1,000,000 or more	1965	9.6		220.5		929.5	
	1970	18.4	92	778.0	253	2008.9	116
	1975	24.6	34	878.8	13	2185.0	9
500,000– 1,000,000	1965	10.4		164.7		1008.5	
	1970	18.2	75	533.8	224	1981.3	96
	1975	20.1	10	592.4	11	2459.6	24
250,000– 500,000	1965	7.2		121.9		1045.3	
	1970	14.7	104	320.6	163	1797.1	72
	1975	17.6	20	473.0	48	2556.2	42
100,000– 250,000	1965	6.4		73.1		871.2	
	1970	10.0	56	198.9	172	1684.5	93
	1975	10.9	9	282.6	42	2177.3	29
50,000– 100,000	1965	3.5		48.5		674.6	
	1970	5.2	49	110.2	127	1114.5	93
	1975	7.2	39	189.4	72	1723.1	29

Category	Year						
25,000–50,000	1965	3.1		32.9		561.7	
	1970	4.2	36	82.3	150	940.1	68
	1975	5.7	36	129.6	58	1417.7	51
10,000–25,000	1965	2.3		18.6		461.8	
	1970	3.3	44	42.2	127	785.0	70
	1975	4.4	33	81.6	93	1199.0	52
Less than 10,000	1965	2.0		11.8		368.9	
	1970	2.6	30	23.6	100	630.6	71
	1975	3.9	50	49.4	109	1037.5	65
Suburban communities[a]	1965	2.7		28.1		544.6	
	1970	3.8	41	58.3	108	871.7	60
	1975	5.4	42	93.4	60	1321.0	52
Rural communities	1965	4.2		9.9		308.4	
	1970	5.5	31	13.3	34	477.2	55
	1975	8.4	53	24.9	87	872.6	83

[a] Some of the suburban communities also appear in the specific size categories.

SOURCES: Federal Bureau of Investigation (1965, Table 6; 1970, Table 9; 1975, Table 14).

rates, especially rates of violent personal crime, are
relatively high in central cities and decline with distance from the core. This is not a new pattern; it has
been observed since the earliest statistical studies.
Furthermore, the period of rapid suburban migration of
middle-class whites out of central cities coincides, at
least in very general terms, with a period of rapid
increases in crime rates. Table 1 illustrates the first
pattern, showing murder, robbery, and burglary rates for
the community-size (or community-type) categories provided
in the *UCR* for 1965, 1970, and 1975. The following major
conclusions can be drawn from the *UCR* data:

1. Crime rates are higher in larger communities. The
concentration of crime in larger communities is greatest
for robbery but is apparent for both murder and burglary.
The relatively high rate for murder in rural areas is the
most striking deviation from this pattern and is typical
for this offense.
2. All three crime rates have increased over time.
This trend accounts for about 85 percent of the variance
in the crime rates in the table.
3. The largest changes occurred in the first time
interval. For the 1965-1970 interval, the average percentage change for murder is 56 percent, but for the 1970-
1975 interval, it is only 33 percent. The comparable
values for robbery are 146 percent as contrasted with 59
percent, and for burglary, 77 percent as contrasted with
46 percent (see Table 2).
4. There is a noticeable interaction in the rates of
change. The effect of community size reverses between the
two time intervals. This can be seen clearly in Table 3,
in which we have grouped the community-size categories
into two classes and computed means of the percentage
changes in crime rates. In the first interval (1965-1970)
large communities have the largest changes in crime rates,
but in the second interval (1970-1975), it is the smaller
communities that change the most.

Figure 1 provides a dramatic illustration of the second
type of pattern. It shows the homicide rate and the white
population of the city of Detroit between 1926 and 1976.
Clearly, the two series are negatively related; during the
period prior to 1950 the homicide rate was falling or
fluctuating around a low mean of about six homicides per
100,000, and at the same time the white population was
increasing. In the second period (after 1950), the trends
are a decreasing white population and a very rapidly risin

TABLE 2   Mean Percentage Changes in Crime Rates, 1965-1970 and 1970-1975

Time Interval	Murder Rates	Robbery Rates	Burglary Rates
1965-1970	56	146	77
1970-1975	33	59	46

NOTE: Calculated from rates in Table 1.

homicide rate, especially after 1960. These data are extreme, both in choice of crime and in choice of city, but
they illustrate a pattern that has greatly influenced opinion about relationships between crime and intraurban migration. These data are generally consistent with the hypothesis that the risk of criminal victimization is one of the
factors that contributes to the flight of whites from
central cities.

   In spite of what many observers take to be an obvious
link between fear of crime and selective migration to

TABLE 3   Mean Percentage Changes in Crime Rates by
Community Size, 1965-1970 and 1970-1975

Community Size	Percent Change in Murder Rates		Percent Change in Robbery Rates		Percent Change in Burglary Rates	
	1965-1970	1970-1975	1965-1970	1970-1975	1965-1970	1970-1975
100,000 or more residents	81.8	18.2	203.0	28.5	94.2	26.0
Less than 100,000 residents[a]	34.0	42.1	107.7	79.8	64.7	59.5
Difference[b]	48	-24	95	-51	30	-34

[a]Suburban and rural communities are treated as smaller than
100,000 residents, even though the *UCR* does not define the
specific sizes of these communities.
[b]Numbers have been rounded.

NOTE: Calculated from rates in Table 1.

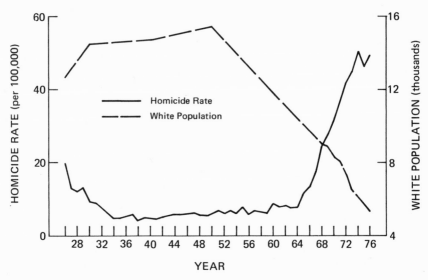

FIGURE 1 Homicide rate and white population of Detroit, Michigan, 1926-1976, based on data from Boudouris 1970. The series is extended to 1976 by regressing Boudouris series on the *UCR* series in order to obtain estimates of the Boudouris series.

peripheral locations, there is reason to believe that subjective estimates of the magnitude of this influence may be exaggerated.

A major problem with data such as those in Table 1 and Figure 1 is that they do not encourage one to see crime in relation to a model of metropolitan community structure and change. The size/type categories used by the *UCR* do not correspond to the functions that communities perform in urban spatial systems. Almost none of the existing research takes into account the fact that observations in a spatial or temporal series are not independent replications of the events being studied. They are part of a system that is linked in space and time in such a way that recurrent patterns appear not only because relationships are functional, but also because the units are open at the edges and are mutually influential. Subjective standards, which are acquired from experience with data that are independent observations, can be highly misleading in assessing the statistical significance of these patterns because conventional means of estimating standard errors do not apply (Berry 1971, Cliff and Ord 1973). When the data are interpreted within the framework of a model of

urban growth, it becomes evident that the ordinary mechanisms
of change in community structure can create a relationship
(in time and space) between levels of crime and middle-
class out-migration, even where there is no causal link
between them.

In suggesting an alternative interpretation of the
correlation between crime and selective migration, I do
not argue that criminal victimization has no influence on
population distribution. Certainly crime lowers the
quality of life and undoubtedly has some impact on family
decisions about housing. However, many estimates of the
magnitude of this influence are biased upward because they
do not take into account the indirect relationship that
is generated by the spatial dynamics of urban systems.
The nature and magnitude of the direct relationship is,
of course, crucial for social policy makers who want to
know how much influence a change in the crime rate in a
given area would have on the composition of the population
in that area.

The indirect relationship between crime rates and
mobility patterns has two major components: (1) a tendency
for criminal opportunities and for high-risk populations
to be located relatively close to urban centers, and (2)
a tendency for residents who have the financial and ethnic
requisites to move to peripheral locations. Both patterns
are well documented. Using data from 128 census tracts in
St. Louis, Boggs (1965) shows that environmental opportunities account for the concentration of certain types of
property crimes in commerical areas. When crime rates
were standardized by environmental opportunity factors
such as the business-to-residential land use ratio, crime
rates were no higher in commercial than in residential
areas. Pyle et al. (1974) demonstrate the same type of
variation in crime rates standardized by different types
of land use in their study of Summit County, Ohio (which
includes the city of Akron). In addition, they present a
series of maps that show how the pattern of crime is
influenced by the locations of businesses and homes that
provide opportunities for criminal activity.

Central cities also appear to have higher crime rates
because they are used by the residents of the whole metropolitan region and thus population "at risk" far exceeds
the numbers of residents used in calculating conventional
crime rates. Gibbs and Erickson (1976) have shown that
for 180 singular cities [i.e., largest cities in a standard
metropolitan statistical area (SMSA) with only one central
city] there is a positive correlation between all seven

index offenses and a measure of dominance (the ratio of
SMSA population size to the central-city population size).
This is consistent with the studies done by Lottier (1938)
in Michigan that show that many offenses are distributed
in a declining gradient pattern throughout a region
extending 200 miles from the center of Detroit.

The concentrations of high-risk populations (the poor
and minorities) in central cities and the preference of
low-risk populations for more peripheral locations is
also well documented and is attributed, in large part, to
the spatial structure of urban housing markets. New, low-
density housing is less expensive and therefore more available in peripheral areas. This radial variation in housing
costs, which is ultimately tied to the limited supply of,
and demand for, access to central locations (Berry and
Horton 1970), combines with factors such as discriminatory
real estate practices, the development of freeways, the
movement of jobs and services to suburban areas, and the
aging of housing stock in central cities to generate a
pattern of selective out-migration of middle-class whites.

Some studies attribute high crime rates in areas with
high levels of migration to the destabilizing or disorganizing effects of migration itself (Clinard 1964, Edward
Green, unpublished data). While there seems to be little
evidence supporting this type of migration effect, there
is one statistical mechanism by which the process of
selective out-migration can contribute to the correlation
between crime rates and middle-class out-migration. Consider
a neighborhood with a relatively stable number of crimes
that are committed disproportionately by low-income residents. If high-income residents migrate out of the neighborhood, the crime rate (crimes per resident) must increase
because the residents with a high propensity toward crime
are becoming a greater proportion of the population. This
will occur even if the number of crimes remains the same,
assuming that the higher income migrants are not replaced.
If they are replaced by low-income migrants, then the
magnitude of the effect will be even greater.

There are four studies that, to some degree, have
addressed the issue of whether there is a direct influence
of crime levels on migration flows. None is complete or
definitive, but all four suggest that crime contributes
little, if anything, to patterns of population redistribution

Droettboom et al. (1971) report micro-level evidence
from a national longitudinal survey of residential mobility
conducted in 1966 and 1969. The survey indicates that
there is a strong relationship between the perception of
crime as a serious problem in a neighborhood and the desire

to change residential locations, but there is no relationship between that perception and actual migration from the
neighborhood. More important, for our purposes, is the
finding that there is little difference in the perceived
seriousness of crime problems in a neighborhood between
people who have changed residence from central city to
suburb and those who have not. Among middle-class whites
residing in central cities in 1966, those who perceived
crime and violence as "very serious" were no more likely
to have moved to the suburbs in 1969 than those in the "not
so serious" category. In both cases, 20 percent moved
from the central city to the suburbs. Similar findings
are reported by Garafalo (1977) from his analysis of the
National Crime Survey data from eight cities. Very few
respondents indicated that their neighborhood was dangerous
enough to make them think seriously about moving. Even
among low-income blacks who had been victims of crime and
perceived their neighborhood as either somewhat or very
unsafe, less than half said that the danger was serious
enough to make them consider moving. When households that
had moved in the last 5 years were asked why they moved
and what was the most important reason for the move, only
about 3 percent indicated that crime was the reason.

Two macro-level studies of intrametropolitan migration
flows provide estimates of the effects of crime levels on
city-suburb migration that are consistent with the micro-
level data (Frey 1977, 1978; Guterbock 1976). The estimates
are derived using quite different statistical procedures,
theoretical models, and measures of the magnitude of
suburban migration, but the results of both studies are
consistent with a model in which there are no direct effects
of crime rates on the migration flows from city to suburbs.
Frey's second study (1978) extends his first analysis by
estimating the effects for migrants with six different
levels of education. The patterns suggest that suburban
propensity rates (the proportion of residential movers who
move from the city to suburbs) for high-education groups
are much greater in older northern SMSAs than in southern
or western ones. However, his estimates for the effects
of city crime rates on suburban propensity rates for migrants
in all six education groups were small and not statistically
significant by conventional standards.[2]

[2]Frey did not report standard errors or significance levels
because he was dealing with the universe of SMSAs that were
of interest. However, he kindly provided a copy of his
computer output and none of the crime effects are statistically significant by conventional standards.

In sum, I suspect that intuitive estimates of the
magnitude of the effects of crime on population redistribution are biased upward. To many observers it appears
obvious that the white middle class is fleeing the dangers
of the central city for the relative safety of the suburbs.
When the indirect relationship between levels of crime and
middle-class migration is taken into account, however,
this interpretation is much less persuasive. On the other
hand, it is unlikely that crime exerts no influence on
population distribution. There are many potential links
between crime and population distribution that have not
been investigated systematically. For example, high levels
of crime may prevent people from moving into certain areas
even though it has little influence on the out-migration
of current residents. Also crime may be a very important
factor in rare but important local instances that are not
represented in national surveys, but that have a powerful
influence on public opinion. Nevertheless, with regard to
selective middle-class out-migration, the evidence suggests
that nationally the process is dominated by ecological and
economic factors and that changes in crime rates would
have only a very small impact on the process.

A NOTE ON AGE, RACE, AND GENDER

Before beginning a discussion of the effects of changes in
the distribution of population, I will discuss the relationship between changes in the age structure of the population and levels of crime. While this is a compositional,
rather than a distributional trend, it appears to be a
factor of great importance that may interact with distributional factors in ways that will be important to
subsequent discussion. Table 4, which has appeared in
several frequently cited discussions of the effects of age
structure on crime, shows typical estimates of the effects
of age on arrest rates, which are generally used as proxies
for offense rates. Note that for all offenses the rates
are higher for individuals under age 25 than for those
over 25, and that the difference between age-specific rates
is much greater for property offenses than for person
offenses. For example, the arrest rate for homicide is 1.8
times greater for persons age 10-25 than for persons over
24, but for automobile theft the rate for the younger group
is 22.3 times greater than the rate for the older group.
    Although studies generally show that changes in the age
structure of the population have contributed heavily to

TABLE 4   Age-Specific Rates of Arrest for Index Offenses, 1965

| Crime | Rate of Arrest per 100,000 Population | |
	Age 10-24[a]	25 and Over
Criminal homicide	7.7	4.4
Forcible rape	14.0	2.7
Robbery	64.2	9.9
Aggravated assault	71.2	34.2
Burglary	321.4	27.3
Larceny	592.5	63.8
Auto theft	182.8	8.2
Total[b]	1,253.9	150.4

[a]The volume of arrests is reported in *Uniform Crime Reports* for the age-group under 25.   Since arrests of persons under age 10 are so few, the population 10-24 has been used as the base for this rate.
[b]Rates shown do not sum exactly to this total because of rounding.

SOURCE: Morrison (1972, p. 14).

changes in crime rates in recent years, estimates of the magnitude of this contribution vary widely.   Several studies conducted during the 1960s estimate that between 10 percent and 50 percent of the increase in index crime in the period between 1950 and about 1965 can be accounted for by changes in age composition (Ferdinand 1970, President's Commision on Law Enforcement and Administration of Justice 1967, Sagi and Wellford 1968).   It is possible that these studies underestimate—perhaps by a large margin—the magnitude of these effects.   The issue is complex and unresolved at the present time because age-specific offense data are not available for the nation as a whole and must be inferred from arrest data.   The major source of age-specific arrest statistics, the *UCR*, has several serious liabilities that restrict the usefulness of the data for these purposes: (1) arrests are available separately by race, gender, age, and community size, but these factors are not cross-tabulated; and (2) the reporting area of the arrest data is significantly less than complete and has changed over time.   The first problem has led analysts to treat the factors (age, race, gender, and

community size) as though they have additive effects on
crime rates, in spite of evidence to the contrary. As a
result of the second problem, arrest rates have been
underestimated, but as coverage increases, a spurious
rise in arrest rates occurs. For example, the arrest data
used in the calculations of the arrest rates in Table 4
are based on reports from 4,062 agencies representing only
69 percent of the U.S. residential population. The population data, on the other hand, are derived from Census
estimates of the total population in each age category.
Clearly these calculations underestimate the arrest rates,
and changes in coverage will produce a change in the *UCR*-
based estimates, no matter what happens to the true arrest
rate.[3]

The only study that is not affected by the reporting
area problem and controls separately for the effects of
age, race, and gender, allowing for interactions among all
factors, found that demographic factors account for all of
the trend in male crime rates (Blumstein and Nagin 1975).
Two statistical techniques are used in the paper: one esti
mates a model that controls for variation in the intensity
of police activity over a 6-year period for each of eight
age, gender, and race groups; and the second is an analysis
of variance of the crime rates for the age, race, gender,
and time categories. Surprisingly the only significant
increase in rate, given controls for the other factors, was
for females. The age, gender, and race factors and their
interactions account for 99 percent of the variance in the
arrest rates. This study is limited because it is based
on a single city and a short time period, but it, along with
some other studies from local areas (Chilton and Spielberge:
1971, 1972), suggests that the magnitude of the effects of
age structure on crime rates is much larger than had previously been estimated.

Putting aside the methodological problems, one might
guess that as the smaller birth cohorts born in the 1960s
move into the crime-prone age-groups and the larger cohorts

[3]Surprisingly, coverage has not increased regularly over
time. The trend is toward greater coverage, but the 1974
coverage was 30 percent lower than the coverage for 1973
for some tables. The distribution of rural-urban coverage
also shows irregular variations. Rosenthal and Steffensmei
(1978) provide a description of the coverage between 1960
and 1964 and a useful discussion of the use of arrest rates
for estimating patterns of offense.

of the postwar decades move into the lower risk age-groups, the U.S. crime rates will decline dramatically. Figure 2 shows the trends in the size of the male white and nonwhite cohorts age 15-19 and 20-24. The white males age 15-19 reach a peak size in 1977 and decline thereafter; for those 20-24 years old the peak is in 1981 with a similar decline following that point. By 1989 there will be 17 percent fewer white males age 15-24 than in 1979. The nonwhite cohorts are much more stable in size; they peak later than the white cohorts and remain relatively stable throughout the 1980s. In 1989 there will be only 2 percent fewer nonwhite males age 15-25 than in their peak year, 1981. Nationally there will be 15 percent fewer males 15-24 years of age in 1989 than in 1979.

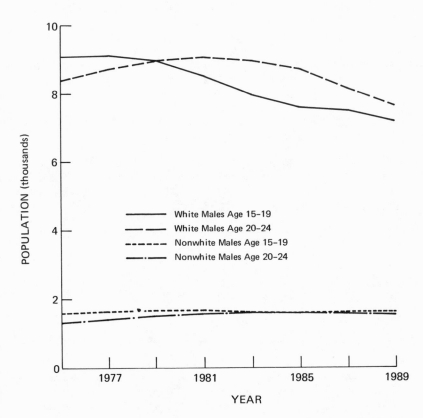

FIGURE 2 Projected number of males age 15-19 and 20-24, 1975-1989 (U.S. Bureau of the Census 1975b).

Two factors may, however, reverse or offset expected reductions in crime rates resulting from changes in the age structure: the first is the high rate of crime in the relatively stable nonwhite population, and the second is the apparent trend toward higher crime rates for women. Table 5 presents a simple illustration of how the relatively stable age structure of the nonwhite males combined with a higher crime rate could produce a much more stable crime rate than might be expected if such differentials were not taken into consideration. I use the 1970 race, age, and gender-specific arrest rates that Blumstein and Nagin (1975) estimated for Pittsburgh and the Census Bureau's annual population estimates (U.S. Bureau of the Census 1975b) to derive the number of arrests that would be expected in the 15- to 24-year-old groups each year if the rates were to remain constant until 1989. For purposes of this illustration, it is assumed that the pattern of arrest rates reflects variation in crime rates and that the ratio of crimes to arrests is approximately the same for all groups. The Pittsburgh arrest rates are selected because they are the only available estimates specific to age, race, and gender groups. Since they reflect only urban patterns they are

TABLE 5 Expected Arrests for Index Crimes Among Males Age 15-24, and Age-Specific Arrest Rates, 1975-1989

| | Number of Arrests | | | Arrest Rate (per 1,000) |
Year	White Males Age 15-24[a]	Nonwhite Males Age 15-24[b]	All Males Age 15-24	All Males Age 15-24
1975	418,320	513,710	932,030	45.8
1977	423,680	539,560	963,240	46.2
1979	421,470	559,420	980,880	46.6
1981	407,370	567,880	975,750	47.0
1983	387,190	562,270	950,470	47.4
1985	371,620	560,380	932,000	47.9
1987	361,150	561,980	923,140	49.1
1989	343,240	553,760	897,000	50.1

[a]The actual rates are 34 per 1,000 for white males age 15-19, and 13.1 per 1,000 for white males age 20-24.
[b]The actual rates are 195.2 per 1,000 for nonwhite males age 15-19, and 158.5 per 1,000 for nonwhite males age 19-24.

SOURCES: Population estimates from U.S. Bureau of the Census (1975b, Table 7); crime rates from Blumstein and Nagin (1975, Table 2).

probably too high. The patterns, and not the exact levels
of crime, however, are the important point.

In this hypothetical population the number of arrests is
greater for the nonwhite population in every year in spite
of the fact that there are many more white than nonwhites
in the population. Over time the number of arrests decline
for both groups, but the rate and size of the decline is
greater for whites. The number of arrests for whites in
these age-groups would decline by 19 percent between its
peak year, 1977, and 1989, yet the number of arrests for
nonwhites would decline by only about 2 percent between
its peak year, 1981, and 1989. An examination of the total
number of arrests expected for both white and nonwhites
reveals the dampening effect of the nonwhite population on
the decline in the number of arrests. The total number
of crimes would not peak until 1979 and then would decline
only about 8 percent by 1989, rather than the approximately
15-percent decrease that would be expected from the decline
in the size of the 15- to 24-year-old group. It is also
interesting to note that because the nonwhite population would
become a larger proportion of the 15- to 24-year-old group,
the age-specific arrest rate would increase by 9 percent
by 1989. If to this is added the tendency of youthful,
low-income, minority populations to concentrate in central
cities (see Berry and Dahmann in this volume), where crime
rates are the highest, it would be quite possible for
increases in the number of crimes committed by nonwhite
youths to offset completely the reduction in the number of
crimes committed by white youths.

The second trend that could offset the decline in crime
rates expected to result from the smaller size of crime-
prone age-groups is the apparent trend toward higher offense
rates for women. Studies of the *UCR* arrest data and arrest
data from local police departments indicate that female
arrest rates have increased at a higher rate than have male
rates during the past 2 decades (Blumstein and Nagin 1975,
Norblit and Burcart 1976, Simon 1976, Steffensmeier and Jordan
1978). There is significant disagreement about the nature
and causes of these trends. For example, it is not clear
whether the disproportionate increase in female arrests
applies to both property and violent crimes. Most studies
indicate that women have not gained over men in the proportion of violent offenses, but one study (Norblit and Burcart
1976) found that for women under 18 years old, both violent
and property arrests have increased at a much higher rate
than for men. Also, a major study of self-reported delinquent behavior (Gold and Reimer 1975) found no change in

male and female offenses between 1967 and 1972 when offenses for drinking and the use of marijuana are excluded. Another problem is the selection of an appropriate measure of the relative change in arrest or crime rates. Table 6 illustrates this problem. The data are arrest rates for property offenses in cities with a population greater than 2,500. Female rates rose by 221 percent during the decade, while male rates rose by only 58 percent, but the difference between the male and female rates increased from 714 arrests per 100,000 persons in 1960 to 967 arrests per 100,000 persons in 1970. In other words, the probability of a random male being arrested increased more in absolute terms than did the probability of a random female being arrested.

Most analysts agree that changes in the social role of women influence both the behavior of law-enforcement officials and the opportunities that women have to engage in illegal activity. Because changes in the role of women can be expected to diffuse more widely in the near future, crime rates will probably rise as women participate more equally in crime and the criminal justice system. Although it would be difficult to assess how much of the change in the future overall crime rate will be attributable to changes in the age structure, changes in the racial mix of cohorts, or changes in the crime rates for women, the relative stability of the age structure of the nonwhite

TABLE 6   Arrest Rates (per 100,000 persons) for Property Offenses in Cities with a Population Greater than 2,500, by Gender,[a] 1960 and 1970

Gender	Arrest Rate 1960	Arrest Rate 1970	Percentage Change 1960-1970	Average Yearly Rate of Increase
Females	98	315	221	12.4
Males	812	1,282	58	4.7
Difference (males-females)	714	967		

[a]Because population data were not provided separately by gender, the calculations assume that the ratio of males to females is 1.0.

SOURCES: Federal Bureau of Investigation (1960, Table 19; 1970, Table 36).

population and the increasing crime rates for women will
clearly offset a substantial amount of the declines that
would be expected from the decline in the youthful population.

CRIME AND CRIME CONTROL IN DECLINING AND STABLE AREAS

The next two sections deal with the consequences of the
trends in population distribution identified by Berry and
Dahmann for crime and crime-control institutions. The
general thesis is that changes in population distribution
are both a cause and a consequence of changes in community
structure and that both crime and crime-control institutions will reflect these changes.
     I use a simple model of the criminal justice system,
which is divided into three simultaneously determined
components:

     1. *Criminal activity;*
     2. *Law-enforcement activity,* including all public and
private reactions to criminal activity, of which the most
important are the activities of police, courts, and
correctional institutions; and
     3. *Community demand for law enforcement,* which is
reflected, to some degree, in expenditures for crime control but is more complex and differentiated than such a
measure would imply. It is the willingness of residents
and officials to pursue particular law-enforcement policies.

Note that in this terminology the "criminal justice system"
includes both criminal and crime-control activity. The
following discussion starts with the criminal-activity
component of the system and then proceeds to law enforcement
and community demand. The joint determination of the
variables make verbal descriptions difficult and sometimes
repetitive, because changes in one component imply changes
in others. For ease of presentation one component at
a time is discussed. The reader should keep in mind that
this is a simplification and that changes in one variable
generally cannot be considered in isolation. Indeed, the
existing literature on law-enforcement activity and that
on the demand for law enforcement are so closely linked
that they are treated together in the relevant sections of
this paper.

Crime

It is expected that older central cities will experience stable but high levels of criminal activity, in terms of volume and rates, in the near future. As already noted, the changes in arrest rates for women and the relatively stable size of young nonwhite age cohorts will tend to offset reductions that might be anticipated from changes in the age structure of the population. These trends should be at least as large in central cities as in other areas.

Furthermore, patterns in housing markets, services, and job locations will continue to reinforce the selective out-migration of whites and middle-class blacks so that central cities will contain a greater proportion of poor and minority residents. Out-migration accounts for most of the changes in the composition of central cities (Long 1975), but the inflow of southern blacks continues to be an important factor contributing to the composition of northern cities. Although the South has recently experienced net-migration gains and increases in return migration, the rate of out-migration for blacks in the South was virtually the same between 1955 and 1960 as it was between 1965 and 1970 (Long and Hansen 1975) and the volume increased by about 5 percent.

Economic conditions in central cities will also contribute to crime as opportunities for unskilled and less educated residents become more scarce. The greater incidence of abandoned, poorly maintained, or unsupervised property will also provide more opportunity for larceny, arson, and vandalism. Furthermore, crime rates are generally higher in older cities than in newer cities (Chapman 1974). Central cities will also continue to attract non-resident offenders who contribute to the number of offenses committed in central cities but not to the residential population.

Is there reason to believe that the thinning of the population or associated changes in population composition and community structure will modify cultural or ideological support for criminal behavior in declining areas? Although we will consider two arguments that would lead to such predictions, the evidence suggests that changes in culture will either be very minor or that they will have little impact on criminal activity.

The first argument is that a reduction in out-migration from the southern region of the United States will lead to a reduction in violent crime in traditional receiving areas

such as the urban Northeast and the Midwest because
Southerners are exposed to a distinctive regional subculture that emphasizes personal violence--a lack of regard
for human life and an exaggerated sense of personal honor.
In this view, the high rates of homicide and assult that
characterize the southern pattern of crime are a result of
this violent subculture, and the rise in violent crime in
areas adjacent to the South has, to a large extent, been
a consequence of the migration of Southerners into those
areas (Gastil 1971, 1975, Hackney 1969). There are two
reasons, however, why changes in migration patterns will
have negligible effects on the level of crime. First, the
thesis of a distinctive southern regional subculture of
violence is probably not valid. Evidence does not support
the contention that violent behavior is more frequent among
Southerners (Doerner 1978, Erlanger 1975), and there is
one study that shows that economic and social characteristics
of the South provide an equally plausible explanation for
the geographic distribution of violent crime (Loftin and
Hill 1974).

Although the regional subculture theory primarily has
been used to explain violent crime, some authors have
generalized it to other offenses, attributing generally
higher rates of crime and delinquency to southern migrants.
The evidence, though fragmentary, also contradicts the
generalized version of the regional subculture theory.
Southern migrants seem to be significantly less likely to
be involved in property offenses than nonmigrants. Savitz
(1970) found that migrants--most of whom were from the
South--had lower rates of delinquency in Philadelphia than
did native residents. Similarly, studies by Long and
Heltman (1975) and by Friedlander (1972) suggest that black
males born and raised in northern cities are more likely to
pariticipate in illegitimate occupations than are southern
migrants.

Second, even if southern migrants do have higher offense
rates than native residents of other regions, the reduction
in out-migration from the South is not great enough to
produce a very large effect, especially if the social composition of the migration streams are taken into account.
The substantial increase in net migration to the South
between the late 1960s and the early 1970s is primarily due
to an increase in in-migration to the South rather than to
a decrease in out-migration. The number of migrants from
the South to the Northeast and North Central states remains
substantial (U.S. Bureau of the Census 1975a).

A second theory that might predict a reduction in cultural

support for criminal behavior in declining areas is Fischer's (1975) subcultural theory of urbanism. According to Fischer, urban areas nurture and sustain unconventional behavior and beliefs for much the same reason that they provide conventional services. That is, the aggregation of population provides a "critical mass" of people large enough to support deviant subcultures and to sustain a market for the goods and services of criminal specialists. Small towns and rural areas are less likely to develop deviant subcultures simply because there are not enough consumers and participants to build and sustain the social groups that are necessary for a vigorous subculture.

Since the dynamic element in this theory is population size, it would seem to follow that reductions in population would tend to weaken deviant subcultures by reducing not only the number of subculture members but also potential victims and targets of criminal activity. In effect, the members of deviant subcultures should follow general population trends to nonmetropolitan and Sun Belt areas, leaving weakened subcultures and less criminal activity in declining areas.

This is a very interesting possibility, but it is unlikely that population changes of the magnitude that we are considering will significantly influence the viability of deviant subcultures. It is simply more likely that deviant patterns of behavior will spread more widely as the fields of influence of urban areas extend. The resulting pattern may be one in which urban centers are less distinctive from peripheral areas with respect to criminal activity, but this will be a consequence of increasing criminal activity in the periphery, not increasing conformity in the center.

One of the most popular hypotheses in the study of crime is that urban growth causes crime. Some studies posit a particular mechanism (e.g., changing patterns of social interaction, strain, anxiety, changes in informal social control, etc.) that is thought to be a consequence of urban growth, but more typical are global statements positing a structural relationship between "urbanization" and crime. For example, one frequently cited study suggests that the relationship between city size and crime is such as " . . . to raise the possibility that a cost-effective long term method [of controlling crime] is to redirect the population toward more nearly optimum sizes . . . " (Morris and Tweeten 1971, p. 48). Clinard (1965), who has written extensively on these themes, notes in the context of urbanization in developing countries that " . . . crime would probably be reduced if the size of urban concentrations

were controlled by decentralization . . . " (Clinard and
Abbott 1973, p. 277). A slightly different variation on
the same theme is: "A community might seek to reduce the
costs of crime by instituting arrangements which would
discourage in-migration" (Pressman and Carol 1971, p. 222).

All of these studies were carried out during a period
of time when urban areas were growing rapidly and population concentration was the dominant trend in population
distribution. Given that the populations of many metropolitan areas are currently stable or declining, these
theories would now predict major reductions in crime rates.

Clearly, current trends provide a new opportunity to
evaluate these theories. Although complete evidence is
not yet available, such effects appear to be unlikely.
The most frequently cited evidence for the relationship
is a bivariate tabulation of crime rates and population
size such as Table 1, but such evidence is inadequate because many variables that are related to population size are
also related to crime and might explain the observed relationship. Second, more sophisticated multivariate models
produce estimates of the effects of density and population
size that are very sensitive to variations in the unit of
analysis and the time period from which observations are
drawn. A good example is Skogan's (1977) study, which finds
that the relationships among population size, density, and
crime have changed over the period 1946-1970. In this
period the relationship between city size and crime rates
shifts from moderately positive to near zero and then up
to weakly positive; the relationship between density and
size goes from moderately negative to moderately positive.
Gordon (1976) has commented on the shift in the relationship between crime rates and city size as reported in
studies done by Angell with data collected in 1940 and 1960.
He attributes the change to a change in the distribution
of the black population, but there are many possible
explanations.[4] Because most studies do not consider the
mutual influence of crime and law-enforcement activity, the
indirect effects of population on crime that are transmitted through law enforcement become confounded with the

[4]An interesting example of the sensitivity of the relationship between crime rates and urban growth to variations in
time and space is found in McHale and Johnson's (1976a,b)
study of administrative districts in Imperial Germany between
1882 and 1913. See also Lodhi and Tilly (1973) for a time-
series study in France.

direct effects. The widely different estimates of the
magnitude and size of the effects of population size and
density on crime almost surely mean that existing models
are poorly specified and that variables other than these
are responsible for the observed relationships.

The changes that characterize crime in older metropolitan
areas are more likely to be in the type and spatial distribution of offenses, rather than in the number of offenses.
As the population of an area thins, the offenses that would
have been committed by departing residents will be replaced
by offenses that are a consequence of physical deterioration and a dependent population. Obsolete and physically
deteriorating buildings provide opportunities for vandalism
the stripping of plumbing, and arson that are unique to
sparsely populated areas. Where large-scale abandonment
of property occurs, fires and other threats to public
safety will increase rapidly. Also selective migration
leaves behind a population with a high proportion of disadvantaged persons such as the elderly, the mentally or
physically disabled, and the poor. Not only is such a
population more vulnerable to physical and financial
exploitation, they are more likely to call on the police
for general social services such as emergency medical
assistance and help with suspicious or stressful situations
(Vanagunas 1977, Weicher 1971).

Law Enforcement: Demands, Expenditures, and Services

Population decline is likely to have a greater impact on
the criminal justice system through its influence on law
enforcement than through its direct influence on crime.
The major trends that will determine this influence are
an increasing demand for public law-enforcement services,
increasing costs per capita for service delivered, and
increasing conflict over who will bear the costs of these
services. These factors are not unique to declining
metropolitan areas, but there are indications that the
problems are more severe and that the conflicts are more
difficult to manage in these areas. Although there are
limitations on the studies, there is ample evidence of
each of these trends.

The demand for crime control throughout the nation is
greater than at any time in the past 30 years. Part of
the growth in demand may be attributed to the pressure of
increasing crime and growing awareness of the problem.
However, a larger part should be attributed to a major

shift in the social theory of crime, which probably explains
why social policy has moved quickly toward a more active
attack on crime. The main elements of the shift are, first,
a discrediting of treatment as a rationale for lenient
sentences and, second, a growing belief that crime can be
reduced by increasing the certainty and severity of punishment (Tullock 1974, Wilson 1975). The twin arguments that
have weakened the treatment model of sentencing are that
it leads to capricious and unfair sentences (von Hirsch
1976) and that it does not work (Lipton et al. 1975,
Robinson and Smith 1971). This change in theory is
reflected in professional and popular literature on criminal justice as well as in criminal justice policy. Many
states are attempting to reduce judicial and prosecutorial
discretion by enacting determinate sentencing statutes
and adopting policies intended to limit plea bargaining.
California, Michigan, and Maine have already enacted determinate sentencing statutes, and other jurisdictions seem
likely to follow.

Prison populations throughout the country are suddenly
burgeoning. Since 1930 the imprisonment rate (prisoners
per 100,000 population) has been relatively stable,
fluctuating around a mean of about 110. At the end of
1973 it was 97.8. Three years later, in December 1976,
it was at 125--two standard deviations above the historical
mean (Blumstein et al. 1977). At the end of 1977 the total
number of persons being held in state and federal institutions reached a record high for the third year in a row
(Getlinger 1976, Wilson 1977).

Expenditures show a similar pattern. Between 1971 and
1976, expenditures of criminal justice by local governments
rose at an annual rate of 12.6 percent. The rate of
increase has accelerated within this time period. For
1971-1972, the increase was 11 percent; for 1975-1976, it
was 15 percent (U.S. Department of Justice and U.S. Bureau
of the Census 1976, 1977). A study by Odani (1977) of
police expenditures in 33 large cities during the period
1966 to 1973 shows that the per capita expenditures more
than tripled during that period and that annual growth
rates were about twice as high in the 1966-1973 period as
in the 1959-1966 period. He estimates that about 50 percent of the increase was a result of increases in police
employment.

The impact of the high levels of demand for crime control is particularly great in declining communities because
conditions in these areas increase the costs of each unit

of service delivered. Beaton (1974) has suggested that
the structure of the determination of law-enforcement costs
is unique in cities experiencing population declines. His
argument is that there are statistical interaction effects
between population change and other determinants of law-
enforcement expenditures. Whether this formulation turns
out to be valid, evidence shows that population change has
an additive impact on the costs of law enforcement.
Sternlieb and Burchell's (1973) study of residential
abandonment, which clearly shows that abandoned structures
create public safety problems, illustrates one way that
declining cities make special demands on law enforcement.
Bergstrom and Goodman (1973) found in their study of
municipal expenditures in 10 states that the rate of population change was negatively associated with per capita
expenditures on police--in other words, the decline in
population was associated with high expenditures per
capita. Other studies report similar results (Lind 1971,
Weicher 1970), although some report discrepancies (Beaton
1974, Brazer 1959, Hiibner 1971).

An additional constraint on law-enforcement costs in
declining areas is that the businesses and citizens who
reside in these cities, or at least those who use them,
appear to rely more on public protection against crime
than on private protection. Clotfelter (1977) found that
the best predictor of the substitution of private for public
law-enforcement expenditures was population change:
declining areas have a greater preference for public
expenditures.

The mechanisms that mediate the effects of population
change on law-enforcement expenditures are not clearly
understood, but the demographic composition of these areas
is probably a major factor. As a result of selective
migration, the poor, members of minority groups, the elderly
or others with special needs become a larger proportion of
the population in declining areas (Morrison 1974). Studies
consistently show that this demographic pattern increases
the amount of public resources that a city must expend in
order to achieve a given level of crime control. Pogue
(1975), in one of the clearest discussions of this topic,
shows that cities with a large proportion of poor and nonwhite residents must pay higher costs, either in terms of
crime or social control expenditures, than other cities.
If cities with different demographic profiles are to achieve
a similar level of public safety, the city with a more
dependent population must spend more of its resources on

law enforcement. His findings are supported by many other studies that have investigated the determinants of police expenditures (Brazer 1959, Chapman 1976a, Morris and Tweeten 1971, Swimmer 1974, 1975, Weicher 1970). These studies imply that although the declining population size and density will increase the resources of law enforcement on a per-capita basis, the composition of the population and the nature of the services demanded are such that any gains will be more than offset by the increased costs per capita.

These increases in demands and costs will result in escalating conflict over who will bear the costs of crime control. The financial problems of declining cities and growing opposition to the property tax provide the context for the conflict. The major items of the agenda are (1) the share of budgets to be devoted to law enforcement; (2) the resistance to reductions or redistributions of personnel in areas with declining population densities; (3) the shifting of law-enforcement costs to a wider area or a higher level of government; and (4) the location of new prisons and other correctional facilities.

Incremental budgets, which do not vary the share allocated to particular service functions or geographical areas, are more conciliatory than those that redistribute the shares. Odani (1977), in his study of police expenditures in 33 large cities, found that although expenditures more than tripled between 1959 and 1973, the proportions of budgets assigned to the police have remained remarkably stable. Declining areas, however, will find such harmonious budgets impossible to afford as resources stabilize or grow at a slower rate. In a struggle for changing shares of municipal budgets, law enforcement may gain at the expense of other services, but the battle will be intense. Public opinion more clearly favors cuts in expenditures for welfare, education, and recreation than for public safety.

The only effective argument in the popular press against property tax limitations schemes has been that they would reduce police and fire services. Policy makers are reticent about making cuts in law-enforcement personnel because of possible adverse effects on public safety. Chapman (1976b) has shown that the demand for police (as measured by police per capita) is relatively unresponsive to variations in the wages paid to the police. Chapman's estimate of the elasticity of police wages for a cross-section of California cities was less than 0.5 percent. Regardless of the outcome, the conflict will be evident in more antagonistic labor-management relationships as entrenched and powerful

interests resist the erosion of their share of municipal
budgets.

Conflicts of a different nature will inevitably emerge
as administrators attempt to save money by more efficient
allocation of law-enforcement resources. Thurow (1970),
among others, has noted that there are significant contra-
dictions between standards of equity and efficiency in
crime control. The existing allocation of law-enforcement
resources embodies serious inefficiences as well as marked
inequalities in the distribution of criminal victimization,
probabilities of apprehension, and other costs of crime.
Attempts to reallocate the resources will activate quiescent
conflicts over the distribution of costs. The lines of
the conflict will vary with local circumstances and the
nature of proposed allocations, but several issues are
likely to arise: (1) the degree to which the police should
reduce traditional service functions so that they can
concentrate on criminal activity; (2) whether patrols
should be reduced in low crime areas so that they can be
increased in high crime areas; (3) the use of specialized
undercover or heavily armed law-enforcement units in
particular areas; (4) the creation of consolidated law-
enforcement service districts; (5) the use of state police,
county sheriffs, private security, and even voluntary
personnel to patrol areas in metropolitan areas; and (6)
the use of state and federal funds to pay for police,
courts, and correctional facilities that serve local areas.

Another closely related source of conflict that emerges
with the increased demand for punishment of criminal
offenders is the location of facilities such as prisons,
jails, and community correctional facilities. One estimate,
cited by Wilson (1977), is that there are over 860 penal
facilities (including local jails) currently proposed or
under construction. Given the overcrowded condition of
most state systems and the rapid growth in prison populations, officials are seeking existing structures that can
be converted to prisons. Everything from mothballed ships
to abandoned seminaries has been considered "ideal" for
use as prisons. The presence of prisons is a cost of the
criminal justice system that must be absorbed by some part
of the community. Most citizens resist the location of
prisons in their neighborhoods because of adverse effects
on land values and the quality of the use of other land.
However, the availability of abandoned structures and the
need for employment makes those areas that are experiencing
population declines particularly attractive as potential
locations for jails and prisons.

CRIME AND CRIME CONTROL IN GROWING AREAS

Criminal Activity

Regional patterns of crime in the United States have
puzzled criminologists for several generations. The con-
tinuity of research on the topic is atypical: the patterns
have been analyzed carefully three times since the 1930s
and the literature extends back into the 19th century
(Harries 1971, Lottier 1938, Shannon 1954).[5] However,
the problems with the studies are typical. Conceptual
and methodological errors obscure most interpretable
patterns in the data, making generalizations more difficult.
However, before we attempt to assess the impact of trends
in population distribution, it will be useful to take note
of some general regional patterns.

The one spectacular pattern is the high level of murder
in the South. For example, in 1976 the rate of murder and
nonnegligent manslaughter in the South was 40 percent higher
than in the West (which is the closest competitor) and 67
percent higher than in the Northeast. This pattern has
persisted since at least the 1860s (Hackney 1969, Redfield
1880) and has been consistently documented in every study
of the topic. Other violent crimes also tend to be high
in the South, but the pattern is much more varied. Table
7 presents the mean rates of homicide, robbery, and burglary
for cities with populations over 2,500 by region in 1960
and 1970. Two very clear patterns are evident. First,
the communities in the South and the West have much higher
crime rates than those in the Northeast and North Central
regions. The South leads the West for homicide, but the
West is higher than the South for both robbery and burglary.
Second, the gap between the regions did not narrow in the
decade. If there was a trend, it was toward a greater
difference between the South and West as compared with
the other regions. One study of regional trends in crime
rates finds a pattern of converging regional differences
(Jacobson 1975). However, that analysis combines the West,
the highest crime region, with the North Central and Northeast regions, which have the lowest crime rates, and thereby
obscures the pattern evident in Table 7.

The thesis of regional convergence or balance in
crime is appealing, and is popular among criminologists.
It implies a trend toward relatively lower crime rates in

[5]Harries (1974) provides a good summary of the major studies.

TABLE 7   Mean Crime Rates (per 100,000) for Sample of
Cities in Four Regions, 1960 and 1970

Crime and Year	North- east	North Central	South	West
Homicide				
1960	2.0	2.5	8.2	3.4
1970	5.2	5.8	14.5	7.3
Robbery				
1960	27.4	38.7	49.3	75.1
1970	159.6	171.6	181.3	211.8
Burglary				
1960	402.6	414.1	716.0	768.4
1970	1,164.7	1,104.5	1,450.9	1,793.9

SOURCE: Computed from data provided by Jacobson (1975).

the South and West and relatively higher rates in the
Northeast and North Central regions. However, such a
prediction cannot be deduced from any existing theory of
crime and regional structure and cannot be sustained by
any existing body of evidence. For now, we must settle
for generalizations, such as those in Table 7, and some
preliminary evidence on the effects of growth on crime
and crime control.

In the context of the discussion of declining and
stable areas, the popular thesis that crime rates vary
positively with urban growth was noted. Although it
was found lacking in that case, there may be some reason
to expect that it would operate asymmetrically, predicting
increasing crime rates with urban growth but not decreases
with urban decline.

Not surprisingly the evidence of differences between
migrants and nonmigrants with respect to criminal activity
is mixed. Studies by Kinman and Lee (1966) and Savitz
(1970) in the United States and Clinard and Abbott (1973)
in Uganda report that migrants are less likely to be
offenders or that there are no differences, while studies
by Green (no date), Pressman and Carol (1971), and
Shoham (1962) find the opposite. Criminal populations may
be attracted by the general opportunities that attract
noncriminal migrants, but this is very different from the
mechanism that I have in mind. Clearly the evidence is
deficient, but I find no reason to expect that migration,
independent of other factors, will increase the probability

of criminal activity. There are many versions of the theory, two of which I believe can be rejected: (1) that urban forms of social organization promote "stress" and "social disorganization" and (2) that the process of migration itself has a stressful or disorganizing effect. There is no evidence that urban forms of organization are inherently stressful. Studies of the "pathological effects" of density are flawed by methodological errors, produce inconsistent results, and are generally unconvincing.[6] Furthermore, there is no reason to think that stress, even if it were more characteristic of urban areas, changes the probability of engaging in criminal behavior. With regard to migration, it is difficult to disentangle the effects of the social characteristics of migrants from the effects of the move itself. If all migrants from rural to urban areas, for example, are of rural origins and nonmigrants are of urban origin, do we attribute differences to migration or to place of origin?

A more believable argument is that urban forms of organization drastically modify opportunities for crime and the nature of social control. In this view crime patterns reflect changes in regulation rather than changes in the impulse to commit crime. Major elements of urban growth that are implicated are the increased interactions and dependencies among strangers, the more intensive use of public spaces that are concentrated in a smaller area and that cannot be regulated by private groups (Stinchcombe 1963), and the greater accessibility of movable property.

Several patterns of crime and crime control organization follow from these changes. First, social controls that depend on dense personal networks to sanction offenders and settle disputes are less effective. Consequently, crime may increase to some degree, but more importantly demands will increase for public law enforcement to control public space and to regulate the behavior of strangers. An increase in the use of the police to settle disputes and to maintain increasingly sensitive standards of public order are well-documented changes associated with the development of "modern" forms of social organization (Black 1973, Lane 1969). Second, property offenses increase because offenders can more easily evade detection and because property is more available and accessible. Urban concentration appears to be an efficient organizational form for illegal enterprises just as it is for legal ones.

---

[6]See Choldin (1978) for a recent review.

Third, a major cause of violent personal crime will diminish as private groups increasingly are forced to rely on public agents to settle disputes rather than resorting to the use of force to settle disputes for themselves.

These changes are the result of large-scale modifications in organization. Although there is reason to believe that each has contributed heavily to the patterns of crime and crime control that currently exist in modern urban systems, the scale of current changes in population distribution are not great enough to result in major extensions of the patterns. Changes will occur slowly along existing lines as urban systems expand their fields of influence into rural areas, but the patterns are already widely established.

More important changes will occur in growing areas because of the effects of selective in-migration on their demographic composition. Growing populations tend to be younger than stable or declining ones because migrants tend to be young and, as a result of their youth, tend to have higher birthrates. Approximately 33 percent of all migrants in the United States are in their 20s and 16 percent are children between the ages of 1 and 6 (Morrison 1974). This factor alone, given the higher offense rates for younger people, would increase crime rates. The socioeconomic class composition of some areas may also change radically because of in-migration. Patterns of personal crime will, to a large degree, follow the trend in the distribution of low socioeconomic status groups. Some growing areas will suffer increases in personal crime rates, but most will experience decreases. The net effect for large areas should be a reduction. The high levels of personal violence that are the hallmark of the South can, to a considerable extent, be attributed to a large percentage of the population at the very low end of the distribution of socioeconomic resources, as reflected in such things as the percent of the population with less than 5 years of education, infant mortality rates, and the percentage of families with very low incomes. Homicides are highly concentrated in this end of the distribution and fall rapidly as one moves toward the middle (Loftin and Hill 1974). Growth in the region should moderate the rates of violent crime, assuming that the distinctive socioeconomic patterns are, in fact, eroded by growth. Some reservations should be noted, however, because there is some question as to whether economic growth in the Sun Belt has reduced inequalities (Firestine, 1977). Property crime may respond differently to growth since it is sensitiv

not only to the proportion of potential offenders in the
population, but also to the opportunities to obtain valuable
property at low risk. Economic growth and expansion provide more targets for property crime and spread property
over a wider area making it more difficult to protect.

Law Enforcement

Although they are more indirect, the effects of population
growth on crime that are transmitted through law-enforcement
activity may be more important than those that operate more
directly. Even if crime rates were to remain fixed in
areas that are experiencing population growth, crime control resources--police, judges, prosecutors, correctional
facilities, etc.--would be consumed more quickly and spread
more thinly across the larger population. As law-enforcement
resources lag behind population growth, crime rates should
rise in response to declining levels of law enforcement
per capita. There is considerable debate concerning the
effects of law-enforcement activity on crime. For example,
a persistent finding is that estimated effects of police
expenditures and personnnel on crime are positive (Greenwood
and Wadycki 1973). These "perverse" findings are not a
result of simultaneity bias. Even studies that simultaneously estimate the effect of crime on law enforcement
and law enforcement on crime find that both parameters are
positive. Refinements such as including arrest rates or
other sanction variables and the use of distributed lag
models produce results that are more consonant with theoretical expectations (Ehrlich 1973, McPheters and Stronge
1974, Pogue 1975), but the nature of the effects is still
uncertain. For present purposes it is assumed that the
effects are negative and that crime rates will rise in
growing areas because the resources of the criminal justice
system will lag behind the levels that would be necessary
to maintain them at a constant level. The failure of law-
enforcement resources to keep pace with population growth
may explain why population increases and migration are
positively related to crime in spite of the common finding
that migrants are not more likely to engage in illegal
activity than nonmigrants. It is, perhaps, a type of
"social disorganization," but it is very different from
the commonly held view that migration contributes to personal confusion or disorientation, which increases criminal
activity.

In absolute terms, expenditures on law enforcement will

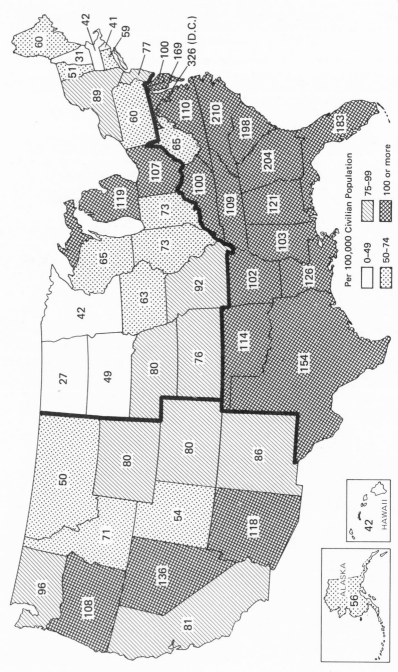

FIGURE 3 Sentenced prisoners in state and federal institutions: number per 100,000 population, December 31, 1975 (National Criminal Justice Information and Statistics Service 1977).

rise in response to growing crime rates and increasing
demands for crime control. In per capita terms, however,
the picture is more complex. There are some studies that
find that population change is positively related to police
expenditures per capita, while others find a negative
relationship. Beaton (1974) argues that the discrepancies
are explained, at least in part, by the interaction between
population size, direction of population change, and per-
capita expenditures. For growing cities under 10,000 in
population, he finds that police expenditures are relatively
high because of high "start-up costs," but larger cities
that are growing benefit from lower police expenditures
per capita (Beaton 1974, p. 342). The evidence is not
clear-cut, but it appears that growing areas experience
lower costs per capita than declining areas. Part of the
reasons is the contrasting demographic profiles of the two
types of areas. In spite of their relative youth, growing
areas are proportionately more prosperous, contain fewer
dependent citizens, and experience lower demands for police
services per capita. Furthermore, residents and businesses
in growing areas appear to invest more heavily in private
crime protection than older areas (Clotfelter 1977).

Lower per-capita costs of crime control and expanding
tax bases may moderate conflicts over who will bear the
costs of law enforcement, but they will not prevent growing
areas from experiencing such conflicts. The location of
courts and correctional facilities, the allocation of
responsibilities and costs among governments with over-
lapping jurisdictions, the financing of new services in
the face of growing public resistance to property taxes,
and the allocation of services to areas with changing
social composition are typical issues in growing areas.
Since local areas gain the most by passing the costs to a
higher level of government, one can expect considerable
pressure to have the state and federal governments assume
more responsibility for law-enforcement expenditures.

Regional patterns in law-enforcement personnel or expenditures per capita are not at all distinctive. Community
size and character are much more important (Harries 1974).
However, the tendency of a state to incarcerate offenders
as measured by inmates in state institutions has a regional
distribution that overlaps remarkably with the Sun Belt
states. Figure 3 shows the number of sentenced prisoners
in state and federal institutions per 100,000 residents of
states as of December 31, 1975. The pattern would be even
more striking if the rates had been averaged over several
years because Michigan and Ohio joined the group with

TABLE 8 Estimates of Change in Number of Inmates in State Prisons by Region, 1976-1980

Region	January 1, 1976		I. January 1, 1980[a]		II. January 1, 1980[b]	
	Number	Inmates per 100,000 Persons	Number	Inmates per 100,000 Persons	Number	Inmates per 100,000 Persons
Northeast	35,657	71.8	51,780	104.2	54,129	109.0
North Central	49,153	85.3	102,478	177.9	74,618	129.5
South	105,668	160.1	156,366	236.9	160,409	243.0
West	35,104	96.0	60,893	166.5	53,290	145.7
Total	225,582	107.5	371,517	177.0	342,446	163.1

[a]Assumes that the rate of change will continue to be the same as 1975-1976 for each state.
[b]Assumes that the rate of change for the total U.S. 1975-1976 is applicable to each state.

SOURCE: Based on data from Getlinger (1976).

imprisonment rates of over 100 in 1974 and California left
the group temporarily in the same year. Over time, the
pattern is much more stable in the South than in the West,
but western states clearly tend to incarcerate more offenders
than do the North Central or Northeast states. Table 8
(column 1) presents 1976 data from a survey conducted by
Corrections Magazine. The pattern in the table is the same
as on the map. The imprisonment rate is 123 percent higher
in the South than in the Northeast; and 67 percent higher
than in the West, the next highest region. The South contains only about 32 percent of the U.S. population, but has
48 percent of prisoners held by states.

It is interesting to speculate about what will happen
to correctional systems and courts in the South as the
population of the region increases. These two factors--
spectacular incarceration rates and a growing population--
if allowed to operate unchecked, would drastically increase
the size of the prison populations. If we project the
1975-1976 rate of change in prison populations through
1980 (see Table 8), the imprisonment rate in the South
would increase to a value of over 230 inmates per 100,000
residents. If we add to this the expected increase in
population and volume of crime, the consequences in terms
of prison populations are huge.

Clearly, rises in prison population of this magnitude
will not occur. The interesting question is how the
criminal justice system will adjust to these pressures.
Will average sentences be shorter? If they are, what
consequences will this have for the crime rate? Other
possible adjustments include decreasing the average rate
at which offenders are incarcerated, more use of diversion,
and lowering the probability of incarceration. These circumstances would seem to provide a unique opportunity to
examine the dynamics of the crime control system.

CONTENDING WITH CRIME IN GROWING AND DECLINING AREAS:
SUMMARY AND CONCLUSIONS

The changes in community structure that are associated
with population growth and decline produce distinctive consequences for the criminal justice system. Some effects
are the result of changes in crime rates and the type of
criminal activity. Declining cities continue to experience
high levels of criminal activity, in spite of population
losses, because of the effects of selective out-migration,
shrinking economic opportunities, the relative youthfulness

of the nonwhite population, the presence of social networks
that support criminal subcultures, and the intensive use
of cities by nonresidents. Some growing areas experience
changes in crime rates that are a result of changes in the
age and class composition of the population and the failure
of law-enforcement resources to keep pace with population
increases, but all experience rising levels of criminal
activity because of the increase in the number of residents

More important effects of growth and decline are transmitted through changes in the demand for law enforcement,
the costs of crime control, and the organization of law
enforcement. In cities that are losing population the
national trend toward the more active use of criminal
justice sanctions combines with perceived and actual declines in public safety to create very high demand for
law-enforcement activity. These services, if they are to
be provided, are delivered in the context of increasing
costs per unit of service delivered, declining fiscal
resources, and escalating conflict over who will bear the
social costs of public safety. The problems of law enforce
ment in growing areas are largely a result of the need to
provide new services to a growing population. In most
cases law-enforcement resources lag behind increases in
population, and therefore crime rates rise. In response,
the community demands more crime control, and law-
enforcement expenditures rise. The demand for law enforcement may also rise independently of crime rates to the
extent that residents perceive that resources are lagging
behind population growth.

Generally growing areas operate in an environment that
is less constraining than that of declining areas. A
growing tax base, a less dependent population, and more
investment by residents in private security reduce the per-
capita costs of law enforcement. Therefore, conflict over
the social costs of law enforcement may be more easily
managed and moderated. Nevertheless, persistent change
will continue to raise issues such as the location of
courts and correctional facilities, the allocation of
services, and the appropriate level of enforcement.

REFERENCES

Beaton, W. (1974) The determinants of police protection
     expenditures. *National Tax Journal* 27(2):335-349.
Bergstrom, T., and Goodman, R. (1973) Private demands for
     public goods. *American Economic Review* 63(3):280-296.

Berry, B., and Horton, F. (1970) *Geographic Perspectives on Urban Systems.* Englewood Cliffs, N.J.: Prentice-Hall.

Berry, B. (1971) Problems of data organization and analytical methods in geography. *Journal of the American Statistical Association* 66(335):510-523.

Black, D. (1973) The mobilization of law. *Journal of Legal Studies* 2(1):125-149.

Blumstein, A., and Nagin, D. (1975) Analysis of arrest rates for trends in criminality. *Socio-Economic Planning Science* 9(5):221-227.

Blumstein, A., Cohen, J., and Nagin, D. (1977) The dynamics of a homeostatic punishment process. *Journal of Criminal Law and Criminology* 67(3):317-334.

Boggs, S. (1965) Urban crime patterns. *American Sociological Review* 30(6):899-908.

Boudouris, J. (1970) Trends in Homicide, Detroit: 1926-1968. Unpublished Ph.D. dissertation, Wayne State University.

Brazer, H. (1959) *City Expenditures in the United States.* National Bureau of Economic Research Occasional Paper No. 66. New York: National Bureau of Economic Research.

Chapman, J. (1974) Violent crime rates: the influence of city age. *Annals of Regional Science* 8(3):61-69.

Chapman, J. (1976a) An economic model of crime and police: some empirical results. *Journal of Research on Crime and Delinquency* 13(1):48-63.

Chapman, J. (1976b) The demand for police. *Public Finance Quarterly* 4(2):187-203.

Chilton, R., and Spielberger, A. (1971) Is delinquency increasing? Age structure and the crime rate. *Social Forces* 49(3):487-493.

Chilton, R., and Spielberger, A. (1972) Increases in crime: the utility of alternative measures. *Journal of Criminal Law, Criminology and Police Science* 63(1):68-74.

Choldin, H. (1978) Urban density and pathology. Pp. 91-113 in *Annual Review of Sociology.* Vol. 4. Palo Alto, Calif.: Annual Reviews.

Cliff, A., and Ord, J. (1973) *Spatial Autocorrelation.* London: Pion.

Clinard, M. (1964) The relation of urbanization and urbanism to criminal behavior. Pp. 541-558 in E. W. Burgess and D. J. Bogue, eds., *Contributions to Urban Sociology.* Chicago: University of Chicago Press.

Clinard, M. (1974) *Sociology of Deviant Behavior.* 4th ed. New York: Holt, Rinehart and Winston.

Clinard, M., and Abbott, D. (1973) *Crime in Developing Countries: A Comparative Perspective.* New York: John Wiley.

Clotfelter, C. (1977) Public services, private substitutes, and demand for protection against crime. *American Economic Review* 67(5):867-877.

Doerner, W. (1978) The index of southerness revisited: the influence of wherefrom on whodunnit. *Criminology* 16(1):47-56.

Droettboom, T., Jr., McAllister, R., Kaiser, E., and Butler, E. (1971) Urban violence and residential mobility. *Journal of the American Institute of Planners* 37(September):319-325.

Ehrlich, I. (1973) Participation in illegitimate activities: a theoretical and empirical investigation. *Journal of Political Economy* 81(3):521-565.

Erlanger, H. (1975) Is there a "subculture of violence" in the South? *Journal of Criminal Law and Criminology* 66(4):483-490.

Federal Bureau of Investigation (various years) *Uniform Crime Reports for the United States.* Washington, D.C.: Federal Bureau of Investigation.

Ferdinand, T. (1970) Demographic shifts and criminality: an inquiry. *British Journal of Criminology* 10(2):169-175

Firestine, R. (1977) Economic growth and inequality, demographic change, and the public sector response. Ch. 5 in David C. Perry and Alfred Watkins, eds., *The Rise of the Sunbelt Cities.* Beverly Hills, Calif.: Sage Publications.

Fischer, C. (1975) Toward a subcultural theory or urbanism. *American Journal of Sociology* 80(6):1319-1341.

Friedlander, S. (1972) *Unemployment in the Urban Core.* New York: Praeger.

Frey, W. (1977) Central City White Flight: Racial and Non-racial Causes. Discussion paper, Institute for Research on Poverty, University of Wisconsin, Madison.

Frey, W. (1978) Class-Specific White Flight: A Comparative Analysis of Large American Cities. Paper presented at the Ninth World Congress of Sociology, International Sociological Association, Uppsala, Sweden, August.

Garafalo, J. (1977) *Public Opinion About Crime: The Attitudes of Victims and Nonvictims in Selected Cities.* Washington, D.C.: U.S. Department of Justice.

Gastil, R. (1971) Homicide and a regional culture of violence. *American Sociological Review* 36(3):412-427.

Gastil, R. (1975) *Cultural Regions of the United States.* Seattle: University of Washington Press.

Getlinger, S. (1976) U.S. prison population hits all-time high. *Corrections Magazine* 2(3):9-20.

Gibbs, J., and Erickson, M. (1976) Crime rates of American

cities in an ecological context. *American Journal of Sociology* 82(3):605-620.

Gold, M., and Reimer, D. (1975) Changing pattern of delinquent behavior among Americans 13 through 16 years old: 1967-1972. *Crime and Delinquency Literature* 7(4):483-517.

Gordon, R. (1976) Prevalence: the rare datum in delinquency measurement and its implication for the theory of delinquency. Ch. 8 in Malcolm W. Kline, ed., *The Juvenile Justice System*. Beverly Hills, Calif.: Sage Publications.

Green, E. (1970) Race, social status, and criminal arrest. *American Sociological Review* 35(3):476-490.

Green, E. (no date) Internal Migration and Crime. Unpublished paper.

Greenwood, M., and Wadycki, W. (1973) Crime rates and public expenditures for police protection: their interaction. *Review of Social Economy* 31(October):138-151.

Guerry, A. (1833) *Essai sur la Statistique Morale de la France.*

Guterbock, T. (1976) The push hypothesis: minority presence, crime and urban deconcentration. Ch. 6 in Barry Schwartz, ed., *The Changing Face of the Suburbs*. Chicago: University of Chicago Press.

Hackney, S. (1969) Southern violence. *American Historical Review* 74(3):906-925.

Harries, K. (1971) The geography of American crime, 1968. *Journal of Geography* 70(4):204-218.

Harries, K. (1974) *The Geography of Crime and Justice.* New York: McGraw-Hill.

Hiibner, C. (1971) Determinants of Municipal Policy: A Florida Case Study. Unpublished Ph.D. dissertation, University of Florida.

Hindelang, M. (1974) The Uniform Crime Reports revisited. *Journal of Criminal Justice* 2(1):1-17.

Jacobson, A. (1975) Crime trends in southern and northern cities: a twenty-year perspective. *Social Forces* 54(1):226-242.

Kinman, J., and Lee, E. (1966) Migration and crime. *International Migration Digest* 3(1):7-14.

Lane, R. (1969) Urbanization and criminal violence in the 19th century: Massachusetts as a test case. Ch. 12 in H. D. Graham and T. R. Gurr, eds., *The History of Violence in America: Historical and Comparative Perspectives*. New York: Bantam Books.

Lind, R. (1971) Determinants of Local Public Expenditures: A Study of Rhode Island's Thirty-Nine Cities and Towns. Unpublished Ph.D. dissertation, University of Maryland.

Lipton, D., Martinson, R., and Wilks, J. (1975) *The*

Effectiveness of Correctional Treatment: A Survey of Treatment Evaluation Studies. New York: Praeger.

Lodhi, A., and Tilly, C. (1973) Urbanization, crime, and collective violence in 19th century France. *American Journal of Sociology* 79(2):296-318.

Loftin, C., and Hill, R. (1974) Regional subcultures and homicide: an examination of the Gastil-Hackney thesis. *American Sociological Review* 39(5):714-724.

Long, L. (1975) How the racial composition of cities changes. *Land Economics* 51(3):258-267.

Long, L., and Hansen, K. (1975) Trends in return migration in the South. *Demography* 12(4):601-614.

Long, L., and Heltman, L. (1975) Migration and income differences between black and white men in the North. *American Journal of Sociology* 80(6):1391-1409.

Lottier, S. (1938a) Distribution of criminal offenses in metropolitan regions. *Journal of the American Institute of Criminal Law and Criminology* 29(1):37-50.

Lottier, S. (1938b) Distribution of criminal offenses in sectional regions. *Journal of the American Institute of Criminal Law and Criminology* 29(3):329-344.

McHale, V., and Johnson, E. (1976a) Urbanization, industrialization, and crime in Imperial Germany. Part I. *Social Science History* 1(1):34-78.

McHale, V., and Johnson, E. (1976b) Urbanization, industrialization, and crime in Imperial Germany. Part II. *Social Science History* 1(2):210-247.

McPheters, L., and Stronge, W. (1974) Law enforcement expenditures and urban crime. *National Tax Journal* 27(4):633-644.

Morris, D., and Tweeten, L. (1971) The cost of controlling crime: study of the economics of city life. *Annals of Regional Science* 5(June):33-49.

Morrison, P. (1972) Dimensions of the population problem in the United States. Pp. 3-28 in U.S. Commission on Population Growth and the American Future, *Population Distribution and Policy*, Sara M. Mazie, ed., Vol. V of Commission Research Reports. Washington, D.C.: U.S. Government Printing Office.

Morrison, P. (1974) Urban growth and decline: San Jose and St. Louis in the 1960's. *Science* 185(August):757-763.

National Criminal Justice Information and Statistics Service (1977) Prisoners in state and federal institutions on December 31, 1975. In *National Prisoner Statistics Bulletin* SD-NPS-PSF, p. 3. Washington, D.C.: U.S. Department of Justice.

Norblit, G., and Burcart, J. (1976) Women and crime: 1960-1970. *Social Science Quarterly* 56(4):640-657.

Odani, M. (1977)   Recent employment and expenditure trends in city police departments in the United States. *Journal of Criminal Justice* 5(2):119-147.

Pogue, T. (1975)   Effect of police expenditures on crime rates: some evidence. *Public Finance Quarterly* 3(1): 14-44.

President's Commission on Law Enforcement and Administration of Justice (1967)   *Crime and Its Impact--An Assessment.* Task Force Report. Washington, D.C.:   U.S. Government Printing Office.

Pressman, I., and Carol, A. (1971)   Crime as a diseconomy of scale. *Review of Social Economy* (March):227-236.

Pyle, G., Hanten, E., Williams, P., Parson, A., Doyle, J., and Kwofie, K. (1974)   The Spatial Dynamics of Crime. Department of Geography Research Paper no. 159. University of Chicago.

Quetelet, L. (1842)   *A Treatise on Man.* Gainesville, Fla.: Scholars' Facsimiles and Reprints.

Redfield, H. (1880)   *Homicide, North and South.* Philadelphia: Lippincott.

Robinson, J., and Smith, G. (1971)   The effectiveness of correctional programs. *Crime and Delinquency* 17(1): 67-80.

Robinson, S. (1966)   A critical view of the Uniform Crime Reports. *University of Michigan Law Review* 64(6):1031-1054.

Rosenthal, A., and Steffensmeier, D. (1978)   A Method for Converting UCR Arrest Statistics into Refined Arrest Rates.   Paper presented at the Eastern Sociological Association meeting, Philadelphia, April.

Sagi, P., and Wellford, C. (1968)   Age composition and patterns of change in criminal statistics. *Journal of Criminal Law, Criminology and Police Science* 59(1):29-36.

Savitz, L. (1970)   Delinquency and migration. Pp. 473-480 in M. Wolfgang, L. Savitz, and N. Johnson, eds., *The Sociology of Crime and Delinquency.* 2nd ed. New York: John Wiley.

Shannon, L. (1954)   The spatial distribution of criminal offenses. *Journal of Criminal Law, Criminology and Police Science* 45(2):264-273.

Shoham, S. (1962)   The application of the "culture conflict" hypothesis to the criminality of immigrants in Israel. *Journal of Criminal Law, Criminology and Police Science* 53(2):207-214.

Simon, R. (1976)   American women and crime. *Annals of the American Academy of Political and Social Science* 423 (January):31-46.

Skogan, W. (1977)   The changing distribution of big-city
    crime: multi-city time-series analysis. *Urban Affairs
    Quarterly* 13(1):33-48.
Steffensmeier, D., and Jordan, C. (1978)   Changing patterns
    of female crime in rural America, 1962-75. *Rural
    Sociology* 43(1):87-102.
Sternlieb, G., and Burchell, R. (1973)   *Residential Aban-
    donment: The Tenement Landlord Revisited*. New Bruns-
    wick, N.J.:   Center for Urban Policy Research, Rutgers
    University.
Stinchcombe, A. (1963)   Institutions of privacy in the
    determination of police administrative practice. *America
    Journal of Sociology* 69(2):150-160.
Swimmer, E. (1974)   Measurement of the effectivenss of
    urban law enforcement--a simultaneous approach.
    Southern Economic Journal 40(4):618-630.
Swimmer, E. (1975)   Relationship of police and crime:
    methodological and empirical results. *Criminology*
    12(3):293-314.
Thurow, L. (1970)   Equity and efficiency in justice. *Public
    Policy* 18(3):451-462.
Tullock, G. (1974)   Does punishment deter crime? *The
    Public Interest* 36(Summer):103-111.
U.S. Bureau of the Census (1975a)   Mobility of the popu-
    lation of the United States: March 1970 to March 1975.
    Series P-20, No. 285 in *Current Population Reports*.
    Washington, D.C.:   U.S. Department of Commerce.
U.S. Bureau of the Census (1975b)   Projection of the popu-
    lation of the United States, 1972-2050.   Series P-25,
    No. 601 in *Current Population Reports*. Washington,
    D.C.:   U.S. Department of Commerce.
U.S. Department of Justice and the Bureau of the Census
    (1977)   *Expenditure and Employment Data for the Criminal
    Justice System: 1975*.   Law Enforcement Assistance
    Administration.   Washington, D.C.:   U.S. Government
    Printing Office.
Vanagunas, S. (1977)   Socioeconomic class and demand for
    urban police services not related to criminal incidents.
    Journal of Police Science and Administration 5(4):430-
    434.
von Hirsch, A. (1976)   *Doing Justice: The Choice of
    Punishment*.   New York: Hill and Wang.
Weicher, J. (1970)   Determinants of central city expendi-
    tures: some overlooked factors and problems. *National
    Tax Journal* 23(4):379-396.
Weicher, J. (1971)   The allocation of police protection
    by income class. *Urban Studies* 8(3):207-222.

Wilson, J. (1975) *Thinking about Crime*. New York: Basic
   Books.
Wilson, J. (1977) Changing criminal sentences. *Harper's*
   255(1530):16-20.
Wilson, J., and Boland, B. (1976) Crime. Ch. 4 in William
   Gorham and Nathan Glazer, eds., *The Urban Predicament*.
   Washington, D.C.: The Urban Institute.
Wolfgang, M. (1963) Uniform Crime Reports: a critical
   appraisal. *University of Pennsylvania Law Review* 3(6):
   708-738.
Wolfgang, M. (1968) Urban crime. Ch. 8 in James Q. Wilson,
   ed., *The Metropolitan Enigma*. Cambridge, Mass.:
   Harvard University Press.
Wolfgang, M. (1970) *Youth Violence*. Washington, D.C.:
   U.S. Department of Health, Education and Welfare.
Zeisel, H. (1971) The future of law enforcement statistics:
   a summary view. In *Federal Statistics: Report of the
   President's Commission*. Vol. II. Washington, D.C.:
   U.S. Government Printing Office.

THE SOCIOLOGICAL IMPLICATIONS
OF POPULATION REDISTRIBUTION

William A. Sampson

INTRODUCTION

A great deal of discussion has recently been focused on
the geographic shifts of the nation's urban population.
Scholars, journalists, the public, and public officials
have seen the need to talk and write about this movement,
which may perhaps best be understood in terms of an analysis of the areas with declining populations and the areas
with growing populations. Essentially, as Berry and
Dahmann point out, there are two types of areas with
declining populations: central cities and the Northeast
and North Central regions. There are three types of areas
with growing populations: suburbs, exurbs, and the South
and the West. This paper focuses on the ways in which age,
income, and racial groups affect and are affected by these
patterns of decline and growth.

AREAS OF DECLINING POPULATION

Since 1970, population has increased 6.3 percent in non-
metropolitan areas and 3.6 percent in metropolitan areas
(U.S. Bureau of the Census 1975). Cities such as Baltimore,
Chicago, Cleveland, Detroit, Philadelphia, Pittsburgh, and
St. Louis have declined in population since the 1950s (see
Berry and Dahmann in this volume).

Growth rates in the Northeast and North Central regions
have declined since 1970, although both regions are still
experiencing modest growth. Between 1970 and 1974 the

William A. Sampson is Associate Professor of Sociology
and Urban Affairs, Northwestern University.

populations of the Northeast and North Central regions
increased 1.2 percent and 1.3 percent, respectively, compared with a 4.1 percent increase for the nation (U.S.
Bureau of the Census 1975). As Berry and Dahmann state:
"Only three divisions of the country have exhibited significantly declining shares of the nation's new population
growth since the 1950s." The three divisions--East North
Central, Middle Atlantic, and New England--comprise the
North Central region and the Northeast region; the North
Central region also includes the West North Central division, which has experienced a decline in the rate of
increase since 1970.

When examining how these declines affect and are affected
by various age, income, and racial groups, we should bear
in mind the relationships among the variables themselves
(Blau and Duncan 1967).

Age

Without a doubt, people in their 20s are more likely to
move than people in other age brackets. Young people are
entering the labor force for the first time, getting
married, or moving to go to school in other locations.
The elderly move less for a number of reasons: in most
cases, they are no longer in the labor force and thus are
not moving to take new jobs or to complete their education;
neither are they moving to establish new families. Because
there is virtually no societal pressure on them to achieve,
there is no reason for them to move in order to achieve.
This picture of a "static" older population applies only
to migration to suburbs or exurbs and does not apply to
interregional migration. We will deal with these shifts
a bit later. Generally, the movers from central cities
and older suburbs tend to be the young. Increasingly,
the central cities of the Northeast and North Central
regions are populated by the elderly, who are left, in
many cases, without vital services and often become the
victims of criminals (Hauser 1975, National Commission on
the Causes and Prevention of Violence 1969).

The plight of the elderly is related to the migration
of younger people. As young families move to small and
nonmetropolitan areas, they take with them their money,
their vitality, their sense of civic responsibility. Money
is probably the most important loss. Grocery stores,
department stores, pharmacies, and specialty shops typically follow the population, particularly the buying

population. They are following the younger population to
outlying areas and leaving the elderly with fewer and fewer
facilities, making it necessary for the elderly, many of
whom are nonambulatory or semiambulatory, to travel greater
distances to get the goods and services they need.

Elderly residents of central cities are easy targets
for criminals who use force. This has always been the case,
but as city neighborhoods cease to be neighborhoods and
simply become areas in which the immobile live (Stein 1964),
they lose the civic spirit that in the past has helped to
protect neighborhood residents.

The elderly in central cities are left powerless. They
tend to vote less than younger people (Milbrath 1971).
They are less able or likely to attend meetings held to
accomplish neighborhood goals. There is little economic
or political incentive for political and governmental units
to serve them (although this may be slowly changing as the
conditions in which the elderly live become more and more
the focus of national attention).

All of this has important policy implications for educational, economic, and criminal justice institutions. As
central cities lose the young, they lose school-aged children, and schools in central cities and older suburbs are
closing in many areas of the country (Downs 1970). The
buildings often become a drain on public funds, and sometimes cannot be sold. At the same time, many elderly
people clamor for education that might retrain them for
jobs or offer opportunities for personal growth. Perhaps
educational institutions should begin to consider seriously
the premise that education does not stop at 18 or 22 or 25
years of age. On the other hand, the erosion of property
tax bases in central cities makes the funding of education more difficult for all ages.

Profit-making institutions are not generally in the
social service business. Although it is socially desirable
for stores to remain in central cities and within easy
reach of older people, it is often not profitable. What
can urban governments do to keep local pharmacies, grocer-
ies, hardware stores, and even hospitals within their original neighborhoods? How can the criminal justice system
protect a population that is increasingly unable to protect
itself either physically or by means of neighborhood
cohesion and spirit?

There are also implications for housing, lending institutions, and transportation. The housing, financial, and
transportation needs of the elderly are not the same as
those of younger people. Older people need less space

because they generally have fewer persons in the home. Lending institutions are reluctant to offer 30-year mortgages or 4-year car loans to people 70 years old who are living on pensions. The elderly generally do not need rapid transportation so much as they need door-to-door transportation. These are issues that should be addressed.

However, we must remember that the cities are a long way from being decaying retirement homes. Although younger people are leaving, so also are some of the elderly, while some younger people are coming to cities. The middle-aged population cannot be forgotten. In other words, it is easy to go too far with the implications of trends. We must be careful to maintain perspective as we grapple with the implications of migration trends.

Income

As younger, middle-income residents move out of the central cities and older suburbs, they leave the poor and the wealthy behind. The poor are left because they cannot afford to go anywhere else and the wealthy remain because they can afford to isolate themselves from most urban problems and still have the geographic, cultural, and recreational advantages of the city. The median family income of suburban dwellers is $14,007; the median for central-city families is $11,343 (see Berry and Dahmann in this volume). As of March 1974, 17 percent of all central-city families had incomes over $20,000; but central cities also contain 37.4 percent of all people below the poverty line, and 1 in 10 central-city families receives some form of public assistance. In a sense then, central cities are becoming both rich and poor as a result of population movement. The poor cannot move for economic reasons (and perhaps, in many cases, racial restrictions). The wealthy or upper middle-income residents often see no reason to move. As long as there are private schools, private security forces, and exculsive condominiums and housing areas, the advantages of central cities may outweigh the disadvantages. Furthermore, for the younger, middle-income residents who are moving back to older sections of some cities to buy and renovate older houses, the city offers attractions that cannot be found elsewhere (Coleman 1978). It is too soon to assess the impact of this trickle back to the city, but it bears watching and may have major repercussions for social, political, and economic institutions in the cities in which this phenomenon is taking place.

Nonetheless, as large numbers of younger, middle-income residents flee the city, taking their property taxes and buying power with them, central cities are finding it increasingly difficult to pay for the higher levels of service required by the older, poorer population that remains (Downs 1970). The middle-income population is less likely than the poor to "use" the criminal justice system, the public welfare system, public or low-income housing, the fire department, and public hospitals. The elderly and the poor need all of these services more, but are less able to afford them (Lashoff 1968). Obviously, states and the federal government will have to provide a greater share of the funding for these services if these population movements continue.

Race

Blacks still live primarily in urban areas. Fifty-eight percent of all blacks reside in central cities, compared with 25 percent of all whites. However, recent trends suggest that important changes are taking place. Since 1970, the average rate of growth of the black suburban population has increased to 5.2 percent per year. The annual rate of growth for the white suburban population has decreased to 1.6 percent. Black suburbanization rates are increasing and white suburbanization rates are falling. At the same time, the growth rate of blacks in central cities is declining; the concentration of blacks in the central city is dropping. Seventy-four percent of all blacks living in metropolitan areas now live in central cities, compared with 80 percent in 1970. It seems, then, that blacks are moving out of the central city along with whites, although blacks are moving to the suburbs while whites are moving to the exurbs.

This movement has a number of important social, political, and economic implications for blacks, for cities, and for the nation as a whole. Perhaps the most obvious implications involve the integration process in schools and other areas of life. It is obviously difficult to integrate schools or neighborhoods racially when there are "not enough whites" within the boundaries of a municipality. While the federal government continues to strive for racial integration, the population mix makes this task increasingly difficult. Cities such as Gary, Indiana, Detroit, Michigan, and Washington, D.C., vividly illustrate the problem (U.S. Commission on Civil Rights 1974). If racial integration is

so desirable, how does the government justify literally
giving up on places such as Gary and Washington that are
largely black?   Integration has, of course, rarely been an
issue in places that were basically all white.

Furthermore, as middle-class nonwhites move out of
cities to areas vacated by more socially mobile whites, we
may not be able to move toward economic or social integration.   This movement tends to leave only relatively immobile people in central cities--the poor, the old, and the
young.   How do we achieve economic or social integration
when we have few middle-class residents of any race in the
central city?

Of greater concern for many blacks is the question of
black political and cultural leadership within the cities
of the North and the East.   From the 1920s to about 1970,
many urban black communities, although economically depressed, managed to thrive culturally.   Since the mid-1960s,
they have, to some degree, also flourished politically
(Cruse 1967).   This has been due in large measure to the
legal, social, and economic discrimination that forced
almost all members of the black population to reside within
a relatively small area.   Black teachers and physicians
lived next to black musicians and factory workers.   The
children of postal workers went to school with the children
of college professors (Drake and Cayton 1945).   Black
political efforts had to be concentrated in these areas,
and the areas gave birth to black leadership, both political
and economic.   This concentration, of course, had its advantages and disadvantages (Drake and Cayton 1945).   Whereas
it promoted cultural and political growth and awareness,
it made it easy to manipulate blacks economically and
politically.   A distinct advantage of this concentration
was the promotion of community diversity and economic
integration.   As middle-class blacks leave the ghetto, the
ghetto doesn't disappear.   The ghetto will always have its
opportunists and hustlers, as will any other area, but
the quality and quantity of ghetto leadership will diminish.
I am not suggesting that the ghetto should remain intact
as a base for this leadership or as an example of economic
integration--the price is too high.   However, I would argue
that the ghetto will be with us for some time, but its few
advantages will disappear.

Largely as a result of federal policies, housing opportunities for blacks have improved.   However, as more and
more blacks have moved into the middle class (Farley 1977,
Sampson and Milam 1976) and have had more contact with
whites in housing, schools, and jobs, attacks upon

affirmative action programs have increased. These programs are often considered responsible for black economic and housing gains (Jones 1977). Attempts to keep the black population "in its place" have become more subtle and economically oriented. Policies to counter these attacks will have to emerge soon if gains are not to be eroded (Jones 1977).

Furthermore, the federal government will have to rethink its urban policies. Population trends are changing the nature of the city's population, and urban policies must reflect these changes. Affirmative action and housing integration, as policies, have in part been responsible for the departure of increasing numbers of middle-class blacks. What can these policies do for those who will remain in 10-15 years? New policies must be developed to benefit people of all races that are not part of the middle class. We may have to be more concerned with job creation and rent control than discrimination in promotion and mortgage policies. We must recognize the fact that we are, or will be, dealing with a different central-city population.

Before I discuss areas of increasing population, it is important to point out that although this section is entitled "Areas of Declining Population," it generally deals only with cities and not with regions. As I discuss the relationships of the relevant variables to areas of growth, I will make reference to regions of decline. It seems easier to discuss regional growth and decline at the same time given that the two trends appear so dependent upon one another.

AREAS OF INCREASING POPULATION

Berry and Dahmann indicate that the South is "experiencing net migration gains from all other regions in numbers that are more than double the net gain to the West--the only other region now experiencing a net migration gain." Furthermore, the South is gaining blacks from other regions (14,000 between 1970 and 1975). Blacks continue to move from rural areas to metropolitan areas but are moving more from the central city of metropolitan areas to the suburbs, and are beginning to move from metropolitan areas of the Midwest and the East back to the South. The West continues to experience the highest growth rate, but the most rapid growth is now occurring in the mountain areas. The migration from the Northeast and North Central regions has almost

doubled since the last half of the 1960s. There has been
a 34.1-percent increase in migration from the North to the
South and a 17.3-percent decrease in migration from the
South to the North. Coupled with these interregional shifts
has been the movement from metropolitan areas to nonmetropolitan areas.

Age

The elderly, generally among the least likely to move, have
become a very significant part of the population of the
"retirement states" of Arizona and Florida. Not all of
the elderly are "static." Middle-class blacks are moving
not only to the suburbs, but to the South. Presumably,
middle-class blacks are also remaining in the South.
Middle-class whites are moving beyond suburbs to nonmetropolitan areas, to smaller metropolitan areas, and to the
South and the West. As jobs move to these areas, so do
people.

Blau and Duncan (1967) indicate that special advantages
are needed to induce people to move from larger to smaller
places. Consequently, if one moves in this direction, he
or she must benefit greatly from such a move. Berry and
Dahmann indicate that the special advantages are not really
so special after all. They are part of " . . . the accelerated decentralization of manufacturing and related activities out of central cities--especially out of the nation's
largest ones--that is occurring during the 1970s." In
other words, increasingly, the advantages for the upwardly
mobile lie outside the big cities, and outside the Northeast (and to some extent, the North Central region), assuming that we define "advantages" as better job prospects.
Obviously, some groups are less affected by job prospects
than others. The unemployed are greatly affected, but the
elderly are not; when they change regions or metropolitan
status, it is generally not for employment purposes. Those
persons employed in industries that offer seniority are
less likely than others to change regions, even though they
may have to travel greater distances to work.

The harsh winters and problems of mobility in the cold
and the snow of the North Central and Northeast regions
certainly contribute to the desire of many elderly persons
to move from these regions to more temperate regions. This
movement, however, appears to be quite selective. We see
increasingly larger concentrations of the elderly in Florida
and Arizona, for example. In both of these states, an "aged

industry" has emerged as more and more elderly persons
migrate to retirement communities. Most experts on the
subject suggest that this type of age segregation is not
good for the elderly or for those younger persons deprived
of contact with the elderly.

Frequently, when an area is developed as a recreational
center, its population increases greatly. Recreational
centers in the Mountain and Pacific regions, in the South,
and to some degree in the North Central region have shown
us that the nation's population moves to maximize its
recreation time. The development of such facilities may
be aided or impeded by governmental action. Therefore,
governments can, to some degree, influence population
shifts by controlling recreational development. However,
because we cannot manipulate the weather very effectively,
the South and the West will continue to have an advantage
in terms of recreation over the other regions of the
country. The South and the West, therefore, may continue
to lure people with ample time for recreation, such as the
elderly or people with money to spend for recreation.

Income

For years the upwardly mobile (fairly young whites from
middle-income families with strong educational backgrounds)
have fled the city for the suburbs. Consequently, the city
has increasingly been populated by the less socially (and
thus geographically) mobile. The local area has, however,
remained largely economically and racially integrated. If
these same mobile people now flee metropolitan areas and
the most metropolitan regions, will we ultimately end up
with some cities and counties that are entirely comprised
of the poor, old, and nonwhite, others that are integrated
(the South and the Pacific region), and others that are
entirely comprised of young, upper-middle-income whites
(Nevada, for example)? In other words, cities of the North
Central and Northeast regions are losing population to the
South and West *and* to nonmetropolitan and smaller metropolitan areas within the regions. This loss is, however,
not random. It results primarily from the migration of
middle-income, white families in their childbearing years,
although a significant number of blacks are migrating to
the suburbs (as opposed to nonmetropolitan or smaller metropolitan areas) and many elderly are moving to warmer states.
Thus the larger central cities in the North Central and
Northeast regions are becoming increasingly poor and nonwhite.

The exurban communities receiving these young, middle-income, relatively well-educated migrants also face important issues. What is the impact on the political, educational, and social service systems of this influx of upwardly mobile people? The sudden increases in the population of these smaller places require increases in school facilities and public services (trash collection, police and fire protection, etc.); they also lead to increases in public revenues. Many communities are not politically equipped to make these large-scale changes rapidly. Furthermore, these upwardly mobile immigrants often carry with them a political sophistication that is absent in smaller towns and cities. Frequently, political conflicts develop over economic issues such as the pace of growth. This influx may also force out some older residents if property taxes go up to meet the need for additional services, and as a reflection of growth. Long-time residents of the area may not be able to afford these tax increases and may feel forced to sell land to developers who are happy to accommodate the desire for more housing.

Furthermore, the residents of the receiving communities may express some hostility to the newcomers who may significantly differ from older residents. The newcomers tend to have more education and higher incomes than natives (Blau and Duncan 1967). They are perhaps more likely to be politically liberal than older residents. These changes may lead to changes in the political composition of receiving communities, just as the movement of these people out of central cities has led to changes in the political composition of many of the cities. For example, in terms of local politics, Chicago, Milwaukee, and Pittsburgh are almost one-party areas.

The ways in which such hostilities are worked out have important implications for population movement. Some of these communities have adopted a no-growth policy to limit the number of outsiders coming in. In other cases the fight has been over whether to encourage or allow shopping-center development (which is actually a growth versus no-growth issue). If growth in a community is limited by zoning ordinances, sewer regulations, or other restrictions, the upwardly mobile movers will have to go elsewhere. It is possible that this movement could be specifically channeled (or slowed considerably) if regional planning authorities had greater power. They could use that power to plan for and guide growth rather than simply reacting to it. However, Americans do not seem ready for much planned growth.

If we assume that economic integration is desirable, then recent population shifts may be seen in a negative light as they tend to exacerbate economic segregation. As stated above, increasingly we see the rich and the poor remaining in the central cities of several areas of the country. We further see the central city getting poorer and the exurbs getting richer. Poor youngsters are increasingly left with other poor people as role models (Liebow 1967). However good these role models may be as human beings, they are not likely to be good examples of success or achievement. We must question how middle-income or wealthy people will develop compassion and empathy in their insulated worlds. How will the two groups relate to one another? How will an antipoverty attitude be spawned and nurtured in the absence of relationship?

Blau and Duncan (1967) also indicate that smaller cities provide exceptional opportunities for the migrant, in large part because the migrants are precisely the ones most able to take advantages of the "special opportunities" needed to induce movement of people from larger to smaller places. Such special opportunities, particularly for the middle-class professional worker, need not be job related but often are. Smaller communities, whether they be in the South or North Central region, are generally less congested than others, are perceived as having more responsive government than others (Altshuler 1970), and have less crime than others (National Advisory Commission on Civil Disorders 1968). They have a lower population density than other communities. But they are also less likely than other larger, more urban communities to be racially or economically diverse. The federal government will have to shape its integration policies to apply to smaller communities as well as big cities.

Given the size and the relative homogeneity of smaller communities, whether in the South, the West, or the North, the influx of politically sophisticated, upwardly mobile people is likely to have immediate political consequences. Smaller, nonurban communities will have to face educational, housing, and social integration to a greater degree than they have in the past. In most cases this will involve integration of whites of different backgrounds; in some cases integration of blacks and whites will be necessary. How will school systems accustomed to the needs and desires of a small-town (often antiurban) population handle the educational demands of the Piagetian, open-classroom generation? How will the relatively affluent newcomers spend their money in these smaller, less cosmopolitan areas (most of which are not recreational communities)?

Race and Integration

I have already noted the increase in the black suburban
population. Since 1970, the South has gained 14,000 blacks
from other regions. Although black migration does not
represent a rush back to the "New South," it is a significant movement. While there are as yet no data to tell us
who these "returnees" are, I think that it is safe to
assume that they are, for the most part, middle-income and
upwardly mobile people.

I am certain that black politicians in the South are
keeping a close watch on this recent population movement.
Changes in both the black and white population may threaten
black political gains in some southern areas. Elected
political officials are faced with a new and different
constituency, perhaps more urbane and certainly more economically and educationally mobile. The loss of black
leadership in Northeast and North Central cities is, in an
increasing number of cases, the gain of southern cities.
Those in power, however, will have to find ways to deal
with the changed population.

The movement of blacks to southern cities is still a
trickle, albeit a highly significant one. As I meet and
talk with my black colleagues and friends, I am impressed
by the consistent and oft-heard references to moving "back
to the South." The people who voice this desire are young,
middle-class professionals with children. They talk about
clean air and lots of land in the South. They talk about
plentiful jobs and a sense of community in the South.
They talk about the huge house they can buy with the profit
from the sale of their small one in Chicago, or Philadelphia,
or Milwaukee. These are people who are politically aware
and active. They owe no allegiance to what I call the
"Morehouse Mafia" in Atlanta (Maynard Jackson, Andy Young,
John Lewis, Julian Bond, etc.), or to the Fords of Tennessee.
They will have to be won, and they are hard to sell.

How will suburbs handle the influx of blacks? The
policies of the nation over the past 20 years have affected
jobs, housing, education, transportation, and racial problems (Farley 1977). Increasing numbers of blacks are moving
to the suburbs. However, a relatively large, mostly nonwhite central-city population has remained unaffected.
Public assistance programs have not provided incentives for
recipients to move or to improve their status. These people
are not likely to benefit much from changes in transportation, housing, or job discrimination policies. We may be
on our way to the formation of what I have called a permanent

underclass, and what others have called the lumpen proletariat, in cities of the North Central and Northeast
regions. As a result, economic and racial integration
may become impossible in cities like Gary, Detroit, Newark,
and Washington. However, cities in the South and West,
such as Atlanta and Nashville, will increase their potential for racial and economic integration as their middle-
class black and white population grows.

Solutions to urban problems will become more costly and
more difficult politically as the central city and older
suburbs become increasingly populated with those people
most (and least) in need of city services and least able
(or willing) to pay for them. In contrast, smaller metropolitan and nonmetropolitan areas will have to deal with
rapid growth. If, indeed, a number of cities in the North
Central and Northeast regions reach a point at which they
can no longer be integrated racially and economically,
and if racial integration through housing and education
remains a national goal, what then are we to do? Some
form of metropolitan-wide integration appears to be one
alternative. However, if the Milliken decision is any
indication, the courts may limit this possibility. Local
governments outside central cities limit metropolitan-wide
integration by generally refusing to allow sufficient numbers of low-cost, low-income housing units to reduce the
concentration of the poor in the central city and put them
closer to jobs. These governments also refuse to enter
into integration agreements with central-city school systems
I am not arguing that racial integration is necessary or
even desirable. However, integration of government-
sponsored activities is the law of the land; and therefore,
attempts must be made to accomplish it, or the law should
be changed. The question is whether it may be accomplished
at all given recent population trends and political realitie

Economic integration is a quite different matter. Although blacks or Hispanic Americans may thrive in communities that are all black or Hispanic, I suspect that they
cannot thrive in communities that are all poor, whether or
not such communities are racially or ethnically integrated.
Funds are needed for social services, housing, food,
clothing, etc. Furthermore, success models are needed for
poor youngsters. These models need not be of different
races, but they must be available. Since the economically
mobile nonwhite middle class has become geographically
mobile, where will these models come from?

This discussion has dealt with different types of integration. In the case of movement to smaller metropolitan

and nonmetropolitan areas, it has dealt with integration
of lifestyles, and, to some small degree, races. In the
case of the central cities of metropolitan areas, it has
dealt with integration of income levels, lifestyles, races,
and stages in the family cycle. For southwestern and
mountain states such as Arizona, Nevada, Utah, and Oklahoma,
integration is a problem insofar as there is relatively
little racial or ethnic diversity. These states have
native American populations that have been relatively
"controlled" and not integrated very well. Indeed, native
Americans remain "out of sight" of the majority of the
population.

This discussion assumes integration to be generally
positive (though, I could argue, I think convincingly, that
some forms of racial integration may be harmful for blacks
or Hispanic Americans). It accepts integration as the law
of the land and does not fully examine the benefits and
shortcomings of integration. However, it is important to
place the need for integration in some perspective. I
have already cautioned restraint with respect to consideration of the effects of the movement of blacks either to
the South or the the suburbs. The trends are very important,
but the numbers are relatively small. It is important to
note that not all middle-class whites moving beyond the
suburbs or to smaller cities and towns will have to be
fully integrated into those communities. Many of them,
particularly in the Pacific region, the North Central region,
and the Northeast region, are commuters to the central city.
They go to the central city to earn money, to spend money,
to shop, and to enjoy cultural activities. Their children
may be integrated, but they may not. They may take no
active part in the political, social, or cultural affairs
of the receiving community, preferring to "get away from
it all." We must distinguish between these people and those
who altogether shun the big city--its jobs, its money, its
culture, and its social activities. One group requires
integration, and the other does not.

PERCEPTIONS AND MOTIVATIONS

Before I consider some of the public policy implications of
the characteristics and relationships detailed above, I
think it wise to consider briefly the related issues of
the perceptions and motivations of movers. It is easy to
accept the notion that variables are really constants. I
have described the movement of blacks to the central city

and suburbs almost as though the motivations for the moves
were the same--improvement of living conditions. In a
broad sense, this is true. However, we should also bear
in mind that some blacks are moving from the rural South
to the urban North in order to find jobs, while other
blacks with secure jobs are moving from the urban North to
the suburbs of northern cities, and still others are moving
back to southern cities. Both groups are moving, but for
far different reasons.

We should not assume that all whites leaving northern
and northeastern central cities are doing so to avoid contact with blacks. Certainly, some are; however, others
are moving because of perceived differences in the quality
of schools or the value of land. Not all of the elderly
remain in central cities due to lack of alternatives.
Some remain there by choice--because they find things
about central cities and/or the region that they like.

My point is that we should remember that differences in
perceptions and motivations occur among the members of
any large group. Groups of movers are no exception.
While these groups may have age, income, or race in common,
it cannot be assumed that the motivations for similar moves
are the same. In order to fully understand and appreciate
these moves we need to examine closely the perceptions and
motivations of the movers.

POLICIES AND PROSPECTS

As far as race is concerned, the trends seem to suggest a
dispersal of the black population throughout the metropolitan region and some black migration to the South.
Where movement to the suburbs occurs, it is likely to be
to older suburbs. The South will retain a higher percentage
of its black population than it has for some 50 years.
However, the trends also suggest a geographic and economic
gulf between the black population and the white (which is
not at all new), and between the black "haves" and the
black "have-nots." Whether this gulf is related to intra-
racial antipathy is not clear (Sampson and Milam 1976), but
it does not bode well for black communities or for central
cities.

This movement of whites and middle-class blacks out of
central cities, could, within the next 15 years, leave the
central city with a permanent underclass living on public
funds, and with a decreasing property tax base to pay for
the increasing number of social services needed by such a

population. The notion of scattered site housing within
a central city may not mean very much if there are few
middle-class or white neighborhoods left. Less attention
will need to be paid to red-lining than to rent control
because an increasing percentage of city dwellers will be
renters if homeowners continue to leave metropolitan areas.

If the nation remains interested in racial and economic
integration, ways may have to be found either to increase
the number of whites and middle-class blacks in the central
city or to enlarge the scope of integration to include areas
beyond the boundaries of central cities. Ways will also
have to be found to employ those remaining in the cities.
Indeed, perhaps we should consider ways to move relatively
immobile people to places where the jobs are--to the suburbs
of the North Central and Northeast regions, and to the South,
Southwest, and Pacific regions. Travel funds, relocation
expenses, and incentives for employers to move blue-collar
and unemployed workers to new locations do not seem like
outrageous ideas.

It does not seem unrealistic to use federal revenue
sharing funds to facilitate economic and racial integration.
Why should exclusively white, upper-middle-income suburbs
get money they can often do without when they refuse to
build low- or moderate-cost housing so that central-city
residents may be within traveling distance of jobs? This
hurts not only the central-city residents but the economy
as well. Attractive interest rates could spur builders to
construct such housing and attractive mortgage terms could
be offered to those whites and blacks willing to build or
to buy single-family homes in urban or suburban neighborhoods that include a specified percentage of low- and
moderate-income housing. No one can or should force
people to live where they do not want to (as Federal
Housing Administration policies, transportation policies,
and racism have forced many blacks to do), but the federal
government can offer enticements that might make some areas
more attractive than they might otherwise be. We could
stop encouraging movement to areas that are farther and
farther from the central cities by ceasing to build highways or public transportation systems in these areas.

There are not many ways to mitigate the effects of
interregional movement. The government can provide assistance to the unemployed who migrate to areas where jobs
are available and can try to attract employment opportunities
and people back to the Northeast and North Central regions.

Since the elderly are generally not looking for jobs,
our concern for them is not with job policies. However,

the elderly do need accessible and relatively inexpensive
transportation. They often also need to be close to goods
and services because their physical mobility has diminished.
For this reason, cities would appear to be excellent places
for many elderly people. Indeed, this is an important
reason why so many elderly people remain in the city.
However, to make life bearable for those who choose to
remain, we will have to control crime, and provide door-to-
door, inexpensive transportation and increased medical
care. If we do not deal with these problems, we may see
in 10 to 15 years a sort of bipolar distribution of the
elderly. The more affluent elderly will be "hidden" away
in retirement complexes in the Sun Belt and Florida, and
the others will be concentrated in central cities, living
in fear.

As I have stated previously, upwardly mobile people are
more likely than others to move, whether from city to
suburb, suburb to exurb, or North to South (Blau and Duncan
1967). Movers tend to have higher incomes and more education than nonmovers. We have heard a great deal in the
past 10 to 15 years about the erosion of the property tax
bases of larger, older cities, particularly in the North
Central and Northeast regions, as middle-income people
move away. Actually, these tax problems should be examined
more carefully since presumably many of these people are
selling homes at a profit. Under these circumstances,
little or no decrease in property values should occur, at
least in the short run. Of course, if large numbers of
middle-class homeowners move out of a neighborhood very
quickly, values and tax revenue may drop sharply.

Perhaps even more important than property taxes is the
fact that central cities are becoming increasingly the
homes of the very rich and the very poor, with the middle-
income family preferring suburbs and exurbs. The very poor
have little money to spend in the city and generally pay
no property taxes. The very rich may spend little money
in the city in which they reside (we need to look into
this further) but do pay property taxes. Currently, in
some cities such as Chicago, Philadelphia, and Washington,
we are witnessing a return to the city by young, upper-
middle-income whites. What becomes of the low-income renters
or owners of the houses that are purchased by these young
returnees? Where do they go? Where can they go? In some
cases, they can no longer afford the ghetto, at least not
the same one, because property improvements have increased
the value and thus the rents. Cities should be very
careful about encouraging this return until they are quite
certain that those people displaced are adequately cared for.

If central cities continue to become places for upper-income people who can often insulate themselves from the city and the poor who cannot, who will provide civic leadership and initiative? Are all decisions to be made by the upper-income minority for the majority who have lower or no incomes? This is a political rather than a governmental issue, but each impacts upon the other. Something must be done to attract and retain jobs in central cities. Housing must be made available near jobs in suburban and exurban areas, in the Sun Belt, and in the Northeast and North Central regions. I am not certain that the nation can afford to continue to allow business and industry to move at will with little regard for the consequences. If this freedom is to be maintained, strong incentives will have to be developed and used to provide jobs in the private sector for the majority of urban residents who may be poor in 10 or 15 years.

This of course takes us back to the issue of the urban lumpen proletariat or permanent lower class--people passed over by the civil rights revolution and by boom periods. These are people with no jobs, no skills, no hopes, who are, to a large extent, concentrated in northern cities where strong labor unions and seniority do not greatly help their causes. They are not helped much by making accusations of racism, because a lot of blacks have now made it out of the ghetto (at least economically). It is not simply a question of race, but neither is it simply or largely a question of economics. Racially oriented solutions (like affirmative action) are good, but primarily help the upwardly mobile (many of whom would eventually make it without such solutions). They do not help those at the bottom or poor whites. Economic solutions generally ignore the existence of racism. It may be that we have reached a point at which it is not really in the economic or political interests of the nation to help these people. They do not vote very often (Milbrath 1971), and provision of jobs for them will cost government some money, either in direct salary payments or in the form of incentives for business and industry to relocate, develop, or expand. I think that rising crime rates and the resulting economic losses as well as rising costs for courts, jails, welfare, and police, economically justify these governmental expenditures. Simple human concern justifies them on a moral basis.

My last point relates to the classic distinction between class and status. People who move do so not only for market-related (employment) reasons but also for status.

Some are seeking the prestige of a particular school or
community. Some are looking for a particular type of house.
Others are simply "movers"--for example, military personnel
or academics. Others are moving away from blacks or Hispanics. Some blacks may be moving toward other blacks.
In these cases, job considerations may be secondary.

If people do in fact move for reasons of prestige or
race, then urban policy should take this into account. If
schools in declining cities such as Cleveland could be
upgraded to gain a national reputation for excellence, I
am certain that many middle-income whites would move to
(or back to) these cities. Provision of jobs and adequate
relocation efforts for those displaced by people moving
in would have to be provided. It would be interesting to
find out the extent to which education and race affect
movement, but I am not certain that asking people is the
best way of acquiring this information. Perhaps an "experi-
ment" is a better way of doing this. If middle-income
whites can be lured to Cleveland, Gary, or Newark by quality
schools and are willing to live in integrated settings to
use the schools, we may learn about the relative importance
of race and education. Obviously, this would require careful planning. But, my main point is not that we should try
this with shcools, police services, or recreational facilities, but that variables other than employment affect decisions to move to one place or another. Policies affecting
movement or affected by movement should consider manipula-
tion of these variables.

REFERENCES

Altshuler, A. (1970) *Community Control: The Black Demand
    for Participation in Large American Cities.* Indianapolis
    Ind.: Pegasus.
Blau, P., and Duncan, O. (1967) *The American Occupational
    Structure.* New York: John Wiley and Sons, Inc.
Coleman, J. (1978) Can we revitalize our cities? In
    C. Leven, ed., *The Mature Metropolis.* Lexington, Mass.:
    D.C. Heath & Co.
Cruse, H. (1967) *The Crisis of the Negro Intellectual.*
    New York: William Morrow & Co.
Downs, A. (1970) *Urban Problems and Prospects.* Chicago:
    Rand McNally.
Drake, St. C., and Cayton, H. (1945) *Black Metropolis.*
    Vol. 2. New York: Harcourt, Brace, and World.
Farley, R. (1977) Trends in racial inequalities: have the

gains of the 1960's disappeared in the 1970's? *American Sociological Review* 42(2).

Hauser, P. (1975) Chicago-urban crisis exemplar. *Urbanism Past and Present* 1.

Jones, F. (1977) *The Changing Mood in America.* Washington, D.C.: Howard University Press.

Lashoff, J. (1968) Medical core in the urban center. *Annals of Internal Medicine* 68(2).

Liebow, E. (1967) *Tally's Corner.* Boston, Mass.: Little, Brown and Company.

Milbrath, L. (1971) *Political Participation.* Chicago: Rand McNally.

National Advisory Commission on Civil Disorders (1968) *Report of the National Advisory Commission on Civil Disorders.* Washington, D.C.: U.S. Government Printing Office.

National Commission on the Causes and Prevention of Violence (1969) *Violent Crime: Homicide, Assault, Rape, and Robbery.* Washington, D.C.: U.S. Government Printing Office.

Sampson, W., and Milam, U. (1976) The intra racial attitudes of the black middle class: have they changed? *Social Problems* (December).

Stein, M. (1964) *The Eclipse of Community.* New York: Harper Torchbooks.

U.S. Bureau of the Census (1975) Mobility of the population of the United States: March 1970 to March 1975. In *Current Population Reports.* Series P-20, no. 285. Washington, D.C.: U.S. Department of Commerce.

U.S. Commission on Civil Rights (1974) *Milliken vs. Bradley: The Implications for Metropolitan Desegregation.* Washington, D.C.